Managing the Sales Function

**McGRAW-HILL
SERIES IN MARKETING**

Consulting Editor
Charles Schewe
University of Massachusetts

Britt and Boyd: MARKETING MANAGEMENT AND ADMINISTRATIVE ACTION
Buzzell, Nourse, Matthews, and Levitt: MARKETING: A Contemporary Analysis
DeLozier: THE MARKETING COMMUNICATIONS PROCESS
Howard: CONSUMER BEHAVIOR: Application of Theory
Lee and Dobler: PURCHASING AND MATERIALS MANAGEMENT: Text and Cases
Redinbaugh: RETAILING MANAGEMENT: A Planning Approach
Reynolds and Wells: CONSUMER BEHAVIOR
Russell, Beach, and Buskirk: TEXTBOOK OF SALESMANSHIP
Shapiro: SALES PROGRAM MANAGEMENT: Formulation and Implementation
Stanton: FUNDAMENTALS OF MARKETING
Star, Davis, Lovelock, and Shapiro: PROBLEMS IN MARKETING
Stroh: MANAGING THE SALES FUNCTION
Wright, Warner, Winter, and Zeigler: ADVERTISING

Managing the Sales Function

Thomas F. Stroh
Professor of Marketing
Florida Atlantic University

McGraw-Hill Book Company

New York   St. Louis   San Francisco   Auckland
Bogotá   Düsseldorf   Johannesburg   London   Madrid
Mexico   Montreal   New Delhi   Panama   Paris
São Paulo   Singapore   Sydney   Tokyo   Toronto

Managing the Sales Function

1 2 3 4 5 6 7 8 9 0 D O D O 7 8 3 2 1 0 9 8 7

This book was set in Palatino by Black Dot, Inc.
The editors were William J. Kane and Barbara Brooks;
the designer was Joseph Gillians;
the production supervisor was Leroy A. Young.
The drawings were done by ECL Art Associates, Inc.
R. R. Donnelley & Sons Company was printer and binder.

Library of Congress Cataloging in Publication Data

Stroh, Thomas F
   Managing the sales function.

   (McGraw-Hill series in marketing)
   Includes index.
   1. Sales management. I. Title.
HF5438.4.S87   658.8'1   77-22570
ISBN 0-07-062219-1

To
Audrey Merritt Stroh,
my partner in life.

CONTENTS

PREFACE

As the title indicates, this work is intended to be more enlightening than the usual approach to sales-force management. The functions of sales management, such as skimming the cream off the top of a market, often dictate how a manager will direct the sales force. Therefore, the function of sales management is stressed particularly in the first part of the book, "Planning and Innovating," and is reinforced throughout the text. While others have traditionally placed sales management subservient to marketing management, this book stresses that it is the sales manager's responsibility to strongly influence all other phases of any organization—including marketing, production, and finance.

The many facets of sales management have been included in a schematic model which, through word and graphic presentation, gives a summary of the complex job of managing the sales force and the qualities needed to succeed. This work is descriptive of the real-world sales management alternatives and is prescriptive, guiding the reader by recommending specific actions. These recommendations have often generated heated discussions in the classroom, and they also make easy and lively reading.

The author's personal experience in sales management enables him to contribute realistically to the discussion of organization, human relations, morale, forecasting, quantitative analysis, and budgeting. In addition, this book is profit-oriented, with current management and quantitative techniques together with concepts from the behavioral and information sciences. It emphasizes the importance of appraising the probable results and dollar costs of adopting a proposed course of action.

Other differences from the usual approach include the psychology of communications, time management, on-the-job coaching, directing the sales force to sell key target accounts, situational analysis, and decision making. The author clearly shows the importance of a sales manager's changing his or her style of leadership to fit the needs of different sales representatives.

To enrich the learning process, fifty-four practical but brief cases were written for class discussion. Concise learning objectives are stated at the beginning of each chapter, and a series of interesting discussion questions conclude each chapter. The selected references are contemporary, as are the recommended films and video-cassette programs which make the learning process more entertaining and effective.

The author is indebted to many sales managers, to other faculty members, and to the many students who worked with this material. Particular thanks are due to Joel Ross, Robert Murdick, Barry Hersker, Mike Kami, and Alexander Sklar, all from Florida Atlantic University and each of whom contributed valuable materials. Also, Robert Vizza of Manhattan College, Robert Collins of Oregon State University; Roy Klages of the State University of New York at Albany; Guy Gordon of the University of Washington; and James Littlefield of the University of North Carolina each gave constructive criticism as the work progressed. Jared Harrison of the General Electric Company and George Doremus of the Xerox Corporation also contributed tremendously to enlightening the author. Grateful acknowledgment is also given for the substantial help which was received from William Kane and Barbara Brooks, both of the McGraw-Hill Book Company, in putting together the final work.

Finally, the author assumes full responsibility for the synthesis and, of course, any errors in either logic or content.

Thomas F. Stroh

Managing the Sales Function

Part 1

PLANNING
AND INNOVATION

Sales management is once again becoming the key to
business expansion and growth as business attempts
to satisfy potential customers at a profit. The
functional approach to the study of sales management
has been the foundation of marketing. But today the
focus has shifted from looking at the various isolated
functions of management to concentrating on the
needs and wants of the potential customer. This
change involves market research, test marketing, and
operations research.

Today research lies at the very core of the
functional activities grouped under sales
management. A decade ago market research was not
included under sales management. Forty years ago,
few sales executives knew about it. Long-range
planning, together with research and development,
represents the heart of modern sales management.
Technological changes in the past ten years alone
have made traditional sales management obsolete.
Modern sales management should have strong
influence over almost every facet of a business today
and in deciding where a business will be headed in
the future.

The Sales
Manager's Concepts

▶ Objectives

The reader will understand that sales management deals with much more than managing the sales force. He or she will be able to utilize the basic marketing tools of market segmentation and product differentiation to direct the sales force to better profit opportunities. The reader will be able to analyze the existing function of distribution and the alternates possible to increase sales and profits. The reader will appreciate how a modern sales manager accepts the responsibility of directing or influencing many other functions of the organization.

A sales manager with years of experience has some degree of knowledge about where the markets are and some of the ways to reach the customers. In addition, the size of the sales force and the financial clout of the company may enable the manager to make certain strategic decisions, or they may limit the choices. But how a manager looks at the possible markets or how he or she evaluates alternate market segments can make a tremendous difference in the effectiveness of the sales force.

Certainly sales managers have a great deal of knowledge about their products and their competitors' products. How the sales managers look at product differentiation and relate this to possible target market segments can make the job of the sales force easier or more difficult.

With experience the sales manager knows how the company and industry have traditionally used various independent manufacturers' representatives, brokers, wholesalers, and retailers. The manager may accept what is commonplace in the industry as the norm and give it little or no further thought. He or she may look at the various functions being served and evaluate their cost. Traditional sales agents and channels are not necessarily the best ones for today or for tomorrow. Judging the optimum number of agents is another decision which should be reevaluated frequently by the sales manager.

A sales manager's ideas and thinking about the basic functions of the job can help or hinder the efforts of the sales representatives. If the manager ignores these questions, the sales rep may never learn better ways to satisfy customers and increase profits. At best, they may learn by lengthy trial and error, but that way is not economical and competition may easily win the business.

MARKET SEGMENTATION: A BASIC STRATEGY

When a product or service can be used by most people, traditional sales managers urge their sales representatives to make more calls per day. If one in ten people may buy, for example, a representative must see one hundred people to sell ten. Make more calls! Modern sales managers, on the other hand, realize that some groups of people are better prospects than others. They identify segments of the general population and direct their sales representatives to these selected target groups. They help build sales messages which will have the strongest appeal to the targeted segments. They train their representatives to spend time learning about the target groups and cultivating their friendship. *Market segmentation is the identification of subgroups of potential customers who may provide disproportionately high profit opportunities.*

Segmentation by Use Through market research the Bayuk Company, manufacturers of Phillies cigars, found that a very few men smoked most of the cigars sold. When industry sales declined 4 percent, Phillies concentrated its sales promotion on these heavy users. They offered a complete line of merchandise in a catalog similar to an S & H Green Stamp catalog. The heavy user was urged to save his Phillies cigar bands and redeem them for merchandise. When cigar smokers wrote in for the catalog, their addresses were put on the computer so that post office zip codes could be used to identify the geographical concentration of heavy users. The sales force was then directed to get point-of-purchase displays into tobacco shops in these identified areas.

Heavy cigar smokers responded immediately. While industry sales were down, Bayuk's sales went up 40 percent in one year. The product and price remained constant. Only the promotion and sales direction changed from being directed to all adult males to targeting just the heavy users.

Campbell dominates the canned soup market in the United States with nearly 90 percent of the market. As a result, Campbell directs its marketing effort at the medium user. Packaging and sales promotion are

	Heavy user	Medium user	Light user	Nonuser	Specifies brand	Makes purchase
Male under 12 Female under 12						
Male 13–24 Female 13–24						
Male 25–34 Female 25–34						
Male 35–54 Female 35–54						
Male 55–64 Female 55–64						
Male 65+ Female 65+						

Market Segmentation to Identify Profit Opportunities. A grid analysis of this type identified the retired adult users of soft baby foods as well as identifying young females as a new target for National Brewing Company. The sales force can be directed to use their time more productively on selected target segments.

designed to remind the family cook, who it is assumed, serves soup occasionally, to use more Campbell soup for variety and economy. The company furnishes recipies to show how to enrich meals by using Campbell soups. During an economic downturn or inflationary period, many occasional users serve soup more often than they do in prosperous times.

Light users or nonusers are often selected as customer targets by other companies. Through research, breakfast cereal manufacturers found that many adults did not eat their products because they were too sweet. General Mills, Kellogg's, and Quaker Oats began marketing natural cereals, promoting their healthful, nutritional value. An entire new line of products was successfully launched without taking sales away from older products. This is good basic marketing strategy.

Segmentation by Industry The Shaw-Walker Company, manufacturers of office furniture, filing equipment, and systems, identified insurance companies and banks as its primary customers. While any office could use its products, Shaw-Walker sales representatives are directed by sales management to concentrate their efforts on these two target industries. They are taught the language and systems used by such companies and they become experts in these areas. This preparation gives the sales representatives a sharp competitive edge. As banks build new branches, many furnish each new branch exclusively with Shaw-Walker products. Segmenting growth industries is a highly profitable sales management strategy.

In the United States, Sony Corporation of America won over domestic companies in the videocassette market by identifying the education market and company training departments as desirable segments. They directed their dealer sales representatives to these profitable target segments and gained the dominant position. At the same time a number of large American companies lost over $50 million trying to sell to the mass consumer market.

Bendix Corporation, Avionics Division, in Fort Lauderdale, Florida, used market segmentation to break into the highly competitive field of instruments for general aviation. The company identified helicopter pilots as a customer target for small radar. Offshore oil rigs are serviced by helicopter, and Bendix radar increased the aircraft usage by 300 percent in several cases. Other target segments successfully reached were police departments and forest rangers using helicopters for surveillance and rescue work. Alert sales management identified these profitable targets and directed its sales force to seek them.

Segmentation by Age   In the United States, manufacturers of baby foods were concerned about future sales when the population growth began to level out. Through market research they discovered that old people who had lost all their teeth were secretly eating soft baby foods. Old people like the small portions and they appreciate the nutritional value of these foods as beneficial.

Unfortunately, old people were ashamed to admit they wanted baby foods. After this target group had been identified, advertising and point-of-purchase materials were designed to show grandparents feeding babies and tasting the food themselves. The message reminded older people to buy baby food for unexpected visits by grandchildren. Having established this target segment, the manufacturers were able to provide a logical reason or excuse for older people to buy their product without embarrassment. Sales representatives with territories composed of many retired people were able to participate enthusiastically, getting the instore promotional materials accepted and used by store managers.

Young adults are a target segment for some companies. Through market research, the National Brewing Company found that the taste preferences of young people were changing. The Pepsi generation was not switching to beer as they matured, as older generations had done before them. National therefore developed a number of sweet-tasting malt drinks for this young segment. In test markets, sales management found that the new products sold well without hurting the firm's beer sales.

Before going national with a new product, modern sales managers insist on test marketing in a limited area. If the new product sells well with a reasonable amount of effort on the part of the sales force, managers look to see if the new product is *cannibalizing*, or eating into the sale of their other products. If it is not, a new and additional segment of the market is being reached.

Segmentation by Geography   One interesting example of market segmentation occurs in the overseas travel market in the United States. Government statistics show that residents of only four of the fifty states are issued half of all passports. Another five states account for an additional 17 percent. Airlines can easily maximize the effect of their promotional dollars and sales effort by using geographic market segmentation in this situation.

Because hardness of water varies in different areas of the United States, many laundry products are promoted differently according to geographic region. A heavy, thick pancake syrup is preferred in one region while a much thinner syrup is preferred in another. One major coffee supplier has exploited the regional taste differences by blending a stronger, darker coffee for people who live in the western part of the United States.

The United States is large enough to have climate differences that affect marketing of clothing and sports equipment, among other products. Also, many countries throughout the world have sharp differences by region, with warm coastal cities and cool mountain ranges. Modern sales managers seek ways to segment markets in order to build more appealing and economical promotional strategies.

Other Ways to Segment Markets One of the most common ways to segment markets is by income. For example, many prestigious universities in the United States can be afforded only by the wealthy, while the masses attend state universities.

Social mobility is used to segment the innovators or style setters. These people are first to adopt new products and new styles. They lead the masses, so manufacturers court them to gain acceptance of new products. They were the people in the United States who first purchased small foreign-made automobiles in the early 1950s. They purchased 90 percent of all stereo equipment when it was first introduced. They are socially, economically, and geographically mobile, moving steadily ahead by leading the mass of followers.

Some mass markets are segmented by the level of job responsibility. Business executives have certain needs and tastes that are different from those of the medical profession, for example. Blue-collar workers, while making higher income than average, have different tastes from those of either of the above groups. Their preferences in food, alcoholic beverages, restaurants, clothes, autos, and many other things also vary by group. The successful sales manager carefully identifies the best target segments for the sales force.

Combining Segments Sales managers dream of having their products universally accepted, much as Coca-Cola has done. But that seldom happens. As a result, modern sales executives use the basic strategy of market segmentation. They search for distinct groups which their products can serve best. They direct the sales force to call on these target groups who are more likely to need and want their products than the masses might.

Frequently several different groups can be combined and the sales representatives can be taught to modify their sales message to better suit the needs of the individual prospect. Unfortunately, too often what appeals to one targeted segment automatically offends another. It takes knowledge and discretion to intelligently combine compatible segments. Such knowledge in the past was gained through years of sales experience. Modern sales executives rely more on market research studies.

PRODUCT DIFFERENTIATION: A WAY TO REDUCE COMPETITION

Successful sales managers today are working more intelligently, not necessarily harder, to beat competition. One of the basic tools they are using is product differentiation. While many products and services look alike and claim to perform the same functions, the best sellers have obtained a distinction which makes them unique. This marketing strategy is a good way to reduce competition. *Product differentiation is the identification and promotion of unique differences in products which make them more attractive to specific groups of potential customers.*

By combining market segmentation with product differentiation suppliers are able to offer innovative products and marketing programs which appeal to specific groups of customers. Jack Wishnick, president of Crowell Designs, Inc., for example, designed a high-capacity bilge pump with an electronic switch for boats. He gave it a one-year unconditional guarantee. All of this was new to that industry. In just two years he captured the major share of the boat manufacturers in the United States. He then designed a smaller pump, painted it white, and put pictures of flags around the top. This smaller pump could be displayed on counter tops in marinas and was successfully marketed in this way. Product differentiation tripled the business in two years.[1]

[1]*Crowell Designs, Inc., Marketing Case History,* Intercollegiate Video Clearing House, Miami, Fla., 1976.

Intelligent sales managers find out from their product designers what components are in the final assembly and why certain metals, shapes, and sizes were selected. Very often there are real differences between competing products which make one superior in performance. It is then necessary for the sales managers to build a promotional strategy for the sales force to communicate this information to the selected customer targets.

"D" Features John Gockley, vice president of the Fibre Box Association, was the innovator of plastic-coated corrugated packaging. This product enabled the corrugated box to perform well in a wet environment. Gockley says, "We needed to get higher profits for value added. We did it by demanding 'D' Features or demonstratable differences in our product. Our Cora Cool box was the solution."[2] With this innovation

[2]*Westvaco Cora Cool Marketing Case History,* Intercollegiate Video Clearing House, Miami, Fla., 1976.

Figure 1-1 Product Differentiation. In sharper contrast to the 25-cent disposable razors being marketed by Gillette and Bic, Warner-Lambert's Schick Super II Classic razor sells for $12.95 and was designed by International Silver Company with a "rich antique pewter handle." The product is positioned in the luxury gift market. *Courtesy: William Esty Company.*

they were able to take over much of the poultry shipping container business, their initial targeted industry. From there they moved into the produce industry, where such vegetables as celery and lettuce are shipped packed in ice, another wet environment.

It takes competition several years to copy a major innovation such as this, and good sales managers take advantage of this lead time. They quickly enter new market segments where they can honestly exploit the demonstratable differences in product superiority. As competition tries to catch up and offer a "me too" package, Gockley searches for other innovations for specific uses. He says, "Product differentiation is the best way I know to reduce competition in the box business."

Inferior May Be Superior

After analyzing product differences, some sales managers realize their products are not superior in quality or performance. The problem they face is to position the product so that it will be most appealing to a selected group of customer targets. The Gillette Company did exactly this when it introduced the French-made Cricket cigarette lighter in the United States. This butane lighter could not compete with the expensive silver and gold jewelrylike lighters then on the market. Gillette wisely promoted its lighter as an inexpensive "use and throw away" product. The Cricket lighter has become a very successful and profitable addition to the Gillette product line of convenience items.

The best posthole-digging machine in the world may be ideal for a telephone company or an electric utility company. On the other hand, the man who wants to put a fence around his yard only needs to dig a very limited number of holes. He does not want a big, heavy piece of machinery that will last for thousands of uses. He is the proper target for the inferior manual posthole digger as long as it will honestly do the job. In between these two extremes is the small machine which is sold correctly to companies that rent construction equipment to home owners.

Modern sales managers analyze their products and services to identify whatever may be their unique product advantage. This need not be a superior feature. When they find they have a lemon, good marketing men are able to sell lemonade. When they identify something different about their product, they promote this difference to make it attractive to a select target segment. In some cases a minor modification of a product will make it different. Tareyton cigarettes, for example, promoted their charcoal filters as being better than others. Benson and Hedges boasted of being "a silly millimeter longer" in their humorous advertising campaign to appear different.

Total Product Offering   Some products, such as raw materials, may be in fact identical. Many successful products attract competitive copies which are nearly identical. In these cases intelligent sales managers look at the total product offering to differentiate their goods and services. *Total product offering is the physical characteristics of the product, the packaging, the guarantee, and all the services which a vendor may offer.* For example, Squibb Corporation's Life Savers were promoted in 1975 in a vacation-oriented prepack containing five rolls of Life Savers candy and gum plus a foldout sheet of ten games. It was put together in decorative cardboard bus packages. This total product offering clearly distinguished Life Savers from similar candy.

The amount and kind of inventory which is carried by a vendor can differentiate the total product offering. For example, a Ford automobile dealer may stock a large variety of Ford autos in many colors to offer most buyers immediate delivery. Another Ford dealer in the same city may stock a large range of Ford trucks and feature this inventory to a different group of customer targets. Each Ford dealer may offer exactly the same vehicles for approximately the same prices. However, intelligent sales managers elect to legitimately serve different market segments by using their inventory to differentiate their total product offering and hence their image.

Another variation of using inventory control to differentiate the total product offering occurs when a manufacturer decides to build many new parts for future maintenance. General Motors has for many years used this basic strategy worldwide, making it difficult for competitors to gain much of their market. The value of their used cars stays relatively high because of the availability of new spare parts.

While IBM has dominated the computer market throughout the world, few people outside of business realize how IBM product differentiation is achieved. Beyond their obvious research and development, IBM is probably the largest educator in the world. Its annual training budget is bigger than that of most universities in the United States. They train customers and future customers to get better usage of their IBM computers. This training, free in most cases, is a standard part of IBM's total product offering, and it has certainly reduced their competition.

Xerox has used another variation of total product offering to remain the leader in the copy industry. They use a field service force which is almost as large as their sales force. This enables Xerox to assure prospects that their new copy machine will never become obsolete because they constantly install innovative improvements in every machine in the field. Competitors who do not have a large field service organization cannot match this strong product offering.

A strong guarantee or service warranty can also differentiate a product from its competitors. American Motors Corporation in 1976 offered the free use of a rental car if the customer's new car had to be kept in the repair shop overnight while covered under its strong guarantee. In the industrial field, Bendix Corporation offers to fly in technicians and parts for many of their sophisticated instrument customers. This minimizes the risk of expensive downtime when equipment cannot be used. Overnight repairs and rapid transport of field service technicians are part of the total product offerings.

Large American retailers, such as The Allied Chain and Federated department stores, have learned to differentiate their total product offering through services. They make it easy for customers to spend many hours shopping, and many United States consumers do like this. They provide convenient parking, restaurants, nurseries, and children's play areas. For those consumers who cannot spend much time shopping, the same stores offer telephone mail-order privileges to make it easy for them to buy their merchandise. Of course, Sears, Roebuck and Company grew the other way from mail-order catalogs to super shopping centers. In both cases, however, services were used to differentiate the successful retailers from their competitors.

In economic recessions, another service can be used effectively to differentiate a supplier. When there is a shortage of capital or a reduced cash flow, many prospects put off buying many items they really would like to have. A supplier who offers several optional finance plans can often generate business where the competitors cannot. Crowell, discussed earlier, developed a seasonal dating plan on its new line of bilge pumps for the marine industry.[3] Boat manufacturers could get the pumps

[3]*Crowell Designs, Inc., Marketing Case History,* op. cit.

during the slow winter season and not pay for them until the busy spring season started. Crowell had to borrow from banks to finance their accounts receivable under this plan, but the cost was less than they were able to save in steady year-round production. Good differentiation!

Combining Differences . Modern sales managers attempt to identify real differences in their products, psychological differences which seem important to their customers, and real differences in services. They then combine those elements which fit their company strengths and will also appeal to their selected customer targets. In this manner a total product offering can be constructed, by design and planning, which is truly unique.

Many companies are not aware of the various elements in their total product offering. Product and service policy decisions are often made at different times and by different executives, and the result is a confusing mess which may be self-defeating.

Of course, these situations can be corrected. Products can be modified. Services can be expanded or contracted. Policy can be changed. It requires a knowledgeable sales manager who can handle a number of variables at the same time to achieve a clear objective.

Customers usually benefit when the sales function becomes more efficient. By segmenting groups of customers and using product differentiation, intelligent marketing people can offer greater customer satisfaction and generate more profit in the process. These procedures also make the sales force significantly more efficient and more productive.

SELECTING DISTRIBUTION CHANNELS BY THEIR FUNCTION

"The only way to reach customers," some business executives say, "is through traditional channels. Every manufacturer distributes this way. Who are we to question this practice?" Modern sales management seriously challenges this position. They identify what function is needed. Then they search for someone who can perform it most effectively and most efficiently. In many cases, the traditional channel is not very effective and it is more expensive than it needs to be.

Many large companies grew because they analyzed the functions served by their distributors. An American shoe manufacturer, Maxie

Jarman, decided his wholesalers and retailers were not worth the percentage they were charging. He purchased several retail shoe store chains. This was the beginning of today's giant Genesco Corporation, worldwide manufacturer and retailer of department store merchandise.

Sears, Roebuck and Company is another example of vertical integration. In this case the company began as a retailer and expanded into manufacturing their own tires, for example. When suppliers do not seem efficient enough, a giant retailer has the financial strength to move into manufacturing. A & P and Safeway are good examples of this. A number of industrial marketing people have looked at weak functions and found other facilities that could serve their needs better than they could themselves.

S FUNCTIONS OF A DISTRIBUTION CHANNEL

1 ST FUNCTION

Sales Expertise   The Pall Corporation, manufacturer of stainless steel porous filters, was very successful in the aircraft industry. They were easily able to prove better filtration in a lightweight and small space unit. But when they tried to sell filters to the automotive industry, they could not interest a single manufacturer. Finally they got an agreement with a small manufacturer of hydraulic equipment to distribute Pall filters. Their sales force knew the automotive industry. They were able to sell the superior filters to every major manufacturer of tractors and earth-moving equipment. By purchasing sales expertise, Pall increased its earnings by 500 percent!

Crowell Designs, Inc., the small manufacturer of water pumps noted earlier, sold its product directly to boat manufacturers. Two representatives could easily cover the sixty major boat builders in the United States. When the manufacturer wanted to sell to boat owners, they realized that the marine wholesalers had the experienced sales organization which was essential. They selected one large wholesaler in each of the key states. In two years they were able to double their sales.

Itek Corporation, through its Univis Division, sells bifocal lenses to the processing laboratory. The labs grind the lenses to the doctor's prescription. Thus they serve as processors and wholesalers to the doctor. The doctor serves as their retailer. A large competitor, Bausch and Lomb, elects to use its own processing labs and do away with the wholesaler's function. Their labs and sales organization are more efficient than most small independents.

2 ND FUNCTION

Advertising and Sales Promotion   The Holiday Inns in the Caribbean islands of Curacao and Aruba found it too expensive to advertise in the

United States and in Venezuela and Colombia as well. The regional marketing manager, Mike Picot, analyzed the function to be performed and recognized a good solution. He was able to persuade Eastern Air Lines, Inc., to share the advertising costs. They also helped Holiday Inns with their computer reservation system and with their sales promotion materials. Eastern is the major United States carrier to these destinations from the States, and the joint advertising serves both companies.

Wilkinson Sword, the British manufacturer of razor blades, tried for several years to enter the U.S. market against the giant, Gillette. They needed help in positioning their product in the minds of U.S. shavers. Colgate agreed to do the advertising and sales promotion and quickly won a profitable share of the market.

Expediting Delivery Manufacturers supplying hardware retailers have generally found economies in shipping carload lots of heavy tools to wholesalers. The latter, in turn, take smaller orders and ship by truck to retailers. The major function of the middleman is physically delivering heavy equipment at the lowest cost possible.

International Paper Company uses large dealers in a similar way: They ship heavy carload lots by train to regional dealers. Dealers sell primarily to business accounts and ship by truck. Westvaco, being a relatively smaller paper manufacturer, can be more selective in seeking accounts. They ship not only carloads but complete trainloads to a few large customers.

General Electric sells its white goods (ranges, washing machines, refrigerators, etc.) through factory-authorized dealers. The primary function is to deliver and install the products in the home with necessary plumbing and electrical work. For large developments, such as Fontaine-bleau Park in Miami, they join in financing the developer and sell directly to him in bulk quantities. His subcontractors do the necessary installation work.

In the food industry in the United States it is common practice to use routemen to service the local supermarkets. Coca-Cola–franchised independent bottlers hire these men to fill orders as required, but their primary function is not sales; it is physically delivering the product. Bread and other baked goods, eggs, and many dairy products are also sold and delivered by routemen in the same way.

After-Sale Service Bendix Corporation, Avionics Division, as previously noted, manufactures communication and instrument components for the aviation industry. It is one of the giants serving the military and commercial airline markets. When it wanted to sell to the small plane owner, it was faced with the problem of supplying local service after the sale. Herb Sawinski says, "We identified two key distributors who had the required government certification to install and service our equipment. Overnight we had nine hundred licensed outlets through these two key distributors. They can supply local after the sale service at every major United States airport."[4]

In the office equipment field, giants such as IBM and Xerox prefer to maintain their own after-the-sale service force. Smaller manufacturers must rely on a dealer organization to provide local service. Dealers in this industry are selected partly for their sales ability as well as for their service capability.

Financial Support The Alumafold Company is a small manufacturer of hurricane shutters in Florida. With less than $40,000 in capital it was unable to expand as rapidly as it wanted. The owner then decided to franchise local dealers to raise more capital. In one year he was able to sell six franchises at $25,000 each. This increased his net worth 400 percent and enabled him to expand the plant facilities immediately.

Sawinski of Bendix says, "Part of the reason we selected our two key distributors was the fact that they were large enough to handle credit problems which we were not prepared to do."[5] Bendix needed this financial support from its dealers in order to reach the general aviation market. The distributors were willing and able to extend credit to the owners of small planes all over the United States.

Function versus Form When distribution channels are looked at as a form of physically handling a product, companies tend to use traditional methods. Intelligent sales managers today are changing this by looking at the many functions which can be served by a variety of distribution channels. When they identify the essential function to be served, they can often see new opportunities to market more efficiently.

[4]*Bendix Avionics Marketing Case History,* Intercollegiate Video Clearing House, Miami, Fla., 1976.
[5]Ibid.

DISTRIBUTION: EXCLUSIVE, SELECTIVE, OR INTENSIVE?

How many wholesalers, jobbers, or retailers should a sales manager have? The answer is *not* always, "As many as possible." Intelligent sales managers first identify the primary function which will be served by the channel. This may limit the number of alternates possible. Next they look at the kind of coverage which will best serve their needs at that point in time. As business situations change, they review channel decisions for possible changes.

Exclusive Distribution   Jefferson Electric Company is a large industrial manufacturer of transformers and other electronic components. When they developed a line of consumer clocks, they had no consumer marketing organization. Al Sklar, vice president, says, "I decided to pick the fifty largest wholesale jewelry dealers in the United States. In order to induce them to take our line of products I had to give them exclusive sales rights for one year. They accepted and we immediately had over three hundred salesmen experienced in this market."[6]

The small manufacturer discussed earlier, Alumafold Company, makes a patented line of hurricane shutters for high-rise apartment and condominium buildings. They wanted to sell franchises to dealers to raise capital. As an inducement to the dealers they had to offer exclusive sales territories. Any order the factory received for installation in a dealer's exclusive territory had to be credited to that dealer. Many large builders have projects in many territories and order direct from the manufacturer. This inducement was sufficient to sell the franchises.

In marketing industrial goods in the international market it is fairly common practice to offer exclusive rights to one agent for an entire country. The local agent knows the laws, language, and business customs of his country, and this is essential in marketing. In some cases his political connections permit sales to be made which might not be possible in any other way. "Ethical values vary widely around the world," says J. Kenneth Jamieson, newly retired board chairman at Exxon, "but honesty is not subject to criticism in any culture."[7]

[6]*Jefferson Electric Company Marketing Case History,* Intercollegiate Video Clearing House, Miami, Fla., 1976.
[7]*Fortune,* August 1975.

Delmar Jewelry Manufacturing Company in Miami makes a line of costume jewelry. Barry Hersker, a partner, says "Being small and unknown, we had to offer our retailers exclusive sales rights. Only one dealer in each city. This worked very well until our retailers began opening branch stores in each other's territories. Then we had to change the whole system."[8] Hersker strongly recommends formal written agreements which state the length of time a dealer is to have exclusive rights and the conditions for automatic termination.

Selective Distribution As new products and services become established, some manufacturers may prefer to move away from exclusive distribution. Being dependent on a single organization in each area can be risky and expensive. It may also limit sales. GM, Ford, and most automobile manufacturers prefer to have several competing agencies in each sales territory. They contract enough auto agencies to provide good service to the public yet limit the number in each area to ensure that each dealership will be profitable.

Watch manufacturers such as Benrus and Hamilton use selective distribution to enhance their product image. Only the best stores are permitted to carry their products. They keep track of population shifts, however, and do add more dealers as geographic areas increase in population density.

Jefferson Electric Company's Al Sklar notes, "In our second year of consumer marketing we were able to move away from selling exclusively through jewelry stores. We added many of the better department stores on a selective basis. Sales increased so dramatically that we could not keep up with demand."[9] Since they had limited their exclusive wholesalers to one year, they were able to add other wholesalers to broaden their markets.

The problem with having several dealers in the same area is the threat of price deterioration. A weak dealer who is not checked from selling below cost may hurt the reputation of the manufacturer. Most selective dealership aggreements provide for termination if poor practices are observed by the manufacturer's sales representatives.

[8]*All or Nothing,* Intercollegiate Video Clearing House, Miami, Fla., 1976.
[9]*Jefferson Electric Company Marketing Case History,* op. cit.

Intensive Distribution   When a manufacturing company has earned good acceptance, management may want to increase sales by making it more convenient to buy the company's goods. They will then move to intensive distribution and encourage any dealer meeting minimum standards to carry their product line. Typically, a good credit rating is the only requirement. In some industries—gasoline, for example—cash on delivery is traditional, and anyone is offered a dealership. This may soon change.

Timex, in distributing their low-cost watches, initially captured most of this end of the market by offering them to drugstores and food supermarkets.[10] This made it easier for the public to buy watches any place they could buy cigarettes. They have 150,000 outlets, ranging from auto supply dealers to drugstores—in the United States alone. For a relatively low-priced item, intensive distribution is a logical choice.

Intensive distribution is used when a company employs a "pull" marketing strategy. For example, Heublein's slick advertising builds strong demand for its Smirnoff brand vodka and other popular liquors. Retailers are forced to carry them. With this strategy Heublein pulls the product line through the distribution channel, and practically all legal retail outlets and restaurants want to carry their popular brands.

Intensive distribution frequently provides economies of scale. Timex sells 40 million watches a year, so they can produce watch cases more cheaply than anyone else. "The consumer will spend money for an inexpensive watch with the Timex name on it," says Howard Levine, a distributor of Timex watches in the New York metropolitan area.[11]

TIME FACTORS

The number of wholesalers and retailers a marketing organization should have is dependent on several time factors. In industrial marketing the targeted segments may be small and a few manufacturers' representatives may quickly cover all prospects. In the office machines and

[10]"Timex," *Business Week*, Aug. 18, 1975.
[11]Ibid.

equipment market the industrial prospects are everywhere and many dealers are needed to sell and service them as business executives demand.

2. The second factor is the stage of the product's life cycle. A new product may begin with exclusive distribution channels. As it earns market acceptance, it may be moved into selective distribution channels. Finally a product with strong demand may be moved into intensive distribution channels in its mature stage.

3. The third factor is the desired broadening of markets as companies expand their capacity to produce at lower costs. A small organization with limited funds cannot attempt to serve broad markets. The intelligent sales managers with these companies seek only the most profitable target accounts, occasionally selling direct. As their companies grow, they reevaluate distribution-channel alternate possibilities. Sales managers had better realize one must be flexible in making channel decisions, because business situations are constantly changing.

NATURE AND SCOPE OF SALES MANAGEMENT

In 1948 the definitions committee of the American Marketing Association said that sales management meant "the planning, direction, and control of personal selling, including recruiting, selecting, training, equipping, assigning, routing, supervising, paying, and motivating as these tasks apply to the personal sales force." This has been the traditional and narrow view of the nature and scope of sales management.

In fact, modern sales managers not only deal with the sales force, as above, but also get involved with innovation, research, planning, budgeting, pricing, channels, advertising, sales promotion, production, and even plant location.[12] This broad view of sales management makes it synonymous with marketing management except for one important difference. The top executive in charge of the sales force is primarily

[12]Rodney E. Evans, "Field Sales Executives through Their Own Eyes," *Oklahoma Business Bulletin*, vol. 39, pp. 14–21, September 1971.

concerned with the implementation of policy and strategy decisions *in the field.*

The cost of managing and operating a sales force is the largest single marketing expense for most companies—typically double the expense for advertising. Executives cannot manipulate a sales force as they can advertising, for example. Management may cut advertising costs by 50 percent one year and double them the next with few qualms of conscience. They would not dare fire half the sales force or attempt to double its size so quickly.

2. Another important distinction between sales management and management of other marketing functions—advertising, sales promotion, and market research, for example—is the functional loyalty. That is to say, good advertising managers are all advertising—it is their career. Generally they will seek a job as ad manager with a larger company rather than a promotion out of advertising with the same company. While this functional loyalty is true for other marketing specialties, the modern sales manager is becoming the broad generalist. Regardless of the job title, the executive in charge of the sales force is the one in the best position to make, or strongly influence, overall marketing decisions and, more broadly, overall top-management decisions.

3. Finally, when people use the term *sales manager* they may refer to the top marketing executive, a vice president of sales, a divisional sales manager, a regional sales manager, a branch sales manager, or a product sales manager. In a large company there are many people in sales management at a number of levels. Conversely, when one speaks of the *management* of advertising or the *management* of credit, for example, there are relatively few people involved.

The traditional view of the functions of sales management is not only important but crucial to the success of most companies. A considerable portion of this text is devoted to the management of the sales representatives. However, in the modern view, that is only part of the job of sales management. Operating in a partial leadership vacuum, tomorrow's successful sales managers can and should influence every plan and every function of their companies. While a person may be hired to manage the sales force in the narrow sense, one should seek to influence everything relating to customers and potential customers. Top management will usually accept input from an intelligent sales manager and broaden the job as that manager demonstrates knowledge and abilities.

QUESTIONS

1 How can a sales manager use the concept of market segmentation to improve sales and profits? Illustrate with a product or service of your choice.

2 What are "D Features," and how can a sales manager identify and use them?

3 Describe the five functions of a distribution channel other than physically handling the product.

4 What determines how extensive a distribution system should be? Illustrate with products of your choice.

5 How does product maturity influence the sales manager's choice of alternate distribution systems?

6 How can a sales manager influence decisions in engineering, manufacturing, finance, and advertising?

SELECTED REFERENCES

Dunn, Albert H., Eugene M. Johnson, and **David L. Kurtz:** "The Sales Management Process," chap. 1 in *Sales Management,* General Learning Corporation, Morristown, N.J., 1974.
Jefferson Electric Company Marketing Case History, ³/₄-in. videocassette, 50 min, b&w, Intercollegiate Video Clearing House, Miami, Fla., 1976.
Johnson, H. Webster: "Sales Management Functions," chap. 1 in *Sales Management,* Charles E. Merrill Books, Inc., Columbus, Ohio, 1976.
Kotler, Philip: "Marketing Strategy," chap. 3, and "Market Segmentation and Targeting," chap. 7 in *Marketing Management: Analysis, Planning, and Control,* 3d ed., Prentice-Hall, Inc., Englewood Cliffs, N.J., 1976.
McCarthy, E. Jerome: "Marketing's Role within the Firm," chap. 2 in *Basic Marketing: A Managerial Approach,* 5th ed., Richard D. Irwin, Inc., Homewood, Ill., 1975.
Spitz, A. Edward, ed.: *Product Planning,* Auerback Publishers, Princeton, N.J., 1972.
Stanton, William J.: "Markets: People and Money," chap. 3, and

"Product Planning and Development," chap. 8 in *Fundamentals of Marketing,* 4th ed., McGraw-Hill Book Company, New York, 1975.

———— and **Richard H. Buskirk:** "The Sales Manager as an Administrator," chap. 3 in *Management of the Sales Force,* 4th ed., Richard D. Irwin, Inc., Homewood, Ill., 1974.

Still, Richard R., Edward W. Cundiff, and **Norman A. P. Govoni:** "Determining Sales Policies," chap. 3 in *Sales Management,* 3d ed., Prentice-Hall, Inc., Englewood Cliffs, N.J., 1976.

▶ **Case 1-1**

BARNES, LTD.

Al Johnson joined the field sales staff of Barnes, Ltd., liquor and wine department as a field salesman in 1971. During the final interview for the job he was told that he would be responsible for the sales, promotions, and servicing for all the company's accounts in the Montego Bay area in Jamaica. He would also be reporting directly to the manager of the sales department, which was located 150 miles away in Kingston.

The sales force consisted of Mike Magee, sales manager, Tom Sharp, assistant sales manager, and five salesmen. It was not very long before Al Johnson realized how badly organized the department was and the problems he was to encounter. His first problem was that he had three bosses, the sales manager, the assistant manager, and the manager from the plant that housed the branch office in Jamaica from which he worked. Al found it impossible to communicate with the sales manager, who was located in Kingston. The manager was either too busy or would have Al talk to his assistant, who for the most part was drunk. The assistant sales manager would relay telephone conversations as he interpreted them.

Although Al was instructed to solicit new accounts, there was no application blank provided for credit. Final authorization for credit had to come from the sales manager. This was a long and tedious operation, because if the manager did not know of this new customer, he would not give credit.

Another problem area was that of expenses for entertainment. Al would have to spend his own money, then submit a report which would be approved by the manager. These reports would be left on his desk for weeks before they were approved and sent to accounting, after which reimbursement checks could be made out.

Al often visited some of his bigger accounts only to learn that the manager had sneaked into town and visited these accounts. The manager would take their orders and not even try to contact Al. Sales meetings were infrequent and, when held, had no directions, values, or objectives. New products were introduced without Al being informed, and the only time he knew of these new products was when a shipment of goods came to his branch, where a sizable amount of inventory was kept.

Al had found some overlapping in his territory with another salesman, and when he asked about this, he was told that the manager wanted Al to concentrate on the hotels and duty-free shops in the area. In 1976 Al Johnson quit and the manager advertised for an experienced salesman. Although the manager was not related to the owners, he had worked for them for twenty-five years and was a trusted employee. The operation was very profitable and the owners were satisfied with the manager.

1 How would you evaluate this sales manager?

2 What would you do to correct the situation?

▶ **Case 1-2**

BENDIX CORPORATION AVIONICS DIVISION

Bendix Corporation Avionics Division, located in Fort Lauderdale, Florida, has specific policies when setting up dealerships to handle their line of instruments for general aviation. The normal steps taken to be qualified as a dealer are as follows:

1 Salesman recommends a dealer to become part of the Bendix organization.
2 The intended dealer then fills out the following:
   a Contract request
   b Shop form (type of equipment he has)
   c Credit application

3 The contract is then sent to the sales administrator in Fort Lauderdale, who processes it. He, in turn, sends it to Wichita, Kansas, where it is approved or disapproved.

4 The Wichita office then sends it back to Bendix, who then send it to the dealer.

Problems occur when the following happens: A salesman sells a unit of equipment to a customer and tells him to purchase it from Joe's Electronics. Meanwhile Joe is not authorized to sell Bendix equipment. Now the salesman has to have Joe qualified in order to sell to his customer. The salesman calls the plant and informs them that he is setting Joe up as an authorized representative. This the salesman wants done right away, because he has just made a sale.

It takes an average of thirty days for any new dealer application to be processed. The new dealer must apply for specific dealership. This is governed, by FAA regulations, by the type of equipment he has to install Bendix units. This is determined by the shop form that he fills out. He is not permitted to apply for any dealership which his equipment cannot handle. He not only has to sell the units, but he must be able to install them and provide future service if they need repair.

Meanwhile the customer is waiting for his unit. Because of this lack of understanding between the field salesman and the plant sales administrator many customers cancel their orders. This causes both a bad image and a loss of business.

1 What sales management policy would you adopt to improve this situation?

2 What guidelines would you recommend for salesmen to solicit new dealerships?

▶ Case 1-3

GLEANWOOD, INC.

A few independent manufacturers' representatives from my territory just happened to have finished their day in the same area and were having a cocktail at one of the golf clubs.

I had had some problems that day, and before I did anything hasty, I wanted to get some other views on the subject.

It was obvious from the look on my face that I was a little provoked, and when I sat down next to the rep from U.S. Royal, he said, "Jimbo, you look like you could use some Gator Aide."

"You're right as rain. Pards, if that little S.O.B. isn't redirected, one of these days I'm going to take him fishing and use him for bait."

"What do you mean?" my friend retorted.

"Well," I explained, "as you know, I represent Gleanwood, Inc., and it is a division of Wovencraft, Inc., with Gleanwood being the Pro Shop line and Wovencraft being the Store line."

My friend nodded understandingly.

"My territory includes all of the golf and tennis pro shops in the five counties. I am supposed to have an exclusive on anything delivered to any of these shops, and yet it doesn't seem to be working in all cases."

"What do you mean?" my colleague questioned.

"To be perfectly frank," I commented, "there are several pretty good-sized accounts that are being serviced by the guy who is supposed to be calling on the stores. Now, I don't call on any stores, and I wish he would keep out of the pro shops."

"What does the sales manager have to say about the situation?" my friend asked.

"It seems that his hands are tied," I responded. "It seems that this other guy has been representing the company for some fifteen years and writes a considerable amount of business. There has been quite a turnover in Pro-line reps, and the company honored the other guy's orders because they needed the business. Any restrictions placed on the Store rep would have to come from the company president, and for some reason it is difficult to approach him on that subject. As you know, even with this problem, I will write a lot of business with this company, and I really don't want to lose the line."

"Since you service these same accounts with your other lines, can't you get them to buy from you, instead of him?" my friend asked.

"Yes, in some cases I have been able to do this, but in some of the larger accounts I haven't been able to do it because he sells at Store-line prices, which are considerably lower than Pro-line prices. His price is about 50 cents a dozen under mine, and with an order for thirty to a hundred dozen, this can really mean something to the Pro, as the retail is the same and it means added profit for him."

"Jimbo, if I had the problem, I would darn sure get it straightened out or drop the line," my friend commented.

"Well, I sure don't want to drop the line because, like I said, I still write a lot of business, but I sure think someone should do something about it."

1 How should the sales manager handle this situation?

2 How might the independent manufacturer's agent clear up this problem?

▶ **Case 1-4**

SOUTHLAND FLOORS, INC.

Since its beginning in July 1974, Southland Floors had been struggling to make a dent in the Atlanta wholesale floor covering market. It was well financed by its parent company, Northern Carpet and Linoleum, of Brooklyn, New York, but the sale of floor coverings was quite different in Atlanta from what it was in the North—from the color which people preferred to the type of salesmanship expected. Nevertheless, Northern had been successful in New York and felt they could be successful with the Southland Floors venture.

The owners of Northern Carpet and Linoleum and John Marshall, Atlanta sales manager, chose the type of goods Southland would carry. The first line of products sold at Southland were Amtico tile products and various accessories. Later, a private line of cheap pure vinyl tile was introduced under the name of Kent Tile.

The first carpet lines of certain select fabrics to be stocked at Southland were supplied by Downs Carpet Company. All other fabrics were offered from the mill. Other carpet lines were supplied by certain mills and shipped under a private Southland name, Sunstream Carpets.

Carpet padding was supplied by Ludlow Corporation under the name of Ludlow Cushion. Lastly, artificial grass carpeting was supplied by Whitecrest Mills under the Sunstream name.

Since Southland Floors was a new company, there is very little sales history, but in the first six months it was estimated that total sales were about $600,000, with 80 percent coming from the tile business.

The Wholesale Carpet Market

The wholesale carpet market can be divided into two basic segments: contract carpet and domestic carpet dealers. The main difference between the two is that in contract carpets the ultimate user does not choose the carpet. For example, when a condominium or office building is built, the carpet is chosen and installed by the developer; whereas in the domestic market, the ultimate user usually chooses the carpet, as in a single-family-unit dwelling, where the family buys and installs the carpeting.

In Atlanta, the number of dealers who compete in each market is quite different. In the contract carpet market, only the large dealers seem to compete well for large contract deals such as condominiums and office buildings. This means the number of dealers in the contract market is minimal compared with the domestic market. In the domestic carpet market, there are large numbers of individual consumers, so that this market lends itself to many dealers. These dealers are known to carry many samples and not much inventory, relying almost totally upon the wholesalers' inventory.

Southland's Policy

Since the beginning, Southland's strategy about carpet was to first get the carpet samples into the retail stores, and then somehow to get the dealers to buy from the samples. Promotion was handled almost entirely by the individual sales representative in his or her own territory. It was believed that, as the samples were pushed, sales would soon result.

John Marshall arrived at the pricing policy, basing his figures on a 30 percent margin. For example, as shown in Exhibit I, Award carpeting with Jute backing sold for $2.75 a square yard, meaning that Southland's cost was $1.93 per square yard plus freight charges. John Marshall set these prices at 30 percent margin, figuring that he had plenty of room to bargain with the dealers and still make a profit. The sales representatives complained that the prices were too high; however, when they asked if they could bargain with a discount of their own, Marshall usually intervened and stopped their dealings. John Marshall wanted to sell all discounts on carpeting himself and often told the sales personnel that it

Exhibit 1 PRICES OF STOCKED CARPET LINES TO RETAIL
DEALERS, JANUARY 1976 (All prices per square yard)

Sunstream			Downs		
Line	Cut	Roll	Line	Cut	Roll
Award (J)	$3.00	$2.75	Silver Star	$ 7.50	$ 7.00
Award (HD)	3.25	3.00	Penn Centre	7.15	6.75
Westbury (HD)	3.60	3.35	Ocean Reef	8.00	7.25
Westbury (J)	3.30	3.15	Emerald Isle	11.00	10.25
Malibu (J)	4.25	4.00	Diamond Glow	11.18	10.25
Malibu (HD)	4.50	4.25	Bonnet Lane	8.25	8.10
Symphony	5.60	5.25	Palm Court	9.00	8.65
Woodmore	7.50	7.35	My Favorite	6.75	6.45
Allure	8.27	8.10			
Sagwest	5.15	5.00			
Classique	9.00	8.65			
Park Ridge	4.25	3.90			
Capri	6.00	5.50			
Ultima	5.75	5.30			
Nitrile Grass	3.00	2.80			
Durogan Grass	3.50	3.25			

was not their job to set Southland sales policy. By keeping control on all carpet discounts, Mr. Marshall believed that he could better control carpet profit margins, in addition to giving all salespersons an equal chance at any carpet promotions which he would institute.

In January 1976, Mr. John Marshall, sales manager for Southland Floors, Inc., was in the process of deciding upon which way to promote its carpet product line. Over the previous few months, Southland's hard-surface flooring business had been enjoying a steady increase. But the soft goods line, or carpet, was not moving very well. To help him make a decision, Mr. Marshall called a sales meeting and asked for suggestions as to how to promote the existing carpet lines. From this meeting came three serious suggestions:

1 Give a 5 percent discount on all carpet cuts for certain carpet lines to all dealers.

2 Give certain soft goods buyers all carpet cuts at one roll price.

3 Make one carpet line the carpet of the month and sell to all dealers carpet cuts at roll price and rolls at a 5 percent discount.

Each month the chosen carpet would be backed by heavy advertising.

1 How well do you think the sales manager handles the price policy?

2 Evaluate each of the three suggestions made by the sales representatives.

2

Integrating Sales Management with Other Marketing and Management Functions

▶ Objectives

The reader will be able to recognize the many ways a sales manager can and should integrate functional decisions on new product development, production, pricing, market research, and test marketing. The reader will understand the classical techniques to broaden a product line with minimum risk and when and how to thin a product line to increase profits. He or she will know alternate pricing strategies and how to use them, and will be able to construct test-market plans to evaluate quality perceived by customers, price range, channel acceptance, and promotional costs. Beyond quantification, the reader will be able to encourage the use of the creative input of the sales force for innovative ideas.

Traditional managements in most United States companies have divided the responsibilities of conducting their business into production or operations, finance, sales or marketing, and other functional specialties such as legal, advertising, and research and development. In many companies today, top management decides it wants to produce and market a complete line of new products. Production managers frequently decide how a product shall be produced and what materials shall be used. The finance department frequently dictates price increases and audits profit and loss of individual products to advocate an early termination of losses.

Modern sales management's *minimum responsibility is* to influence the decision-making process in all areas relating to the customer or potential sales. When such decisions are made by a number of executives with diverse functional responsibilities, the result is usually a hit-and-miss, haphazardly developed mess. It is essential for tomorrow's success that sales managers assume as much leadership in the decision process as possible. This does *not* mean one should give the customers whatever they demand at any price. It does assume, however, that a good sales manager knows the market best and should be responsible for seizing profitable opportunities to serve those markets.

There are a number of tried and proven techniques and strategies which can guide the prudent sales manager in broadening or contracting a product line. Other techniques are known which will help the manager in making pricing decisions and forecasting sales and profit success. A strong customer identification is a good philosophy; but when the sales manager wants to influence financial decisions, facts and figures are essential. The manager of the future will be equally concerned with innovation for success.

BROADENING THE PRODUCT LINE: CLASSICAL TECHNIQUES

When a company achieves success in selling a few products, it can grow rapidly by broadening its product line. But the risk of failure is high unless management follows some fundamental strategies. Of the hundreds of thousands of new products introduced in the United States annually, perhaps 60 to 80 percent fail. This would indicate that many people in management either do not know some basic principles or elect to ignore them.

An intelligent sales manager analyzes the company's strengths and weaknesses. Where possible, new products are added to match company

(1) BROADEN THE PRODUCT LINE

strengths. When a weakness is identified, it is not ignored but is held up to inspection and offsetting action. For example, as noted earlier, when the British-manufactured Wilkinson razor blades were first sold in the United States, they had limited acceptance and high distribution costs. The company was attempting to challenge the sleeping giant, Gillette, in its own back yard. It might have been disastrous if they had not acknowledged their weakness. Wilkinson contracted with Colgate-Palmolive Company to distribute their blades. Colgate's knowledge of the market and its promotional strength brought success for the imported blades.

2. Build on Past Successes When the Bilge King pump became a success for Crowell Designs, Inc., the company was able to rapidly broaden its new product line by simply adding a smaller bilge pump to its line called the "Mini King." This was an exact replica of its successful product scaled down for small boats. The same salespeople sold it to the same wholesalers and marinas with very little extra effort.

Cahners Publishing Company of Boston, Massachusetts, published *A Basic Guide for Buyers,* which was a simple how-to-do-it guide for beginners.[1] Surprisingly the book sold 70,000 copies in its first two years. Since Cahners also published *Purchasing* magazine, they were actually building on their own successful publishing experience. In September 1975, Cahners published *The Purchasing Agent's Guide to the Naked Salesman* as a companion book.[2] It deals with dirty tricks and unethical sales practices and the human, creative side of buying and selling. Clearly, Cahners marketed the new book on past successes through heavy advertising to loyal customers.

3. Innovation Is Essential When considering the addition of new products, it is essential for the sales manager to consider whether these honestly contribute something unique or different to the customers. The innovation does not have to be an invention or something new under the sun, but it should be new to that manager's industry.

The Intercollegiate Video Clearing House of Miami, Florida, offers

[1] James Dowst, *A Basic Guide for Buyers,* Cahners Publishing Company, Boston, Mass., 1973.

[2] Barry J. Hersker and Thomas F. Stroh, *The Purchasing Agent's Guide to the Naked Salesman,* Cahners Publishing Company, Boston, Mass., 1975.

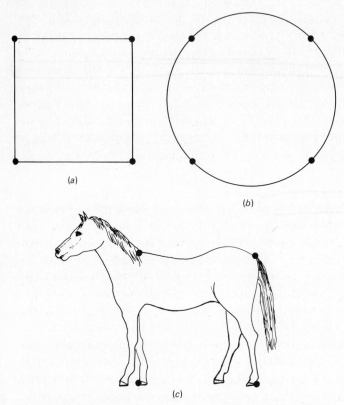

(a)

(b)

(c)

Connect Four Dots. To encourage innovation the sales manager can remove normal constraints. In step *a* the dots are connected simply in a box shape without any use of the imagination. Step *b* is more creative because the connecting line goes outside and beyond the area covered by the dots. Step *c* is innovative because it creates a new form—a horse—from the same four dots.

educational programs to universities. In 1976 it obtained an excellent series of films on international business produced by the Caterpillar Tractor Company. This series was new to the university market in videocassette format and was well received. The distribution company broadened its product line by offering something that was unknown to its customers.

In 1975 it was forecast that by 1980 digital watches would account for 30 percent or more of the world market, with United States companies selling about half of this business and perhaps two-thirds of the uncased watch module production.[3] Significantly, it was not the old American watchmakers who finally found a way to beat the Swiss. It was a bunch of newcomers to the industry, such as Texas Instruments, who saw that the way to win was to go back to the laboratory and invent a new way to tell time. Without the hundreds of small parts that make the mechanical watch a labor-intensive product, the digital watch is assembled in minutes at low cost. In addition, it is more reliable and accurate than the clockwork mechanisms. In a similar way, this United States industry had recaptured the consumer calculator market from Japan a few years earlier.

Identification Any new product considered by a sales manager should be naturally identified and accepted by the target market. A satisfied user of a Black and Decker electric drill, for example, can easily recognize Black and Decker's electric sanding machines and many other power tools. These items are sold in the same hardware stores. The customer willingly looks for new products where he habitually shops. He attaches the same high-quality image of products he has used in the past to the new ones being offered.

Because identification is so important in broadening a product line, many companies spend millions of dollars protecting their brands. They dare not introduce a poor-quality product under the family name. The world-famous "Heinz 57 Varieties" of pickles now has been generalized to cover over 2000 food products under the Heinz 57 label.

New products sold through retail stores receive increased consumer acceptance when the point-of-purchase displays identify them with the older successful products. Whether the display is a simple card hanging overhead or a large stand, identification increases consumer acceptance. Del Monte foods, for example, found that this identification concept increased sales over 200 percent as compared with the same new products sold in the same chain but in stores that did not use the point-of-purchase materials.[4]

Sears, Roebuck and Company also uses the identification concept

---

[3]"Beating the Competition," editorial, *Business Week,* Oct. 27, 1975. See also: "How TI Beat the Clock on Its $20 Digital Watch," *Business Week,* May 31, 1976. (Texas Instruments, Inc., estimated 20 million units would be made worldwide in 1976.)

[4]Point of Purchase Advertising Institute, Study No. 23, 1971.

when broadening its product lines. The company offers good-quality, better-quality, and best-quality items for many product categories. This triples the product line of Sears' own brands and is a real aid to customer choice.

5. **Compatibility** For a sales manager to make a recommendation on a new product, it is essential first to decide whether or not the plant has the right machines with enough idle time to produce it. Do the factory workers have the necessary skills? Procter and Gamble Company applies a detailed checklist before deciding to turn out a new product. This list includes compatibility in manufacturing and its distribution. Procter and Gamble determines whether the new product will be sold through the same wholesalers and retailers as its other products. The company also makes sure the sales force can sell the new product without expensive training. Of course, new products are test-marketed, but Procter and Gamble has used compatibility as an early discriminator of the likely success or failure of many new products.

Reader's Digest magazine also uses the criterion of compatibility in judging new products. Educational and entertainment books and records for family audiences fitted in naturally, thereby increasing its product line and profits substantially. By choice and intent, the direct-mail distribution system is the same for all products.

Incidentally, it should be noted that none of these criteria are rigid and none automatically cancels a new product idea. They are flexible. However, they do call management's attention to possible problem areas early in the planning stage. For example, a sales manager wishing to persuade an executive committee to broaden a product line should know what additional machines the plant will need, at what cost, and how long it will take to train the operators. This need not be a permanent obstacle to the proposal if the manager is well prepared.

6. **Systems Orientation** Another fundamental strategy to broaden a product line is known as *systems orientation*. When a customer is about to use a product, what else does he need with it?

For example, when the Bilge King pump was to be installed in a boat, the manufacturer knew the following items would be needed and wisely decided to package them in one kit: (1) water hoses, (2) clamps, (3) an outlet nozzle, (4) an electronic switch, and (5) wire. These accessories are all essential for installing an automatic bilge-pumping system. They are also highly profitable additions to the product line.

Brazilian-born Michael Kami, when he was an IBM vice president, used the systems concept when planning a computer product line. He realized that the complete system in use would require input devices, remote terminals, display terminals, and high-speed printers. It was designed to later expand the memory and manipulation devices to perform more functions with larger amounts of data. Dr. Kami says, "The systems orientation is a fundamental principle in planning to broaden a product line."[5] He used this concept again with Xerox as vice president of long-range planning and still uses it today in working with many small companies.

While the systems orientation sounds new, it is really an old, time-tested strategy to broaden a product line. For example, when a man buys a new suit, he wants to look his best. When he wears it, he will also need good shoes, a shirt, tie, underwear, and socks. The systems orientation is simply the adding of accessories to the main product purchased. If all the extras can be purchased conveniently from the same source, they become natural product additions. Individual accessories are relatively inexpensive compared with the main product. But they are readily accepted and usually generate high profits.

PRODUCT LIFE CYCLE: WHEN TO THIN A PRODUCT LINE

A new product may fail because not enough funds are committed to launch its sales promotion. A successful product may begin to decline in sales and considerable funds may be wasted in attempting to revive it. As these two extremes indicate, the familiar product life cycle is often forgotten by executives. The intelligent sales manager knows how to manipulate the factors which influence the product's life cycle.

Product Life Cycle The idea is based upon the fact that a product's sales volume follows a typical pattern of four phases. After its birth, the product passes through a low–sales-volume introductory phase. Advertising and promotional funds often exceed total revenue from the product

---

[5]*Crowell Designs, Inc., Marketing Case History,* op. cit.

2ᴺᴰ STAGE

at this stage. During the following growth stage, sales volume rises sharply, revenues exceed the break-even point, and profits rise. In the third stage, sales volume is stabilized although profit margin usually begins to decline. Increased competition and price cutting often occur during this third phase. Eventually, in the obsolescence stage of the product, the sales volume and profits decline. *4/ 7ᵀᴴ STAGE*

3 RD STAGE

The length of the life cycle, the duration of each stage, and the shape of the sales curve vary widely for different products. In most cases obsolescence occurs because the need declines, because a better or cheaper product fills the same need, or because a competitive product suddenly gains a decisive advantage.

Manipulating the Curve When the Pall Corporation, manufacturer of industrial filters, introduced a new superior filter, it wanted to hasten the first phase. George Feely, vice president of sales, says "We knew we had to prove our superiority by demonstration. This meant expensive field tests and heavy marketing spending. Without this commitment of funds we might not have succeeded."[6] Their new porous stainless steel filter system quickly made competitors' inferior systems obsolete.

[6]*Pall Corporation Marketing Case History,* Intercollegiate Video Clearing House, Miami, Fla., 1976.

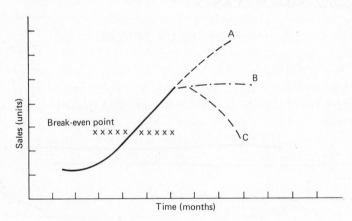

A By adding new target segments, sales to new users can be increased.
B By continuing to improve the product, steady sales can be maintained.
C By doing nothing differently, sales will eventually drop to unprofitable levels.

Product Life Cycle

During the growth period a marketer has a competitive edge and wisely exploits it. Westvaco introduced plastic-coated corrugated boxes to replace wire-bound wooden crates. Dick Alexander, the product manager, says, "We figured the product life cycle was about seven years from introduction to price-deteriorating maturity. We entered the produce market, the fish market, the meat market, and the hardware market all in the first year. We were able to accelerate the growth stage to profitable levels in a very short time."[7]

When the sales curve begins to level off, intelligent marketing people look for ways to increase sales. They search for new targets who are not using their products. Ed McNulty, of International Papers, says, "When we experienced a tapering of sales growth in our milk carton division, we looked at what else might be put into our package. Through some product modification we were able to capture much of the Coca-Cola syrup packaging replacing the glass gallon jug."[8] They are constantly searching for other new target segments to prolong the growth phase.

During obsolescence, cost control is the key factor in generating profits. Sam E. MacArthur, board charman of Federal-Mogul, worldwide manufacturer of engine parts, says, "We analyzed our product line and eliminated the low-volume items. We increased our production and marketing efficiencies to become the best low-cost producer and distributor of bearings and engine components. Our products enjoy a profitable old age long after competitors have disappeared from the scene."[9]

Revitalizing Mature Products The shape and duration of a product's life cycle can be changed sharply in the mature stage. Len Casey, of E. I. du Pont, tells how they were the strongest producer of cellophane from World War II into the 1950s. Then polyethylene film threatened to replace cellophane unless strong corrective action was taken. Casey says, "Du Pont launched a series of product modifications to reduce costs and increase product usage. In spite of predicted rapid sales decline, we were able to extend the life of cellophane at least fifteen years at a steady sales

[7]*Westvaco Cora Cool Marketing Case History,* op. cit.

[8]*International Paper Company Marketing Case History,* Intercollegiate Video Clearing House, 1976.

[9]Address to Marketing Club, Florida Atlanta University, Boca Raton, Fla., 1976.

volume.''[10] At the same time Du Pont recognized the maturity of cellophane and developed a strong position in polyethylene and other packaging materials.

When Procter and Gamble entered the cake-mix market in the United States, competitors felt the market was overcrowded and in a mature stage. Procter and Gamble introduced a large number of different cake mixes. This actually increased demand because more consumers were interested in variety and were persuaded to bake them more often. It took intelligence from Procter and Gamble to expand their cake-mix product line rather than cut it back as others were considering doing. Their research showed the product had not yet reached the mature stage, which competitors had incorrectly assumed.

Auditing Product Life Cycles   Intelligent sales managers can manipulate the life cycle of their products when they make periodic reviews or audits of each product and of the range of products. Many begin by developing historical trends of unit and dollar sales, profit margins, market share, and price. They then look at the numbers of competitors and new product introductions or modifications. By projecting sales and profits over the next three to five years they can typically see when profit margins will deteriorate.

Once a product has peaked in sales and is becoming obsolete, most of the advertising and sales promotion budget can be cut. These funds may be used for research and development or they may be put directly into profit. Sales will go down regardless of the spending level of promotion or of the efforts of the sales force.

Thin-Out Line for Increased Profits   A small candy company in New York City had a product line of almost 800 different items. Sales of almost every item were declining and the company was in serious trouble. By analyzing the life cycle of each item they were able to identify only four growth products. They decided to put all their promotional budget on these four items and discontinue all other products. They shifted production from early-obsolescence to growth products. Today they are one of the most profitable operations in the confectionery business.

Westvaco makes kraft paper and converts it into the familiar brown

[10]Ibid.

grocery bags. This same grade of paper, however, is also used in the manufacture of laminated products such as Formica, Micarta, and Textolite. Today demand for the newer product is strong and highly profitable. Westvaco increased production of the new products and happily reduced allotments of the low-profit grocery bags. Most other paper producers have found that strong demand for newer products has enabled them to reduce or eliminate grades of paper which yielded little or no profit.

Thinning out a product line can reduce inventories, make them more manageable, and permit an increased production of the remaining items at lower costs. This is not simply an accounting or financial decision. There are situations in which *loss leaders* may be essential. These may be desirable to give good service to large customers and to build loyalty and regular buying habits. Loss leaders give sales managers the opportunity to obtain highly profitable add-on sales. The decision to thin a product line should be done by a knowledgeable sales manager who is familiar with customer needs and with the competition. It should not be made solely by production or finance managers. A sales audit of the product cycle is the key.

PRICING METHODS FOR LONG-TERM PROFIT

A basic method of pricing is *cost plus* a fixed percentage. For example, a large United States manufacturer of office furniture has tight cost controls for every manufacturing process. They add a fixed percentage for their manufacturing profit, and this results in their wholesale price to their dealers. Since they also sell direct, they divide the wholesale cost by 6 and multiply by 10 to set the retail price. For example, if wholesale cost is $72, the retail price would be $120, giving the retailer a fixed 40 percent gross profit margin. This method is easily understood and accepted.

A second method of pricing is called the *flexible markup*. It is used when markets are unstable or highly competitive. Each gasoline retailer, for example, wants to cover costs and earn as much as possible above that figure. When supplies are plentiful, the retailer's price must be kept competitive because consumers feel all gasoline is the same. When supplies are short, the retailer can increase the markup, and people will still line up at the pumps. Regional independent dealers of off brands are permitted to price their product a few cents below the name brands. If they cut the price more than the few cents allowed, the name brands match the lower price in a price war. Without collusion, the off-brand dealer quickly learns to adjust prices to stay within the permissible few cents' difference from name brands.

For new products, a third method of pricing is often used. It is called the *research method of pricing.* Market researchers ask prospective customers what they think about a forthcoming product. They attempt to find out the value of the new product as customers view it and their intentions about possible purchase. Al Sklar, vice president of Jefferson Electric Company in Illinois, says, "We used market research to determine price elasticity. We found there was a great demand for our Golden Hour Clock at $19.95 and substantially lower demand at $24.95. We were able to get our costs down through the economies of large-scale production. At the lower price we were hard pressed to fill all of the orders."[11]

Experimental pricing is a fourth method used by some marketing men. In this method the product is offered for sale against all competitive efforts in several test cities. In each city the price is different and sales are measured against competition. Fred Wynn of Texize Corporation says, "We used experimental pricing in three areas of California and another in Iowa to gauge demand at various price levels and to measure repeat purchases of our new Spray 'N Wash laundry product. With this information we were then able to launch our product nationally and we enjoy the lion's share of that product category."[12]

Intuitive pricing is a fifth method. It relies heavily on executive experience. Based on years of working in one industry, some sales executives have a feeling for pricing. They seem to know how much people will pay for certain innovations. Univis is a manufacturer of bifocal lenses for eyeglasses. Their product manager, Frank Brink, says, "We developed a new machine which could save our customers lab processing time. Based on years of experience selling to these people, we knew how much money they could save. We decided to charge them half of the savings."[13] In two years they captured more than 50 percent of the

[11] *Jefferson Electric Company Marketing Case History,* op. cit.

[12] *Texize Spray 'N Wash Marketing Case History,* Intercollegiate Video Clearing House, Miami, Fla., 1976.

[13] *Univis Division, Itek, Marketing Case History,* Intercollegiate Video Clearing House, Miami, Fla., 1976.

market. At that point they announced a price reduction to prevent potential rivals from entering this lucrative market. Because of their long-term pricing policy, to date no competitor has entered this field.

The sixth and final method of pricing is called *multistage pricing.* Intelligent sales managers begin with the selection of market segments or targets. Next they decide upon a brand image. Then they compute the cost of promotion to achieve stated goals. This, together with manufacturing costs, enables them to figure the break-even point at various price levels. Test marketing may be necessary for some products at this point. Executive experience may enable others to set firm prices. Most companies will have a broad policy on pricing, such as "above average market price." This then influences the final selection of a specific price.

Sears, Roebuck and Company uses this multistage pricing with a unique variation. For most of their product lines they offer Good, Better, and Best. While each category is intended for a different market segment, the greatest sales should always be of the middle-priced merchandise. If there are more sales of the Best item than either of the others, prices are too low. Conversely, if there are more sales of the lowest offering, prices are too high. This method is used in selling many industrial products with categories such as Economy model, Standard, and Deluxe. Clearly, if the pricing is right, the standard model should be the best seller.

In the computer industry one can see IBM using "umbrella pricing," or pricing intentionally high to protect the entire industry. This also reduces the risk of legal prosecution. They will tolerate and protect small competitors. Any large-scale threat to their share of market is met very quickly and strongly.

Another example of a broad pricing policy is the "Gillette Concept." You can afford to give the customer the razor if he will then buy your blades for many years. This pricing policy is used by one sales manager of office products and systems. The company will often bid low on steel files when they are confident they will get the file folder business for many years to come. Heavy industrial equipment can often be priced at or near cost provided there is a profitable long-term service contract along with it.

For long-term profitable operations, experienced sales managers have a policy for pricing in a declining market. First, they want to drive unethical companies out of the market. For their own survival they meet the lowest price offered. Second, they are willing to take a short-term loss and help their dealers. They do not *lead* a price decline. The sooner unethical producers leave the market, the quicker profitable operations can resume.

Conversely, in a booming market, prudent sales managers are careful not to become greedy. High profits tend to invite government inquiries. Suppliers of raw materials want higher prices. Organized labor may demand higher wages. Unusually high profits also attract potential rivals and increase competition. The old adage, "Charge all the traffic will bear," is no longer appropriate.

The criterion of a good price is best recognized by the limits of extremes. A price is too low when it is below cost or when customers would readily pay more. When sales are too easy or when salespeople can make their quota working half-time, prices are probably too low. On the other hand, if a *slight* reduction in price would increase sales greatly, it is likely that prices are too high. Finally, if a very *substantial* price reduction would be required to stimulate sales *slightly,* price certainly is not too high.

FORECASTING SALES BASED ON VARIOUS LEVELS OF SUPPORT

Sales managers are frequently embarrassed in executive committee sessions when asked, "How many units can your sales reps move the first year?" While the answer is obvious—that it depends on price, promotional support, competition, and customer acceptance—this knowledge is of little value to the committee.

Early in the process of new product development, sales managers should urge that plans be made to test-market at various prices and at various levels of promotional support. When executed properly, such test-marketing data will generate facts and figures which will indicate a probability of certain sales volumes over a period of time at relative costs. Given such data, an executive committee can decide on various options, knowing approximately how much risk is involved. If the tests were well designed, the basic inferences will be valid and the sales manager will be well respected. If the tests were poorly designed or the manager supplies "guestimates" off the top of his head without factual support, he loses respect. Such are the demands on sales managers today which were not stressed ten years ago.

Test Marketing: One Variable per Test Area   When broadening a product line under a well-established name or brand, there is always the risk of a new product failing. This may seriously hurt the family brand name. If the new product seems cheap, or of poor quality, customers may think the entire line has been cheapened.

Some new products require lengthy promotions to gain acceptance. Frequently the introductory costs on a national level are so great that they outweigh the profit potential. In other cases, a product may be so different that there are no guidelines for pricing it. The marketing executive wants to know how many people will buy it at several different possible prices.

For these and many similar reasons, effective marketing people test new product candidates in competitive small areas before spending millions of dollars on a national introduction. Inexperienced managers often try one marketing mix in one small marketing area. They foolishly let the results of the one test area dictate their decision on whether or not to introduce the new product on a national basis. A cardinal rule in test marketing is to test *one variable* in each small test area.

Quality Perceived by Customer   The Bic Pen Corporation of Milford, Connecticut, has a 70 percent share of the ball-point pen market in the United States. It also has a 33 percent share of the disposable butane lighter market. With such broad distribution and consumer acceptance of their brand name, they were reluctant to market panty hose without test marketing. The hosiery is manufactured in France by Dim S. A., in which Bic Pen Corporation has a controlling interest. They wanted to sell through the company's traditional United States outlets, using its existing sales force.[14]

For eighteen months they tested the panty hose in a number of different small Midwest cities under the name of Fannyhose. That name was used to protect the Bic brand in the event it did not succeed. After data were accumulated on dealer margins, pricing, and promotional spending, they decided the new product could succeed.

[14]The Bic illustration is taken from *Advertising Age,* July 7, 1975, p. 1.

According to John L. Paige, vice president of marketing, "The line was renamed Bic pantyhose after testing to capitalize on the widespread consumer recognition of the Bic brand name."[15] It was then launched, beginning in October 1975, in fifty major United States markets.

Price Range During the eighteen-month testing period, Bic used five different small cities to test price elasticity. They priced slightly above competition at $1.39 in one city and 10 cents lower in each of three others, down to 99 cents in the fifth city. In all cities the line was sold under the Fannyhose trademark.

Toward the end of the testing period it was decided that the 99-cent price would generate ample increased sales. In each of the five cities they withdrew Fannyhose at various prices and introduced Bic Pantyhose at 99 cents. Sufficient sales volume was obtained in these test cities to enable Bic to set a goal of a 5 percent share of the estimated $800 million panty hose market within one year.

Channel Acceptance In other test cities during this same time period, Bic tried to find out how much it would cost to get good retailer support. The best-selling competitive brand was L'eggs, which offered retailers a 35 percent gross profit. In one city, all retailers were offered Fannyhose at the same profit margin.

The second best-selling competitor, No Nonsense brand, was offering retailers 42 percent gross profit. In a second test city, all retailers were offered Fannyhose at 42 percent gross margin.

In a third test city Fannyhose was offered to all retailers at a higher gross margin of 50 percent. Sales analysis over a period of time showed this offer was essential to get good retailer acceptance and cooperation. Retailers willingly gave the requested floor space and used point-of-purchase materials at this high markup. Increased volume permitted the passing along of savings to the retailer.

Promotional Costs In July of 1975, the Pillsbury Company of Minneapolis, Minnesota, announced it would test-market in five cities a new product called Egg Baskets. These are refrigerated dough shaped into cups. Eggs are broken into them and put in the oven for baking.[16]

Using the well-established Pillsbury name, they were clearly testing

[15]Ibid.
[16]Ibid.

the promotional level necessary to achieve success. In the five cities they tested five levels of promotional spending. They used spot television, direct-mail coupons, and local newspaper advertising. The use of a number of cities permitted them to reasonably bracket the promotional costs required to generate desired sales volume. This result was then projected on a national basis to determine the likelihood of success before spending millions of dollars.

Incidentally, in the Bic panty hose testing, the line was supported with a heavy spot-television and Sunday-supplement newspaper campaign. They projected, based on testing costs, that it would require a $7 million advertising budget nationally to achieve $40 million in sales in the first year. Their thorough test marketing provided the facts necessary to make this sizable commitment.

Cannibalizing Your Own Sales The National Brewing Company, brewers of a number of famous-brand beers, wanted to reach non-beer drinkers in order to increase sales. They developed a sweet-tasting malt liquor named Malt Duck Liquor. One of their major fears, however, was that the new product would be purchased by existing customers and the new brand would simply cannibalize, or eat into, existing sales.

Before taking this risk nationally, they wisely decided to test-market the new product in seven cities. The first phase was to give free samples of six bottles of Malt Duck Liquor to young adult females in supermarkets. Eighty-four percent of those given samples later reported they liked its taste. The second phase of the test was to offer it for sale at a range of prices and in two bottle sizes. Of those who had tried the free samples, 75 percent actually purchased more of the product.

While their initial target market segment was young adult females, they found in test marketing that young adult males were also buying in equal numbers. In all seven cities they also monitored the sales of beer and wine for the three-month test period. They found there was no loss of sales in either beverage in any of the test cities. National concluded that the new sweet-tasting product was hitting its new target without taking sales away from their other successful products.

Based on test-market data, they were confident enough to launch a $4 million national campaign to introduce this new product. The test-marketing data also indicated the best price and most desirable small-bottle size. They successfully reached their sales target of 4 million cases sold the first year without cannibalizing their other product lines.

Testing Changes in Old Products While most test marketing is concentrated on new products, many companies test changes in old products before announcing the change nationally. For example, Spray 'N Wash, noted earlier, was being sold in 8-ounce bottles at a price equal to Procter and Gamble's 16-ounce competitive product. Texize reformulated their spot-remover laundry product so that they could also offer the 16-ounce size at the same price. They were afraid consumers would not believe the new formula was as strong and effective as the old.

Fred Wynn, then Texize Group Product Manager, said "We test-marketed the new formula in two cities. We sold out the entire old stock and could not keep up with demand for the new formula in just three months." Today his products dominate the United States market in their categories. Sales manager Wynn says, "The only way I know to beat giant competitors is to constantly improve your products and test-market thoroughly before making any national commitments."[17]

BRAINSTORMING TECHNIQUES FOR INNOVATION

Traditionally, Americans are intrigued with numbers, measurements, and statistics. These are assumed to be objective evidence of some achievement—such as the tallest building, the longest bridge, the largest share of the market, or the largest advertising budget. There is no question that objective numbers *are essential* to every sales manager. But, in our quest for objective numbers, too often we Americans ignore the role of creativity and innovation in making products and services into commercial successes.

Creativity is not new to management, but its potential has hardly been scratched. More and more companies are holding brainstorming sessions in their management training programs, and creativity is fast becoming a mark of the professional manager.

Contrary to popular belief, every normal person has a considerable amount of latent creative talent. The creative process is the constructive exercise of one's imaginative powers to develop a new idea. In a selling situation, imagination can help the sales representatives to visualize new

[17] *Texize Spray 'N Wash Marketing Case History,* op. cit.

applications and new target segments for their products. Imagination can help the sales manager to visualize improved product features to give customers greater utilization or satisfaction. It can provide ideas for new solutions to customer problems. While sales managers cannot be expected to teach creativity, they can certainly encourage the regular use of imagination to further development of creativity in every sales representative.

Relatively few people use their imagination to the extent to which they might. Many feel they do not have an imaginative mind or do not recognize how situations could benefit if imagination were applied to them. To be creative, a person must be able to look at a situation without the normal constraints. For example, when told to connect four dots on a piece of paper, the less imaginative person will probably draw a square or a straight line. Another person, using more imagination, may draw a circle with the dots on the circumference, or some more elaborate figure, or an animal, for example.

Brainstorming   The manager who is interested in developing creativity in the sales force, other marketing managers, or the executive committee encourages the group to dream up as many imaginative ideas as they can without exercising value judgments. For example, the sales manager of a manufacturer of corrugated boxes held a brainstorming sales meeting in which he asked the sales force for possible uses of their product. The only rule was that there be no criticism or judgment of anyone's suggestion. The first twenty to thirty suggestions concerned novel uses of boxes, but then someone suggested the material be used as flooring and wall covering. Thus stimulated, someone else suggested that the material be used for point-of-purchase three-dimensional displays. Another suggested it be compressed into fireplace logs, while another suggested adding a plastic coating and using the product to make living room furniture. Within the hour allotted for the session, several hundred creative ideas were put forth by the sales force.

Brainstorming sessions do not have to be limited to a few strange characters on Madison Avenue. When the rule book and constraints are thrown away, sales representatives can use their minds as imaginatively as any other group of people. The group process tends to release inhibitions, and almost everyone in the room gets caught up in the creative spirit. Many an idea suggested in jest at such a session has turned into a multimillion-dollar market. Indeed, the industry created by the point-of-sale display idea noted above is now estimated to gross $2 billion per year.

As mentioned earlier, creativity and innovation do not necessarily mean developing something new under the sun; rather, they mean identifying an idea or a process which is new to an industry. For example, a teaser campaign to introduce a new product might be appropriate in an industry that had not used this technique in twenty years or more. A series of announcements or interesting pieces of mail might very well stimulate the prospect to look forward to the new product. But competition is quick to imitate success, and novel ideas rapidly become boring. Therefore, the sales organization which encourages creative thinking is more likely to build a series of novel campaigns to stay well ahead of the traditional followers in an industry.

Subconscious Creativity Much of a person's thinking occurs in the twilight zone just below the conscious level. In this area the artificial restrictions and constraints do not operate very well, and the mind is free to associate thoughts that it otherwise might keep separate. Consequently many people have found it practical to "forget" about a problem for a while or to "sleep on it" before making a decision. Often they will hit upon a unique idea or solution when their minds are consciously on another topic. A chance remark by a friend may trigger the solution to a problem which had been put on the back burner to simmer a while. Many people go through life without thinking about the creative process, while others intentionally utilize this power of the subconscious mind.

Whether the use of creative thinking and innovating is encouraged by direct methods such as brainstorming or by indirect or delayed methods such as presenting a problem one day and asking for ideas a week later, all participants should be praised for any contributions. When someone uses a creative idea on the job and has success, this should be well publicized and praised in order to reinforce the creative process. In other words, the creative effort should always be rewarded and never judged on the basis of its practical or commercial applications. Out of several hundred creative suggestions made, someone else or an executive committee may decide which few are worth pursuing at this time. Decision making is a different skill and should not be confused with the creative process.

SUMMARY

In a typical business many responsibilities are divided into functional organizations with a specialist managing each separate function. This often leads to many different managers making decisions at different times which will affect customers and sales. Whether the business climate is highly competitive between managers or highly cooperative, it is the sales manager's minimal responsibility to at least attempt to influence every decision made which will affect customers and future sales. The sales manager should know the customers and their needs better than any other executive in the same company.

There are guidelines or classical strategies tried and proven which can help the sales manager influence decisions regarding broadening a product line. These include the concepts of identification, compatibility, and systems orientation. In a similar manner the concept of the product's life cycle can guide the sales manager in recommending actions regarding contracting a product line.

Many pricing decisions can be strongly influenced by a sales manager who understands price theory and who is able to plan and conduct valid test-marketing programs. Given such data, the manager can more reasonably forecast sales volume based on various levels of price and various levels of promotional support.

Finally, in their search for statistical data to support influencing decisions, the sales managers of the future will find it essential to encourage and utilize creative thinking and innovating. In the long run these subjective areas may have a greater impact on success than will the objective measurements and controls. At the least, one would not dare to ignore them.

QUESTIONS

1 In broadening a product line of your choice, show how you would use the concepts of (*a*) identification, (*b*) compatibility, and (*c*) systems orientation.

2 Show how a sales manager might manipulate the product life cycle curve (*a*) early in its introductory period and (*b*) late in its maturing stage.

3 What factors should be considered when deciding on thinning out a product line to increase profits?

4 Describe the six alternate methods of developing a pricing strategy and note when they can be appropriate.

5 Show how a sales manager can test-market several variables in the marketing mix simultaneously.

6 How can a sales force be encouraged to submit numerous ideas and suggestions for new products or new uses for existing products?

SELECTED REFERENCES

Hersker, Barry J., and **Thomas F. Stroh:** *The Purchasing Agent's Guide to the Naked Salesman,* Cahners Publishing Company, Boston, Mass., 1975.

Heskett, James L.: "Formulating Marketing Strategy," chap. 12 in *Marketing,* The Macmillan Company, New York, 1976.

Johnson, H. Webster: "The Sales Manager," chap. 3 in *Sales Management,* Charles E. Merrill Books, Inc., Columbus, Ohio, 1976.

Kotler, Philip: "Product Life Cycle Strategy," chap. 11, and "Price Decisions," chap. 12 in *Marketing Management: Analysis, Planning, and Control,* 3d ed., Prentice-Hall, Inc., Englewood Cliffs, N.J., 1976.

McCarthy, E. Jerome: "Overview of Marketing Strategy Planning," chap. 4 in *Basic Marketing: A Managerial Approach,* 5th ed., Richard D. Irwin, Inc., Homewood, Ill., 1975.

Pall Corporation Marketing Case History, $3/4$-in. videocassette, 50 min, b&w, Intercollegiate Video Clearing House, Miami, Fla., 1976.

Stanton, William J.: "Product Line Policies and Strategies," chap. 9, and "Price Policy and Strategies," chap. 12 and 13 in *Fundamentals of Marketing,* 4th ed., McGraw-Hill Book Company, New York, 1975.

Still, Richard R., Edward W. Cundiff, and **Norman A. P. Govoni:** "Sales Department Relations," chap. 7 in *Sales Management,* 3d ed., Prentice-Hall, Inc., Englewood Cliffs, N.J., 1976.

▶ **Case 2-1**

WHYO RADIO STATION

In October of 1974 WHYO radio station had established itself as a top contender for the young adult listening audience (aged 17 to 25) in its area. After being on the air only one year in a competitive market with thirty-three stations, WHYO carried an impressive 60 percent share of the total listening audience. Only three other stations competed for the same target audience.

The tremendous growth of this new station was attributed to the comprehensive marketing plan that was created. Through the use of billboards, trade-outs with newspapers, trade magazines, and television, and promotions such as $50 cash calls, slogans, T-shirts, and car stickers, the station literally captivated the young adult listening audience. In November 1974 with the advent of the Christmas season, the market-place was at its highest potential. The management of WHYO set its monthly goal at $100,000 in advertising sales with a sales force of eight salespeople. This goal was reached successfully, and in December the goal was $150,000 as a result of the surge of business attributed to the peak holiday rush. This goal was also obtained and even marginally surpassed.

In January 1975 the business entity as a whole regressed and sales dropped considerably on the local market. National representation, however, because of the tremendous growth of the past rating period, increased their advertising budget to WHYO, resulting in the prime-time advertising space being bought by national accounts for much higher rates than the local trade was paying. This occurrence had rather immediate effects on the overall objectivity of the sales management. The first step they took was to establish a concrete decree to the sales force. As of February 1, 1975, there would be no exceptions of the new rate card that was introduced as of that date. The new rate card was 25 percent higher across the board in all categories. Also, the management required all new orders to be sold BTA (best time available) unless the retail establishment was willing to pay equal rates with national ads.

For the next two months, local sales dropped to the lowest they had been since the beginning of the operation, resulting in a 90 percent turnover in the sales force.

1 How might the sales manager have handled this situation to retain the best of his eight salespeople?

2 What additional promotions might be used to maintain audience loyalty?

▶ **Case 2-2**

PLYMOUTH GOLF BALLS, SHAKESPEARE GOLF CLUBS

Shakespeare, the parent company, has been in the golf club construction business for thirty-seven years. Plymouth Golf Club Company has been manufacturing golf balls since 1916 and is the world's largest exclusive manufacturer of golf balls. On a contract basis they manufacture golf balls for most of the major golf club companies.

Shakespeare had experimented with the glass shaft for golf clubs (it was too heavy to be practical) and the aluminum shaft (it was unsuitable because of the fatigue factor). Finally the engineering department was charged with the task of coming up with a shaft better than steel, lightweight steel, or carbon steel, the shafts currently in use by most manufacturers of golf clubs.

At the same time, or thereabouts, the president of Plymouth called his engineers together and stated that, since Plymouth manufactures most of the balls, "Why can't you people come up with a ball that we can put our name on and get a piece of the action for us?"

After nearly five years' research and testing, Shakespeare introduced the first graphite shaft. They really had something. It was lighter than steel and it was stronger. How could they possibly go wrong?

About the same time Plymouth announced the Sigma Ball. It was a surlyn-covered, tightly wound ball that was, as stated in their advertising, "as good as any ball."

The national sales manager for Shakespeare/Plymouth announced at the sales meeting, "We have got it captured, we have the hottest thing in golf. We not only have the best shaft in the world, but we also have a ball as good as any ball out there."

Sales were fantastic at first; orders simply could not be filled. Three years later, Shakespeare/Plymouth ranks about twelfth behind Exxon, Graftek, Aldila, and Sceptre, to mention only a few.

Performance tests prove that the Shakespeare is a superior shaft and the Sigma is "as good as any ball." It is more than apparent that much went wrong, because, although the goals were accomplished as far as products were concerned, they certainly fell short somewhere.

1 How might market research help solve their problems?

2 What kind of national sales promotion might build consumer interest?

▶ Case 2-3

GOLDEN YAMAHA

Mike Alvarez is the sales manager of Golden Yamaha in Hollywood, California. He has fifteen employees, three of whom are sales reps. This franchise was established in 1967 and has grown to be one of the most reputable and successful motorcycle shops in Southern California. Its success and popularity can be attributed to many factors, according to Mr. Alvarez. One main factor, he feels, is the stressing of fast service in his advertising. Service is done by skilled mechanics who are extremely knowledgeable concerning motorcycle racing, in which they specialize.

Instead of spending his advertising allocation ($2000 per month) for newspaper or magazine advertising, Mr. Alvarez has determined that radio spots and the sponsoring of the company racing team are the most effective advertising media. Up until about nine months ago, the bulk of their advertising was done in newspapers and magazines.

At the beginning of this year Mr. Alvarez added another advertising program. He created a campaign in which he spent a lot of money to introduce the idea that Golden Yamaha would not only sell you a fine motorcycle, but would also take your old bike or automobile as a trade-in on the sale. Mr. Alvarez believed that this was a much-needed selling tool. He and his sales force agreed that this would cut down on lost sales because the consumer would now be able to exchange titles right there in the shop without having to leave the sales rep.

Signs were made and advertisements written which would promote this idea. Unfortunately, the used car business did not run as smoothly as desired for Mr. Alvarez and his sales force.

The new campaign did cause new sales to increase, but the used car trade-ins were not selling. Mr. Olson soon found himself with a growing number of used cars that were filling up his already too small parking area. The additional cars made accessibility by customers even harder and also increased the danger of driving out onto the main highway because the cars were blocking customers' view of on-coming traffic.

The cars also cheapened the appearance of Golden Yamaha Company. The old clunkers that were received as trade-ins were far from attractive and were often very close to breaking down completely.

Mr. Alvarez also found that his sales reps were eager to take trade-ins but were not so eager to spend any time trying to sell them. His sales staff was paid on a 100 percent commission basis and were more interested in selling motorcycles, not only because they received less on the trade-in sale, but because they were not that knowledgeable about the cars and often were afraid to sell them for fear that they were bad merchandise.

Another problem was that the already overworked mechanics could not find time to clean and repair the autos, nor were they skilled auto mechanics.

The idea of trade-ins to increase sales was very successful, but Mr. Alvarez soon realized that neither his sales force nor his service department was able to operate the used car business efficiently enough to break even.

Mr. Alvarez does not yet feel that he has lost money on this new campaign because sales have increased greatly. He does not want to drop it because of the sales increase, and also because he has already spent much of this year's advertising budget on the trade-in campaign. Mr.

Alvarez is thinking about the future. He cannot continue to honor his trade-in promise if operations continue as they are at present.

1 What might you recommend to Mr. Alvarez to improve this situation?

2 Would the campaign be as appealing if it were restricted to used motorcycles only?

3

The Planning Process, Market Research, and the Sales Manager's Input

▶ Objectives

The reader will be able to recognize the value of good planning, as well as its limitations and pitfalls. He or she will understand the planning process from analysis, projections, objectives, strategy, and tactics to control. The reader will know the causes of planning failure and two ways to reduce the chances of failure. He or she will be able to construct market research to improve the sales manager's input to the planning process.

In the introductory chapters, the wide range of sales management decisions was indicated with emphasis on one executive coordinating everything that relates to customers and future sales. If this had to be accomplished on a daily basis, as various problems occurred in random order, it would be very hectic indeed. The accepted tool to attempt to control the direction which a business will take is the formal plan. For the sales manager, planning is the process which can enable a generalist to coordinate the many and diverse activities of the specialists within the same company. Good planning is also the basis for management by objectives, as well as being fundamental to constructing strategic operational sales plans.

Of course, rapidly changing conditions may force management to revise plans or possibly to discard them for entirely new ones. When top management is unsure of the direction it wants the company to take, lesser executives may feel frustration over a planning exercise. Skeptical, traditional managers often say they are too busy generating profits to bother with planning. While all of these situations and changes may occur, the company operating without any plan is not likely to achieve long-term success. In a similar way, a rudder on a ship in a storm may be of little value for that time, but the rudder is essential for the ship to safely reach port after the storm. The planning process includes changing directions when events so dictate, but it is the rudder which can guide a business safely past the rocks and shoals to reach long-term goals. Modern managers prefer to use the planning process as a guide to control their long-term operation.

TYPES OF PLANNING

Good business plans are not created by one person isolated in an ivory tower, nor are they drawn up by committee compromises. They are formulated by many levels of management in a continuous, ongoing process, usually under the supervision of one effective executive. This leader may be the chief executive officer (CEO), the vice president of planning, or the vice president of sales, or she or he may have any number of other titles. In American business, opportunities can be seized by many competent managers who are willing and able to assume the risks. Which executive leads the planning process often depends upon the type of plan being considered.

Long-Range Plans Long-term company planning usually involves from two- to five-year objectives, although the top managements in many companies in 1975 were beginning ten- and twenty-year plans. As population projections and energy shortages were forecast, many presidents' annual reports to stockholders discussed broad company plans for the long term, to 1985, to 1990, and some to the year 2000. The main benefit of long-range planning is the determination of profitable new opportunities which a company selects as its goals. As these opportunities are identified, technology can be directed to provide the new tools which will be required. For example, a fertilizer manufacturer may get into oceanography for mining deposits thousands of feet below the ocean surface. Electric utilities are moving more broadly into all possible sources for capturing and converting energy. Food processors are moving into synthetic and nourishing chemical substitutes. Waste disposal companies are looking forward to becoming raw material suppliers as technology in recycling increases. The possibilities are endless.

On a functional level, Bendix Corporation Avionics Division design engineers, for example, work three to five years with potential customers before any sale can take place. This means decisions made today will affect sales five years in the future. In a similar way, companies serving the United States space program, such as the Pall Corporation, work with five or more years' lead time before they can bid on a job. If they make the sale, it may still require eighteen months or more to produce the products.

Even a nonprofit organization can benefit from making long-term plans. Public libraries, for example, are looking at future plans to store, identify, and retrieve information and to display it other than on printed paper. This involves computers, numerous photo processes such as microdots, and televisionlike display terminals with optional hard-copy printout of still frames at the push of a button. It also involves closed-circuit television with two-way voice communications to serve invalids in their homes. Because of the expense and new technology required, long-range planning is essential.

Functional Planning Since most companies are functionally oriented, most long-term plans attempt to coordinate future actions in financing, research and development, marketing, production, materials handling, and other areas. These areas each contribute sections to the overall long-range plan. In addition, functional subplans are developed within each of the major primary areas. For example, included in the marketing plan major subordinate plans might be submitted on the following:

1 A *market research plan* to explore in depth two promising profit opportunities each year for five years.

2 A *product research and development* plan to guide new investments in technology and the direction of these efforts.

3 A *test-marketing plan* to establish parameters for go no-go

decisions on launching new products or making major modifications.

4 A *product mix plan,* which might indicate allotment of several years to exploit new marketing opportunities and gradually phase out less profitable lines.

5 A *sales force plan,* which might indicate a shift to sales engineers in the future to better serve the newly emerging customer targets and improve effectiveness.

6 A *distribution plan,* which would involve channel evaluation and anticipated changes as well as changes in physically moving and storing products.

7 A *customer service plan,* which might indicate changes in guarantees, field service personnel, stocking of spare parts for so many years, and the like.

8 An *advertising and sales promotion plan,* which should reflect the broad changes in communication and stimulation required to complement any of the above and to measure and improve its own effectiveness.

9 A *pricing plan,* which should anticipate raw material shortages, inflationary costs, consumer demand, government controls, competitive actions, and company production capacity changes, for example.

10 A *public relations plan* as it relates to obtaining free publicity directed at customers and future sales. This would indicate the broad strategy, the preference in media, measuring and improving effectiveness, and so on.

Some companies are organized by product lines, so that their long-range planning would be modified. For example, a pharmaceutical division might have all the above functional plans within the division's long-range plan. The cosmetic division of the same company would have its own unique functional plans for its division.

Other companies are regionally oriented; thus the South American region might have long-range plans which would be different from the African region's plans. Each would normally include the functional subplans described above.

The point is that long-range planning is done for a variety of purposes at many different levels of responsibility. In the process, many individuals become involved and subsequently committed to achieve the goals. While the active participation of many specialists is highly desirable, notice how many of the functional areas relate directly to the sales manager's responsibility. The chief sales executive can and should influence others in formulating their long-range plans.

Short-Range Plans Short-term plans are usually annual operating plans, schedules, and budgets common to most organizations. Unfortunately, too often they reflect emphasis on current problems or on avoiding last year's mistakes. A short-term or annual plan really should indicate the progress to be made this coming year on the long-term goals. The one-year functional plans are very specific in terms of numbers of people and dollars allocated to specific tasks as well as projected income and profit anticipated. The components can be modified as conditions warrant.

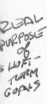

[handwritten margin note: REAL PURPOSE of SHORT-TERM GOALS]

Short-term plans may be evaluated monthly or quarterly, usually comparing year-to-date actual performance with targeted goals. These are too often ulcer-producing sessions with each manager in the frying pan or sitting on the hot seat attempting to explain any deficiencies. This is a gross misapplication of the planning process. Planning is designed to keep a business safe and steady, to guide it, not to whiplash managers when trouble occurs.

THE PLANNING PROCESS

Authorities generally agree, no matter who is doing the formal planning and what the type or level of the plan is, the process is composed of a sequence of decisions.[1] These include:

1. *Analysis:* Where is the organization today, and why?

[1] The author is indebted to Michael J. Kami for direct personal recommendations for this chapter. Also, for an excellent explanation, see "Marketing Planning," chap. 8 in Philip Kotler's *Marketing Management: Analysis Planning, and Control*, 3d ed., Prentice-Hall, Inc., Englewood Cliffs, N.J., 1976.

2 *Projection:* If we continue what we are doing, where will we go?

3 *Objectives:* Where do we want to be headed?

4 *Synthesis:* How do we put it all together?
   a *Strategy:* What is the best way to get there?
   b *Tactics:* What action is required, by whom, and when?
   c *Control:* What measurements will indicate progress?

Analysis   The planning process starts with a broad situational analysis of where the company is in relation to its earlier-stated goals, if any, in relation to competition, and in relation to political and economic conditions. Typically, it is sales management which generates much of the input for data inside the company. This would include exact unit and dollar sales, share of market and recent trends by product, by family of products, by territory, by customer-targeted category, or by other breakdowns. Other internal information also required would be profit levels for the same groupings and related manufacturing data showing costs and plant utilization analysis. Market research data showing earlier benchmarks and subsequent changes would also be included. For example, a study one year ago of consumer brand awareness on product A may have shown that 30 percent of a sample of consumers were aware of that brand. Nine months later research may have shown brand awareness was up to 35 percent.

External data are essential regarding existing competition and potential competitors. Trade associations are a common source of information about the entire industry from which any one company can compute its share of market and relative strengths and weaknesses. Political and economic conditions reflect such things as inflation, energy shortages, governmental controls, tax incentives, international trade, and tariff policies. A number of government and association studies are published regularly concerning many of these variables, showing figures for the latest week, previous week, month ago, year ago, and ten years ago, as appear weekly in *Business Week* magazine, for example. *Dun's Review* magazine also publishes ratios for manufacturers, wholesalers, and retailers by standard industrial code classification. This enables a wood furniture manufacturer, for example, to compare his sales and return on investment with those of other manufacturers of similar size in his industry. *Fortune* magazine publishes much of this kind of informa-

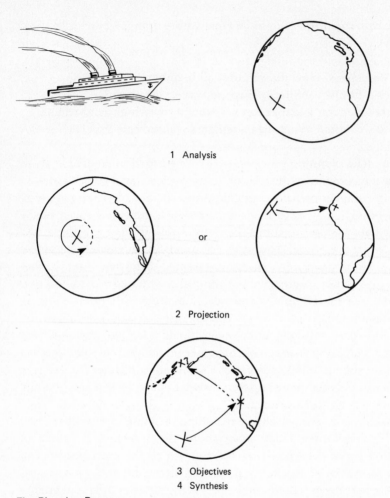

1 Analysis

2 Projection

or

3 Objectives
4 Synthesis

The Planning Process

tion annually about the top 500 in companies in industry, banking, retailing, and other fields.

The point being made is simply that a sales manager, or anyone else, attempting the planning process has access to a considerable amount of external information. Much of it is free and most of it will help the planner to determine where his or her company is today. All the publications cited also carry important articles about the economy and about trends in domestic and foreign political events and their possible impact on business.

Projections Once the planner has reasonably estimated the organization's present position, it is possible to project where it is most apt to go if present policies and trends remain constant. In other words, if the planner's company and its competitors continue the same basic product mix, with the same relative promotional support and the same trends in pricing, where will this course take them? Conversely, if known changes are about to occur in the major variables, the planner attempts to assess their likely impact on the company and on its sales.

The pitfalls here are numerous and can be catastrophic. Many assumptions must be made without complete information. Many competitors will change course abruptly in the future. Political and economic conditions can change with the wind. For these and other reasons, critics of the planning process are suspicious of its value and feel the time spent on it is wasted. This would be similar to a ship captain saying, "Throw the map or chart away because all of the rocks and shoals are not marked and the weather is unpredictable." Modern pilots know that sandbars shift in the best-charted ports in the world, and they take radar or sonar readings continuously. Much is known today about the future, and steps can be built into the plan to provide safety in the event some assumptions are false or that unforeseen conditions occur.

In business a planner begins with a *projection of industry sales* over the future planning period. Industry sales may be reasonably predicted in some cases where sales follow another event. The government uses ten

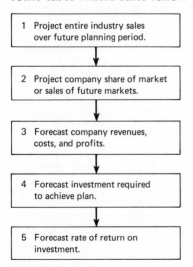

```
1  Project entire industry sales
   over future planning period.
        │
        ▼
2  Project company share of market
   or sales of future markets.
        │
        ▼
3  Forecast company revenues,
   costs, and profits.
        │
        ▼
4  Forecast investment required
   to achieve plan.
        │
        ▼
5  Forecast rate of return on
   investment.
```

Planning Projections

"leading indicators" to predict the general economy. The number of new housing starts is the leading indicator for many household goods. In some industries, the capacity to produce is a good indicator of future industry sales in units if not in dollars. Market research of customer attitudes, confidence in their own future income, disposable income, and the like, is often essential in predicting industry sales. In any event, many authorities with sophisticated computer analyses and techniques will publish their projections, and the planner can use judgment concerning which of these seems most appropriate for one particular industry.

The second step is a *projection of company sales* or its share of the future market. It is at this point that the sales manager can exert tremendous influence in the planning process. The sales representatives know what their customers are saying about future orders and competitive offerings and actions. In a well-organized sales unit, this information readily flows to the sales manager, who collects it to document his or her recommendations. The collector is then in a position to suggest that the company will hold its share of the marketing mix or new product and service offerings. This input is frequently essential in the ultimate success of any business plan.

When the sales manager has conducted test-marketing studies prior to planning, it is possible to be very explicit in projecting the results of various courses of action. There will probably be on hand some information about competitive test marketing and competitive reactions to the tests. With this combined information, the sales manager may very well be the single most knowledgeable person in the company able to make a reasonable forecast of company sales from the assumed industry sales.

Converting sales to profits is the next logical step in planning. It is simply *forecasting company revenues,* costs, and profits. The exercise is simple enough, although the number of calculations may require a computer. The value of the results, however, is dependent upon assumptions made about prices to be received and the accounting manipulations made to estimate costs to produce and distribute the products. As noted earlier, pricing should not be a simple financial decision made by accountants, comptrollers, or other financial personnel alone. The sales manager should have a strong voice in setting price levels, discounts, return privileges, and credit terms to be extended. Each of these can affect demand and the actual revenue to be received, and it is the sales manager who may know the most about these things.

Given reasonable agreement on the setting of prices, the planner then multiplies unit sales forecasted times anticipated price levels to generate forecasted revenue. Forecasting costs implies estimating how much will be spent to produce, distribute, and market the products. The sales manager may or may not get into production costs, but it is essential that a strong input about distribution and marketing costs be had. Once the cost levels have been fixed, they are subtracted from forecasted revenues to yield forecasted profit.

The projected success of a plan is not simply the forecasted profit. Several divisions of a large company might propose a number of plans each yielding a different profit, for example. Since a company has just so much money, it usually must choose between plans. Most often this is done on the basis of the rate of return on investment (ROI) required to implement each alternate plan. For this reason the planner should include a *forecast of total investment* which includes capital outlay for new or additional equipment and the amount of support necessary to achieve the projected sales and profits.

The last step in the formal planning process is a *forecast of rate of return on investment.* Most executive committee decisions are ultimately based on where the organization will get the best return on its money at an acceptable risk. If one division is asking for $2 million to achieve $400,000 annual profit (20 percent ROI) and another is asking for the same amount to achieve $300,000 annual profit (15 percent ROI), clearly the first proposal is more attractive. The variable here is crucial to the sales manager, and that is the expression "at an acceptable risk." A well-prepared sales manager will often have test-market data which document the projected sales, costs, and profits. The old-time manager, typically, would be forced to defend his proposal on the basis of opinion and years of experience. These are not quantifiable risks, and top management is more and more reluctant to invest substantial sums when there is little or no documentation.

The outcome of any plan will be affected, partially at least, by the accuracy of the assumptions built into it. For this reason, authorities in this field recommend one extra step in the planning process. They suggest three forecasts of ROI be made, using optimistic assumptions, most likely assumptions, and pessimistic assumptions. For example, suppose new housing starts remain relatively stable, which is most likely at one point in time. Then ROI can be projected to yield a given percentage. But suppose the government decides to release billions of dollars for low-interest mortgages, an optimistic assumption. Then presumably a much higher ROI would be projected. Conversely, if unemployment goes up sharply—a pessimistic assumption—the ROI would be projected downward. When a forecast shows little sensitivity to the three kinds of assumptions, top management has the most confidence in the plan. That is, if a plan is apt to succeed regardless of the most optimistic and pessimistic assumptions, it is looked upon most favorably.

An experienced sales manager has one additional insight into the planning process which permits the plans to be tailored to the specific company. That is, the manager's personal knowledge of the members of the executive committee. For example, one such member may be enthusiastic and want to double the investment to double the return. More likely, there will be one or more members who want to reduce the investment, arbitrarily, by 10 or 20 percent and achieve almost 90 percent of the return. The sales manager will be able to show that doubling the investment may be a total waste and that reducing it may achieve little or no return. In other words, the test marketing will show: what happened when a reasonable amount was spent; what little additional revenue was produced for a greater amount; and how disastrous results occurred after spending slightly less.

Objectives The planning process continually recycles back to where the company wants to go. If in the analysis and projection stages top management decides it does not like where it is today and where it is heading, it must elect new goals and new targets. These are redefined objectives which determine the marketing area for the coming period and establish specific sales goals. For example, a domestic hardware manufacturer may elect to broaden the marketing base to include international markets and to broaden the product base to include paints. In this case, actual dollar or unit sales figures would become part of the new objectives.

Often in the planning process, some product groups are recognized as being in the declining stage of their life cycle. The best the sales manager may project is to hold their share of the declining market at a lower cost to maintain their contribution to profit. Recognizing the situation, top management, at the demand of the owners or stockholders, may choose new products or new markets, or some combination of both. Intelligent sales managers are most apt to influence these choices.

Objectives, then, are the goals or destinations of a company, as a ship on the ocean has destinations. Although they are top-management decisions, they can be influenced by lower management. Sales goals in number of units or dollar volume should be realistically targeted on the basis of documentation and some testing, if possible, rather than on wishful thinking.

Strategy For each defined objective or target destination of an organization, the next logical step is to determine what is the best way to get from here to there. This clearly begins with the analysis of where one is today and the prevailing competitive and environmental conditions. Next, company strengths and weaknesses must be correctly identified to build on the strengths and to avoid trouble by providing alternates for the weaknesses.

A particular company strategy might call for reducing production but holding price levels in a declining market. Another might be to increase quality and increase price. A third might be to reduce the number of products but mass-produce the remaining ones at a lower price. The number of alternatives is almost without limit.

Many small companies simply follow the one or two leaders in their industry, and the entire industry moves through the future period as a school of young fish. The followers usually do not know where they are going or what dangers await them. They feel safety in numbers and are willing to place their future in the hands of the leaders.

On the other hand, there are those who are willing to take a risk and bet they can improve their position. They search for areas in which the customer is not being satisfied or where the customer might realize greater satisfaction at the same or lower cost. This is called *positioning* a company or a product; it follows the concepts of market segmentation, product differentiation, and broadening a product line as discussed in the first two chapters. In sales management, it might suggest a strategy of creaming the market or selling only to the most profitable large accounts and conceding all smaller accounts to competitors. Conversely, it might suggest using many more salespeople than competitors use and selling to the greatest number of accounts.

Strategy decisions provide the overall game plan to serve customers better, to take advantage of competitors' weaknesses, and to use a company's strengths to their optimum capacity. Careful analysis and documentation should be used in planning strategy rather than making off-the-hip assumptions.

Tactics   In the planning hierarchy, the objectives determine the destination and the strategy determines the route. The tactics indicate the day-to-day operation of the organization or the short-term program to achieve targeted results. These are often the subplans concerning the hiring and training of sales representatives. It would include a timetable of putting them into certain territories with certain incentives and cost projections, for example.

The tactical plan would also indicate the advertising and sales promotional support, showing a detailed schedule of media frequency, size of ads, trade shows, kind of point-of-purchase materials, and the like. The tactical plan would also indicate how the public relations campaign will work, how often, and in what media to reach selected target segments.

These are the functional subplans which underlie and justify the higher-level planning. Since they all concern the customer and will have some effect on future sales, the modern sales manager will influence their content before they are finalized. The more knowledgeable one is in these specialty functional areas, the better one can communicate with and influence the other managers.

Control   Included in the tactical plan are budgetary constraints on which department can spend specified amounts of money, as well as personnel constraints on expanding each function and at specified rates. While these constraints are essential to ensure a smooth cash flow, they do not in any way measure progress in achieving targeted results.

Built into any good plan are a series of objective measurements which will monitor ongoing progress toward specific goals and will signal deviations as early as possible. These are necessary for management to provide help for troubled areas, to reward superior performance, and, most importantly, to *adapt, modify, or change objectives* as the result of unforeseen events occurring.

For example, if the sales force had a goal of signing up 200 dealers in the next twelve months, their functional plan might target the top twenty dealers in the first three months, the next sixty in six months, the next eighty in nine months, and the last forty in the last quarter of the year. At the end of the first three months, if only six dealers have signed up, this signals something is wrong. It might be that the salespeople are using the wrong approach. It might be that a competitor has changed dealer commission rates drastically. It might mean that the economy has fallen sharply and the sales force is doing a superior job signing up just a few dealers.

Measurements should be objective and quantifiable whenever possible so that each sales representative knows what is expected, when, and to what degree. For example, a goal to increase sales next year by 6 percent is much too vague to monitor effectively. Which product lines are expected to increase, say, 10 percent, to offset which declining product lines? Which territories are expected to grow faster than average to help those holding steady and to offset the declining ones? At what rate during the year are they expected to grow? How will we adjust for seasonal variations? What kind of sales training or incentive program will be used at what point in time to assist the sales force? Many of these questions point up the need for information gathering, storing, and manipulating. Ten years ago this was only wishful thinking for most sales managers. Today, with low-cost technology, it is available for the asking even in small companies.

CAUSES OF PLANNING FAILURE

When executives or committees are considering alternate plans for the future, they look at forecast, strengths, and possible choices. Much analysis and computation may go into this phase of the work. Some companies develop elaborate computer simulations to find the optimal course of action for reaching desired objectives.[2]

But despite all the high-skilled effort invested, failure frequently results. The fiascos are not limited to small companies or to management's lacking knowledge. Large, sophisticated corporations make big

[2]This entire section is adapted with permission of Alexander Hamilton Institute, Inc., New York City, James Jenks, publisher, from "New Approach Increases Chances for Successful Planning," *Modern Business Reports,* vol. 3, no. 6, October 1975, p. 1.

mistakes, too, as Xerox and RCA both revealed when they gave up their costly efforts to compete with IBM in the computer business.

Perhaps the most common cause of failure lies in the basic assumptions in each of the planning forecasts mentioned. For example, the sales manager assumes that the market for a given product will reach a certain level in two years. The manager of research and development assumes he or she cannot solve a particular problem for at least five more years. Another executive assumes that the company's most important strength is one that it does not have. Often these assumptions turn out to be faulty. Of course, astute executives have always known they should keep checking and revising key assumptions. A new approach has been suggested, called *dialectical planning,* by Richard C. Mason of the University of California, Los Angeles. *Dialectic planning is a logical discussion about the truth or validity of the underlying assumptions in a forecast.* Basically, it calls for an entirely different set of assumptions to be made during the planning process.

This technique requires managers to do more than simply identify and reconsider the assumptions used. It requires them to do more than raise discerning questions about a strategic course. It even requires much more than the so-called "devil's advocate" approach employed at ITT. Under the leadership of Harold Geneen, wherein every plan offered by a division or department of the company is challenged rigorously at every key step and point in the presentation. A staff planner under Robert S. McNamara, who employed the "devil's advocate" approach when he was head of Ford Motor Company, once likened the process to "being picked over by bees." What the new approach calls for is consideration of a second plan contrary to the first one. Along with the best plan, management is presented a "counterplan" based on ideas and assumptions that are quite different from those used in the first plan. These assumptions need not be farfetched, heretical, or "blue sky." They may simply be ones that had to be disregarded at some earlier point because only one course could be elected. In fact, veteran observers of planning like David W. Ewing of *Harvard Business Review,* George Steiner of the University of California, Los Angeles, and consultant Michael Kami, say that almost always the "one best" plan chosen by management is based on a series of fairly arbitrary choices, most of which could be contested.

When management considers two opposite and contrasting courses of action, there is less chance of its getting tunnel vision and sweeping aside minority points of view. It may still elect the optimal plan, but if it does the choice will not have been made without a good look at the alternatives.[3]

The dialectic approach to planning often increases uncertainty and delays decision making. It also places two appealing alternates before top management, increasing the temptation to compromise parts of both. This may be disastrous for both. If it helps to avoid fatal assumptions, it is well worth the extra effort required.

Since all planning for the future is based on a group of assumptions and "most likely" expectations, only with the passing of time can their value be judged. In reality, many assumptions will not be valid and the "most likely" expectations—of competitor's reactions, for example—will not occur.

To reduce the risk of a major problem in the future, some companies are beginning to build *contingency plans.* These are really secondary or back-up plans to the one adopted and will be called into play *if* certain things occur which the first plan cannot handle. For example, a hotel chain in the Caribbean established a marketing plan based on the assumption that native nationalism would not disrupt the tourist business which most islands need. However, because some executives consulted domestic authorities, grave doubts were placed on the underlying assumption of native cooperation. Therefore, they constructed a contingency plan which called for specific management and marketing actions if and when native arrogance or disruptions threatened the tourist trade.

Old-time sailing vessels carried extra masts and repair parts for a broken rudder. In the space age, the scientists speak of "redundancy systems" or "back-up systems" in the unfortunate event of failure of the primary systems. This is contingency planning and has been proven in operations. It is expensive and time-consuming, but its value is not

[3]Ibid., p. 2.

questioned. Business planners would be well advised to adopt and practice this concept to reduce future failures.

BASE PLANNING DECISIONS ON MARKET RESEARCH

Sales management planning decisions today require highly specialized and quantified information and analysis. When companies were small with limited markets, sales managers knew their customers personally through years of experience of direct selling to them. So many companies today sell to such diverse customers spread all over the country that direct observation is no longer possible or adequate. Large companies such as Sony Corporation of America, with over 300 dealers, claim they do not even know the end customer of many of their products. As a result of increased need for information and sophisticated low-cost technology to handle data, many companies have created a specialized functional group known as *market research.*

Sales managers concerned with planning, decision making, and control should work closely with market research.[4] Indeed, the seven top areas of market research include:

1. Development of market potential
2. Market share analysis
3. Determination of characteristics of a market
4. Sales analysis
5. Competitive product studies
6. New product acceptance and potential
7. Short- and long-range forecasting

While market research is essentially a staff function, it often

[4]See Dik Warren Twedt, ed., *A Survey of Market Research: Organization, Functions, Budget, Compensation,* American Marketing Association, Chicago, 1963. See also Andre L. Delbecq, Andrew H. Van de Ven, and David H. Gustafson, *Group Techniques for Program Planning,* Scott, Foresman and Company, Glenview, Ill., 1975.

operates independently of the line sales organization and serves many masters. Thus in many companies the sales manager must compete with advertising and product research and development, for example, for the services of this group. In any case, the sales manager would be wise to stay close to the research group to influence the selection areas to be probed that might otherwise not be included in proposed studies.

Market Research Steps Authorities generally agree that the market research process goes through the following four steps or procedures:

1. Problem definition
2. Project planning
3. Data collection
4. Data interpretation

Problem definition is the first and probably the most difficult step. It involves a broad situational analysis, a clear statement of company goals, and a fine look at a unique situation. Parameters or limits are established which put boundaries around the search area to minimize costs and to obtain the most pertinent data for decision making. Sales managers often have a personal and very practical contribution to make at this stage.

Project planning includes the processes of assuming the results of research and thinking of the possible alternative actions which might then take place. For example, suppose only 2 percent of a representative sample say they would be interested in purchasing a new home entertainment electronic unit. This low favorable response might still indicate a go decision if that segment were willing to pay a substantial price for the product. Therefore, in constructing the research plan, the range of consumer pricing acceptable would be an essential part. The sales manager would also like to know where customers might expect to shop for such a unit, so that the sales force could be directed to the proper kind of dealers. A well-constructed research plan will serve the sales manager as well as the managers of advertising, product development, and others in decision making. It also will establish the cost and accuracy and the time schedule of the information required.

Data collection involves another series of mental exercises to be gone through before any action is taken. There are many sources of secondary data or information already obtained internally or being obtained regularly externally which might serve another company's needs. As noted earlier, government studies and major business publications frequently release results of their primary research data to anyone interested. In a similar manner associations often do primary research, and their data can be obtained by members of the association. Library research may obviate the need and expense of a company doing expensive original, or primary, research.

Data collection may be done through the existing sales force; this is often called *grass roots research.* It may be done by the company's market research staff itself or by outside consultants.[5] Decisions must be made on the appropriate research instrument and format, such as personal interviews, group interviews, telephone interviews, or direct-mail questionnaire. By knowing the firm's customers and targeted segments the sales manager can often make valuable suggestions in these areas.

Data interpretation is the final step in the market research process which reports the findings in quantitative form and attempts to explain their meanings or implications. Statistical data can be very important in making marketing decisions. However, they are not always reliable, and even when they are reliable, they are not necessarily valid. If the survey were repeated, would the company get the same basic responses? If so, the results are reliable. But if we get the same information again and again, does this necessarily mean we are asking the right questions to get at the heart of the matter? Not necessarily. It is at this step that the sales manager's direct knowledge of a situation can contribute measurably to the interpretation of the research findings.

While a number of large companies have a corporate market research department serving all divisions, many have found it more useful to decentralize the research down into each operating unit. This tends to reflect the importance of the input of sales executives in the line organization and the need for almost daily contact with them in designing, carrying out, and interpreting the results of market research.

[5]See *Advertising Age,* July 11, 1977.

SUMMARY

Planning is simply deciding in the present where one wants to be in the future and then developing the overall broad strategy and detailed tactics to get there. The best plans also include an ongoing method of monitoring progress to correct deviations before they become large enough to cause major problems. Such monitoring measures objective achievements which are most meaningful to top management.

The sales manager can be the single most knowledgeable executive in a company regarding the kinds of data which are essential for decision making. He or she is closest to the customers and knows the most about their future intentions. The sales manager knows their language and how to best communicate with them. He or she knows the capabilities of the existing sales force and the potential of the future sales force. For these reasons, the sales manager can and should have a major influence on the overall planning process and in many details of the strategic and tactical subplans.

Most planning today is based upon documented evidence of historical sales trends, direct observation of current events, and various samplings of future intent. These are the tools of the market researcher, and, when computer technology is used, they can be quite sophisticated. However, being technically oriented, the researcher can benefit from suggestions of the practical sales manager.

The difficulty in producing valid, workable plans lies in making correct assumptions today about future events. The more knowledgeable the planner, presumably the better the assumptions. In any case, many things predicted as most likely to occur in the future do not turn out that way. Dialectic planning and contingency planning are two methods used by some companies to reduce the risk of failure. More important, however, is the need to continually revise and update plans to adjust for changing conditions. Good planning should be a guide to get from one place to another, not a permanent, unchangeable fixed course.

QUESTIONS

1 How can formal planning help a sales organization which is operating under drastically changing conditions?

2 What are the series of decisions to be made in constructing a formal business plan?

3 What are the different purposes of building a strategy, tactics, and controls?

4 What sequence should a manger use to project sales and profits for a future period?

5 Why is the return on investment (ROI) projection important in submitting a proposed sales plan?

6 What is the difference between a dialectic plan and a contingency plan?

7 What are the major areas in which market research can help a sales manager in building long-range plans?

SELECTED REFERENCES

Buzzell, R. D., R. E. M. Nourse, J. B. Matthews, Jr., and **T. Levitt:** *Marketing: A Contemporary Analysis,* 2d ed., McGraw-Hill Book Company, New York, 1972.

Crowell Designs, Inc., Marketing Case History, 3/4 videocassette, 30 min., b&w, Intercollegiate Video Clearing House, Miami, Fla., 1976.

Delbecq, Andre L., Andrew H. Van de Ven, and **David H. Gustafson:** *Group Techniques for Program Planning,* Scott, Foresman and Company, Glenview, Ill., 1975.

Drucker, Peter F.: *Management: Tasks, Responsibilities, Practices,* Harper & Row, Publishers, Incorporated, New York, 1973.

Johnson, H. Webster: "Market Research as an Aid in Sales Management," chap. 15 in *Sales Management,* Charles E. Merrill Books, Inc., Columbus, Ohio, 1976.

Kotler, Philip: "Market Planning and Budgeting," chap. 8 in *Marketing Management: Analysis, Planning, and Control,* 3d ed., Prentice-Hall, Inc., Englewood Cliffs, N.J., 1976.

McCarthy, E. Jerome: "Applying Market Gridding," chap. 6 in *Basic*

Marketing: A Managerial Approach, 5th ed., Richard D. Irwin, Inc., Homewood, Ill., 1975.

Newman, William H., and **E. Warren Kirby:** *The Process of Management,* Part 3, "Planning," Prentice-Hall, Inc., Englewood Cliffs, N.J., 1977.

Stanton, William J.: "Market Planning and Forecasting," chap. 27 in *Fundamentals of Marketing,* 4th ed., McGraw-Hill Book Company, New York, 1975.

———— and **Richard H. Buskirk:** "Sales Planning," Part 4 in *Management of the Sales Force,* 4th ed., Richard D. Irwin, Inc., Homewood Ill., 1974.

▶ Case 3-1

WYXA RADIO STATION

In June of 1976, Bob Andrews, general manager of WYXA-FM, was confronted with the problem of obtaining advertising for his station through advertising agencies. It seems his predecessor was relieved of the general manager position because advertising agencies were not placing ads with the station.

Advertising agencies usually base their selection of a radio station to use for their clients on the Arbitron Rating Service. This service rates the number of users based upon two efficiency rankings. In using the Diary method of sampling listening habits of a given area, the ratings are broken down into SMA (Standard Metro Area) and TSA (Total Survey Area). This information in turn is translated into the number of listeners in these two efficiency areas. The reach of the station in power output has little effect—if any—upon the ratings. The ratings were based years ago on the United States government's methods of reporting the nation's metropolitan and rural population. Because of a lack of updating population growth, many areas of the United States are metropolitan in actual population count but not listed as such with the United States government. The result is that Arbitron Rating Service will not use any area as metropolitan for its ratings until the United States government changes its method of reporting for those areas.

WYXA Station

WYXA, Stereo 610, is an affiliate of OK Stations, a nationwide company. It is a bright, up-tempo, and refreshingly unique station. The music is the best of yesterday, featuring more than 2000 of the top hits from 1955 to 1975. WYXA's sounds are heard twenty-four hours a day.

A limited commercial policy guarantees more music for the listener and provides a promotional showcase for advertisers. The maximum is ten minutes of commercial content per hour—never more than two minutes per break. News, weather, and sports come often enough to keep the audience in touch with events. Wire service is supplemented by UPI Audio and local features.

The lively sounds of Stereo 610 blanket a five-county area. The antenna is over 1000 feet above the average terrain, and power is a full 100,000 watts. There is no stronger FM signal in this market.

Most important, WYXA offers a unique sound and advertising opportunity in one of America's most competitive radio markets. Of the thirty-eight radio signals in the area, WYXA, on a radio spectrum as of March 1, 1976, represents the only "oldies" station in this market. The strong appeal cuts across all economic and social barriers. WYXA appeals to all people who relate to "the best of yesterday."

WYXA's retail rate card No. 7, effective April 5, 1976, lists advertising rates as meeting all competition. WYXA offered weekly package planning, weekly circulation planning, and consecutive week discounts, all of which are competitive.

Advertising Agency Call

"Mr. Andrews, we appreciate your 100,000 watts power and your reach into the surrounding areas, but in your metro rating from Arbitron your Nassau County listening is only 12,000 while WLTF's is 20,000.

"True, WLTF only reaches Nassau County due to their low watts, but we buy only in the county where the antenna is located. We have to keep it local, you know."

"Yes, but, Mr. Rogers, WYXA has in the Arbitron TSA a listening reach of 20,000 in Queens County and 10,000 in Suffolk County in addition to Nassau's 12,000. Based on this and our rate structure, your clients can have their advertising dollar reaching more people without duplication of radio stations in other counties, and the total cost is less."

"Sorry, no, Mr. Andrews. Arbitron is our bible and does not break the area in metro areas other than on a countrywide basis. True, this is a unique marketing situation, but that's the way it is."

"Well, Mr. Rogers, your traditional line of thinking, along with Arbitron's antiquated ratings, is costing the community a lot of advertising money, if only from the standpoint of national promotional test marketing of products."

After exchanging goodbyes with Mr. Rogers, Mr. Andrews left.

Determined to get to the bottom of this, Mr. Andrews matrixed WYXA and WLTF metro ratings from Arbitron as follows:

	Queens	Nassau	Suffolk	Total Reach
WYXA	20,000	12,000	10,000	42,000
WLTF	*——	20,000	——	20,000

*Note: WLTF could not reach Queens or Suffolk Counties because of very low station wattage.

1 What is Mr. Andrews' problem?

2 What marketing strategy should Mr. Andrews use to convince advertising agencies they should use his station?

3 What in particular should Mr. Andrews do to obtain Mr. Rogers' advertising agency business?

▶ **Case 3-2**

THE SHOPPER'S GUIDE

The Shopper's Guide is a weekly advertising publication that has no news stories or other types of news information besides advertising.

The sales force of *The Shopper's Guide* presently consists of five sales representatives, three female and two male, who visit accounts weekly. These salespeople are under the supervision of the sales manager, Tony Bellefond, the owner's son.

Tony says that the main problem he faces in managing his sales force is due to interference in the supervision of the salespeople by the general manager of the company. The general manager, Shirley Jordan, is in charge of hiring salespeople. After the salespeople are hired, Tony is supposed to have full authority over their activities. Tony feels that, because of his age, 24, and because of the overbearing personality of Shirley, he lacks real control over his subordinates. Tony says that if a salesperson has a problem, he or she generally will consult the general manager as to what action is to be taken. He feels that the salespeople may have good reason for doing this because in the past most of his decisions have been contradicted and overruled by Shirley if she was aware of any problem. Although Shirley has no authority over the sales force, she takes it upon herself to constantly question the sales force on their activities. In speaking with members of the sales force about the problem of serving two bosses, Tony says he finds that the salespeople respect his judgment but are afraid of Shirley and what she may do if they follow his instructions instead of hers.

Another problem that Tony cites is that Shirley attempts to handle all complaints from customers. Shirley has instructed the receptionist and the sales force that any complaints should be directed to her because she "knows the business." Tony feels that, since he is in charge of the sales force, he should have the responsibility of handling these complaints.

Although he has complained to his father, he has had no results because his father feels that Shirley has a good track record and that what has worked in the past will work for the future. Tony does not feel that this is correct, because since the company began operations three years ago, circulation has gone from 12,000 to 45,000 papers and advertising accounts have increased 400 percent. Tony feels that Shirley cannot handle this increase in volume and adequately perform her assigned functions of distribution manager and bookkeeping responsibilities. He also feels that the sales force would perform better if they were not confused as to who their immediate supervisor is.

1 How might Tony's father plan an orderly transfer of authority from Shirley to Tony?

2 Is Tony mature enough at this time to accept full responsibility for the sales force?

► Case 3-3

ALL PLASTICS

All Plastics is a firm located in Fort Lauderdale, Florida. It is owned and operated by Rob Steavens. The firm has been in operation for only one and a half years. All Plastics manufactures plastic furniture for both home and office use.

Steavens is also the sales manager and has five manufacturer's representatives that work for him. One works in the Florida area, two work in New York, and the other two are located in Pennsylvania. The salespeople work for themselves in that they carry other lines of plastics furniture and do not report directly to Steavens. They work on a strictly commission basis. Plastic furniture is a highly competitive business, and the sales reps who carry All Plastics products also carry anywhere from twenty to thirty other lines of plastic furniture.

Steavens is only 25, and the sales reps are all at least 40 and have over fifteen years' experience. He feels that some of the reps have taken advantage of his inexperience, often demanding a higher commission. Another problem he has with them is that they try to run his business for him. They want him to make some products that he is not able to produce at a competitive price. Sometimes they demand that a group of products be finished at a specific time, earlier than is possible.

With all the different lines of products that the salespeople carry, Steavens feels that if he were able to employ reps who carried his line exclusively, he would be able to increase sales volume and profits for his company. The firm is too small at this point to handle a sales force of its own. Steavens would like to build a better relationship between himself and his representatives. He dares not offend them by telling them to let him run the business and stop asking for things that he is unable to give them. He fears that they might leave him, and he cannot be in business without them.

1 How might long-range planning help young Bob Steavens?

2 Where might Steavens find other independent manufacturers' representatives who could handle his furniture?

4

Building the Tactical
Operational Plan:
Sales MBO and MIS

▶ Objectives

The reader will now be able to move from broad generalizations down
to constructing specific tactical-operation sales plans. He or she will
understand and be able to use management by objectives (MBO) and
management information systems (MIS) as tools for both planning
and control of the sales functions and the sales force. The reader will
better appreciate how a sales manager can influence the entire
organization through the planning process.

At whatever level sales managers participate in, or influence, the
formulation of broad company plans, ultimately good high-level planning leads directly to the blueprint of next year's sales management
tactical game plan. In well-managed companies, the strategic planning
cycle concludes about three months before the final operational plans are
due. This means that top management has agreed upon specific goals
and a general strategy or course to achieve those goals. For example, the
executive committee may have elected one plan for expanding the

business into new product areas because its goals are to yield a 20 percent increase in sales, a 7 percent increase in net profits after taxes, and a 20 percent ROI within acceptable levels of risk. Now the sales manager is expected to develop the tactical details on how he or she plans to do the sales manager's part of the job.

In most organizations, broad policy decisions are made at a high level of management and the details are left to the functional specialist to work out. For example, it is assumed the corporate treasurer knows best how to use surplus short-term funds. The head of manufacturing knows best how to maximize machine use and to minimize downtime. In a similar way, top executives will assume the sales manager knows the kind of sales force, tactics, and support needed to accomplish the sales goals. Each functional plan will be reviewed in a well-managed company, but the burden of constructing it is on the operating manager and, in this instance, specifically the sales manager.

Unfortunately, not all companies have good top management, and many organizations are operated without any long-term planning. While this may seem challenging to some executives, for most it is confusing and often frustrating. However, it is no excuse for a modern sales manager to fail in proper tactical sales planning. In the absence of higher-level planning, the modern sales manager will independently set up his own tactical one-year plan. This is management by objectives, which is essential to running an effective sales organization.

TACTICAL DECISION: PUSH VERSUS PULL

One of the most common errors of sales managers is to ignore the *tactical* question of how the entire company should approach target customers. This fundamental decision of the sales manager must be made before meaningful advertising objectives can be formulated. It must be achieved before realistic sales promotional targets can be established. It is mandatory if the sales force is to be effective. Yet, similar to their failure to make a conscious choice of channels of distribution noted earlier, sales managers typically do not examine their company's basic approach to markets. Most commonly they accept what has been done in the past without any further thought. In the absence of a decision by the sales manager generalist, the specialists in advertising and other fields assume certain things and select goals which may or may not be in harmony or may not be nearly as effective as they might have been.

Push Selling Strategy[1]   The most common industrial sales strategy is to focus all attention and effort on the professional buyer—to get the buyer to push the products through the purchasing function to the user. Sales managers using the push strategy will direct their representatives to the professional buyer or purchasing agent. They will write sales promotional literature and catalogs that are intended to inform and persuade an objective professional decision maker. Technical specifications and research and test data are all made available to the buyer. In a push strategy the sales representatives encourage the purchasing agent to visit the firm's other customer installations to see their products in use. They invite the buyer to visit their own manufacturing plant and facilities to assure the buyer that they are capable of handling the buyer's orders properly.

When product demonstrations or in-plant trial uses are appropriate, the sales representative is taught and directed to work with the purchasing department. The representative requests the buyer to set up a joint appointment with the head of the department that will use the product.

Together the purchasing agent and the sales representative work out test or comparison criteria and give the product a fair and objective trial. The professional buyer is kept fully informed and is in control of the situation all along the way.

When the buyer issues a purchase order to a supplier using this push strategy, he maintains complete control of shipping instructions, dates of deliveries, rush orders, and so on. The sales representative has no further contact with the user unless the purchasing department requests it and is kept informed.

As any experienced buyer knows, many salespeople do not operate in this manner, and life is not always so perfect for the hard-nosed industrial buyer. Even paradise may be relative.

In a similar manner, many consumer products are sold by pushing

---

[1] This entire section is adapted from B. J. Hersker and T. F. Stroh, *The Purchasing Agent's Guide to the Naked Salesman,* Cahners Publishing Co., Boston, Mass., 1975.

them through wholesalers and retailers. The manufacturer's sales force works on the intermediary agents or the resellers.

Pull Selling Strategy When a sales manager directs the company's efforts primarily at the industrial user, an attempt is being made to persuade department heads to requisition the firm's products and pull them through the purchasing function. If the strategy is successful, the professional buyer loses much of his control and power. He may become frustrated, angered, and a dangerous adversary against that supplier in the future.

Clearly, a sales manager should not knowingly risk alienating the professional buyer unless the rewards are high or the risk minimal. For example, in a one-time (nonrepetitive) purchase where everything is won or lost on a single decision, the sales representative can exert tremendous pressure on a buyer and the users without fear of retaliation tomorrow. There is no tomorrow! It's now or never! In the long term, the sales representative and the sales manager may get their "comeuppance." But in the short run they may very well be successful and will run the risk of incurring the purchasing agent's wrath.

More commonly, a pull strategy in business and industrial selling is more delicately handled. It wears a velvet glove. Advertising is written for the user or department head who can requisition the products. The ads are placed in magazines or trade papers that are normally read by the user. Mailing lists are purchased to obtain the names and titles of individuals within the selected target accounts. Direct mail and personal visits are used to get sales promotion literature into the hands of the user.

The promotion is written in language that will appeal to the user; hence the message is long on benefits with little or no technical data to support the claims. Users are asked to write or phone for more information, and they do.

Sales representatives working for a manager using a pull strategy are taught to avoid the professional buyer and focus their attention on the user or requisitioner. Free samples, demonstrations, and trial uses are arranged directly with the department manager, often without any contact whatsoever with the purchasing department. The users are wined and dined. The sales representative attempts to get the firm's products specified on the requisition.

This is so-called back-door buying by nonprofessionals, and it is very common in business and industry. Sales managers electing the pull strategy simply cater to this demand.

Push-Pull Selling Strategy Over the years, sales management has reduced the use of slick fast-buck artists in favor of customer service-oriented professional sales representatives. In a similar way, purchasing has reduced the hard-nosed low-price buyers in favor of creative, value-oriented professional purchasing agents. Although their needs may never be identical, at least the two parties are becoming more compatible every day.

Enlightened sales managers have evolved what is known as a *push-pull* strategy, which attempts to gain the best of both extremes. The sales manager directs the primary strategy at informing and persuading the professional buyer. The sales promotional literature is technical and factual. The sales representatives are directed to call on the buyer before making any other contacts. The approach is to demonstrate capability and service to the professional purchasing agents.

In using a push-pull strategy, the sales manager's secondary effort is directed toward the user and requisitioner. Once again, additional advertising and sales promotional literature is written differently for this audience. However, it is compatible with the technical data given to the professional buyer. Leads are solicited and obtained from users.

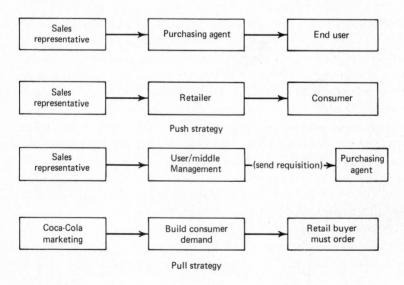

Operating under this strategy, the sales representative is taught to take the user request to the purchasing department first. The P. A. is fully informed and invited to join the sales representative in a three-way interview with the user. If it is an insignificant item, the P. A. may wave the sales representative on, asking simply to be informed after the interview. If the product is expensive or may have a significant impact on the P. A.'s company, the P. A. has the opportunity to stay on top of the situation and control the three-way interview. In either case, the P. A. is fully informed of what is happening and there is open communication, not conflict of interest.

Sales Manager's Option   Because of past experience and current contacts, the sales manager knows the kinds of professional buyers and sales situations which the sales force must face. Therefore it is logical that the sales manager should consciously decide which tactical approach the company should take. By direction or persuasion, the sales manager should influence the goals and tactical plans of the advertising manager, the manager of sales promotion, the head of public relations dealing with customers, the service organization, and so forth.

It should be apparent to the reader that once the sales manager makes this primary decision, he or she will know the kind of training and direction that must be provided for the sales force and the kind of support that will be needed.

Some authorities claim this kind of interdepartmental decision should be made at a higher level than the sales manager. It is this writer's contention that the sales manager is in the best position to observe the firm's customers and the current situation in the field. An intelligent sales manager can and should make this decision. Perhaps the argument is academic, however, because in too many companies *no one* consciously makes this decision. Each department assumes different things, synergism is lost, and many marketing dollars are wasted. Each oarsman cannot steer the lifeboat, much less the ship.

DETERMINING TOTAL PRODUCT OFFERING

As indicated earlier, a knowledgeable person in a company should examine what is to be included in the total product offering. This determination is also essential *before* the sales manager begins to construct the tactical or one-year operational sales plan. In most situations, however, this determination cannot be made unilaterally by the sales manager. But the sales manager is the one most affected by it; thus he or she has a strong incentive to cause others to cooperate in building a cohesive and comprehensive plan. This exercise will take the sales manager far afield of where traditional sales management was permitted to venture in the past. Intelligent modern sales managers can and should get involved with manufacturing decisions, and many other areas of their companies. The sales manager is the only executive with day-to-day personal contact with customers and future customers, and that should be the only justification needed for looking into somebody else's business that is basically the sales manager's business.

Services to Consider In general terms, the product is the total offering of the physical product and accessories needed by the customer as well as the normal services of guarantee, delivery, installation, and related elements. Service, on the other hand, is everything of value given to the customer beyond the product offering. Service includes, but is not necessarily limited to, the following:

1 *Product performance-enhancing services* such as aid in the selection, adjustments to make the product work properly, altering the product to fit a special need, instruction in optimum usage.

2 *Prolonging the product life* by stocking parts over a long period. If this year's model Ford is to be produced up until July 15, how many more front left fenders should be produced to provide new spares for the next five years?

3 *Risk reduction by purchasing* through return privileges and warranty. Under what conditions will a paper manufacturer, for example, accept rejects or grant allowances for paper that is lighter in weight than promised?

4 *Reduction of purchase effort* through phone and mail-order privileges, parking facilities, taking orders at trade shows, and the like.

5 *Reduction of capital required* through credit terms, selling on

consignment, floor-plan financing of inventory for retailers, and several years' contractual financing of retailers' furniture and fixtures.

6 *Efficiency-increasing services* whereby the manufacturer does accounting for the manufacturer's representatives; the wholesaler performs inventory control for the retailer; and the retailer provides restaurant and nursery facilities for the consumers' convenience.

7 *Sales-increasing services* for the reseller such as training retail salesclerks, specialist's advice in advertising locally, and floor traffic control through layout.

8 *Meeting customers' intangible need to feel important* by such means as courtesy, prompt attention, and friendliness in handling complaints; and asking for opinions about possible new products and services.

Customer service and product offering are often difficult to separate, as the service is merely an extension of obtaining or using the product. It is important, however, for the sales manager to think through the various areas in which the company now offers, or could offer, these services. Such decisions can be coordinated to put the company in a strong competitive position or they can be permitted to be disjointed and without reinforcing effect.

SALES MANAGEMENT BY OBJECTIVES

Having analyzed and explored the numerous alternates possible and with this unique company, the sales manager is now in a position to begin to outline the basic tactics to achieve the "20–7" and 20 percent ROI mentioned early in this chapter.

Management by objectives is the planning tool most often recommended at the lowest operational level because it involves the workers—the sales representative, in this situation. The sales manager has agreed with top management that they will increase net sales by 20 percent. Perhaps it was calculated that three-fourths of the increase would come from the additional product line and the remainder would have to come from an increase in sales of existing products. The new product line itself was probably adopted because of its high profit potential, but the sales manager knows it will be necessary to improve profits on the existing line as well to meet the overall goal of increasing net profit after taxes by 7 percent. Finally, the sales manager knows whatever budget is proposed, it must generate a 20 percent net ROI. These, then, are the parameters within which the sales manager will operate for the coming year.

Traditional sales managers would simply raise all quotas by 20 percent and perhaps place bonus incentives on selling high-profit items. Modern sales managers use MBO techniques to individualize the process so that each sales representative can and will contribute as much as each is able.

Odiorne's Cycle   The sales representative and the manager together agree on goals which can be attained in one territory. Criteria for measuring performance for this one individual are also decided jointly and in advance of the period. Authorities in this field, such as George S. Odiorne, state that this process has two advantages.[2] First, it permits the sales representative to participate in determining on what basis his or her efforts will be judged. Second, involving the sales representatives in the planning process will increase their commitment to the goals and objectives which are established. Odiorne's cycle of management by objectives is reprinted in Figure 4-1 to symbolize this theory.

This technique goes well beyond the traditional typical dollar-volume sales quotas. The modern sales manager will appraise each individual sales representative's current ability and the potential of each territory. Then the individual goals might be different for each representative. Objectives might include a combination of many of the following kinds of measurements:

1   Find and sell x number of new accounts, each ordering in excess of y dollars.

2   Reactivate z number of former accounts.

---

[2]George S. Odiorne, *Management by Objectives*, Pitman Publishing Corporation, New York, 1964. See also Anthony P. Raia, *Managing by Objectives*, Scott, Foresman and Company, Glenview, Ill., 1974.

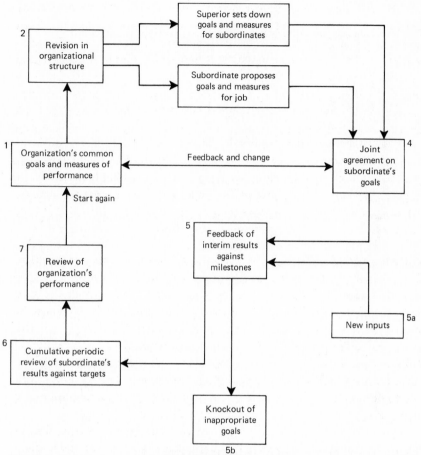

Figure 4-1 Odiorne's Cycle of Management by Objectives. *Source:* George S. Odiorne, *Management by Objectives,* Pitman Publishing Corporation, New York, 1964.

3 Increase average order size by 15 percent.

4 Sell 20 percent less Class III (small) accounts.

5 Sell 40 percent more Class I (large) accounts.

6 Sell 25 percent more of product A (high-profit item).

7 Sell 115 percent of quota of new product B.

8 Lower selling costs by 8 percent.

9 Increase after-sale-service calls by 10 percent.

10 Reduce cancellations and returns to below 2 percent.

11 Increase effective listening skill by 80 percent.

12 Increase face-to-face customer contact by 20 percent.

13 Learn new skill of key target account selling.

Each objective is thoroughly defined so that the sales representatives know exactly what is expected of them and how their individual progress will be measured. The modern sales manager will probably include some personal development objectives to make each representative a better producer and a better person as well.

Inexperienced sales managers may hesitate to permit the sales representatives to set their own goals; however, experience has shown that sales personnel tend to *over*estimate what they will accomplish. Normally, the sales manager should persuade each representative to lower the selected sales target to a more feasible but still challenging level. When the sales manager and the individual sales representative agree on the goals for the coming period and how they will measure performance, the sales manager can be very honest, straightforward, and objective in future performance appraisals. This procedure enables the sales manager to praise good work and progress frequently, and it provides a real opportunity to develop each sales representative individually. Clearly, the total performance will not be perfect, and the sales manager should use caution in disciplining or correcting weaknesses. This point will be covered in detail in Chapter 14.

Experienced sales managers who have successfully used MBO for a number of years advise other managers to begin each planning session with an open discussion of where that unique individual feels he or she can make the greatest contribution to help meet the overall goals. One person may be particularly good at selling new accounts while another might be very adept at reactivating old accounts. Properly applied, the MBO system is flexible and allows for individual differences and desires.

As the sales period progresses, the MBO system provides for changes due to new information such as competitive reactions and for the dropping of inappropriate goals as realities replace certain false assumptions. These are steps 5a and 5b on Odiorne's cycle. If these two steps are ignored, many abuses may occur.

An example of abusing the MBO system occurred recently in a company with sales in excess of $1 billion annually. They use "deviation from standard" as a whip. Whenever one of their salespeople's performance falls below a prearranged norm, the salesperson must explain why it is off and what steps are being taken to recover and prevent a recurrence of the deviation. When production machines break down, the salespeople get ulcers. When sales are off in an entire industry, these salespeople are forced to double their working hours and efforts. This ·kind of pressure or rigid discipline may cause many of the familiar psychosomatic illnesses. It may also cause high blood pressure, strokes, and heart attacks.

Conversely, when a plant machine works faster than anticipated, the production manager may "bank" some of the excess against future breakdowns. When an entire industry realizes a seller's market, the sales representatives for this company can play golf two or three working days a week. These salespeople have learned to live with a *rigid* goals system, but they do not enjoy their jobs and they realize very little personal satisfaction for their achievements. For MBO to work properly, it must be *flexible,* and steps 5a and 5b do provide this flexibility.

THE TACTICAL OPERATIONAL PLAN

Building the tactical operation plan for the next year simply puts the sales manager in the subordinate role of the MBO system just described. The manager understands the corporate or divisional goals and measures of performance which will be used, step 1. He or she then decides if it is necessary to add people to the sales force, for example, or to reorganize the training, the supervision, and the territory assignments, step 2. Together with his or her supervisors, the sales manager charts what basic approach will be taken and what complete package of products and services will be offered next year, step 3. When they are in agreement, step 4, the sales manager explains it all to the sales force and earns their commitment individually. In the latter process the sales manager generates the massive computations of how many units in each category will be sold and at what prices, and also generates projected income and sales expense to derive a projected contribution to profit and ROI. This is the administrative part of planning and may require several assistant sales managers, several clerks, and a computer in a large sales organization. In a small sales unit, the manager will work overtime many nights to work out the tactical plan each year.

Alexander Sklar, internationally known management consultant, uses six specific guidelines for writing good objectives, as follows:

1 Relate to higher management's objectives.

2 Start off with an action verb.

3 Identify a single key result for each of the objectives.

4 Establish a realistic target date.

5 State verifiable criteria which signal when the objective has been reached. Be precise—quantify where possible—dollars, units, percent, and so on.

6 Be sure the objective is challenging and controllable by the person or group setting the objective; if not totally controllable, at least isolate the part that is.

Sklar states that a good objective will contain extraordinary results. For each objective, the sales manager should develop alternate methods of achieving it. This is a form of dialectic planning noted in the previous chapter. Sklar adds an interesting variation at this point. He advises using factor analysis to make a choice between alternate methods to achieve the same objective.

Factor Analysis Every plan has intangible costs which, to all intents and purposes, cannot be measured in terms of dollars. Moreover, a comparative quantitative analysis of alternates is sometimes a standoff, with no one plan having a clear-cut financial advantage over the others. Additionally, decisions are frequently required as to which alternatives to intensively study when one is faced with a large number of choices.

Sklar's factor analysis method follows the industrial engineering concept of breaking down the problem into its elements and analyzing each one. This makes it more objective. Essentially, the procedure involves the following:

1 List all the factors which are considered important or significant in the decision of which alternate should be selected. Commonly used criteria include:
   a Investment required
   b ROI
   c Probability of success
   d Time required to make the decision profitable
   e Growing market
   f Advantage over competitors
   g Within technical competence
   h Compatible with existing marketing organization

2 Weigh the relative importance of each of these factors against each other. Sklar suggests the most effective way of setting weight values is to pick the factor which is considered most important and give it a value of 10. Then relate the weight of each of the other factors to 10.

3 Rate the alternative ways of achieving the same objective, one factor at a time. Using Figure 4-2, *always rate across* the form, considering each of the alternates for one factor at a time. For example, factor item 2, ROI, should be rated Excellent (4), Good (3), Average (2), or Poor (1) for alternate A, then for alternate B, then for C, and so on across the page. This is important, for it is easier to keep one factor in mind for several plans than the reverse. Sklar cautions that, if one rates vertically for one plan at a time, there is a temptation to rate highest on the preferred alternate. Rating across, or horizontally, yields greater objectivity.

4 Extend the weighted and rated values and compare the total value of the various alternates. This is simply multiplying the weight of the factor by the sum of the ratings horizontally.

Sklar's factor analysis for choosing alternatives is a variation of the Bayesian approach. Each makes a systematic evaluation out of many otherwise subjective views and is therefore particularly adaptable where quantitative information is not available and a direction is sought. Some of the rejected alternates may be held as contingency tactical plans in the

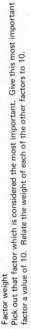
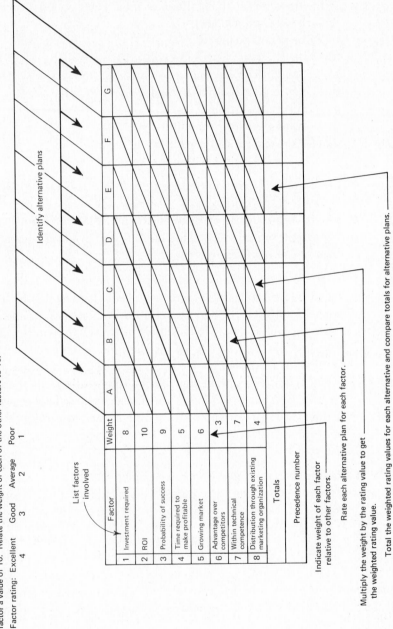

Factor weight
Pick out that factor which is considered the most important. Give this most important factor a value of 10. Relate the weight of each of the other factors to 10.
Factor rating: Excellent 4 Good 3 Average 2 Poor 1

List factors involved

Identify alternative plans

Factor	Weight	A	B	C	D	E	F	G
1 Investment required	8							
2 ROI	10							
3 Probability of success	9							
4 Time required to make profitable	5							
5 Growing market	6							
6 Advantage over competitors	3							
7 Within technical competence	7							
8 Distribution through existing marketing organization	4							
Totals								
Precedence number								

Indicate weight of each factor relative to other factors.

Rate each alternative plan for each factor.

Multiply the weight by the rating value to get the weighted rating value.

Total the weighted rating values for each alternative and compare totals for alternative plans.

Figure 4-2 Factor Analysis Chart. *Source:* Alexander Sklar Associates, Fort Lauderdale, Fla., 1976.

event that changing conditions during the period cause the value weights to change.

To conclude the MBO exercise, Sklar uses an Action Plan Summary, Figure 4-3, which provides an outline format to fill in the specific quantitative and qualitative information. Many experienced executives and sales managers using MBO for the first time have found Sklar's forms invaluable in building their individual tactical operation plan.

SALES MANAGEMENT INFORMATION SYSTEMS

While MBO was touted as management's newest and most effective tool during the 1960s, *management information systems,* or MIS, is being proclaimed the tool for the 1970s.[3] In this approach to tactical planning

[3]See Joel Ross and Robert Murdick, *Management Information Systems,* Prentice-Hall, Inc., Englewood Cliffs, N.J., 1976.

ACTION PLAN SUMMARY

Date _____

Objective:

Goals/Milestones:	When	Measurements
1		1 Quantitative—use existing company records.
2		2 If not available, crude measurements are serviceable.
3		3
4		4

Action Steps (Major)	When	Expected Results
1 Start each action step with a verb.		1
2 Examples: "review," "test," "accumulate,"		2 Narrative—such as: "Establish a base from which to measure progress."
3 "Prepare," "deliver," "design," "check,"		3
4 "Make," "rearrange."		4

Figure 4-3 Tactical Operation Plan Outline. *Source:* Alexander Sklar Associates, Fort Lauderdale, Fla., 1976.

the manager analyzes what information is needed for various decisions, where it will come from, how it will be stored and used or manipulated, and what will be the outcome or required actions. As in MBO, this system is also a complete circuit which continually recycles the decision-making process. Typically, an MIS plan is charted showing the sequential steps and flow of information. It is useful in problem solving and in ensuring a meaningful data communication system. Figure 4-4 shows a hypothetical MIS for a sales manager's information needs and is intentionally simplified to promote better understanding.

In a well-managed organization, research information flows to and from many parts of the country, and, as noted, top management does not make decisions in isolation from subordinate units. In too many companies, however, steps 1 and 2 (Figure 4-4) do not occur in any systematic and planned way, and the sales manager is forced to make certain assumptions without this input. In this event, the modern sales manager will begin the MBO Tactical Plan (step 3) with whatever research information can be learned from others within the company and outside of it.

The sales manager builds his or her tactical plan by deciding what the basic approach to customers will be and what level of support from management is believed feasible. This includes the range of services discussed earlier. With some agreement from top management and other functional areas, the sales manager can proceed with getting the input and the agreement of each member of the sales force.

In the early contacts with sales representatives, one of the prime decisions to be made is the selection of target customers (step 4 of Figure 4-4) who promise to yield high profit opportunities. Some sales representatives may need special training for this task; thus the tactical plan will provide for it in both time and budget allotments.

The next logical step is that the selected target accounts are sold (step 5 of Figure 4-4) or not. If they are not sold, there is another series of decisions, as covered in Chapter 12, all of which recycle back to the tactical plan. If the accounts are sold but there are cancellations before delivery (step 5A), the trouble may be too much pressure from the sales force (recycle back to 3) or it may be because there is too long a wait for delivery (go to 6A).

If satisfactory sales are made, the information is sent to order processing (step 6), which notifies inventory control (6A) and manufacturing (step 6B), and it then becomes input for their own MIS.

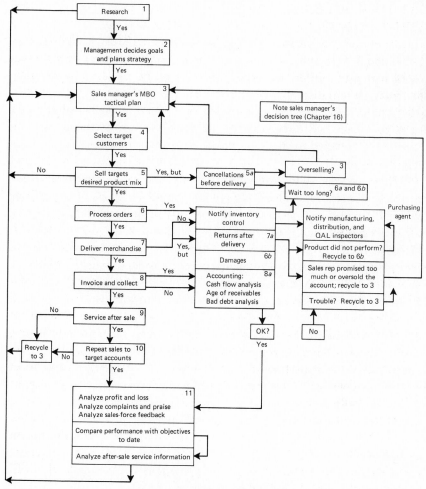

Figure 4-4 A Sales Manager's Management Information System.

The next step, 7, is to deliver the merchandise. If this cannot be done, the problem is sent back to 6A. If the merchandise is delivered and there are returns on rejects, the problem goes back to 6B if the products were defective or back to 3 (the sales manager) if the sales force oversold or promised the product would do more than it could.

If the merchandise delivered is acceptable, the next logical step is to invoice the customer and collect the bill, step 8. If this is done without problems, the information goes to 8A for cash flow analysis, aging of accounts receivable, and so forth. If there are bad debts, the frequency and amount may be caused by too loose credit or poor selection of target accounts. This difficulty would be recycled accordingly.

After-the-sale service, step 9, is essential in most sales organizations, and if it is not provided, the problem should be recycled back to the sales manager. Often customer complaints go directly to the sales manager, automatically signaling this problem.

With proper after-the-sale service, one would logically expect repeat sales to target accounts, step 10. If they are not forthcoming, this problem is recycled to the MBO tactical planning of the sales manager, step 3.

In any event, all transactions are finally analyzed for profit and loss, customer complaints, sales force feedback, and comparison of performance with targeted objectives in accord with the agreed criteria, step 11.

This information is recycled to research, top management, the sales manager in a continuous manner. Obviously, in addition to this input, the sales manager receives regular reports on calls, prospects, expenses, and so forth, from the sales force. He or she also gets occasional feedback from supervisors and individual reps on their progress or problems.

By thinking through and charting the management information system the sales manager is able to establish priorities for various actions and to pinpoint the probable cause of a problem. The general rule is to go as high as possible in dealing with policy or decision-making problems and as low as possible in analyzing problems with execution or carrying out of the decisions. For example, when defective products get out into the marketplace, the problem should immediately go to the quality acceptance limits (QAL) inspectors. If they are passing products within the limits accepted as determined by management, this policy problem should be triggered to higher management.

This formal system can take some of the politics and "knifing in the back" out of a poorly managed company. It pinpoints responsibilities, sequential events, and problems. It also provides for instant communication to all appropriate parties, as well as correction mechanisms to cut losses and improve profits.

Management information systems and management by objectives need not be in conflict. Indeed, as was illustrated, each can operate within the same sales organization to build a better, more efficient, and more humane place to work. They do require intelligence and extra effort; thus they have been shunned and sabotaged by traditional sales managers, but they are used wisely and profitably by modern sales managers.

SUMMARY

In constructing the tactical operational plan, the sales manager has the responsibility of leading and directing the sales force. This means consciously deciding how the company should approach customer target segments. Since this is the sales manager's specialty area, other executives are apt to accept his or her decisions with little or no arguments. By thinking through the various *push and pull options,* the sales manager will have a strong rationale to justify the recommendations made.

In addition to leading and directing the sales force, the sales manager has the responsibility of gaining the necessary support for them in terms of the most competitive and attractive *total product offering* with compatible and comprehensive services. This will involve decisions normally reserved to other executives; hence the sales manager should be diplomatic in the efforts made to persuade them to cooperate. Frequently they will cooperate because, in many companies at least, no one else has taken this leadership position.

Using *management by objectives,* factor analysis of alternate ways to achieve the same objectives, and other decision aids, the sales manager builds the tactical plan in detail. This involves clear objectives for each sales representative, with timetables and criteria for objective measurement as part of the plan. Most sales managers also find that charting the firm's *management information system* helps to prevent problems in the future and to plan a communications system which will signal problems, progress, and achievements.

QUESTIONS

1   Describe the difference between a push sales strategy and a pull sales strategy. Show how they may be used simultaneously.

2   What services can be added to the total product offering to better serve desirable customers target segments?

3   What are the seven steps in management by objectives as used by modern sales managers?

4   What are the six guidelines for writing good objectives for the sales force?

5   How can factor analysis assist one in evaluating alternate plan proposals?

6   Describe a management information system as used by modern sales managers.

SELECTED REFERENCES

Kotler, Philip: "Market Research and Information System," chap. 9 in *Marketing Management: Analysis, Planning, and Control,* 3d ed., Prentice-Hall, Inc., Englewood Cliffs, N.J., 1976.

Manager Wanted, 30 min, 16 mm film, color Roundtable Films, Inc., Beverly Hills, Calif., 1968.

Newman, William H., and **E. Warren Kirby:** "Operating Objectives," chap. 17 in *The Process of Management,* Prentice-Hall, Inc., Englewood Cliffs, N.J., 1977.

Odiorne, George S.: *Management by Objectives,* Pitman Publishing Corporation, New York, 1964.

Oxenfeldt, Alfred R.: *Pricing Strategies,* American Management Association, Inc., New York, 1975.

Raia, Anthony P.: *Managing by Objectives,* Scott, Foresman and Company, Glenview, Ill., 1974.

Ross, Joel, and **Robert Murdick:** *Management Information Systems,* Prentice-Hall, Inc., Engelwood Cliffs, N.J., 1976.

Sales Management (semimonthly), Sales Management, New York. "Survey of Buying Power" every July issue and "Survey of Industrial Purchasing Power" every October issue.

Stanton, William J.: "A Market Information System and Market

Research," chap. 26 in *Fundamentals of Marketing,* 4th ed., McGraw-Hill Book Company, New York, 1975.

Univis Division, Itek, Marketing Case History, 3/4 in. videocassette, 40 min, b&w, Intercollegiate Video Clearing House, Miami, Fla., 1976.

Westvaco Cora Cool Marketing Case History, 3/4 in. videocassette, 60 min, b&w, Intercollegiate Video Clearing House, 1976.

▶ **Case 4-1**

SUNDAY PUBLICATIONS, INC.

Sunday Publications was established in Norfolk, Virginia, in 1974, to provide printing services mainly for religious organizations. The main organization is located in Clinton, New Jersey, with Sunday Publications being the first branch established. The major part of the business consisted of the printing, and designing when necessary, of service bulletins, letterheads, envelopes, and special notices.

Since then they have expanded their services to include all areas of the printing business. They serve many types of customers, from business organizations to the general public. The services they provide include "quick" printing, design work, placement of advertising in local newspapers, and any other printing service which can be produced with their present equipment.

There are twenty persons presently employed in the Norfolk branch. Twelve of these are office staff, and there are a president, vice president, regional sales manager, and five sales reps.

The five reps and the regional sales manager make calls on established and prospective customers daily. The reps report primarily to the sales manager, and the sales manager reports to the vice president.

The main problem that seemed to be affecting the sales function of the organization was in the area of direction.

The sales force was paid a fair salary and received a commission on all orders which they received. This did not seem to be the most important factor.

There were no regular meetings between the sales reps and the sales manager. Generally, the sales manager would report to the office in the morning and see the president or the vice president; then he would go out into the field. If the sales staff had any contact with him, it was for only a brief period of time, and the only matters that were discussed concerned the prospects the sales reps might call on. There was no real feedback to the reps concerning how they were doing in comparison with the other salespeople or any suggestions about how they might improve their performance. As a result, sales are decreasing and the sales manager does not seem to know what the problem is.

1 How might a strategic operational plan give direction to this sales force?

2 What elements would be essential in building a sales plan for this company?

▶ Case 4-2

GENTRY ASSOCIATES

Gentry Associates represents firms that manufacture electronic equipment and products used by electronics industries. Most of the manufacturers that Gentry represents are small firms that cannot afford to maintain their own sales force. Gentry represents firms that offer a variety of products. Anything from computer punch paper tape to very complicated and expensive testing equipment is included in Gentry's product mix.

Gentry was incorporated in Florida in 1960. The home office is still located in Orlando, Florida. The firm has grown to six regional offices: Atlanta; Winston-Salem; Huntsville, Alabama; St. Petersburg, Florida; Melbourne, Florida; and Orlando. An additional office in New Orleans is scheduled to open soon. Gentry is an organization of fourteen people. Half are the sales force and the other half are the clerical staff. Each regional office is run essentially by one person assisted by a secretary.

Revenue is received as commissions on sales. In 1975, Gentry had gross sales of $7 million. Five sales reps own all the stock of Gentry and receive their compensation in the form of profit sharing. The other two reps receive a salary plus commission.

The Southeastern electronics market is small. There is a variety of types of business within the market as well as within the different regions covered by Gentry. For example, the Winston-Salem region requires equipment that can be applied to the textile industry, in contrast to the Orlando and Melbourne regions, which require computer and space-oriented products.

Because there is one contract between Gentry and a manufacturer, all the regional offices represent the manufacturer and are expected to push the product. This causes the problem of having a product in regions where there is no need for it. On the other hand, there is also the problem of not carrying a product needed in only one region, a situation which results in lost sales and loss of goodwill.

Gentry wishes to capture a larger share of the market. But management feels that in order to do this, the firm must find a way to balance their line without becoming specialized.

1   What kind of strategic sales plan would help Gentry expand its line of products?

2   Where could management look for additional manufacturers to represent, which would fit into their operational plans?

► **Case 4-3**

SPEEDFAST, INC.

Speedfast manufactures and sells industrial fastening equipment and supplies through fifty representatives and distributors across the country. The company, which is fifteen years old, has experienced its most dynamic growth in the past two years, with the development of heavy-duty equipment which could cross into many areas: the construction industry, packaging and crating, furniture manufacture, millwork, mobile homes, and many others.

On the West Coast, Speedfast equipment was selling well to contractors and builders, but not to mills or furniture manufacturers. In the Midwest, 92 percent of sales were confined to the packaging and furniture industries. And in the East, better than 80 percent of sales were for millwork.

The sales force was doing a good selling job. Many sales representatives had been with the company since it started. Their competence was unquestioned; their sales were up substantially each year. But when Speedfast developed equipment that could expand their sales into other industrial areas—areas not within their sphere of experience—they balked. The problem was that the representatives had grown comfortable selling to only one or two of these industries.

The problem facing Mrs. Newman, the sales manager, was how to shake long-time competent sales reps out of their regular routine and get them out selling new markets when new product development indicated a market expansion.

1 Construct a strategic sales plan which would cause the sales force to expand their efforts into new categories of customers.

2 What might be the advantage or disadvantages of expanding the sales force at this time?

Part

2

ORGANIZING AND COMMUNICATING

One ship drives east and another west
    With the selfsame winds that blow.

    'Tis the set of the sails
    And not the gales
    Which tells us the way to go.

Like the winds of the sea are the ways of fate,
    As we voyage along through life:

    'Tis the set of a soul
    That decides its goal,
    And not the calm or the strife.
                              —Wilcox, 1898

5

Organizing the Sales Force and the Sales Function

▶ Objectives

The reader will understand how the function of a sales force can dictate its form. He or she will be able to utilize the management principles for organizing a sales force and to take into account the advantages and disadvantages of organizing territories on the basis of geography, products, or customer categories. The reader will appreciate some of the problems in creating territories with equal workloads and equal sales opportunities.

The author has observed a number of sales departments which represent a combination of components put together almost haphazardly over the years, as once-expedient reactions to the immediate needs of a company and the desires of one or more of a series of sales managers. In other words, some sales organizations have grown as chance directed, without rhyme or reason.

Today, some executives pay little attention to the form or structure of a sales organization. Many executives pay even less attention to the continuous planning or systematic grouping of activities, people, and facilities in a sales unit. In such situations, dramatic improvements are often possible to reduce costs, increase efficiencies, and increase profits.

Modern sales managers, on the other hand, do look at the various components of their departments. They relate these parts to the changing needs of their unique situations and to changing company objectives and strategies. Newly appointed sales managers may blindly accept their existing organizational structures without any further thought. Tomorrow's sales managers will search for opportunities to improve profit by reorganizing or changing some or all of the components.

In the following discussion the word "organizing" is used to describe the planning process of intelligently putting together groups of activities, people, and facilities to serve predetermined functional needs. The word "organization" is used to describe the structure or end result of the planning. It is the organizational chart, or a picture of the structure, as it exists at any one point in time.

ORGANIZING THE SALES FORCE

There is almost universal agreement among business executives and leading educators writing on this subject about the general guidelines for organizing or consciously building a business structure.[1]

1 Activities should be considered, not the individual people currently employed.

2 Authority and responsibility should be assigned to each position, not to individual executives.

3 Each functional position should be coordinated with each of the others, preventing encroaching or empire building.

[1] See William J. Stanton and Richard H. Buskirk, *Management of the Sales Force,* 4th ed., Richard D. Irwin, Inc., Homewood, Ill., 1974; Richard R. Still, Edward W. Cundiff, and Norman A. P. Govoni, *Sales Management,* 3d ed., Prentice-Hall, Inc., Englewood Cliffs, N.J., 1976; and Philip Kotler, *Marketing Management: Analysis, Planning, and Control,* 3d ed., Prentice-Hall, Inc., Englewood Cliffs, N.J., 1976.

4   The span of control and supervision of each position should be reasonable or within the ability of one executive.

5   The organization or structure should be stable but adaptable to change.

Beyond these generalizations, each unique company will have some restrictions and options which may not apply to others. Clearly, the size and financial resources of an organization may permit planning many specialized positions or they may restrict it to planning a very few generalist positions. The level of sophistication in top management may encourage or limit the amount of change which can be planned. Government-regulated industries may have to operate under certain constraints, and more and more white-collar unions are imposing other legal and social restraints on reorganization planning. Once again, the total environment should be considered, as in all planning activities.

Activities Should Be Considered, Not People   As in the charting of a management information system, planners are concerned primarily with the job that has to be done in the organization. They use an objective approach to the activities which will be carried out at different levels of the structure. This avoids the problems attached to the subjective evaluation of the individual executives involved.

At any given point in time, the planning seeks to optimize the company's resources of people, facilities, and finances. This, of course, is the ideal goal, which may never be achieved. It does take into consideration the number of employees at each level of the organization, the financial limitations in the immediate future, and the physical machines, equipment, and space available.

In any sales organization, consideration should be given to the level of sophistication and intelligence of the sales force. This may indicate the amount of first-level supervision required or the number of sales trainers needed to upgrade the sales force, for example. Sales administrative duties are common activities which normally include sales and profit analysis by sales representatives and/or by product. As noted, advertising and sales promotional activities may also be planned within or outside of the sales department. Recruiting and selecting sales trainees may be planned within the sales department or with the personnel function.

After deciding the optimum plan for one point in time with its given constriction, the organizer is then forced to match executives with the essential activities. This may require the temporary combining of closely related activities into a single position until the company can afford the ideal separation. It might require the creation of several subordinate or assistant positions on a temporary basis until these individuals can be developed enough to take over the activities on their own. On occasion, this planning may point out the urgent need to go outside of the company and hire a specialist for an essential area.

In other words, if compromises are needed because of personnel problems, they should occur after the ideal plan is put together. The organizational plan should remain intact with unfilled positions noted and temporary assignments so indicated.

Authority and Responsibility As a sales organization grows, it will often develop a number of market segments and several large accounts. If the size of the potential orders is attractive, the sales manager may want to assign one or more sales reps to work full time on these few accounts. One should, of course, establish quotas for such activities as calls, quotations, dollar sales, and so forth. This is the responsibility given to the particular sales reps. Along with this delegated responsibility, the manager should recognize, is the need for increased authority. The sales reps should have the authority to quote varying prices to meet competition on big-volume orders. They should have the authority to entertain prospects and customers as the market situation demands. They should have the authority to contact manufacturing direct to obtain scheduling and shipping information. In other words, the manager in assigning a task (responsibility) to a sales rep should also give him the tools (authority) to do the job as expected.

The sales force should know which executives have line authority and can, therefore, give them direct orders. For example, on a pricing problem the reps should know which executive can authorize certain concessions. Indeed, all executives should know this, or there will be mass confusion and considerable wasted time. Sales supervisors, sales trainers, sales analysts, the advertising manager, the sales promotion

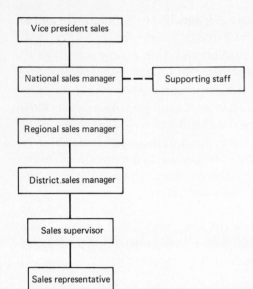

Figure 5-1 Vertical Line Organization—Centralized

manager, and others at different times may want sales reps to do certain things. Without clear lines of authority, some executives will abuse their power and some sales reps will not cooperate for the good of the company.

This problem is compounded when branch sales offices are involved. Any visitor to the branch from the home office carries more power and influence than the local branch sales manager, or so some sales reps believe. In fact, this may not be true at all.

Everyone in an organization should know who has line authority to give orders, directions, and suggestions to which workers or sales reps. No one should be forced to make assumptions or to guess which suggestions are mandatory and which may be considered and disregarded.

Coordination and Balance Organizational theory suggests that groupings of people should be kept small enough so that they can freely communicate on a face-to-face basis. In many companies, a few dynamic executives assume power and encroach on weaker ones. When their positions grow out of proportion to the importance of their functions, the entire organization suffers.

The idea, of course, is to group individuals into the smallest number that can efficiently perform their defined duties. Then each group is expected to cooperate and communicate with all related groups. This often requires training, a management information system, procedure manuals, and other management tools. However, the objective of coordination and balance is best achieved in planning the organizational groups.

In some cases the market research specialist, for example, may be authorized to utilize the sales force to survey selected customers to obtain certain information. The specialist may attempt to use technical research language which confuses the sales force, and thus he or she requires an assistant sales manager to interpret and assist the specialist. This is empire building and a waste of people, time, and money. When functional needs arise which require a temporary use of line authority in a limited area, coordination is essential. An effective sales manager will protect the sales force from abuses from any quarter, and the line organization is all the authority which he needs.

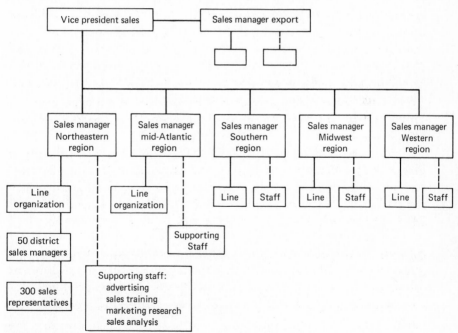

Figure 5-2 Horizontal Line Organization—Decentralized

Span of Control In planning an organization there is a need to coordinate the activities of a number of salespeople under one supervisor, of a number of supervisors under one branch manager, of a number of branch managers under one regional manager, and so on up the ladder. In organizational theory this limit is called the *span of control.* Its purpose is to provide adequate supervision and guidance to the sales force with a minimum of overhead or administrative costs. Because these are relative terms, no precise numbers can be recommended as a general guideline.

If the planners study the requirements of a sales supervisor's job, for example, they may find the supervisor has to spend one full day each week with each newly assigned salesperson. The supervisor may also have to spend one day each month with experienced sales representatives. Obviously, he or she will also have to spend some time on additional coaching, discipline problems, expense problems, and in meetings with the sales manager and other supervisors. The question of how many sales representatives one can adequately supervise then evolves around the number of new representatives and the maturity of experienced representatives. This will vary in time and with the ability of each supervisor; thus, a general rule would not be appropriate.

However, one should remember that the organizational plan and chart represent a picture of the structure for one point in time, or as it should appear for the next quarter, the next six months, or the next year. This enables the planners who are organizing the sales force to optimize the effect of each sales supervisor for the projected short term. The executive span of control and supervision should be within reasonable time and ability demands for the time period projected. It will change as the situation changes.

Stability with Flexibility It should be apparent at this point that a good organizational plan is not a document which rigidly locks into place all jobs on a permanent basis. A good organization is one which allows for expansion and contraction of personnel and of the volume of business. It provides the stability necessary to withstand the shocks of government rulings, competitive actions, and radical shifts in the economy, for example. It provides for optimum efficiency during the projected time period.

A well-planned organization provides for the training and development of subordinates in adequate numbers to afford a pool of candidates for promotion into higher-level jobs. It provides for specific people to perform all necessary activities without duplication or neglect. A good plan will also reduce friction between operating units while maximizing the coordination and cooperation between them.

An organizational change is not mandatory each time a new product, territory, or activity is taken on by the sales force. The plan should provide for anticipated changes during the projected time period. On the other hand, the organizational structure is simply a management tool. If, in fact, it is not appropriate for unanticipated changing conditions, it is time for reorganization.

Within the sales force area, the sales manager usually has the authority and responsibility to operate as he or she deems necessary. Often budgetary restrictions are the only ones that must be considered. Outside of the sales force, however, the sales manager faces entirely different organizational problems and forces. These are related to the sales function, which is often controlled or strongly influenced by other executives.

ORGANIZING THE SALES FUNCTION

Often top-management decisions will dictate and limit the functional purposes which the sales organization can accomplish. For example, a decision made to reduce production of a certain line of products or, conversely, to expand the production automatically imposes decisions on the sales manager. In a similar way, top-management decisions on new plant locations and new distribution centers may have a tremendous impact on the organization of the sales force.

Top managements in many companies also impose checks and balances which limit the sales managers in setting prices and maximizing profits. Credit decisions are often made outside of the sales department by organizational design. This can limit the number and types of new accounts which can be sought by the sales force.

Limited Production   Some executives, often a second and third generation of a family-owned business, will elect to hold production down to existing products and existing capacity. They seem to enjoy what they are doing and to fear venturing into anything new. Many are satisfied with the existing level of profits and are unwilling to risk reinvesting profit in expansion.

One such company with annual sales of more than $20 million apparently evolved such a restrictive policy. A series of sales managers were frustrated and ineffective because they could not adapt their organizations to fit the constraints. Finally, one sales manager recognized the restraint as one which dictated that the function of sales was to skim the cream off the top of the market. He was able to evolve a sales strategy of exclusive selling to the most profitable accounts and of not even calling on lesser prospects. All sales expenses, including salaries, had to be self-funding or generate enough increase in contribution to profit to pay for themselves. The sales manager reduced the size of the sales force and put the remaining best salespeople on salary with a bonus based entirely on contribution to profit.

Maximize Production   A large competitor in the same industry as the family business had entirely different problems. It was engaged in a series of mergers and acquisitions, and top management wanted to increase plant production to capacity and to expand rapidly. Their sales manager recognized that this situation mandated that the function of sales was to generate a high volume and gain the lion's share of the market. He divided the sales force into five product-oriented divisions and opened branch sales offices in all major markets. In a single day one purchasing agent might see three to five different sales representatives from this one company. A saturation sales strategy evolved with intensive coverage by many salespeople—product specialists more knowledgeable than their competitors. Although the large company eventually lost this battle, the point being made here is simply that the function of a sales force often dictates the form of the organization.

Selling Only to Original Equipment Manufacturers (OEM)   In the case of Crowell Designs, Inc., noted earlier, the president of this small manufacturer of bilge pumps decided that his sales force of two could handle the OEM or boat-builders market. There were not more than eighty accounts, and they were well known. Pricing was competitive, and the firm also offered discounts for high-volume orders. In the first year they captured considerably more than 50 percent of the OEM primary market. They then had several options in sales force organization. They might have hired more salespeople. They might have contracted for manufacturers' representatives or they might have contracted with several large wholesalers. Because top management was considering selling the business, they elected to contract with wholesalers, to keep the internal organization lean and highly profitable. Once again it was the function of sales—in this case the short-term maximization of profit—which dictated the organizational form. The options were analyzed for the short-term highest profit to reach the secondary or after-the-sale market through thousands of small marinas.

Selling Service   When one company dominates a market, as the Bell Telephone Companies, IBM, and Xerox do in their respective fields, getting sales is not really a major problem. The function of the sales force is primarily service to get existing customers to upgrade their equipment or to keep competition out of the account. In the cases of IBM and the telephone companies, education is the service offered. Both show the users how to improve the flow of information and increase efficiency.

In the case of selling a new account or upgrading an existing account, they both use the sales strategy of problem solving to prove that their proposals will do a better job. The sales function is still primarily one of providing educational services, and this fact dominates their sales organizational forms.

In a similar way, Xerox has elected to provide field service after the sale so that every copier leased or under service contract will always have the latest improvements installed. One might argue that service cannot be given until a sale is made, so that this should not affect the organization of the sales force. But consider the value to a sales representative of being able to claim this benefit in speaking to his prospect and to prove it. The Xerox field service force of men and women is actually larger in number than the Xerox sales force. The sales function here is to ensure after-the-sale service, and this strongly influences how the sales force is organized. Since service must be fast, local branch offices are mandated, and sales offices go right along to the local level.

Operations Research   On occasion top management may feel there is a better way to organize the sales function but is not sure which way to go. Under these conditions, sales managers can analyze historical data, conduct field experiments—a series of tests in the marketplace—or use simulation to answer "what if" types of questions. These are techniques of operations research using mathematical models to determine an optimal mix.[2] For example, the Shaw-Walker Company, a manufacturer of office furniture and equipment, has conducted operations research in its sales organization for many years. They adapt to changing market conditions as the situation warrants. For example, they sell primarily through a large dealer network which includes many exclusive territory agreements. That is to say, the dealer gets half the profit on any products sold outside his or her area which are delivered into that area. At the same time Shaw-Walker operates its own retail stores with outside, or territory, sales personnel of men and women representatives. These sales branches are located in selected cities where the dealer does not have exclusive rights. This flexibility, together with operations research, enables the manufacturer to warn a weak dealer—one who is not giving adequate service, for example—that his or her exclusive contract will not be renewed next year. If the dealer does not meet company standards, which were established by operations research, the manufacturer can put into the area one or more sales representatives or a large competitive branch, depending on the potential profit opportunities.

Within the sales branches, Shaw-Walker also experiments with various sales organizational structures. In smaller cities the sales force may be organized on a geographic basis. In larger markets the sales force may include some representatives who are organized by customer segments, such as those serving insurance companies or savings and loan institutions, for example. Operations research is an excellent tool for the modern sales manager to explore, promising new forms of organization and developing cost and profit figures mathematically on a small or local level without disrupting the entire organization.

CONSTRUCTING TERRITORIES

At the level of the individual sales representative, a sales force can be organized around company geographic territories, products, customers, or some combination of the three. Reorganization at the local level can

[2]For a more technical discussion see David B. Montgomery and Glen L. Urban, "Personal Selling Decisions," chap. 6 in *Management Science in Marketing*, Prentice-Hall, Inc., Englewood Cliffs, N.J., 1969.

be very difficult because it usually has a direct and strong impact on the individual representative's income, workload, and way of life. Sales managers should exercise a great deal of caution and restraint in this area. However, reorganizations at this level can be done with the support and continued loyalty of the sales force.

1. **Territory-Organized Sales Force** A traditional method of sales organization is one where each sales representative has an exclusive geographical territory in which he or she sells all the products made or handled by the company. It is a method that is used commonly because it clearly defines the sales representative's responsibilities, it encourages the building of good customer relations over the long term, and it provides incentive for the representative to take pride in building a good territory. In addition, travel expenses are usually minimized when territories are relatively small with efficient local transportation.

If the sales manager has a good method of estimating territory potential, the sales representative knows that the credit for relative success or the blame for failure in that one territory goes to the representative insofar as the effects of personal selling make a difference. Various approaches to estimating territory potential are discussed in detail in Chapter 14.

The territory-structured sales organization works quite well in situations where the product line is small or relatively easy to learn and where most customers are of a similar type. As product lines broaden into diverse specialty or technical areas and customer-target segments become very different from each other, this form of organization becomes less efficient. Good sales representatives know their products and their customers, but there is a limit to how much they can be expected to learn.

2. **Product-Organized Sales Force** The second traditional method of sales organization is one where the sales force is divided into two or more subunits each responsible for selling only a single line of products. For example, a manufacturer of electronic office products might have one sales manager and a specialized sales force selling just a line of computers, another sales manager and a specialized sales force selling just a line of cash registers, and a third sales manager and a specialized sales force selling just a line of typewriters.

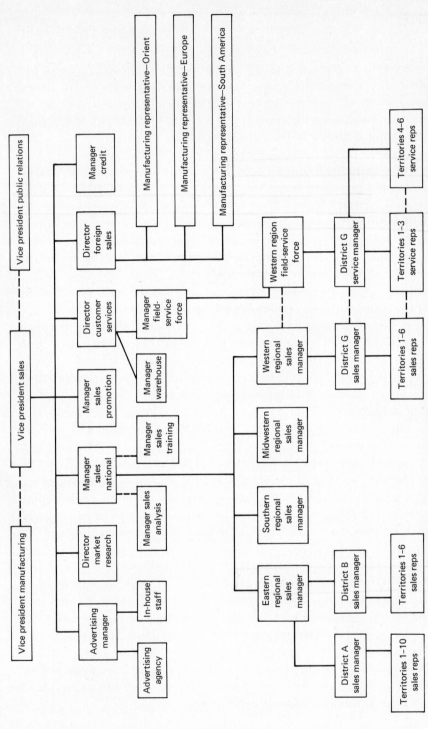

Figure 5-3 Line and Staff Territorial Organization. *Note:* All sales representatives sell all products to all customers in territory.

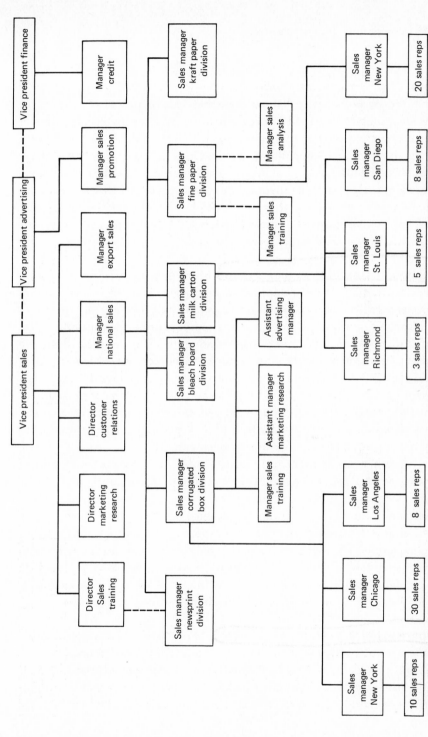

Figure 5-4 Product-Oriented Sales Organization. *Note:* Sales representatives sell only one line of products in each territory.

The major advantage of organizing a sales force by product group-ings is the increased knowledge the sales force has in their specialty area and the exclusive attention paid to that line of products. The major disadvantage of this kind of organization is that several representatives must often call on the same customer, which is expensive for the selling company and time-consuming and irritating for the customer. It also creates an additional level of administration or management, which may be more costly than is justified. While this cost can be calculated, the very creation of extra sales management positions increases the temptation for, and opportunity of, empire building, with several assistants and specialists for each product sales manager.

3. **Customer-Organized Sales Force** More in line with the marketing concept is the relatively modern form of organizing the sales force to specialize in serving major target segments. Most often each group of salespeople sell the full line of products but confine their attention and efforts to defined customer-target segments. This may be desirable where the segment is both large enough and possessing unique problems and requirements. As noted, the Shaw-Walker Company in some cities has a group of sales representatives who call only on savings and loan institutions and another group who call only on insurance companies. The potential accounts are large, and they prefer a sales representative who has specialized in their line of business.

Another common division of the sales force by customer groups occurs when different channels have different and/or conflicting needs. For example, a paper manufacturer may sell direct to large retail merchants through one group of salespeople, to wholesalers through a second group of salespeople, and to exporters through a third group. A manufacturer of wristwatches may have one sales force selling its expensive line to the finest jewelry stores on an exclusive basis and a second sales force selling its economy line to drugstores, tobacco shops, and wherever it can get space on an intensive-distribution basis.

4. **Complexly Organized Sales Force** Many sales organizations today have various combinations of both traditional and modern units. Proba-bly most of them have evolved slowly over many years of trial and error with little conscious thought or planning. Others have gone through phases of centralizing control and supporting staffs and of decentralizing.

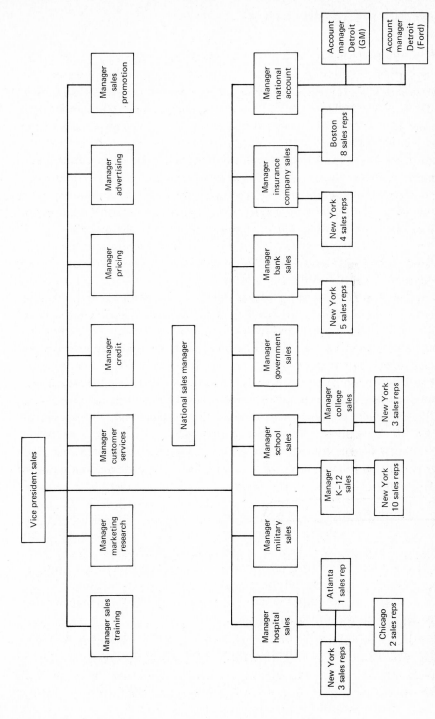

Figure 5-5 Customer-Oriented Sales Organization. *Note*: All sales reps sell all products to one category of customers in each territory.

The unfortunate part of such reorganizing is that once decisions are made, the situation is forgotten—at least until some major problem arises. But organizing the sales force, reorganizing, and planning are simply short-term projections of how the functions, activities, and people should be structured to achieve stated goals and objectives within the constraints of what may be available.

Modern sales managers do not automatically accept their given organization as being ideal to achieve the company goals and sales objectives. They analyze the costs involved in relation to the return on money or time invested to perform the various activities desired. What might have been appropriate ten years ago or even last year may not be the best way today. They constantly recycle the organizational decisions to meet ever-changing conditions in the marketplace today and those anticipated in the foreseeable future.

When analyzing the existing structure and comparing it with the proposed organization, a detailed economic analysis is essential, of course. Perhaps more important is an analysis of the human reactions to any proposed changes. Sales personnel, staff, and management people all perceive organizational changes in different ways. Some will see threats to their income, job security, and basic way of life. Others will see new opportunities for personal growth and career advancement. Some will see them as a futile exercise in shuffling papers and job titles which will achieve nothing. Any substantial human resistance to a proposed reorganization of the sales force can negate the best of plans. The communications involved in proposing such a change and gaining acceptance are discussed in Chapter 7.

 Individual Territory Design In practice, most companies do assign their sales representative to specific geographic territories even when they further specialize one or a group of representatives by products and/or by type of customers. Several contiguous territories are grouped together into *districts,* and these are often further grouped into *regions.* Once again, based upon the desired span of control, a number of sales management levels may be created.

When designing the individual territories, the sales manager generally attempts to provide the following ideal conditions:

1   Territories are easy to administer.

2   Sales potential is easy to estimate.

3 Travel time and expense are minimized.

4 Equal sales opportunity is provided.

5 Equal workload is provided.

It is very difficult, if not impossible, to achieve all of these ideal conditions. In order to provide equal sales opportunity, the sales manager must classify each potential account according to the size of the potential business in each product category, the estimated share of that business from among competitors, and the probability of achieving it. Then one must group such accounts until each territory has approximately the same potential sales volume. (See Chapter 14.) The problem, in fact, is that in urban and industrial areas, the total number of accounts that reach the desired potential are located close to each other. In larger, sparser areas with the same potential, the accounts are spread out, requiring that much time be spent in travel. Clearly, the representative in the urban area can cover his or her accounts in less time than the representative in the sparse area will require. Although the potential may be approximately the same, the workloads are not equal.

If the attempt is made to equalize the workload between representatives, the manager will begin with a similar classification of accounts but then will assign the desired number of calls required for each category. Next to be decided will be what is a reasonable number of calls to be made in each geographic territory which allows for differences in travel time. Finally one must decide on the number of effective calls which can be made by sales representatives of different levels of experience. When this mammoth job is completed with great wisdom, the end result might be equal workloads for all territories but tremendous inequality in sales and earnings potentials.

This very real dilemma has traditionally been resolved by moving the better senior reps up into better and better territories. In some industries sales representatives' unions have demanded that this kind of movement be based solely on seniority. This plan has some obvious disadvantages, however. When a senior representative leaves the sales force, a number of people move up, disrupting many well-established customer contacts. In large geographic areas, this may mean moving the representatives from one city to another, disrupting their entire families, and incurring the expense and annoyance of physically moving and resettling.

Modern managers are attempting alternate solutions to the problem of unequal territories through various compensation programs. One alternative is to pay higher salary and commission or bonus to the representative serving the large, sparse territory with equal sales potential. This plan acknowledges that it is a harder territory requiring more hours to cover but it pays better. The disadvantage, of course, is that it reduces profit in large territories. In the opposite case, where workloads are equal but potential is unequal, sales managers pay a lower compensation rate in the territory with high sales potential. A third alternative is to recognize that as territories really are different, so do the sales representatives differ in experience and ability. These sales managers put the newest representative in the poorest territory, enabling the novice to make mistakes and learn without hurting big accounts. As the trainee earns the manager's confidence, he or she is moved to progressively better territories as vacancies occur.

Compensation and motivation are discussed in detail in Chapter 12, but it should be noted here that territory construction and the assignment of individuals to specific territories are fundamental to both of these problem areas. This is especially true when a highly productive representative can no longer handle a growing territory and the sales manager wants to divide it into two or more territories. Several ways for the manager to handle this problem are discussed in Chapter 12 also. There are also many possibilities of getting around the territory dilemma in utilizing a hierarchy of sales responsibilities, which are discussed in the following chapter.

SUMMARY

Moving from broad planning and encouraging innovation, this chapter delves into the short-term and day-to-day decisions of a sales manager. There is strong agreement on the management principles for organizing a sales force, which include: activities should be coordinated; authority should be given along with responsibility; balance should be maintained between units; span of control should be reasonable; and, finally, the sales organization should be stable in its foundation but flexible and adaptive to changing conditions.

Organizing the sales function, on the other hand, is too often ignored, causing much frustration and many problems. Several examples of function dictating form or structure were considered, including:

1 A top-management decision to limit production or to maximize production

2 Electing to sell exclusively to OEMs

3 Selling service rather than the products themselves

4 Doing ongoing operations research to evaluate function and form

Constructing territories is usually planning the lowest level of the organizational chart. In general, territories can be laid out on a geographical basis, by product lines, by groups of customers, or on some combination of all three. Individual territory construction, however, presents the dilemma of attempting to balance equal sales potential and equal workload. Traditional methods were discussed and modern alternate ways were suggested which lead directly into other sales management areas.

QUESTIONS

1 What are the five guidelines for organizing a sales force?

2 What are the advantages of a well-planned sales organization?

3 Compare a vertical line organization which is centralized with a horizontal line organization which is decentralized.

4 How can operations research be used to test various alternate forms of sales force organization without disrupting a national sales force?

5 What are the advantages and disadvantages of organizing a sales force by geographic territory?

6 What are the advantages and disadvantages of organizing a sales force by product groupings?

7 What are the advantages and disadvantages of organizing a sales force by customer categories?

8 What are the ideal conditions in designing the individual territories, and why are they so difficult to achieve?

SELECTED REFERENCES

Bendix Avionics Marketing Case History, 3/4-in. videocassette, 40 min, b&w, Intercollegiate Video Clearing House, Miami, Fla., 1976.

Dunn, Albert H., Eugene M. Johnson, and **David L. Kurtz:** "Organization of the Sales Force" in *Sales Management,* General Learning Corporation, Morristown, N.J., 1974.

Johnson, H. Webster: "Organizing the Sales Department," chap. 2 in *Sales Management,* Charles E. Merrill Books, Inc., Columbus, Ohio, 1976.

Montgomery, David B., and **Glen L. Urban:** "Personal Selling Decisions," chap. 6 in *Management Science in Marketing,* Prentice-Hall Inc., Englewood Cliffs, N.J., 1969.

Newman, William, and **E. Warren Kirby:** "Organizing," Part I in *The Process of Management,* Prentice-Hall, Inc., Englewood Cliffs, N.J., 1977.

Schnee, Jerome E., Harold Lazarus, and **E. Warren Kirby:** "Organizing: Structural Design," Part I in *The Process of Management,* Prentice-Hall, Inc., Englewood Cliffs, N.J., 1977.

Stanton, William J., and **Richard H. Buskirk:** "Principles and Policies of Sales Organization," chap. 4, and "Typical Sales Organization Structures," chap. 5 in *Management of the Sales Force,* 4th ed., Richard D. Irwin, Inc., Homewood, Ill., 1974.

Still, Richard R., Edward W. Cundiff, and **Norman A. P. Goroni:** "The Sales Organization," chap. 6 in *Sales Management,* 3d ed., Prentice-Hall, Inc., Englewood Cliffs, N.J., 1976.

▶ Case 5-1

NATIONAL BEVERAGE COMPANY

National Beverage Company is a nationwide wholesale distributor of imported and domestic wines and liquors. The company is divided into regional areas with each branch having its own group of salespeople.

They have the territory divided geographically for their salespeople. Ideally this is the way the accounts are to be serviced; however, realistically this is not the case.

The company employs seven wine and liquor salesmen to service the area restaurants, bars, and country clubs; there are also four wine salesmen who service only grocery stores. All the salespeople work on straight commission.

Bob Salonsky came to National Beverage Company from another company and was hired as a wine and liquor salesman. For his initial training program, he went around with one of the company's established salesmen for two weeks.

When he first started his route solo, Mr. Salonsky had approximately 100 accounts. The system was so set up that he had to call in to the branch three times a day for special requests and orders from customer call-ins. The branch was set up on a 48-hour delivery service. From Monday to Wednesday at 2 o'clock he was essentially an order-taker. Within the time period allowed, he did not have any time to "sell" anything. He needed to recall from his memory what the customer usually ordered and mention those items; he then had to hurry to the next customer in order to reach all the accounts by Wednesday. If by chance he missed one customer, that would be the week that the customer called National Beverage Company to complain that they had not seen a sales rep in "weeks" (actually, it was only since the previous week). Then the complaint continued down the chain of command until Mr. Salonsky was reprimanded; it reached the point where he felt as though he did not do anything right!

On Thursday and Friday he had to deliver all orders taken for the week; when he returned to the customer, this was supposed to be his time for "selling." He was expected to promote future deals and weekly specials. Ideally this would have been a great setup. The problem involved was that by Thursday and Friday his customers had already seen him once, and that was enough for that week. The customer had already seen numerous other sales representatives and had other matters to attend to. As it turned out, there was little or no time for Mr. Salonsky to actually increase his sales for more commission.

After a short time Mr. Salonsky realized that the only sales reps who had their accounts divided by territory were the new reps. Actually

National Beverage Company was broken down by seniority. The older salesmen had their choice of customers and naturally chose the higher-paying accounts. Usually a senior sales rep had between thirty-five and forty accounts. So the breakdown turned out to be one of an economical consolidation instead of a geographical consolidation.

Mr. Salonsky was very knowledgeable in wines and knew that, given a chance, he could increase his commission by selling a larger volume and variety of wines. Most of his customers knew very little about wines and needed someone to inform them about which wine to serve with which meal.

After ten months with the company, he had 133 accounts and not enough time to service them properly. He felt that he was working himself to death and getting no monetary compensation. He wanted fewer good accounts and time to work on potential accounts. Instead, he was spending his time running from small account to small account and getting nowhere. It was at this point that he went to his sales manager.

The sales manager told him that there was no other way for the company to be divided. Mr. Salonsky realized how long he would have to wait until he would be among the senior salesmen; it was then that he resigned. The sales manager said that he was disappointed to see him leave, since he had excellent potential with the company.

Because of this policy National Beverage Company has a high turnover of new sales reps, yet they refuse to change.

1 What functions do liquor sales representatives serve besides "taking orders"?

2 Traditionally, seniority determines who gets the best territory in this industry. If you were the sales manager, how would you have handled young Bob Salonsky?

▶ **Case 5-2**

GENERAL FOAM COMPANY

General Foam Company is primarily a wholesaler of products used in manufacturing furniture. Some of the products sold by General Foam

Company are the following: (1) foam (both rubber and polyurethane); (2) zippers, tacks, and thread; (3) plastic laminate; and (4) contact adhesive. When General Foam Company started out, its primary product line was foam. Over the years the company added associated products such as zippers, tacks, and thread, which are used in manufacturing furniture such as couches, chairs, and bedding. General Foam purchases large blocks (3 × 4 × 15 feet) of foam and cuts the foam to order for the local furniture manufacturers. This process involves purchasing the foam by railroad carload, storing the foam in the warehouse until needed, cutting the foam, and delivering the foam to the customer.

Recently, General Foam decided to expand its product line and added General Electric Textolite. Textolite is a plastic laminate directly competing with Formica laminated plastic. The company also added a line of contact adhesives (Trans World Adhesives) which are used to attach the plastic laminate to wood in the manufacturing of furniture and kitchen cabinets. Textolite plastic laminate is purchased from General Electric in sheets which range in size from 3 × 8 feet to 5 × 12 feet. The Trans World adhesive is purchased in containers that range in size from 1-quart to 55-gallon drums. The process of distributing Textolite laminated products and Trans World adhesive is: The materials are purchased generally by the truckload, stored in the warehouse, and then delivered in small lots to the customers.

There are principally five brands of plastic laminate produced on a large scale. All the brands have standardized sizes, similar prices, and approximately the same range of colors and textures. Because of the similarities, the advantage of one distributor over another comes in the service provided to customers.

Ms. Charlotte Foster, the president of General Foam Company, started the company and has nurtured it to its present size and status. The attitude of management was that foam and the associated products were the "bread and butter" of the company and therefore should receive preference over other products.

The warehouse manager not only directed operations in the warehouse but also routed the delivery trucks. Since the foam products were of primary importance to him, the Textolite products and Trans World adhesive orders would be scheduled for delivery only if a truck carrying foam products happened to be going to that area. In some instances, four or five days would pass between the placing of an order for Textolite products and its delivery. Competitors in the local plastic laminate market were guaranteeing one-day delivery. Consequently, Textolite products were not capturing a good share of the market. The sales manager for Textolite products and Trans World adhesive suggested that with improved delivery service, Textolite products and Trans World adhesive sales could be significantly increased. He further recommended that:

1 The warehouse manager set a firm schedule stipulating on which specific days and to which geographic areas delivery trucks will be routed.

2 A van or small truck be purchased to make deliveries to those customers who are not in the scheduled delivery areas.

Ms. Foster felt that the present volume for Textolite and Trans World adhesive did not warrant the purchase of an additional vehicle.

1 Rather than having product divisions, what might be the effect of having all sales reps sell all products?

2 Are the customer categories so different that sales reps should be specialized?

▶ **Case 5-3**

ALBERT DOOR COMPANY

Albert Door was established in 1950 as a small furniture store. Today, it has grown throughout the northern half of the country in the form of a warehouse dealing directly with the consumer. This style of operation eliminates intermediaries, in effect cutting the cost for the consumer. The company was operated by two partners. One chose the Northeast section as his sales territory and the other partner the Northwest. This arrangement lasted for years before the firm's business prospered to such an extent that it became necessary to hire more personnel.

In 1970 the partners assumed managerial roles and hired seven sales representatives. Each rep was given a geographic territory within which to operate. For two years the business continued to expand.

In 1972, each of the sales reps was promoted to manager of his or her region and was instructed to divide the area into several new territories. The regional managers now had to hire new sales reps to cover these territories.

In 1975 it became apparent that two of the newly appointed regions desperately required more sales staff. The partners disagreed on how the new territories should be divided. One partner wanted to revise all the territories because of the inequalities. The second partner was afraid some good reps would quit if their territories were reduced.

1   How can management get a good sales rep to willingly give up part of a territory?

2   How important are the sales-customer relationships in switching territories?

▶ Case 5-4

PALMER PAPER COMPANY

Palmer Paper Company was established in 1860 and became a subsidiary of Hammermill Paper in 1962. Company headquarters are in Erie, Pennsylvania. The company sells printing paper, printing supplies, and printing equipment to the commercial printing industry and to in-plant printers. The local branch of Palmer Paper Company has an annual sales figure of $3 million.

Palmer Paper Company has a sales force of eight salespeople. Four of them sell the entire line of printing products and supplies to selected exclusive customers in the county. These sales representatives are assigned accounts on an individual-customer basis, as opposed to the usual territory-construction method employed by most other companies.

One salesperson solicits all paper products and supplies in the adjoining county. Another serves all customers in the next county. The remaining two are specialized and sell only paper by-products. One of these two reps also sells a special program of printing supplies and equipment to banks in the area.

All members of the sales force are paid on an equal commission basis, which is determined by sales. Annual salaries tend to be approximately equal, with the exception of the specialized salespeople. Their salaries are somewhat less than those of the other reps who sell entire product lines.

The company has matured to the point where it has so many paper products and supplies from different manufacturers (Scott, NCR, and NuArc, for example), that Palmer's sales force cannot adequately sell all the product lines that it now carries.

This has caused the sales staff to more or less become order takers. They cannot devote enough time to each customer to give a fair presentation of what the company has to sell.

The sales force could be expanded, but the added expense might be greater than the additional sales revenue generated.

1 How would you reorganize the branch sales force to increase sales and profit?

2 Are some customer categories important enough to warrant specialized salespersons?

6

Self-Management and
Span of Management Control

▶ Objectives

The reader will understand the importance of a sales manager deciding what major contributions can be made to achieve substantial goals. The sales manager's use of time shows the reader the difference between doing important work to achieve goals as contrasted with doing urgent or busy work. The reader will be able to analyze span-of-control problems and to determine an effective limit. He or she will understand the steps in effective delegation of authority and the benefits derived from it. The reader will be able to determine the appropriate sales force size as well as to construct a career path plan for sales representatives.

An organizational structure, whether well planned or simply grown from expediency, depends on people for its efficiency. A disorganized sales manager or one without functional priorities can easily disrupt the company and the sales force. An effective sales manager knows which activities are most important and blocks out time to do these things. A well-organized manager will also know his or her own limitations and how to use organizational theory to get others to do some of the important tasks. This requires the setting of goals, establishing of priorities, self-discipline, and the delegating of responsibility and authority to others.

SELF-MANAGEMENT

In sales management there are many areas where the local manager has more of less complete autonomy to act with authority. The manager can hire and fire, train in many different ways, reward and punish, motivate, control, and lead. Often there will be guidelines, of course, but a sales manager is usually expected to operate independently of immediate, close supervision. There are always realistic limitations, such as available funds or capital, the sophistication of the product lines, the availability of work force, and competitive activity.

Establish Goals   Within these constraints, the modern sales manager will analyze the situation and make the decision of what major contributions can be made to achieve sizable goals. One common goal is to upgrade the sales force's effectiveness. This might be approached by a plan to direct the efforts of the sales representatives so their efforts will be more fruitful. It might be approached by a plan to retrain the existing sales force so they may sell target segments not previously solicited. It might be approached by a plan to weed out the misfits and to whip the lazy and lethargic salespeople. The goal might be approached in a number of ways combined, depending upon the sales manager's situational analysis.

Another goal desired by many sales managers is to improve profits. This might involve a program to analyze the most economical order size to be sought and the minimum order acceptable. Another profit improvement program (PIP) might call for a mix of products to be sold to each account which serves the customer but also generates higher overall profit. A third example of PIP might call for selectively selling to only certain kinds of accounts which prefer the higher-profit products and services.

A third goal desired by some managers is to increase the face-to-face contact time between the sales representative and the buyer. This goal might be approached by analyzing the routes within territories which sales representatives use and reducing travel time. It might be approached through a training program to enable each representative to see a number of buying influencers or different decision makers on each call. It might be approached by analyzing the paperwork or reporting required and streamlining the system.

Whatever goals the sales manager establishes, they should be of a relatively high leverage or high impact for a minimum of effort. Usually this involves getting the sales force to work smarter, not harder, in ways which will yield relatively quick and clear benefits.

Time Management Perhaps the most significant factor in effective sales management is the way time is used. Many managers establish goals or targets, but somehow these get pushed into the background because there are too many day-to-day problems and crises with which the managers must deal. One salesman needs help in preparing a large bid on a new job. Another wants help in making a presentation to a new account. A third wants the manager to settle a complaint of a major account, and so forth. This kind of sales manager is so busy putting out fires that he never has the time to truly help the sales force to become independent, mature, responsible representatives.

The difference between doing *important* work, as contrasted with doing *urgent* work, should be carefully noted here. Important work is that which will contribute to the achievement of the established goals of significant impact. This would include working out plans and programs, developing people, and making improvements which will help realize the goals. Urgent work, on the other hand, is busy work which demands attention but, when finished, contributes little or nothing to accomplishing the desired goal. A telephone ringing is one such urgent demand. A pile of incoming mail is another urgent demand. Often a superior's request for a report is handled as an urgent demand. Too many meetings are considered urgent demand. Clearly, many phone calls are a waste of time, with rumors, gossip, office politics, and the like, consuming precious time. Most of the written material piled in the in-basket can be weeded out by a clerk. A superior's request for a report may be based on idle curiosity or a real need for a simple conclusion rather than reams of pages and detailed documentation. Many business meetings decide little of value and tend to drag on endlessly.

Authorities in the field of time management recommend that executives record their activities every fifteen minutes in two columns on a sheet of paper. The first column is marked "important activities" and the second is labeled "urgent activities." Starting at 9:15 A.M. on Monday and going to 5 P.M. on Friday, managers invariably find the majority of their time is spent doing things which did not have to be done, which could and should have been done by others, and which contributed little or nothing to the accomplishment of important work.

The next step after this realization is to write a list of important activities to be accomplished, including a priority number. Then the manager begins to work on the first item and does not leave it until it is finished. This may require several days or more, depending upon the number of interruptions; but the sales manager will no longer consciously elect to do some urgent work and postpone the important work. He or she will cut short unproductive conversations and meetings and will delegate to others much of the busy work. Some executives who insist on an open-door policy physically leave their offices for several hours a day to accomplish their goals in solitude elsewhere. By the time they return, many of the urgent calls, messages, and questions have resolved themselves. This change in daily activity requires strong self-discipline and a sense of purpose, but it can be achieved.

Self-development The third part of self-management—improving oneself—requires an objective analysis of one's strengths and weaknesses. Often company records will include aptitude test scores and interview evaluations which personnel people can use to guide the sales manager who seeks their help. Knowledgeable superiors are also a good source of guidance in this area. However, even a branch sales manager off on her own should realize general areas of weakness. Typical areas of need include the studying of management, accounting, electronic data processing, and technical subjects. Too often overlooked, however, are the basic skills of speed reading, effective listening, and effective business writing. These three skills can contribute a tremendous improvement in what can be accomplished when better time management is achieved. These and other self-development areas are discussed in more detail in Chapter 11, but the sales manager should be aware of his or her responsibility to build a plan for self-development.

SPAN OF CONTROL

In examining the organizational structure, it was noted that the span of control should be reasonable for the individual. This refers to the number of people one manager can effectively direct and control. The productivity of sales reps is often a function of how much on-the-job training and help they get from the sales supervisor and sales manager. Turnover of sales personnel has also been related to the number of representatives reporting to one manager. Optimum span of control has been suggested as 12 or 16 to 1 in selling to the trade, 10 to 1 in selling to businesses and missionary selling, and 7 to 1 in technical selling.[1]

A Conference Board survey of what companies actually do reported that the median number of salespeople reporting to a supervisor varied by type of product sold.[2] The median ratios reported were 10 to 1 in selling services, 8 to 1 in selling consumer products, and 6 to 1 in selling industrial products. From these and similar studies there is seen to be a tendency to generalize that span-of-control ratios are reduced as the selling becomes more complex or technical. This generalization is not necessarily true.

Perhaps much more of a factor in deciding the optimum ratio is the degree of maturity and the experience level of the individual sales representatives involved. Clearly, new sales representatives would require close supervision while learning to sell almost any line of products. One supervisor might effectively handle only five trainees in the field. On the other hand, one sales manager has very effectively handled twenty to thirty manufacturer's representatives who were all mature sales engineers on a straight commission basis.

An immature salesperson is passive and relatively dependent on the sales manager. He or she wants to be told where to call and what to say and do. As the salesperson learns and becomes experienced, he or she has increased activity and independence and wants to be on the go and does not want to be closely supervised. The immature salesperson will have only a few behavior patterns, which will be repeated again and

---

[1]See Derek A. Newton, "Get the Most Out of Your Sales Force," *Harvard Business Review,* vol. 47 pp. 130–143, September–October 1969.

[2]Morgan B. MacDonald, Jr., and Earl L. Bailey, "The Field Sales Supervisor," *Conference Board Record,* vol. V, p. 34, July 1968. See also William H. Newman and E. Warren Kirby, Part II, "Human Factors in Organizing," in *The Process of Management,* Prentice-Hall, Inc., Englewood Cliffs, N.J., 1977.

again. A mature salesperson is capable of behaving in many ways and has deep and strong interests in life. He or she can easily adjust to different kinds of people in changing situations. The immature salesperson has a short time perspective and is normally impatient. He or she needs constant pepping-up and inspiration to call back again and again when there is no immediate reward of an order. The mature salesperson, on the other hand, has a long time perspective of both past and future which produces wisdom. He or she knows it takes care and patience to cultivate some business. The immature sales rep has little awareness of self and often acts childishly or impulsively. The mature sales rep is more self-aware and has, therefore, greater control over his or her behavior.

This degree of maturity changes and develops over the years in most salespeople. However, there are many salespeople over 40 years old who still need almost daily direction, inspiration, and a sympathetic ear. They demand as much time and attention of their sales manager as do the young sales trainees. Age and experience do not necessarily equate with maturity.

Thus it can be seen that the number of sales representatives reporting to one sales manager or supervisor should be different depending on the amount of the sales manager's time which is demanded. Since this demand changes over time, even with the same sales force, the optimum span of control will vary within the same sales organization. Clearly, this factor is also changed with a high turnover of the sales representatives. What may be ideal at one point in time may be inappropriate at another time, and the sales manager should be flexible in making such assignments. As the time demands become excessive, additional levels of management can be created by delegating some authority and responsibility to assistants, supervisors, and specialists as required.

DELEGATION PROBLEMS AND PROCEDURES

Many newly appointed sales managers feel that a bulging briefcase taken home every night is the way to top management. They do not realize that effective executives delegate work to subordinates.

Many other sales managers are more than willing to delegate responsibilities but not the commensurate authority. They believe that others cannot possibly perform as well as they can. Other sales managers subconsciously fear that if they delegate too much, their own jobs will be eliminated. Finally, there are some sales managers who enjoy certain activities so much that they reserve them to themselves even when they know they should delegate them. These are the sales managers who are too busy putting out fires because basically they enjoy fighting fires and their egos are flattered when others ask for help. The results of not delegating are (1) an overworked sales manager; (2) some important activities that simply never get accomplished; and (3) a dependent and frustrated sales force, often with low morale and high turnover problems. These are all problems of managing the sales function, and they require self-discipline by the modern sales manager.

Once the manager recognizes that some important activities will not get done otherwise, he or she must delegate part of the workload to others. This does not necessarily involve promoting salespeople into management or hiring outsiders to do staff work. Indeed, it usually means giving additional responsibilities to people already working full time. Maturing people seek such assignments in order to grow and to increase their chances of being promoted.

Steps in Delegation The process of delegating effectively involves the following steps:

1 Define what has to be done.

2 Determine when the activity will begin.

3 Decide how long the activity will continue.

4 Set goals or objectives expected from the subordinate.

5 Determine the kind of person who can now handle the assignment.

6 Determine how much time initially should be spent on this assignment in addition to normal duties.

7 Determine how much time should be spent on this assignment after the breaking-in period.

8 Determine standards of performance and reporting procedures for accountability.

9 Determine what is the benefit to the subordinate who accepts this additional responsibility.

10 Specify the precise limits of authority which will go along with the new responsibility, noting the right of appeal inherent in all jobs.

To illustrate these steps, look at the situation where sales training is taking too much of the sales manager's time. Sales training may be defined to cover only newly hired sales trainees or part or all of the sales force. It may involve assigning one trainee to one sales representative in the buddy system, where no time is lost from selling activities. In a large company, sales training is frequently defined to include recruiting, interviewing, hiring, training, and, finally, placement or assignment within the company.

However it is defined, the sales training may start immediately or at the beginning of next year's slow period and continue every day for one week, or one day per week for three months, or it may be a full-time, continuous process in a large organization. The objectives or goals of training may be as simple as acquiring a knowledge of the product line or as complicated as developing a sophisticated behavioral skill of probing for information and gaining agreement from a hostile prospect. The objectives should be specific and measurable.

The kind of salesperson who can handle this new responsibility should have the education, experience, personality traits, and ambition equal to the challenge. Decisions must be made about how much counseling, training, or preparatory experience the individual may need before assuming the responsibility. He or she may have to write sales training manuals and tests or may be able to use standard published materials.

Preparing the initial sales training plan and materials may require several months. However, once the program is implemented, it may require only one week of the person's time every three months with little or no revision in between, for example. An outside consultant may be used to create a sales training program and assist the experienced sales representative who will actually conduct the classes or on-the-job demonstrations.

Before the delegated duties are assigned, the sales manager should establish standards of performance expected from whoever finally gets the responsibility. This would include various reports of test scores, evaluations, budgetary reports, and so forth, to monitor progress toward the stated objectives.

Next, the sales manager should look at the motivational aspects of this new assignment. Will it seem like more work for the same pay or, worse, a probability of lower sales and earnings? The modern sales manager will be able to point out the opportunities for growth and recognition for achievement which are likely to occur.

Finally, the sales manager must decide on the precise limits of authority which will be given to the new sales trainer. Some companies authorize the manager of sales training to go into the field with any experienced salesperson and critique his or her performance. Others restrict the sales trainer to the classroom and to dealing with new sales trainees exclusively.

Each of these decisions should be carefully written and then discussed with the subordinate so that he or she understands precisely what the sales manager wants and expects. While the illustration we have given here was of a relatively easily understood task of sales training, all delegated functions should go through this detailed mental exercise. In addition, all concerned parties in the company should be notified in writing of the change and told to direct their inquiries or to channel their information accordingly.

When delegation is properly carried out, the sales manager benefits by gaining more productive time and often by developing a specialist who can do the job better. The subordinate benefits by getting a more interesting and responsible set of duties. The company should also benefit because delegation contributes to higher profit and to developing a pool of future managers.

DETERMINING THE SALES FORCE SIZE

The question of how many sales representatives a company should have is best resolved through operations research for each organization. A manager can test how sales volume responds to various sales effort inputs. Typically this revolves around the questions of how many accounts must be contacted, how often, and how long the average call should take. Budgetary constraints often force the sales manager to optimize profit with a limited number of salespersons rather than to maximize sales volume.

Account analysis is the first step in this decision process. For example, in Syracuse, New York, there might be sixty top-rated accounts. Based on the sales manager's experience, these accounts should be called upon at least every two weeks. This would mean twenty-six calls per year times sixty accounts, or 1560 calls. Now a good sales representative who averages five calls per day and works 240 days per year can make only 1200 calls per year. One person could not cover the desired sixty accounts as the manager wanted.

Assume there were another 300 accounts in Syracuse which were rated good and worth calling on at least once per month. Then an additional 3600 calls per year would be required, which means that three more sales representatives should be added. This analytical process would continue through to the smallest accounts desired to arrive at the ideal number of sales representatives required to cover all accounts as the manager desired.

Unfortunately this method does not address itself to the question of returning a profit. A more detailed analysis is required to indicate the sales and profit potential of each account and the probability of achieving them. A leading authority in this field, Robert Vizza, suggests using return on time invested (ROTI) as the deciding factor.[3] ROTI is the actual gross margin per account divided by the cost of time invested in selling to that account. A ROTI of less than 1 would not yield a profit.

Assuming a national average of $65 per sales call, this would mean that a representative would have to have a reasonably good chance of generating more than $65 gross profit on each call over a period of time or should not waste time on that account. It remains a managerial decision to classify each account on a potential profit basis.

It is also the sales manager's responsibility to assign the accounts to individual representatives, and how this is done may very well influence

---

[3]Robert F. Vizza, *Time and Territorial Management—A Programmed Learning Course,* R. F. Vizza Associates, Inc., New York, 1975.

the probability of success. If experienced Joe Jones is given an account, perhaps the probability of selling it is .80, while if it is given to trainee Mary Smith there might be less than a .50 chance of success. Thus even the best of objective forumlas in this area tend to rest on the sales manager's subjective decisions.

In any event, it usually helps to quantify such decisions when possible for a more objective view. Figure 6-1 shows Vizza's recommended form for account analysis.

Perhaps the more common way to determine sales force size in the United States today is the expanding of a sales force as it pays for itself. Xerox, for example, with a sales force of over 3000 representatives, has the financial and work force muscle necessary to open a sales office practically wherever it wishes. In south Florida, for example, they opened one office in Miami. As volume and profits grew, they opened a second office 25 miles away in Fort Lauderdale. Still later they opened a third office in West Palm Beach another 25 miles further away. This very practical expansion method enables a sales force to grow while generating profit. A decision to expand or contract is based on profit potential, not solely on the number and size of accounts to be visited.

Clearly, a sales force that is compensated by commission can be

ACCOUNT ANALYSIS AND CALCULATION OF EXPECTED VALUE

Customer Name/Number (1)	Repeat Sales (2)	Additional Volume (3)	Forecast (4)	Prob- ability (5)	Expected Value (6)	Classi- fication (7)
1						
2						
3						
4						
5						

Prospect's Name/Number	Market Potential	Estimated Share	Forecast	Prob- ability	Expected Value	Classi- fication
1						
2						
3						
4						
5						

Figure 6-1 *Source:* Robert F. Vizza, *Time and Territorial Management—A Programmed Learning Course,* R. F. Vizza Associates, Inc., New York, 1975.

expanded more easily than one which is on salarry or salary plus commission. However, even a small company can expand its market coverage by using independent manufacturers' representatives in selected areas. These are professional salespeople who work on a straight commission basis. Normally they require an exclusive territory, and this requirement becomes the limiting factor in the size of the sales force.

As noted in the opening chapters, most sales management decisions are interrelated with other management areas, and this fact certainly applies to the question of optimizing the size of the sales force. One company creaming the crop might prefer a small, well-paid sales force on salary, while another company in the same industry might prefer a large sales force on commission.

Using operations research, a sales manager can experiment with increasing the number of calls made on selected accounts and compute the increased costs and changes in gross profit. This may be done with one or two sales representatives or with all the entire staff on a small percentage of accounts. Allocation of the sales effort is a good area for operations research. With computer technology, today it is relatively easy to design experiments of this nature and measure the effects. Using Vizza's model or other mathematical models tailored to a specific company, the sales manager can tell the computer specialist what analysis is to be made and what measurements will be meaningful. The manager can test various ideas before committing the entire sales force.

While this discussion has centered on the number of sales calls desired, it should not be overlooked that the *quality* of sales calls can also be varied. The sales manager can influence the quality of the call through training and motivation, which are discussed in subsequent chapters. The effects of training and motivation can and should also be measured through operations research techniques.

CAREER PATHS FOR SALES PERSONNEL

Some sales managers think of a sales career as having three distinct steps: junior sales rep, sales rep, and senior sales rep. Others think of a selling career as having many steps, for example, sales trainee, junior sales rep, territory representative, senior sales rep, industry sales rep, and national-account representative.[4] Many managers create a series of titles through which the sales representatives may pass in their career while still doing the same basic job. These artificial titles, milestones of age or years of experience, mean very little to the sales representative who is thinking about his or her career.

To be meaningful, the steps in a career path should involve real changes in responsibilities. Each step would normally have a unique job description clearly differentiating its duties and responsibilities from those of the step below and those of the next step above it. A territory sales representative, for example, might need a general business background; but before one could be considered for promotion to a specialty, such as selling banks only, he or she would need special knowledge. A formal college course in banking might give the rep the desired level of specialized knowledge.

Given a series of distinct steps with the duties, responsibilities, and requirements clearly spelled out, the sales representatives can see what they must do to prepare themselves for promotion. They can decide whether or not a goal is realistic for them and whether or not they are willing to spend the necessary time and effort required to prepare for it. The importance of career guidance by the sales manager cannot be overstressed. It seems foolish to sit back and watch a man or woman prepare for a career which will probably result in failure or personal dissatisfaction. Perhaps more tragic is the emotional impact on the ones who are demoted or terminated because they were unable to make the grade in the wrong job. The discouragement and loss of pride may stay with the unsuccessful persons throughout their lives.

Career Paths in Large Sales Organizations Usually large sales organizations have many highly responsible and highly paid positions within the sales function. Depending on their backgrounds, interests, and ambitions, sales representatives can plan to prepare for any one or a combination of the positions. For example, in a national sales organization with many lines of both consumer and technical industrial products, the following job descriptions are all within the direct control of the vice president of sales:

[4]This entire section is taken from Thomas F. Stroh, *Training and Developing the Professional Salesman,* AMACOM, American Management Association, New York, 1975.

- Sales representative
- Specialty representative
- Sales engineer
- Specialty sales engineer
- Product specialist
- National account representative
- Sales trainer
- Industry specialist
- Sales analyst
- Sales planner
- Market development specialist
- Distribution development specialist
- Merchandising and promotion specialist
- Sales practices and procedures specialist
- Proposals and quotations specialist
- Contract negotiations and sales specialist

These positions are filled by a progression of people from the sales force. Moreover, there can be a group of people in each of the jobs described, each headed by a supervisor and a manager.

Another large sales organization with a small line of products has the following job descriptions as part of their planned career path:

- Trainee (fifteen weeks)
- Junior sales representative (salary guaranteed for one year)
- Sales representative (commission only)
- Senior sales representative (commission plus override)
- Specialty sales representative (by product)

- Industry sales representative (by customer)
- Government sales representative
- Sales supervisor
- Sales trainer
- District sales manager
- Regional sales supervisor
- Regional sales managers
        Planning and analysis
        Promotion
- Divisional sales vice presidents
        Central training
        Sales forecasting
        Market development
- Merchandising and promotion
- Product development
- Work force development

Once again, this organization has many jobs at each level. At the division or national level, the staff functions are centralized and controlled. This organization permits the line managers to concentrate primarily on direct sales, and they spend from 20 to 50 percent of their time on personally selling to "house" accounts.

From management's point of view, career-path planning is also planning for management development. It ensures that trained people will be available to fill vacancies as they occur and helps to forecast areas where training will be necessary. It also ensures that everyone has a chance to be considered for more responsible jobs and that nobody will get lost in the shuffle. The key tools in the planning of training, promotions, and transfers are executive inventories and replacement charts of the company organization. These show the years of experience and skill limitations of employees, imminent retirements, promotions due, and so forth.

Career-path planning should provide opportunities for sales representatives to obtain both formal, off-the-job training and on-the-job experience before they have the full weight of a new responsibility thrust upon them. For some positions, the sales representatives may go through a systematic job rotation, spending several months or years in various parts of a higher job. In other cases it may be more advantageous to have the sales representative understudy the incumbent directly for three to six months. In either case, sales management attempts to forecast its needs, select sales representatives who have the appropriate capabilities, interests, and desires, and prepare them with training and experience before they are needed. While a perfect record of successful promotions would be impossible, this orderly process has a much better chance of succeeding than the typical sink-or-swim method.

Career Paths in Small Sales Organizations Career-path planning need not be limited to large sales organizations. A retail automobile dealer with ten sales representatives, for example, can prepare a number of job descriptions showing different levels of responsibility and compensation for the young sales representatives who are looking at their career possibilities. After the initial training stage, the first responsibility might be to sell only new cars. The second stage might be selling new cars and new trucks. A sales trainer and a sales supervisor could be added to either of these stages. The position of general sales manager might be followed by a limited partnership with responsibilities for both sales and service. The possibilities of planning a career path for sales representatives are limited only by the creative and analytical skills of the planner. The guiding rule is to have each step distinctly different from every other step in real responsibilities and training or preparation. This provides both an opportunity and a challenge for the experienced sales representatives to grow and develop throughout their careers.

Many self-made executives who own their businesses today have come up through the ranks by their own determination and by capitalizing on opportunities. They usually know the intimate details of most phases of their business because they have learned them from personal experience. They have cut their career path almost alone, without help and guidance from superiors. Today many sales representatives are not aware of their career possibilities; hence they cannot show their determination. Others have a strong feeling of what they would like to become someday but do not know how to prepare themselves for it. Clearly, human resources are wasted if career-path planning is neglected or if paths are simply permitted to evolve as pure chance may dictate. Intelligent and empathetic planning by sales managers seems to be essential in planning a career path for sales representatives.

SUMMARY

To become more effective, modern sales managers plan a program of self-management. This begins with establishing high-priority goals which will make an important contribution to their organization. Next they analyze their use of time and concentrate on achieving important things while minimizing time wasted on doing urgent things that are not really important in the long run. Finally, modern sales managers objectively evaluate their own strengths and weaknesses and then plan a self-development program.

To increase their efficiency, sales managers utilize the principles of the span of control, which indicate how much time can be devoted to various groups of salespeople. Inexperienced and immature sales representatives require close supervision and considerable time in their individual guidance. Mature representatives, on the other hand, work very well on their own with only broad or general supervision.

Delegation is the tool which sales managers can use to lighten their workload, develop subordinate specialists, and do important tasks themselves. Guidelines or a series of steps in the process of delegating are essential for avoiding most of the problems which can arise. These require good two-way communication and motivation to be effective.

Determining the sales force size begins with a clear understanding of the company's goals, its resources, and its compensation system. Then modern managers attempt to evaluate the profit potential of desired accounts and the probability of selling specific amounts of each product category. Finally they must assign the accounts to various sales representatives to optimize profits. Operations research can be used to test various ideas and theories before committing the entire sales force.

Planning a career path for sales representatives is an excellent tool to match individuals' needs to grow with the present and future needs of the company. This is not constructing an artificial list of titles for doing the same job. It is the development of a sequential series of steps in which the basic responsibilities and training or preparation are unique for each higher level. It helps in the development of a plan for self-management for the newest sales trainee on up to the top executives of any organization.

QUESTIONS

1 Describe four important goals which a sales manager might develop to get the sales force to work smarter, not harder, to achieve substantial results.

2 How can a very busy sales manager find time to devote to important activities which never seem to get done?

3 What are the kinds of self-development areas in which sales managers can undertake to improve themselves?

4 What are the determinants of how many sales reps one manager can handle?

5 What are the ten guidelines for effective delegation of responsibility and authority?

6 What are the determinants of optimum sales force size?

7 What should be the difference between steps in planning a career path?

8 How can operations research be used to determine the optimum frequency of sales calls on a particular category of accounts?

SELECTED REFERENCES

Breaking the Delegation Barrier, 16 mm film, 30 min, color, Roundtable Films, Inc., Beverly Hills, Calif., 1968.
International Paper Company Marketing Case History, ³/₄-in. videocas-

sette, 40 min, b&w, Intercollegiate Video Clearing House, Miami, Fla., 1976.

Schnee, Jerome E., Harold Lazarus, and **E. Warren Kirby**: "Designing the Hierarchy: Delegating and Decentralizing," chap. 2 in *The Process of Management,* Prentice-Hall, Inc., Englewood Cliffs, N.J., 1977.

Stanton, William J., and **Richard H. Buskirk**: "The Sales Manager—His Job, His Career," chap 2 in *Management of the Sales Force,* 4th ed., Richard D. Irwin, Inc., Homewood, Ill., 1974.

Still, Richard R., Edward W. Cundiff, and **Norman A. P. Govoni**: "The Sales Executive's Job," chap. 5 in *Sales Management,* 3d ed., Prentice-Hall, Inc., Englewood Cliffs, N.J., 1976.

Stroh, Thomas F.: "Career Development of Experienced Salesmen," chap. 11 in *Training and Developing the Professional Salesman,* AMA-COM, American Management Association, New York, 1973.

Vizza, Robert F.: *Time and Territorial Management—A Programmed Learning Course,* R. F. Vizza Associates, Inc., New York, 1975.

▶ **Case 6-1**

AIRPAX ELECTRONICS COMPANY

The Airpax Electronics Company, a manufacturer of nonconsumer electronic components, was established in 1957. The Controls Division of Airpax manufactures industrial controls used to monitor, control, and measure a variety of industrial events, such as rotation of shafts, mechanical motions, and temperatures of precision furnaces. Airpax has earned a reputation for manufacturing only top-quality products and is well recognized as a leader in the electronics industry.

The major goal of the sales department at Airpax Electronics is to keep business coming to the company. Repeat sales are the major portion of this division's business. The actual selling function is accomplished using outside manufacturer's representatives. There is one sales manager and several in-house sales reps. These reps work with customers over the phone as well as in person in the field. Advertising is done extensively in electronics magazines as well as with Airpax catalogs.

Alan Rogers was one of the most effective salesmen in the small force. His customers liked him, he knew the products, and his sales performance was outstanding. The sales trainees looked up to him for guidance and inspiration. Most of the older reps at Airpax recognized his obvious talents for selling. In the past several months, his territory has not kept pace with similar territories worked by the other reps. He was doing a passable job, but the sales manager knew this territory should have been producing more. Communications between the manager and Alan were minimal. Alan sent in his reports and his orders and little else. His contributions at the sales meetings were also minimal. Problems at home were only rumors. However, the management was pleased with Mr. Rogers, as he had in the past brought in many very profitable orders that were large in size and was presently working on another large one.

The sales manager wondered whether or not to let Mr. Rogers go, at the risk of losing a very large sale, or to keep him on, hoping the problem was lack of communication on his part.

1 Why do you suppose there is a communication problem in this very small sales force?

2 What would you do as sales manager, to resolve this problem?

▶ **Case 6-2**

TELLS ORIGINALS

Joan Kelly has worked for Tells Originals, a family-owned women's department store, for five years. She was hired by the owners to manage the Southland store, which is one of the five stores located in shopping centers throughout two metropolitan counties.

Tells Originals stores handle moderately priced dresses, sportswear, and lingerie for women of all sizes and ages.

As the manager, Ms. Kelly is responsible for a sales staff of twenty, employed on a part-time or full-time basis. Her other management duties include maintaining accurate sales records on a daily basis, selecting current merchandise to be displayed in the windows as well as throughout the interior of the store, and handling customer complaints and returns. She also must hire, with the owners' approval, an assistant to help her with these responsibilities. In the past the assistant managers have been hired from within the company.

Nancy, a local college student majoring in marketing, has worked for Tells Originals under Joan Kelly for over a year. She is 19 years old. During this time, Nancy's sales have been above average, and she has shown an eagerness to learn more about the retail business. Under the guidance of Ms. Kelly, Nancy became quite good at choosing merchandise for displays and arranging racks to take advantage of the general flow of customer traffic. Ms. Kelly became quite impressed with Nancy and soon realized that she had great potential. With added experience and education, Nancy felt she was now ready to be promoted to assistant manager. Nancy approached Ms. Kelly with the idea of promotion only to hear that Ms. Kelly had already spoken to the owners on that subject and they felt Nancy was not old enough to assume the role of an assistant manager. The assistant managers currently employed have a strong sales background and are between 20 and 35 years of age. Ms. Kelly tried to assure Nancy that she felt Nancy was mature enough to handle the job and that she was indeed qualified, but her age was the negative factor keeping her from the promotion.

As time went on, Nancy saw many assistant managers hired who were less qualified than she. Ms. Kelly kept reassuring Nancy that the promotion was only a matter of time. This same situation persisted for some time until Nancy approached Ms. Kelly once again on the subject of promotion. Nancy said she felt she was being held back unfairly and that if she was qualified to handle the job of assistant manager, she should be given the opportunity. Nancy told Ms. Kelly that she appreciated her confidence, but she could no longer watch people who were less qualified than she was being promoted above her just because of age. Nancy said she would find work with another retail firm if she was not promoted. Ms. Kelly, realizing the contribution Nancy could make to the company in years to come, did not want Nancy to quit.

1 How might Nancy be given a promotion without risking a loss in sales and profit?

2 How can young, impatient sales representatives be taught to make themselves more promotable?

▶ Case 6-3

POWER-X COMPANY

Power-X, Inc., is a 3-year-old company whose business is the sale of x-ray equipment and accessories (film, light concentrators, and so on). Doug Morgan, the owner, president, and primary salesman for the company, is 54 years old. He has been in the medical-equipment sales business most of his life and has specialized in the x-ray field for the last six years.

Up until three months ago, Doug and another salesman were the only two salesmen for Power-X and were handling the entire three-county area. Doug realized that his sales volume had stayed at about the $300,000-per-year mark for quite a while and decided to reorganize. Doug elected to handle the southern part of one county himself and give the northern half to the other salesman. This meant he had to hire a new person for the two distant counties.

Through a "friend of a friend," Doug hired Cathy McManus, a 27-year-old who had spent the previous four years selling life and health insurance. The compensation arrangement was one of straight commission on all transactions made within her territory.

The first week of Cathy's association with the firm was primarily spent introducing her to current accounts and other acquaintances in and out of the business and some calls on new customers. Cathy questioned the amount of time spent on seemingly worthless calls and ones where Doug spent an hour chatting to make a $20 sale. Doug's reply was, "You have to know what's happening everywhere."

On the start of the second week of work, Cathy, armed with little technical knowledge and a lot of drive, had her customary morning sales meeting with Doug. At this time she was handed a stack of about fifty proposals that Doug had put together and was told to call them (the prospects) to see if they had bought any equipment yet. Doug explained that he had not had the time to get back in touch with them. There was, however, one problem. Many of the proposals Cathy received to follow up on were anywhere from nine months to a year old.

The next day Doug asked Cathy to come with him to see an important client. Two months prior to the day in question, Doug had made a proposal on an x-ray unit to a Doctor Alterwein. Doug had called the doctor to follow up on the proposal but never spoke to him personally, and the doctor did not return his calls.

About a month later Jim Holly, a salesman for another firm selling medical supplies, was playing golf with Doug. Jim told Doug that he had just sold Dr. Alterwein a special film concentrator to go with a new x-ray machine that the doctor bought from another company, and Jim needed somebody to install it. Doug could not understand why the doctor did not buy from him; but under the guise of good public relations, he offered to drive some distance to install another salesman's equipment. This was the important prospect that they were on the way to see.

Upon arriving at the doctor's office, Doug informed the receptionist that he was there to install the part that Jim Holly had sold them. He was promptly informed that she had already done it herself and it was working fine. As Doug and Cathy left, Doug's reply was, "Well, at least now I know what happened there."

1 How might Doug Morgan analyze his use of time to improve his effectiveness?

2 How can Cathy McManus benefit by observing how her manager covers a territory?

▶ Case 6-4

MATT PETECELLO, INC.

Matt Petecello, Incorporated, is a New York corporation with its headquarters in Syracuse. The company distributes diversified flooring products which include carpets, rubber padding, vinyl tiles, and no-wax sheet goods, as well as electrical appliances. Each category has its own sales manager with a staff of salespeople. The classification which is of interest is the Resilient Floor Division, which sells vinyl tiles and no-wax sheet goods.

Matt Petecello, Inc., has the exclusive distribution rights on Armstrong products sold in this upstate New York area. All Armstrong products sold in this area must go through this distributor. Because of this, and the fact that Armstrong does considerable national advertising, the distributor has enjoyed a favorable sales position.

The division's sales position at present is being threatened by GAF and Amtico, who are utilizing the same kinds of marketing techniques with approximately the same types and quality of vinyl products.

The division sales manager feels that the best way to maintain market position, and hopefully attract new customers, is through additional contact by the salespeople. This could be done by hiring more sales representatives to work in the already established territories. Five areas comprise the counties surrounding the Syracuse area. This territory is, at present, being handled by five sales reps.

The sales staff is opposed to the ideas of the sales manager. They feel that the area is being handled very well, which is evidenced by their high sales achievements. In fact, the sales reps feel that they could handle even a larger area.

This situation presents a problem to the sales manager, as he does not want to lose any of his staff because they are top producers.

1 How might different levels of sales management alleviate this problem?

2 How would you determine how many additional sales representatives should be hired?

▶ **Case 6-5**

AVON SALES MANAGER

Terry Cramer is married and is in her early thirties. Presently she has under her 171 sales personnel who make house calls to sell Avon products. All sales are made on a personal basis.

Ms. Cramer states that her only problem is that she does not have time to do all the things she is required to do.

The sales personnel are required to sell $100 worth of merchandise every two weeks. If this quota is not met, Terry Cramer is required to call each and every seller and find out why he or she did not make the quota. Every two weeks she must call between forty and fifty people.

The sales positions are part or full time, but nevertheless, turnover is high. Last week she trained ten people, and she averages one new seller per day. Training is done on a personal basis. A total of four hours' training time is spent (not including travel time, which is extensive) over the period of a month. Also, there is a sales meeting every fourth Wednesday, lasting an hour and a half in the morning with the evening devoted to discussing new products and sales techniques. The attendance at these meetings is averaging fifty-eight. During the meetings Terry delegates some responsibility and sets up ten team leaders. Their responsibility is to try to call people to come to the meetings. Also, they have started calling people who do not reach the sales quota. There is a prize to the team leader who gets the most people to come to the meetings.

Terry Cramer works a ten-hour day six days a week and is constantly fighting the clock trying to keep up with her work and still open new accounts. She describes the job as a constant thing, always going and requiring a lot of busywork that eats up her time.

From the regional office she receives a printout listing of sellers who do not make their quota. Other than two sales meetings (lasting a week or two) that she must attend out of state, she receives no help at all from the regional office.

In conclusion Terry Cramer states that, despite the time factor, sales are up and there is no problem hiring people.

1   How might a time and duty analysis help Ms. Cramer organize her work more effectively?

2   How might one sales manager better handle 171 sales representatives?

Sales Management
Communications

▶ **Objectives**

The reader will understand the psychology of communications and persuasion with their selective mechanisms and will be able to construct a persuasive message that is most apt to be effective, enabling him or her to provide input to the advertising specialist and to direct the sales force's use of advertising. The reader will also be able to evaluate the use of sales promotions and trade shows. He or she will be able to build an in-house communications network to enlighten, inform, and motivate distant sales reps. Finally, the reader will understand the use of supportive techniques to increase the effectiveness of communication by building loyalty.

If modern sales managers are to become the centers of influence in any business, as was indicated in the earlier chapters, they must build a practical two-way communication system. Information from prospects and customers must be obtained by the sales force and efficiently fed to those people who are doing research and development of new products, for example. The ongoing efforts of research should be reported back to the sales force regularly so they can reassure customers of the company's interest in making improvements. Some information may remain confidential, but most of it can be disseminated to customers with good benefits to all concerned.

Customers and prospects often have difficulty in understanding or believing certain facts and claims. Normally this indicates a need for additional information in a form which is easy to comprehend and which is credible or trustworthy. Since the sales reps are closest to customers, it becomes a function of sales management to guide, if not direct, the advertising and sales promotion planning of the same organization.

In a similar way it can be shown that all departments in an organization need some information and guidance from the sales manager. It is also true that every functional unit can also give the sales force information which it needs to do a better job. This two-way communication flow should not occur by chance or through half-false rumors. The modern sales manager will make it a regular and accurate way of doing business. It has been this writer's experience that in a large corporation the number one or number two executive in every department was willing and eager to conduct a one-hour seminar with the sales force four

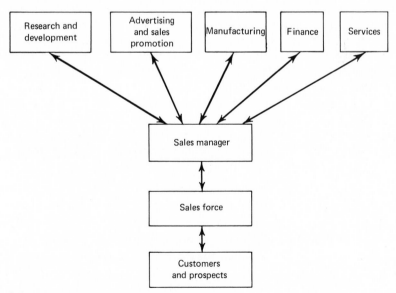

Sales Management Communications

times per year. Such exchanges of information were very enlightening for the sales force and for all the executives.

Finally, there is the problem of communication between the sales force and the sales manager. Many sales reps can hear an identical message and distort different parts so that the received message can be different for each representative. Subsequently, perhaps two weeks later, each sales rep will remember only selected parts of the distorted message and completely forget other parts. At this point there is usually mass confusion regarding what the sales manager wants and why the sales reps should cooperate. This is a very normal behavior pattern, and the modern sales manager will recognize a need to understand the psychology of communications.

THE PSYCHOLOGY OF COMMUNICATIONS

In order to communicate, the sales manager should know something about the personality and predisposition of the audience. For example, a manager who knows the sales reps well enough can phrase the communication in a way which makes the sales reps apt to listen and understand.

Predisposition In the sales management situation, a salesperson's predisposition is a collection of attitudes, opinions, beliefs, interests, and needs as they relate to the line of products being sold, the company, and the sales manager before the salesperson is exposed to any persuasive message. For example, one sales rep may be predisposed to listen to a message suggesting more money while another sales rep may be predisposed to listen to a message suggesting prestige-building titles or promotion. Underlying her predisposition, one particular saleswoman's personality, for example, would lead to her persistent tendency to judge all sales managers as fast talkers who are basically interested only in themselves. Therefore, this saleswoman is skeptical of any programs and promises the sales manager may make. She persistently judges the manager's pep talks and communications in a certain way, and she adjusts to the stress or pressure in a predictable way.

People tend to maintain the status quo and to avoid conflict and frustration. They try to maintain an inner balance. The mechanisms of defense are quite common, and sales reps generally do have a persistent tendency to behave in a fixed or limited manner when faced with conflict. Predisposition includes both the personal needs of each sales rep and the rep's role in the organization. The processes involved in the resistance to persuasion are forms of escape or defense mechanisms, and they form a protective umbrella over the sales rep's predisposition.

Selective Exposure The process of protecting the predisposition of an individual by selectively choosing communications that promise to agree with, confirm, and be compatible with existing attitudes and beliefs is called *selective exposure.* In other words, a sales rep is more apt to listen to a sales manager talking about things which the rep wants to hear than if the manager is talking about everyone making two more calls every day or anything which the rep dislikes. Because their jobs depend on it, salespeople will sit through a sales meeting but mentally may be tuned out in which case they will not hear the persuasive message. If letters and sales promotion materials are mailed to them, the sales reps who are resisting will merely glance at the literature and cast it aside. They will not willingly expose themselves to a message which they suspect will disagree with their existing beliefs.

To gain selective exposure a sales manager might convincingly promise the sales reps satisfaction for the time they take. The manager should appeal to the known predisposition of the individual salesperson's personal needs and role in the organization. The appeal should be genuine and sincere if it is to be effective in repeated future communications.

Selective Perception The process of seeing or understanding in a message only certain selected information that agrees with or is compatible with preconceived ideas, attitudes, and beliefs is called *selective perception.* Sales reps will hear and comprehend that with which they agree and either will not hear or will not accept that with which they disagree. The points of information they like will be seen at a glance, but points of disagreement are often unintelligible or not recognizable. The unwanted opinion or information is obscure or dark and of doubtful meaning, or it may seem too ambiguous. Selective perception is a defense system of the mind which functions to filter out disagreeable information to protect one's self-image or one's preconceived beliefs and attitudes.

Selective Retention The third mental defense is the process of retaining, holding, or remembering the choice information contained in a message that is compatible with preconceived attitudes and beliefs. This is called *selective retention.* If sales reps are compelled to memorize a canned speech which is contrary to their existing beliefs, they will quickly forget or confuse the message so as to make its meaning ineffective. When tested a week later for recall of a simple message of this type, they will not be sure of its content because the information did not seem to make any sense, because it was too exaggerated, or because they felt the sales manager could not be believed.

Information which does not fit the predisposition of the receiver is likely to be recast or distorted to fit not only the receiver's span of comprehension and retention, but also his or her own personal needs and interests. For example, in a sales force of fifty reps, the manager might promise a bonus for the top 10 percent of the sales force who go over quota this month. At the end of the month, the top five sales reps will rightly win the bonus, but some of the top ten reps will claim the manager promised a bonus to the top ten people, not the top 10 percent. The message changes to fit the existing knowledge and attitudes of those who receive it.

In attempting to communicate, a sales manager seeks favorable attention to his message and does not want distracted listening or hostile disregard. If an audience is unobservant, heedless, or inconsiderate, the message may never be heard, much less understood. Second, the manager seeks favorable interest in whatever he or she is saying. One would like a degree of curiosity, an inquiring mind, or intellectual action. The manager's third objective is to get some degree of personal involvement on the part of the audience of sales reps. The manager would like them to be emotionally moved to include or permit the message in their personal thoughts. One would like them to take into active consideration the various points of the message and not sit passively with the blank stare of a dead fish.

Studies by this writer and others show that the average salesperson, passively listening to a ten-minute talk by the sales manager, will forget 70 percent of what was heard immediately after leaving the room. Such studies emphasize the importance of covering a single point at a time, of reviewing periodically, and of gaining understanding and acceptance point by point, throughout a presentation. The sales reps should be allowed—indeed, encouraged—to express an objection or raise questions throughout the conversation. It behooves the manager to perceive sharply the expressions and reactions of the sales force as the presentation progresses. The manager may repeat or emphasize when necessary to reinforce the message and do so in an interesting and entertaining way. It is possible to use questions or to have sales reps role-play situations which illustrate the point. Their active involvement in an animated and lively sales meeting is the key to effective communications.

A direct frontal attack on an attitude or opinion of a sales rep serves to awaken, organize, and stiffen the rep's mechanisms of resistance and defense. Salespeople may become obstinate and angered at the direct or implied criticism of their judgment or professional behavior. They are apt to discredit the source of any such criticism. Once they mentally discredit the sales manager, they will doubt most of the things he or she may say in the future.

If there is a single key to the psychology of communications and persuasion, it is confidence. The sales force must learn to trust what the manager says before they will place any confidence in the manager's propositions or take any action which the manager recommends. A sales force will respond particularly well to specific sources when they consider them to be of high prestige, highly credible, expert, trustworthy, close to themselves, or just plain likable.

An interesting side effect of communication and persuasion is that when opinion conversion works at all, it usually happens through a redefinition of the issues. It generally results from the reinforcement of an associated but subordinate attitude which causes the new one to dominate the old. Creating a new opinion, or persuading, is a procedure in which the selective processes discussed earlier are not likely to be operating. For example, if the manager berates the sales force for being lazy, they are apt to resist a request to work harder for the same pay. On the other hand, if a new way to increase sales without extra time or effort is proposed, they may very well listen to, and accept, the communication.

SALES MANAGER'S INPUT TO ADVERTISING

In most companies, the advertising function is relatively independent of the sales manager because it requires knowledge and experience different from the sales manager's. Specialists in advertising and sales promotion often speak a language which is difficult for sales managers to understand. Many creative people are drawn to the advertising profession; they often have a sophisticated sense of humor and enjoy shocking "straight" people. They prefer to work independently and to be judged on their creative abilities.

Traditional sales managers do not understand the advertising function or its specialists, and they are reluctant to question or criticize. The result, typically, is a joint meeting to help establish advertising goals with some participation by the sales department. Thereafter, the advertising people go back to their world of theoretical specialists and the sales manager goes back to his or her world of tangible realities. There is little communication and less understanding between the two functions.

Modern sales managers, on the other hand, identify segments of the mass market which will yield disproportionately high sales volume and contribution to profit. For each segment noted they will forecast that industry's growth potential to determine how much money and effort should be spent to cultivate the selected segments. These managers note the degree of penetration or market share which their companies have of the target segment. From the sales force they determine what additional information prospects need and in what form it will be believed. This information is then used as the basis for a two-way communication with advertising specialists.

Sophisticated advertising programs are aimed at specific target segments, such as innovators, early product adopters, the majority adopters, or possibly late adopters. One advertising campaign may be designed to create awareness of a product or brand. Another may intend to increase consumer conviction about the superiority of the brand. A third possible campaign may be designed to get prospects to use the product once as a trial. Another campaign might be aimed at getting existing customers to use more of the product. One product of a company may be relatively new on the market and require a large advertising budget, while another product of the same company that is being phased out may receive very few advertising dollars. As a product moves along on its life cycle, the function and cost of advertising should change.

In deciding many of these advertising questions and selecting various alternatives, the modern sales manager is more knowledgeable about, and closer to, the prospect than is the advertising specialist. In other words, the sales manager can be the generalist who decides where he or she wants to go and the advertising specialist can be the staff assistant who points out possible alternate ways to achieve the targeted results. While it may not be possible to dictate advertising decisions in a traditional-bound company, the modern sales manager does have the responsibility to influence such decisions.

Once a national advertising campaign has been launched, early and adequate feedback from the sales force can have a modifying effect while there is still time to do something about it if necessary. Adequate feedback includes direct quotations of customer and prospect statements, reports of incidents, complaints, and the like. In the case of dealer aids and point-of-purchase materials, the sales reps can give direct reports on the ease of getting acceptance or on specific objections and customer suggestions regarding acceptable changes or improvements.

Clearly, such information should flow back through the branch sales managers, who can indicate the relative weight to be placed on statements made by various accounts. These summations, in turn, should flow through the region to the national sales manager. Given enough objective data which are timely, the sales manager can exert a tremendous influence on the advertising and sales promotion campaign.

The evaluation of an advertising program for which one is responsible, however, is often regarded as a personal threat. The advertising and sales promotion specialists may see negative feedback as a personal evaluation of their competence. They may attempt to confuse the goals or to sabotage the feedback system. It is essential, therefore, for the sales manager to create a sincere feeling that the feedback is intended to identify ideas and methods which will help everyone do a more effective job. The specialist who is unable or unwilling to help in this respect should not be tolerated. Such incumbents can be replaced easily from the majority of professionals, who are anxious and able to help.

SALES MANAGER'S USE OF ADVERTISING AND TRADE SHOWS

The traditional sales manager and the typical sales reps out in the field have little understanding of the function of advertising or the purpose of a particular campaign. Most sales reps tend to become critical of their firm's own advertising, and a fairly common attitude is that too much money is being spent on advertising. While these opinions may or may not be justified in a given situation, a sales rep in the field rarely has all the facts, training, and experience in advertising which are essential to make a reasonable judgment. However, all sales reps are entitled to know the objectives of the company's advertising program and how they can personally benefit by using it.

It is a responsibility of the sales manager to inform and educate the sales force. The day has come when the sales managers of industrial companies, even the very large ones, must give more personal attention to their advertising and its effectiveness. Those who do will gain more respect for the potential power of this important marketing tool. They will discover that this "questionable" expense (as they had viewed it, with suspicion) is really an effective way to reduce the overall cost of industrial selling.

From a series of twelve detailed studies conducted by the John Morrill Company over a five-year period comparing the use of advertising and personal selling costs in industry, the following conclusions were drawn:

1 Buyer attitudes affect share of market.

2 Buyer attitudes are affected by sales calls and by advertising.

3 The maximum effect on buyer attitudes, and on share of market, is achieved by sales calls and advertising working together.

4 This combined effect tends to increase sales per call and to reduce selling costs as a percent of sales.

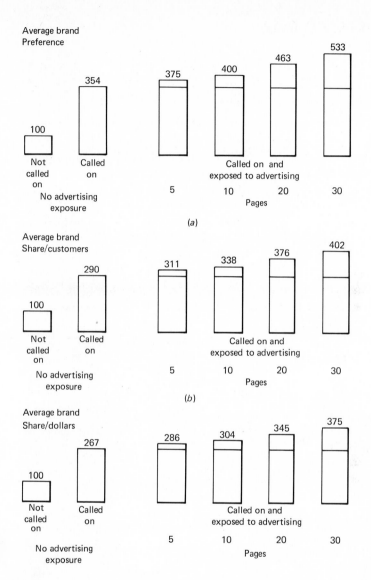

Figure 7-1 Salesmen and Ads Together. *(a)* For every 100 who preferred the brand but were not visited by salespeople, there were 354 who preferred the brand when called on. When sales reps visited *and* customers were also exposed to advertising, preference went up considerably. *(b)* For every 100 who actually ordered but were not visited by salespersons, there were 290 who actually ordered when visited. When salespersons visited *and* customers were also exposed to advertising, number of customers went up considerably. *(c)* For every $100 ordered when not called on, orders increased to $267 when visited by salespeople. When customers saw salespeople and advertising, actual size of orders went up considerably. *Source:* "Advertising's Challenge to Management: A Second Report on The Morrill Study from McGraw-Hill," 1971, p. 5.

5 Good business publication advertising is a profitable investment.[1]

The Morrill studies proved conclusively that sales per call averaging
$100 when the buyer had not been exposed to advertising increase to
$143 sales per call when the buyer had seen a company's ads thirty times
in the previous twelve months. Further, they showed how selling
expense as a percent of sales decreased from 100 percent with no
advertising exposure to 94 percent with five ad exposures and gradually
on down to only 74 percent with thirty ad exposures. Clearly, good
advertising more than pays for itself.

In selling to business and industry, copies of advertisements are
used in a special way. To a number of people, a national advertisement is
somehow proof of claims made because ensuing liability prohibits the
use of false statements. The written word is more credible than the sales
representative's spoken words. The very fact that an advertisement is
published seems to lend authority to what the sales rep says. While this
reasoning may be unsound, a national brand name does carry a
considerable investment, and the manufacturer is not apt to risk such an
expenditure with false or misleading statements.

The same psychological factors apparently are at work in advertisements that appear in technical or trade journals of the type the prospect is

[1] *Advertising's Challenge to Management: A Second Report on The Morrill Study from
McGraw-Hill,* McGraw-Hill Publications, New York, September 1971.

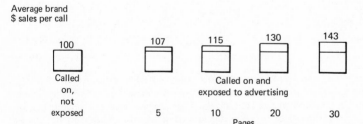

Average brand
$ sales per call

Called
on,
not
exposed

Called on and
exposed to advertising

Pages

Figure 7-2 Sales per Call. For every $100 sales when not exposed to advertising, sales
increased per call from $107 to $143 with both sales reps calling and advertising.
Source: "Advertising's Challenge to Management: A Second Report on The Morrill
Study from McGraw-Hill," 1971, p. 6.

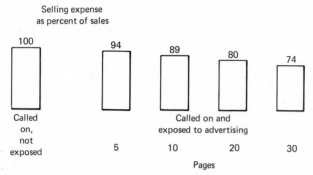

Average brand

Selling expense
as percent of sales

Figure 7-3 Cost of Selling. For every $1 in selling expense with no exposure to advertising, selling expenses decreased from 94 cents to 74 cents with five to thirty advertisement exposures. *Source:* "Advertising's Challenge to Management: A Second Report on The Morrill Study from McGraw-Hill," 1971, p. 6.

apt to be familiar with or to read regularly. Such readership is inclined to be self-selected—for example, all chemical engineers—and the ads are slanted or biased to appeal to that particular audience. Later, when the salesperson uses a copy of the complete magazine as a visual aid, not only is it a form of dramatizing the presentation but it also lends credibility to his or her personal sales message in the minds of some prospects. For many prospects, seeing the ad in their trade journal reminds them that they have seen it before, and often this is a pleasant association.

The modern sales manager is able to explain the purpose of an advertisement and to point out what the target segment is. The sales reps can then selectively visit those accounts who might be most interested in and susceptible to that message. The sales reps can cut out the ads and bring them along on these specific calls or mail them to selected people in the target accounts. Often advertising is read by many people who may influence an order but who rarely, if ever, see the sales rep. If the rep knows the accounts well enough, it is possible to send them copies of certain ads which seem most appropriate for their special situations or personal interest.

Sales Promotion Another form of communication is the sales manager's use of sales promotion, particularly exhibitions, trade shows, and

traveling caravans. It is fairly common, even in tradition-bound companies, for a sales manager to have some responsibility and control over
sales promotion activities as opposed to little or no control over advertising. Because many sales promotion activities require the time and effort
of the sales force, the manager's cooperation is essential. If this function
is outside of the manager's direct control, the sales manager is in a
position to influence what will, or will not, be done.

Sales promotion includes all active promotional efforts other than
advertising, publicity, and personal selling. Such are usually temporary
sales stimulants, such as coupon offers, one-cent sales, and combination
deals, and represent price bargains. The second form of sales promotion
is the means by which a product is drawn to the attention of prospects,
such as free samples given out and trade shows.

A large corporation such as IBM will participate in some 400 trade
shows per year. Beyond the enormous expense of renting booth space
and shipping products in and out is the greater expense of manning or
staffing each exhibit. For example, one show may be open to the public
from 10 A.M. to 10 P.M. and last for five days. This would require the
assignment of many sales reps to ensure that all visitors would be
properly handled.

The major problem for the sales manager is deciding on which of the
many trade shows to use the limited dollars and work force allocated for
the purpose. It is the sales manager's responsibility to identify the target
segment which will yield a disproportionately higher sales volume and
profit. Then one will select only those trade shows or exhibitions which
promise the highest number of prospects within the targeted segment.
The sales manager may delegate this decision to an assistant but should
not abdicate it or allow a promotion manager to make the choice without
the manager's prior approval.

Experienced sales promotion managers evaluate each trade show by
using the rule of thumb that each sales rep staffing a trade show should
talk to the number of prospects per day that would normally be visited in
the field by the rep in one week. While this general rule may not be
appropriate to all companies, it does draw attention to the relatively high
cost of staffing an exhibition and evaluating the results of such a
commitment. All the sales reps should understand the benchmarks, or
how a trade show will be evaluated, and how they can use the advertising
and sales promotion materials to their personal advantage.

IN-HOUSE NEWSLETTERS AND VIDEOCASSETTES

While some sales reps visit a branch office every day, many work out of their homes or travel a large area and do not see the sales manager very often. Successful sales reps are mature and independent people who do not want or need a manager's close supervision. However, they do need the latest information about product changes, delivery schedules, handling of special orders, contest progress, and so forth. They also need reassurance of the good job they are doing and that they are part of a superior team of people.

Obviously the telephone can be used to convey important questions from and information to the distant sales rep. But even a small sales force of five, for example, can benefit by receiving a monthly newsletter which tells of prestigious accounts sold and unique solutions to sales problems. A good in-house newsletter will build a feeling of camaraderie even when the sales reps get together only once a year at an annual sales meeting. They learn of each other's successes and abilities, and this encourages the exchange of leads and ideas between territories.

Many traditional sales managers ignore this potentially powerful communication tool because it does involve considerable time and thought to put together a meaningful message every month. In avoiding its use, however, they risk isolating their sales reps, who may then feel that they are not appreciated or that they are not part of the organization. Distrust and vindictive competition, such as withholding leads from each other, may result.

Another tool used by modern sales managers to communicate with distant field representatives is the videocassette. This equipment permits the sales force to see and hear the communication with the proper inflection and enthusiasm intended by the sender. New product demonstrations, for example, can be replayed as often as the sales rep requires to fully understand all the details. The new advertising program or sales contest can be explained by executives with many visual aids built into the programs.

Videocassette hardware is relatively expensive, but many companies see the communication benefits as well worth the initial expense. The programs can be reproduced for a nominal amount and sent to each branch office through the regular mail service. The sales departments of a number of insurance companies have been quick to adopt this new form of communication. The Ford Motor Company has an in-house network of over 5000 videocassette machines with one at every dealership. Sales reps can see the new models, technical changes, and advertising campaigns before the general public does. When prospects visit or are contacted, the sales rep is knowledgeable and interesting.

With dual audio tracks, videocassettes permit a program to be recorded in two languages or with one technical voice message and a nontechnical message. For multinational sales organizations, such tracks make utilization of its programs much greater at minimal expense. The majority of Latin America, for example, can be reached by using just the Spanish and Portuguese languages in the same videocassette. With the flip of a switch, sales reps can watch the video program in the language of their choice.

BUILDING LOYALTY

In order to build credibility, modern sales managers go out of their way to become experts and leading authorities in their specialty areas. They are more knowledgeable than the competition. Rather than becoming snobbish or proving their superiority, they use basic human relations techniques to build a loyal sales force who have confidence in them. It has been said that loyalty does not well up from the bottom; rather, it trickles down from the top.

A hard-driving sales manager of a company in Boston reprimanded his sales reps unmercifully when they made mistakes.[2] No matter if customers or fellow employees overheard. He felt it keeps them on their toes. To show his sales force he really liked them, however, the sales manager closed the office one day each summer. He took the sales reps and their families to a picnic at the seashore. Refreshments flowed freely, there were games with prizes, and the day ended in song.

But one day of fun did not heal the wounds inflicted over a year of work. Resentful sales reps stole merchandise. Turnover was high. Absenteeism mounted. The situation became so bad the sales manager

[2]This story was reported by Eugene Benge, consulting editor, in "How to Earn Loyalty," *Executive's Personal Development Letter,* Alexander Hamilton Institute, Inc., New York, October 1975.

finally quit, blaming his "ungrateful sales force." While he may have been an expert authority in his technical specialty, this sales manager rightfully earned *dis*loyalty.

Benge says "Praise the sale, not the salesman." Praising one rep may make others envious, but praising the sale will motivate the others to try to do as well themselves. Praise the sale in the presence of other reps or in an article in a newsletter. The latter will enable the salesperson to show family and friends without having to boast.

By asking, "What interesting project are you into these days?" a sales manager boosts morale. Or by saying, "I wish I had your skill to crack an account like that," the modern manager uses supportive and confidence-building techniques. If criticism is unavoidable, give it in private and objectively. Question the salespersons' results, but not the sellers' intention to do good work. Tell them something they want to hear, such as that you have been pleased with their progress. Then insert the criticism, such as an apparent problem with small orders. Finally, end with a suggestion of how to improve and assurance of your confidence in their ability to do so. In this way modern sales managers build loyalty to improve communications.

SUMMARY

Sales management communications are both essential and central in modern business. This includes a steady dialogue with prospects and customers, the sales force, and practically every other department within a company. Most executives of every function in a company are willing and anxious to communicate with the sales force when invited.

To improve communications the modern sales manager will learn of the predisposition of the audience or their mental set before they listen to the message. The manager will understand their normal and healthy mental defenses against persuasion. These include selective exposure, or turning off an unwanted message; selective perception, or understanding only certain parts of a message; and selective retention and recall, or remembering parts of a message correctly and distorting other parts. The manager will attempt to build a new attitude or willingness to act where none existed before so as not to arouse these mental defenses.

Clearly, the sales manager has the responsibility to influence the choice of advertising goals and target prospects and customers. The manager is in the best position to know how prospects think and what information they need and what kinds of words they can understand and believe. The manager, through the sales force, is also in a position to get early feedback which may influence the modification of an ad campaign while there is still time to improve it.

The sales force, on the other hand, has a need to understand and appreciate what the ad program is attempting to accomplish and how it can help them individually. They can be taught how to use the written word to make their spoken sales presentation more believable and persuasive. They can be shown how to reach customer contacts which they normally do not visit and to increase the dollar sales per order.

The use of in-house newsletters is another major tool in sales management communication. It can help bind a sales force together as a friendly superior group which encourages cooperation and team spirit. It can recognize and praise good work as well as inform all of new sales problems. In a similar way videocassettes can be used with the power of visual demonstration and audio variations to highlight, dramatize, and communicate better.

It is not enough to be an expert or authority in one's field. The sales manager with a hard-nosed, demanding attitude will earn disloyalty which will block most attempts to communicate. The modern sales manager will use supportive, confidence-building, good human relations techniques to build loyalty and to increase the effectiveness of communications.

QUESTIONS

1 Describe the selective defense mechanisms which the sales reps normally use to protect themselves from changing their behavior.

2 How can a sales manager gain the acceptance of the sales force to do things differently and more effectively?

3 How can a sales manager influence the design of an advertising program and secure modifications to an ongoing ad campaign?

4 How can a sales manager get the sales force to accept and utilize an ad campaign to increase their effectiveness?

5 What are the determinants of a good trade show?

6 What benefits can be derived from a good in-house newsletter mailed monthly to distant sales reps?

7 Describe some supportive techniques which will increase loyalty and improve effective communications.

SELECTED REFERENCES

Eastern Air Lines Marketing Case History (A), ³/₄-in. videocassette, 40 min, b&w, Intercollegiate Video Clearing House, Miami, Fla., 1976.

Heskett, James L.: "Distribution: The Retailer's View," chap, 8, "The Wholesaler's View," chap. 9, and "The Manufacturer's View," chap. 10 in *Marketing,* The Macmillan Company, New York, 1976.

Johnson, H. Webster: "Conventions, Conferences, Group Meetings, Workshops, Clinics," chap. 8 in *Sales Management,* Charles E. Merrill Books, Inc., Columbus, Ohio, 1976.

Luthans, Fred, and **Robert Kreitner**: *Organizational Behavior Modification,* Scott, Foresman and Company, Glenview, Ill., 1975.

Stroh, Thomas F.: "The Psychology of Getting Your Salesmen to Use Promotion and Advertising More Effectively," chap. 10 in *Effective Psychology for Sales Managers,* Parker Publishing Company, Inc., West Nyack, N.Y., 1974.

————: *The Uses of Video Tape in Training and Development,* American Management Association, New York, 1969.

▶ Case 7-1

SCHWEBER ELECTRONICS

Schweber Electronics sells small electronic components including diodes, resistors, capacitors, integrated circuits, transistors, connectors, and many other parts used in electronic equipment.

The branch sales manager is Rich Erwin, who is in charge of the four inside and eight outside sales representatives. He has been in sales for eighteen years and is very enthusiastic. He enjoys his work of dealing with people.

The outside sales staff is arranged by territory, which gives no trouble to Mr. Erwin, and each rep carries all the product lines of the company. Mr. Erwin has no control over the organization of the sales force, as this is handled by the home office in New York.

Mr. Erwin realizes that the outside staff take up most of his time because they are the ones on the firing line each day and are more apt to run into problems and situations which require his assistance.

The biggest problem he identifies is that the sales reps must discipline themselves against dejection if they do not get an order. Another problem is getting the salespeople to look for their mistakes, recognize them, and then find corrections so that the sale will not be lost the next time.

Mr. Erwin is always looking for new ways to make presentations to customers, as this is another problem for his sales force. The reps never ask the buyers a yes-or-no question. They get the buyer to look at a catalog or talk about a product, and then try to get the sale. The outside reps never carry a price list, so they refer buyers to the inside staff.

There are problems with personality clashes between the inside and outside sales staff, as they work very closely together on accounts. Sometimes there are accusations of one not doing his or her job, and Mr. Erwin must mediate.

The inside sales reps are easier to control because they are right there and can be watched all day. Mr. Erwin's main problem with inside reps is keeping down their phone time with each individual buyer. They have a certain amount of calls to make each day, and he finds the reps are running out of time by the end of the day.

Mr. Erwin says he tries to deal with the sales reps individually according to their own problems, backgrounds, and personalities. Each problem is a challenge, and solving them is something he enjoys doing as part of his responsibilities.

1 What can the branch sales manager do to reduce friction between the inside and outside sales force?

2   What is the communication pattern, and how can it be improved?

▶ **Case 7-2**

SEARS, ROEBUCK AND CO., INC.

Sears, Roebuck and Co., Inc., is one of the largest retail sales chains in the country. Its size, coupled with the diversified nature of the products it handles, ranging from cosmetics to riding lawn mowers, has caused top management to focus on the function of the sales force over the past years.

It is Sears' policy to pay its sales employees in one of three ways. They are paid either on a straight salary, on a straight salary plus 1 percent commission, or on a drawing account, with some of the top sales personnel earning in excess of $20,000 per year.

In a recent local study three basic problems common to most companies were uncovered. They included communication problems, inter- and intra-sales–department coordination problems, and testing problems. Mr. Larry Zeh, the sales manager for one store, was well aware of the first two problems, and he was actively striving to overcome them. The last problem was somewhat overlooked by the sales manager, and it appeared that he was not fully aware of its importance or the overall effect it would have on future operation of the company's sales force.

It was pointed out by Mr. Zeh that there is "no problem getting things done at Sears as long as everyone knows what they are expected to do." This would seem an easy problem to overcome. All one needs to do is to inform everyone of their duties and responsibilities. Although this sounds like a simple solution, it is not quite that easy. Between the time a new goal, policy, or activity is set up by top management and the time it is received and acted upon by the floor salesperson, several things have already occurred.

First, because of defense mechanisms such as selective perception, selective exposure, selective recall, and selective action, much of what management has said has either been forgotten altogether or has been drastically distorted by the time it reaches the sales staff. This break in effective communication is further responsible for problems in coordinating the sales force into a unified organization. These problems are further complicated by the fact that most of Sears' straight-salary sales personnel are part-time employees who work the 6 P.M. to 9 P.M. shift, the store's heaviest traffic time. These people are usually limited by little or no previous sales experience, and they require closer supervision than the seasoned salesperson. However, this is not what they receive, since most of Sears' department sales heads have left the store by 5:30 P.M. Under these circumstances management has to rely on company memos and word of mouth to pass on necessary information. This means of transferring information leaves much to be desired. Proper communication and coordination suffer as a result.

An additional problem that was uncovered relates to Sears' selection and testing process. Each individual store carries out its own selection, testing, and hiring system. Although this is accomplished through the use of set company procedures, who will be hired and who will not is left to the discretion of each store manager. The prospective employee is put through an intense series of math, aptitude, and personality tests which are devised to aid in the evaluation of the applicant's abilities and interests. In conversations with Mr. Zeh, he stated that he places heavy emphasis on the results of these tests. He further stated that anyone who did not fall within the set limits was usually not considered for employment. When questioned about whether he felt that this emphasis on test results was eliminating some potentially strong sales reps, Mr. Zeh responded with the following statement: "Sears is a large company with many years of experience in the selection of sales reps. . . . They know what they are doing." Although this is most likely not a nationwide problem, it points up how some managers base most of their hiring decisions on the outcome of tests rather than using the tests to back up their own experience and personal judgment. In the long run this will undoubtedly cause this store to reject some top-notch sales representatives.

1 How might communications with the evening shift be improved?

2   How does the varied compensation policy affect the communication process?

▶ **Case 7-3**

ALASKAN DISTRIBUTORS, INC.

Alaskan Distributors, Inc., recently entered the highly volatile and extremely competitive Alaska market.

Their business is centered on the sale of merchandise to the retail and wholesale businesses in the area. Alaskan is a merchandise broker who represents various manufacturers in an area where the manufacturers do not directly represent themselves. Alaskan warehouses and delivers some of its own products and promotes and makes new product placements on others. With a small staff of four sales reps, two secretaries, and one warehouse supervisor, Alaskan serves both the civilian and the military community.

Although there exists an abundance of opportunity, Alaskan Distributors, Inc., has its share of problems. A description of the most outstanding of these problems follows.

As a relatively new company in Alaska, it is caught in the web of competition, which, when coupled with its limited size, means the owners are forced to tax themselves and their office staff severely, often to the limit. This causes not only strained relationships, but also a sometimes hostile environment in which the employees must function.

Since the company is sales-oriented, most of the sales representatives' time is spent in creating sales, or "getting the order." The problem is in turning the orders the reps obtain into "delivered goods." One of the most important edicts of selling is that any sale is not complete until the consumer receives the product.

The company is, therefore, constantly striving to cut lead time to the absolute minimum in order to get the product to the consumer first and capture more sales. Thus, it often happens that four different sales reps are shooting orders at the two secretaries and one warehouse supervisor at nearly the same time.

1 How can the company eliminate the mass confusion and arrive at an efficient system for ordering and processing job orders?

2 Is there a management tool which would allow the company, with their limited budget, size, and capabilities, to function more effectively?

▶ **Case 7-4**

NATIONAL DECALS

Jack Taylor works as a manufacturer's representative for a national decal company. He sells to retail outlets and operates on a straight commission with no salary and no business expenses paid. He enjoys this type of work because he works on his own and has no close supervision by his sales manager.

However, today Jack found himself sitting in his boss's outer office. Jack had no idea why his manager had asked to speak with him. Because he is one of the company's top salesmen, he is usually allowed to work on his own, and conferences are infrequent.

"Come on in, Jack," the boss said as he held the door open for Jack to enter. "I guess you're wondering why I've called you here. Let me get straight to the point."

Jack nodded, indicating that his boss should proceed.

"You're in charge of the Neisner's Department Store account. This is an important account to the company, and lately we have been receiving complaints from them. They say that they do not understand our company's pricing policy and that they are not being adequately serviced by you. What do you have to say about this?" asked the boss.

"I have nothing to say about it because I was not aware that Neisner's is not happy with the way I've been dealing with them. The manager of Neisner's has never once complained to me. The company never sends me letters about any customers' complaints. How can I solve a problem with a customer if I am not even aware that there *is* a problem?" Jack said.

The boss was shocked by what he considered to be an attack on the company. "Are you saying that there is a communication problem between the company and the sales force?" he asked.

Jack indicated that this was exactly what he was saying, and then he went on to discuss the communication problem. "Not only am I never advised of customers' complaints; often I am not advised that items have been discontinued by the company. The only way I find out that a decal has been discontinued is by ordering the decal and receiving a notice that it is no longer produced. This company needs to communicate better with its sales force. Have you ever considered that this lack of communication could be the reason for the high turnover rate of employees in this company?"

The boss was overwhelmed by the problem posed to him. He had not realized that a communication problem existed.

1   What new communication system would you recommend for this manufacturer to prevent future problems with the sales force?

2   How can poor communications be the cause of high turnover of sales representatives?

Part

3

Staffing and Human Relations

Sales management is partly a social activity and its effectiveness depends to a large degree on the human skills of the practitioner. Sales managers in the future will rely more heavily on the teachings of psychology, sociology, and organizational behavior. These are the tools of interpersonal relationships as they can exist in a profit-oriented society. Human resources can be both deployed and developed in ways which will cause the individual to grow and the organization to profit.

Each sailor should stand a little taller when he returns from a challenging trip, safely charted by the master.

8

Analyzing Customers to Match Sales Representatives

▶ **Objectives**

The reader will now be able to analyze customer information needs, psychological needs, and sociological needs in order to begin to match sales reps to these needs. He or she will be able to construct a detailed sales job description as well as a matching work force specification sheet. The reader will be able to recognize when several different job descriptions might be necessary for different customer categories.

One of the principles of the marketing concept is that a company should be customer-oriented, not product-oriented. In making decisions about staffing the sales organization, this principle indicates that a modern sales manager will think in terms of what today's customers want and need from the sales rep rather than what the vendor prefers. Of course, if the manager is contemplating changes in his or her product line or choice of target segments, the sales rep must be able to satisfy today's customers and the different types of customers desired in the future.

If a sales manager wants to satisfy customers while simultaneously seeking higher profits, it would seem logical to begin by analyzing customers' wants and needs. Once the physical, psychological, and social needs of the customer are identified and understood, sales reps can be hired who will best fit or be compatible with the customers. Existing accounts can be assigned to those sales reps who best match the customer's needs.

The two basic tools sales managers use in this matching process are (1) the job description and (2) the work force specification. The first states what must be done to satisfy a customer at a profit while the second tool describes the kind of person who can do the job best.

CUSTOMERS' PHYSICAL AND PSYCHOLOGICAL NEEDS

When business executives are planning to open a new office, for example, they have an obvious physical need for desks, chairs, filing cabinets, typewriters, records systems, and a number of specialized office machines. Many office equipment dealers can study these executives' physical needs, recommend the particular items, and quote delivered prices. Most of the vendors are also qualified to floor-plan the location of each item to optimize the use of the office space. Some vendors will also do a complete job of interior decorating, including lighting, wall colors, flooring materials, plants, paintings, and sculptures.

While the customers' physical needs are obvious, their psychological needs for these same products and services are much more subtle. The executives may prefer a high-prestige image to attract better employees. They may want a no-frills, highly efficient appearance to show their stockholders they are a low-cost operation. In some private offices wooden furniture may be preferred to convey a warm, friendly feeling, while in others metal furniture may be wanted to indicate the democratic equality of all employees. In fact, some executives may not have thought about these choices, and often they seem confused when the subject arises.

Need for General Information For major buying decisions there is a need for general information, as is illustrated in equipping a new office.

This kind of information is most often given by the vendor in the form of the benefits to be derived from acquiring selected equipment and services. Competing sales reps will use colorful pictures and brochures which illustrate the overall appearance which the furnished office will have.

In a similar manner, industrial sales reps identify the obvious physical needs of their accounts and recommend specific materials, systems, machines, and equipment. Competing vendors will often have catalogs with pictures, diagrams, and operating specifications showing how there are newer and better ways to do an old job or newer and better materials to be used. Most of this information emphasizes the benefits of acquiring the recommended products and services, such as higher production speed, lower material costs, less wasted material, and lower labor costs. Once again, some sales reps may offer extra services, such as more efficient plant layouts or materials handling flowcharts. In any event, the information at this level of selling is of a general nature.

Need for Technical Information   For most products, highly technical engineering data are available, and *sometimes* this information is essential for making a rational purchasing decision. For example, a steel filing cabinet has several gauges or thicknesses of steel used in various parts. The moving parts may be cadmium-plated steel, and there may be roller bearings or ball bearings made of steel or of permanently lubricated nylon material. The painting process may be by spraying or by submerging in a tank, followed by selected technical drying processes.

In industrial selling, the need for technical information is frequently greater than in selling to consumer markets, and often engineering terms must be used. In many situations an understanding of chemistry is essential to enable the buyer to compare several competitive product offerings. If the buyer is not knowledgeable in the technical area, the sales rep has the additional problem of being the subtle educator, and he uses lay people's terms to describe the technicalities.

For any given line of products, a sales manager has a choice of hiring technically qualified sales representatives who can be independent in the field or of hiring less qualified people who must then be given technical service support. Obviously, the amount and kind of training the manager can provide will influence the decision. Ultimately, it is the customers who will choose the vendor that best satisfies their information needs.

How Much Ego Massage? Another dimension of customer needs consists of the psychological emotions, which may play an important part in a sale. Purchasing agents, for example, are influenced by pride in doing an outstanding job for their employers. They are often quite anxious to learn from the sales rep of new products or of methods to increase efficiency or to cut costs. If the salesperson's idea helps the buyer to look better or show off his or her efficiency, it will be hard for the buyer to resist. Business executives of all ages often buy their clothes to indicate their success. New autos and home improvements are often purchased not because they are needed, but to reflect the family's prosperity.

It is universal that people want to be liked, understood, and appreciated. This includes the desire to be attractive as well as the desire to be accepted in family, social, and business relations. People expend considerable energy to avoid being hurt emotionally or, worse, being ignored. The pressures of group norms often motivate people to maintain a standard of living beyond their economic needs. Many products and services are purchased because opinion leaders have already purchased them. Recognized business leaders, outstanding medical authorities, large corporations, and leading colleges are often cited as using a particular product or service to motivate the mass of smaller or less-known people who want to follow the practices of the group leaders.

Americans are taught that it is admirable to increase their incomes and wealth and to reduce outgo or expenses. The desire to acquire dollars is a common trait in Americans; thus, appeals to this trait tend to motivate the individual to buy. Economy and efficiency are designed to reduce expenses. Buying low and selling high increases income. Often speed and timesaving features are designed to appeal to this emotional motive of acquisitiveness.

Many people have an inner compulsion to prove themselves superior to others in one or more areas and to dominate or "lord it over" others. Professional buyers and business executives often like the power which they can wield over salespeople. They may make the sales rep wait in a reception area simply to show they are very busy and choose to do more important things before allowing the salesperson to enter. Conversely, some buyers enjoy being wooed or romanced by salespeople, and they like being wined and dined in the best restaurants in town.

There are many psychological needs or motives, and a complete list would not be possible. Even if such a list could be prepared, the danger is that each motive would be pictured as separate from the others. In reality, there are usually several psychological needs at work in any given buyer-seller relationship, and the total of combinations possible is infinite. Fortunately most sales managers have found through experience that their products and services appeal more strongly to a few particular common motives. The sales representative, then, should be comfortable in satisfying those psychological needs of the customer.

In some industries, for example, buyers traditionally like to bargain and to negotiate an agreed price. A sales rep who is psychologically comfortable in dealing regularly with this kind of confrontation is apt to be successful. Another rep who is more at ease quoting one price and remaining firm about it will not do as well. Customers who enjoy the bargaining process need sales reps who will play their game. In other industries, buyers want a sales agent who will quote the best price first and remain fixed. With experience in the trade, the sales manager can seek candidates who will best match these customer needs.

Competitive Sales Representatives   Another dimension to the question of matching sales reps to customer needs is the quality of competition. To remain competitive, a sales manager would be required to at least match the abilities of his sales force against the competition. In fact, sales managers would like their people to be superior in ways that customers feel are important.

Traditional sales managers have stressed product knowledge as the criterion for a superior sales rep. Certainly, it is one fundamental requirement, but there are other measures of a good salesperson. Modern sales managers look for a strong feeling of empathy or the ability to put oneself in the buyer's position and see the sales proposition from his or her point of view. Another trait of good sales reps is the ability to listen without jumping to conclusions or becoming argumentative. A fourth trait is the ability to analyze prospects' needs and to develop alternate solutions to their problems. The fifth criterion for an effective salesperson is the ability to search for and develop areas of similarity between oneself and prospects. Being a likable person does not occur by chance; rather, it is developed through conscious effort.

Thus it can be seen that building a superior sales force requires more than a myopic view of the reps' amount of product knowledge. Their human traits often are much more important in building lasting relationships with target accounts. A good salesperson is a friendly authority with a full share of human dignity and pride. There is no reason to be humble, servile, or apologetic when showing a customer how he or she can benefit by using a new product or service.

Good salespeople can command higher compensation than average ones; thus sales managers have practical limitations placed upon them. Modern sales managers do not seek perfection, but they do attempt to recruit and keep the best candidates which their limited budgets will allow. These people must be at least equal to competitors, if not superior to them, in order to have any reasonable chance to succeed.

SOPHISTICATION LEVEL OF SOCIAL-INTELLECTUAL CONTACT

For some sales organizations the range of buyer contacts is easily defined and limited. For example, a detail person sells drugs to pharmacies and hospitals and provides the necessary information to the prescribing doctors. For other sales organizations, the range of possible buyer contacts is wide open. Salespeople in the corrugated box industry, for example, call on practically anyone who regularly ships any product. This may require calls on little family businesses as well as calls on giant corporations. How the sales force is organized, as noted earlier, may also indicate the narrowness of customer contacts or the broadness of contacts.

Within a large account the sales force may contact professional buyers and purchasing agents on a regular repetitive basis. While it might seem to be a narrow and easily defined span of contacts, even this segment has a tremendous range of social and intellectual sophistication. There are still many hard-nosed purchasing agents who want to fill requisitions without any questions and who want the lowest price. Fortunately this profession is being upgraded, and about 30 percent of the incumbents now have master's degrees. These professionals question requisitioners to determine what end result is desired. They search for better ways to achieve goals, and they welcome suggestions and ideas from sales reps. In general they are more open socially and have a good sense of humor as contrasted with the traditional purchasing agent. In addition, many more women are moving into this field today, and they do have the economic power to make or break the sales rep.

Rather than contacting the purchasing department, a sales force may be directed to middle-management contacts in a pull strategy, as noted in Chapter 4. This again changes the social and intellectual needs of the customer. For example, a salesperson may call on a department manager, the comptroller, the manager of systems, and the data processing manager. This situation requires a much more intelligent and flexible sales rep who can adapt the presentation to fit the unique needs of each one of the contact areas. To become a warm, friendly person, the sales rep will have to acquire knowledge about each of the professions or specialty areas of his or her customer contacts.

At many levels of contact the sales force attempts to befriend customers, and this involves eating, and occasionally drinking, in a variety of restaurants. Some sales reps are expected to buy coffee for the warehouse staff who handle their products. These salespeople must be at ease joking with the rough-and-ready men working the loading dock if they want their goods handled with care. The same sales reps may take a middle manager to lunch in a fine restaurant and be expected to discuss exotic foods and rare wines. Effective salesmen in some industries learn to leave their jackets and ties in the car on some calls and to dress their finest on others. They must be able to adjust psychologically as well as physically to meet the social needs and expectations of customers.

Rarely does top management participate directly in purchasing decisions. However, it is becoming more common for a committee of top executives to hear a sales presentation as a group. This requires the sales rep to give a formal talk with numerous visual aids and to handle many questions rapidly and convincingly. Public speaking ability may become a sales job requirement, and this is still another variation of social sophistication. It may be essential to meet some customers' needs.

CONSTRUCTING THE SALES JOB DESCRIPTION[1]

When the sales manager has analyzed a particular sales job and determined what skills are required to perform the job properly, he

[1] This entire section is taken with the kind permission of the publishers from T. Stroh's *Effective Psychology for Sales Managers,* Parker Publishing Company, Inc., West Nyack, N.Y., 1974.

should then write up a detailed job description. The job description includes the job title, such as driver–sales rep, missionary sales rep, engineering consultant, or whatever. It includes management's relation to the sales rep, spelling out in detail to whom he or she reports, the compensation agreement, criteria for promotions and pay increases, the path of advancement, and the like. Most important, the job description spells out in great detail the duties related to the specific job. These should include:

1 Planning. This covers routing, determining the time and methods for new prospecting, and analyzing the market potential. It would also spell out the travel requirements.

2 Actual selling activities. This would include the number and type of calls to be made, specific buying influentials to be contacted, presentation, demonstrations to be given and closing techniques normally used. Social obligations, such as typical customer entertaining, would be included.

3 Clerical and routine duties. Most sales jobs require filling out and promptly turning in various reports and courteously handling customer correspondence. This section would include all key internal relationships with service and management personnel.

4 Self-management. This would spell out exactly how much time is spent on which activities, including improving oneself in selling ability, knowledge of existing and new products, understanding of customers and their industries, changing territory conditions, and the like.

All sales reps should have a copy of the written job description for their level of sales so they will know exactly what is expected of them and how they will be judged. In addition, modern management suggests that successful sales reps also be given the written job description of their *superior,* the sales supervisor, the branch sales manager, or whatever might be the next step upward. This will tell them in detail how they must prepare themselves for more responsibility and greater compensation. It serves as a good motivational tool to excite the sales rep's inner direction.

JOB DESCRIPTION FOR A
CORRUGATED BOX JUNIOR SALES REP

1 Average eight calls daily.

2 Cover territory driving approximately 100–150 miles per day.

3 Average 15–20 minutes face-to-face contact with buying influential.

4 Contact all levels of influences, from shipping clerks to top executives.

5 Make repeat calls on professional purchasing agents over a period of years.

6 Make daily calls generally between 9 A.M. and 5 P.M., plus occasional ones earlier and later to meet customer needs.

7 Entertain important customers and prospects at lunch, dinner, and appropriate social events.

8 Handle repeat business (75 percent) and develop additional new business to expand.

9 Discover customer needs related to sale of corrugated box products.

10 Render service to accounts in the form of helpful suggestions to save time, labor, or materials or to reduce costs.

11 Check customers' inventory, often in dirty warehouses, and prepare orders.

12 Suggest new packaging and printing designs to better serve customers and prospects.

13 Interpret customer specifications accurately.

14 Handle precise measurements and spatial relationships.

15 Handle complaints in customers' plants.

16 Prepare call reports and marketing surveys promptly and completely.

17 Manage territory for economical use of time and expenditures.

18 Operate independently 80–95 percent of time as directed.

19 Continually learn new developments in packaging and equipment—both our industry and customers' industries.

20 Develop solutions to customer problems and needs through office and plant personnel; i.e., Art Department, P.S.C., Testing Labs, Credit, Plant.

21 Utilize both logical and emotional appeals to satisfy customers' needs.

22 Work with associates to improve marketing effort.

23 Replace unprofitable or inappropriate business with that which is more profitable or more appropriate to product mix for specific facilities.

Work Force Specification

Once a specific sales job in a given company has been analyzed and a detailed job description has been written, then work force specifications or hiring specifications can be drawn. These would list the several specific personal skills, qualifications, and characteristics applicants should have in order to be selected for the given job. The sales manager must determine which skills must be possessed and the minimum or range of acceptability.

The major categories included in a work force specification for each type of sales position for each firm hiring new reps would be:

1 Mental—including technical and conceptual skills.

2 Physical—including health, appearance, and verbal abilities.

3 Environmental—including social intelligence, marital status, maturity, and family and social background.

4 Experience—including education and business background.

5 Human skill and personality factors—ambition, industry, resourcefulness, and enthusiasm.

While the job description might require many calls per day with an average of 15 minutes spent on each call, the work force specification then would require a concise talker who is quick and spontaneous with his or her sales presentation. If the job description includes making adjustments for damaged goods or customer claims, the work force specification might require a person who is logical, firm, and tactful. If the job description calls for considerable written contact with customers, then the work force specification should specify high ability in English usage. If the job description includes carrying heavy samples, then the work force specification must include high physical energy, strength, and stamina.

WORK FORCE SPECIFICATION FOR A CORRUGATED BOX JUNIOR SALES REP

1 High physical energy—almost a compulsion to keep busy. Ill at ease when idle over extended period.

2 High degree of stamina and persistence. Strong motivation to make extra calls and work long hours.

3 Clear and concise talker.

4 Able to communicate easily with all socioeconomic levels of buying influentials.

5 Must have inner-resources to wear well on people over a period of years. Sincere interest in people and in helping others.

6 Willing to adapt plans to serve others.

7 Socially adaptable and at ease with all levels of contact—good judgment in recognizing and meeting social needs of others.

8 Persistent and diplomatic in handling both regular accounts and developing new business. Likes challenge and change.

9 Objective, analytical, able to draw prospect out through intelligent questions. Effective listener, oriented to problem solving.

10 Quick to learn own and customer's business and be empathetic to appreciate customer's point-of-view—customer's needs as he or she sees them.

11   Willing to handle details accurately and efficiently.

12   Creative, innovative, inquisitive—willing to solicit ideas and answers from superiors and peers.

13   Superior to high school graduate in ability to read and understand detailed requirements and interpret accurately.

14   Ability to read scales accurately (or learn quickly) and visualize three-dimensional objects.

15   Honest, good judgment, diplomatic but has the courage of his or her convictions.

16   Prompt, complete, but concise reporting, both neat and methodical.

17   Self-starter, operates efficiently with minimal supervision, willing to make responsible decisions on his or her own and direct his or her own efforts, ability to identify opportunity.

18   Has sufficient self-confidence to operate independent of supervision but willing to follow instructions.

19   Eager to acquire knowledge, receptive to new ideas, student of business.

20   Problem-solving oriented and willing to admit need and solicit help from others.

21   Knowledge of—or willingness to learn—the use of selling techniques.

22   Willingness to cooperate on a team for the benefit of others—not totally self-interested.

23   Constantly seeking ways to improve performance—sufficiently self-critical and willing to change. Always on-the-job mentally. Highly motivated to succeed in a sales career.

Clearly, it takes a great deal of the sales manager's time, thought, and energies to develop good written job descriptions and work force specifications; however, they are most useful in identifying the best sales candidates and reducing or eliminating reps who will be marginal or misfits. The job description is also the basis for control and discipline, as covered in the next chapter. The job description and work force specification are the fundamental tools used in interviewing, with appropriate questioning techniques.

SUMMARY

Staffing a sales department is one of the most important functions of a sales manager. Whether inheriting an ongoing sales force or building one from zero, the manager should take the time to analyze the sales job in detail. This writer suggests that the place to begin is in identifying customers' physical and psychological needs.

Various groups of customer targets have different information needs. Some require general information about what the product or service will do for them. Others require more technical information about the materials and engineering components of products. In addition, various customers expect to be educated, entertained, acknowledged as superior, and so forth. Their psychological needs become part of the selling situation, and the sales force should be prepared to deal with this.

There are various levels of social sophistication required for many different sales jobs. Within the buying profession itself there are traditional hard-nosed purchasing agents and a growing highly educated proportion of socially open and friendly purchasing agents. Middle-management customer contacts may prefer sales reps who can converse easily in their field of specialty. A top-management committee may want a formal sales presentation, which requires some facility in public speaking, to be made to a group. Social entertainment is often expected and freely given, and this is another important dimension of the sales job.

The formal written job description is the basic tool used to intelligently staff any sales job. It spells out in detail precisely what must be done with one's time, resources, and energy to sell and service desired customer targets. It includes administrative requirements and self-management activities to keep abreast of one's field.

Finally, the work force specification is the tool used to describe the kind of person who can best perform the required duties. These usually include a minimum acceptable level and a preferred level of mental ability, physical ability, environmental and experiential background, and human skills.

If the organization of the sales force indicates basically different contacts for some reps, separate job descriptions and work force specifications should be written for each category. By matching sales reps to customers' needs, the sales manager can best serve target customers at the lowest cost and gain a competitive edge. This approach is consistent with the marketing concept of satisfying customers at a profit.

QUESTIONS

1 What are the determinants of hiring technically qualified sales representatives or hiring less qualified people and giving them technical support?

2 What are some of the psychological needs of customers which should be considered in attempting to match sales reps to these needs?

3 What competitive factors should be included in the determination of sales reps to match customer needs?

4 What are the five characteristics of a good sales representative?

5 Describe the four main areas of a good written job description. P. 197

6 Describe the five main areas of a good written work force specification. P. 199

7 Show how different job descriptions might be required for different customer categories.

SELECTED REFERENCES

Filley, Alan C.: *Interpersonal Conflict Resolution,* Scott, Foresman and Company, Glenview, Ill., 1974.

Holloway, Robert J., and **Robert S. Hancock,** eds.: *The Environment of*

Marketing Management: Selections from the Literature, 3d ed., John Wiley & Sons, Inc., New York, 1974.

Howard, John A., and **Lyman E. Osland:** *Buyer Behavior: Theoretical and Empirical Foundation,* Alfred A. Knopf, Inc., New York, 1973.

Johnson, H. Webster: "Customer Services," chap. 17 in *Sales Management,* Charles E. Merrill Books, Inc., Columbus, Ohio, 1976.

Karger, Delmar W., and **Robert G. Murdick:** *New Product Venture Management,* Gordon and Breach, Science Publishers, Inc., New York, 1972.

Newman, William H., and **E. Warren Kirby:** "Personal Needs and Organization Design," chap. 7 in *The Process of Management,* Prentice-Hall, Inc., Englewood Cliffs, N.J., 1977.

Stanton, William J., and **Richard H. Buskirk:** "Selection of Salesmen— Determining the Kind of Men Wanted," chap. 6 in *Management of the Sales Force,* 4th ed., Richard D. Irwin, Inc., Homewood, Ill., 1974.

Still, Richard R., Edward W. Cundiff, and **Norman A. P. Govoni:** "Formulating Personal-Selling Strategy," chap. 4 in *Sales Management,* 3d ed., Prentice-Hall, Inc., Englewood Cliffs, N.J., 1976.

The Way I See It, 16 mm film, color 30 min, Roundtable Films, Inc., Beverly Hills, Calif., 1968.

▶ Case 8-1

IBM CORPORATION

Bill Bedell is the district sales manager for a branch of IBM. He is retiring in six weeks and must choose a successor. He has narrowed his choice to three candidates: Jack Casual and John Hatch, his two strongest sales reps, and Bill Greenleaf, presently managing sales in a different district.

    Mr. Casual's success is based largely on securing a substantial volume of orders for modernizing improvements and updated additions to existing systems, as well as heavy reorders on supplies. He maintains frequent and friendly contact with those employees of corporations or businesses who will actually use the equipment. He stresses the company's return/refund and total service policies.

    Mr. Hatch concentrates his sales efforts on establishing new accounts by selling complete new systems (getting new accounts) while maintaining minimal supply reorders and updating-equipment purchases on old accounts. He deals directly and solely with the executives in charge of the actual buying of equipment, usually through some form of social contact. He uses a hard-hitting sales approach and delivers his most successful pitch over a drink or a nine iron.

Both salesmen are successful in their respective tactics, and both bring in comparable sales dollars.

Mr. Bedell feels that each man has the potential to become a capable sales manager. Mr. Hatch's strong sales tactics would prove to be an advantage in the training of a new and unfamiliar sales rep, while Mr. Casual's long-established and friendly contact would be likely to ensure that his new replacement would be met with acceptance and would have a better chance of retaining most of those customers.

Mr. Bedell's last choice is to bring in the new man from another district. While this would allow each of the two sales reps to remain in their fields with predictable continued success, the idea of orienting a new man is not attractive to Mr. Bedell. His hesitation is based on his fears of disturbing a smooth-running, successful operation with the advent of a new person with new ideas. Mr. Bedell admits that a new man may be able to stimulate even further success without endangering the existing prosperous conditions, but he questions whether the risk is worth the possible benefits.

1 How well do the two sales reps match their customers' needs?

2 Does either of the two local sales reps show management potential? How?

▶ Case 8-2

HEARING AIDS, INC.

One field of sales that has caused a great deal of controversy is the hearing aid business. While there are a few charlatans in this field, the majority of the sellers are responsible, fully trained salespeople.

These salespeople for the most part have a thorough knowledge of all parts of the ear and are trained to test hearing and to recognize diseases of the ear. They are required to study, pass a comprehensive exam, and be licensed by most states. One can see that these salespeople must undergo extensive training and instruction in the use of all the various machinery required to determine hearing aid needs and to write prescriptions based upon individual needs.

Unfortunately, it now appears possible that some of these people may be unable to continue in their chosen field if doctors succeed in taking over the hearing aid business as a part of the medical profession. In the past one could obtain a hearing aid for several hundred dollars. Should doctors take over this service, the price of hearing aids and testing may increase considerably, making it impossible for many elderly people on fixed incomes to obtain or change hearing aids.

In order to be successful, the hearing aid sales representative must be considerate, concerned, courteous, and skillful in determining the proper instrument in a variety of cases. Because the salesperson deals mainly with an older clientele, in order to relate to customers he or she must be fairly conservative in dress. Generally a suit and tie with a white shirt, short hair, and cleanshaven appearance are the salesman's choice, while a saleswoman would need to present a neat and conservative appearance. Colorful mod suits or leisure wear, mini skirts, and heavy makeup might discourage some older buyers. Patience and good humor also are definite assets in this business. So one can see that this highly specialized field requires a very special sort of salesperson.

1 Does the sales representative's physical appearance make an important difference to an older prospect? How?

2 How might word-of-mouth recommendations be affected by the rep's physical appearance?

▶ Case 8-3

COMPUTER UTILITIES, INC.

Computer Utilities, Inc., sells computer time. Small businesses that cannot afford to buy and maintain their own computer facilities are sold time on a larger computer. Computer Utilities sales representatives determine the types of program which would help their customers, such as maintaining payroll or inventory records. These programs are sold to the customers for a fee, determined by the amount of computer time that will be needed to run them. The customers provide the information needed and Computer Utilities handles the rest of the operation. The reports are delivered to the customer as soon as they are processed.

There are ten sales reps, who are paid a salary plus a 15 percent commission on all sales.

A problem identified by the sales manager is in the area of the selection of sales reps. The sales manager does not know how much experience a person should have in the computer field in order to be an effective salesperson.

The actual technical knowledge required to perform the sales function is minimal. The types of programs that can be used by a customer can be learned without having any direct experience with computer programming. After a customer is sold a specific service, such as handling of accounts receivable, a computer expert contacts the customer to explain the way in which the information should be compiled in order for it to be processed and to determine if the customer has any special needs, such as account analysis.

The sales manager feels that if the sales reps were more knowledgeable in computer technology they could better evaluate the complete needs of the customer and sell more computer services. However, she is not sure whether someone who is technically oriented could be an effective salesperson.

At the present time, none of the sales reps have any special knowledge in the computer field, and sales have been increasing at a steady rate.

1 What service are customers really buying?

2 In what area of knowledge should the sales rep be strongest?

9

Recruiting
Sales Reps and Staff

▶ Objectives

The reader will understand how a good recruiting program can be a high-leverage opportunity to upgrade a sales force with a minimal effort. One will recognize the continuous need to recruit and the legal restraints involved. The reader will be able to evalute the alternate sources of recruits and to decide which is most appropriate in a given situation. One will be able to evaluate sources of recruits for supervisory and staff jobs on the sales force. The reader will recognize the deployment of people as a combination of economic efficiency and good human resources management.

Under normal business conditions, every large organization has a continuous need to identify, locate, and attract potentially effective sales reps. For a number of reasons, including the aging and promotion processes, there is a continuous turnover, or loss, of salespeople, who must be replaced. Under conditions of rapid growth, top management may want a steady expansion of the sales force. Indeed, even most small companies have the common problem of finding better sales reps.

The candidates recruited become the reserve pool of sales staff from which new sales reps will be chosen. The quality of this reserve group will predict the future success or problems of the sales organization. Future problems might occur in the areas of training, motivation, compensation, discipline, and/or further turnover. Quality, in this context, refers to the degree of matching a number of applicants with the work force specification.

Recruiting should be an ongoing or continuous program so that at any given time the sales manager will have a choice of people to hire amongst those who closely match the needs. Without a good recruiting program a sales manager may be forced to hire the best of a sorry lot of walk-ins or of misfits who respond to a classified advertisement. If there is little or no continuity of recruiting, many good possible applicants are overlooked. A good recruiting program, on the other hand, is a function which has high leverage or the opportunity to get good results for a relatively low cost. It provides the sales manager with the chance to continuously upgrade the sales force.

RECRUITING SOURCES

Possible recruiting sources are determined in part by company strengths and weaknesses and by legal implications. For example, a company which dominates its industry and pays well may attract many good candidates. Another company may be well known for its effective sales training program. Smaller, lesser-known companies may have to offer a substantial future to remain competitive in the labor market.

If a company has a good sales training program, it can recruit inexperienced candidates. If a company does little or no training, it will be forced to recruit experienced sales reps from competitors and other, hopefully related, industries. Small companies frequently have a stated policy of hiring only sales reps who have completed an extensive training program with a specific large competitor. Other companies and sales organizations are so weak that they are willing to recruit anyone who has any sales experience in any field.

When turnover is very high, as in organizations which sell from door to door, any applicant with or without experience is accepted and often paid a bonus to recruit several friends. In other words, it may not be practical to attempt to recruit the theoretically ideal applicant. The sales manager would be well advised to consider company strengths and weaknesses before deciding where to recruit new applicants.

The recruiting process has been tremendously complicated since the passage of the Civil Rights Act of 1964 and its subsequent enforcement by the Equal Employment Opportunity Commission (EEOC) and the Office of Federal Contract Compliance (OFCC), which assist employers in implementing nondiscriminatory personnel policies. These policies cover race, color, religion, sex, and national origin. The Age Discrimination in Employment Act of 1967 protects individuals aged 40 to 65 years against discrimination involving hiring, discharging, or compensating.[1]

An important result of these acts and federal regulations has been that companies must now attempt to balance the employment of women and minority group members in their work force relative to the proportion who reside in the employment area. For the sales manager, these regulations pose new problems undreamed of a few years ago. Sales recruiters must show reasonable efforts to balance the sales force. They must seek out women and blacks in particular, in an *affirmative-action hiring program*. All applicants must be welcomed and handled on an equal basis.

Prior to these laws, this writer recruited many women and blacks for industrial selling jobs but found very few interested job seekers. Of the few later hired, the women did very well and went into business for themselves. The few black men who were hired and trained eventually requested to be transferred into nonselling jobs because *customers* would not mix socially with them as they did with competitive white salesmen. Since that time, a number of major corporations have indeed been active and successful in recruiting blacks for sales positions. In fact, the better black salesmen are in great demand and can move up to better-paying sales jobs very rapidly.

Women have not been very successful in obtaining equal employment in sales in most fields. One outstanding exception is the field of selling real estate, where women are eagerly recruited because they sell as well as, or better than, men. One study shows that women tend to be

[1] See *Guidelines on Employement Selection Procedures,* EEOC, Aug. 1, 1970, and *Proposed Employment Testing and Other Selection Procedures,* OFCC, Apr. 15, 1971.

better listeners than men.² This characteristic enables them to be more empathetic and to see the sales proposition from the buyer's point of view. Unfortunately there is still a strong prejudice against women in outside sales jobs, but one can hope to see this feeling change in this decade.

In any event, recruiters today must seek to balance the sales force with women and with many minority groups. While it may not occur for some time, a sales organization must show that it has tried to comply with the newest laws and agency regulations.

Recommendations by Company Sales Force   To staff distant territories, frequently the salespeople in adjacent territories are the best source of recruits. They meet many local people in their business calls and in their personal lives. Of course, they should be given some guidance about the number of female candidates and minority candidates desired in their areas.

Company sales reps know the job and the company very well and can enthusiastically sell the opportunities to likely candidates. On many of their calls they get to meet noncompeting sales reps of other product lines. Purchasing people comment on the abilities of the better ones, and this feedback increases the chances of selecting those who will best match the work force specification and desired balance of women and minorities.

Unqualified candidates are recruited primarily when the existing sales force does not know precisely what the sales manager wants. These people are predisposed to like the company and may be good social friends of the sales reps. The manager who must turn them down would be wise to explain the reasons to both the candidates and the sales reps who referred them. This courtesy will encourage the sales force to continually seek better recruits and, hopefully, keep the goodwill of the person who was not hired.

Educational Institutions   High schools, adult evening classes, community colleges, and four-year colleges and universities are all excellent sources of good sales recruits. Most have a vocational guidance counselor and a placement office. For distributive education majors, one or more

²Sally Scanlon, "Ms. Is a Hit!" *Sales Management,* Feb. 5, 1973, p. 24. See also "Manage Sales? Yes She Can." *Sales Management,* June 13, 1977, p. 33.

teachers continuously work with both the students and local employers. Contact with professors will often help in matching the student to a sales job in which he or she is likely to succeed.

Most adults attending school recognize their need to further their education; and as each level is about to be attained, they are apt to look for new and better job opportunities. Because of the strong competition for the best graduates, many corporations have created work-study jobs for promising young people in the summer before their last year at school. This work enables the student to size up the company and helps the company to better evaluate a number of recruits firsthand.

James O. Plinton, vice president of Eastern Air Lines, recognized a minority hiring problem which many corporations face.[3] His research showed that when corporate recruiters invited a number of blacks to visit their distant headquarters, many did not show up for the second interview. The students did not have the air fare to pay in advance. Plinton put together a promotion, Travel Reservation Interview Program (TRIP), to resolve the problem. The student makes one phone call to the TRIP desk, telling where and when he or she has been invited to be interviewed. Eastern's reservation desk then calls the corporation to confirm the facts and to have the corporation accept the billing. TRIP then calls the student with information about picking up tickets at the airport for a specific flight. Plinton reports that 99 percent of inquiring phone calls to the TRIP desks have resulted in sales. The program spread to cover all students, not just blacks, and graduates as well. This truly innovative program shows how corporations today are responding to changing business and social conditions.

Internal Transfers   For many sales organizations there is a wealth of good recruits within the company itself. At Shaw-Walker Company, for example, the women who install office systems often are promoted to systems sales, a much higher-paying job. Many service organizations develop specialists who get along very well with customers and who have shown they are dependable working alone in the field. These attributes alone make these people good possible sales recruits. In addition, they already know company policies and have a degree of loyalty. Many

---

[3]See *Eastern Air Lines Marketing Case (B),* Intercollegiate Video Clearing House, Miami, Fla., 1976.

service people, however, are afraid of the insecurity of commission sales. For this reason some sales organizations have modified their compensation programs to attract more of these excellent recruits.

In a similar way, assistant buyers, office managers, and supervisors in production often show superior skill in dealing with people. Some of them make excellent sales recruits and many have gone on to become outstanding sales reps and sales managers.

Many companies have a program to reimburse employees who take job-related educational courses. An alert sales manager knows that completion of a new educational level may be a natural turning point in the career of an employee. Working with the personnel department, the sales manager can identify a number of future sales recruits within the company. It is also good for overall employee morale to know that promotional opportunities exist beyond the confines of one's immediate department.

Employment Agencies Many sales organizations prefer to have an outside specialist do the recruiting job. A number of employment agencies do specialize in recruiting sales applicants, and they perform very well, with many branches covering the entire United States. Unfortunately, others show little concern with attempting to match candidates to company needs.

Sales managers should make sure the agency has both the written job description and the work force specification for the particular position to be filled. In addition, the agency should know how many women and minority candidates are desired. A good supply of company promotional literature is also considered essential by the better agencies.

Good employment agencies do not depend entirely on volunteer applicants who may be unemployed or who cannot land a job on their own. They also search out employed people who can benefit by switching jobs. This is the kind of extra service which sales managers appreciate, and it helps to build long-term relationships.

Armed Forces Discharge centers of the military are another good source of sales recruits. Where a strong or dominant personality is preferred, many veterans have demonstrated leadership characteristics. In addition, many will have learned trade skills which are transferable to several industries. Often veterans are more mature than nonveterans of the same age, and they are willing to work harder for their career goals.

When older sales reps are preferred, retired officers in their early forties may be another excellent source of recruits. With a lifetime pension, they may want additional income and a second career. Many can be attracted to a sales job which offers travel and an expense account. As an example, a retired navy chief petty officer, who had been a corpsman, in two years became the best sales representative for a leading manufacturer of x-ray machines. He knew the medical applications, and his experience commanded the respect of buyers.

Business Organizations Many business organizations operate a placement service for their members. The sales executive clubs (Sales and Marketing Executives International) circulate the résumés of people desiring a sales career. The Jaycees, with their Junior Achievement programs, can recommend many promising young people. The Kiwanis, Rotary, and similar groups are also knowledgeable about many good sales recruits. Participation in such organizations will often provide an alert sales manager with good local recruits.

Advertisements When an open territory must be filled immediately, sales managers often turn to advertisements in newspapers and trade magazines to recruit technically qualified or experienced sales reps. This often causes competitive salespeople to apply, along with many who are not qualified. The danger in hiring a salesperson away from a competitor may be that the person's loyalty is to the highest bidder, and this can escalate the cost for an entire industry. However, good competitive sales reps do have legitimate reasons for switching jobs, and they can be productive in a short time. Vague advertisements will encourage marginal or unqualified applicants and it will take time for the manager to weed them out.

Advertising for sales recruits is usually an expedient measure taken when the sales organization does not have a good recruiting program. Under these conditions the sales manager should exercise caution and invite women and minority group candidates to apply. If this is not done, the problem will probably be compounded by a lack of planning.

Unsolicited Applications For many sales organizations there will be a steady flow of letters from college seniors and a regular number of people who visit without an appointment. Inexperienced sales managers like this kind of unsolicited applicant because they feel it shows a degree of aggressiveness which they like in sales reps. They are often flattered by the number of strangers who want to work for them.

Unfortunately many walk-ins and write-ins could not care less which company they work for, and their actions may be merely methodical plodding rather than intelligent behavior. Experienced sales managers are aware of this important distinction and attempt to separate the two categories of possible recruits. A personalized cover letter stating why the candidate is applying to a specific company will command more respect than the generalized form letter. The same reasoning, of course, would apply to conversations with the walk-in applicant.

SALES SUPERVISORS

The first level of sales management is commonly called the *sales supervisor,* who usually is an experienced salesperson promoted to assist the manager in a limited area. For example, the supervisor may be in charge of five new sales reps in the field, helping them get started. Most often a sales supervisor also has the direct sales responsibility of some accounts of his or her own. Other supervisors may have experienced sales reps reporting to them, and they may or may not have direct sales responsibility.

Typically, a salesperson is picked for this job because of being a good salesperson and not for being a potentially good manager. In addition, the newly appointed supervisor usually works out of the same office in which he or she was a sales rep. As a result, one has the very difficult transition of becoming the boss over one's cronies—the same sales reps with whom one played golf instead of working. The favorite meeting place for morning coffee will be changed, and the supervisor is no longer welcome at lunch. One may be socially ostracized, and this can be an additional psychological burden.

In a small sales organization this situation may be a necessary risk, but many large organizations prefer to promote a sales rep out of one region into a new one. In the new area one can be fair, strict, and demanding without fear of the sales reps' ridicule. In addition, one does not have the temptation of playing favorites with a few of one's closest friends on the sales force.

On occasion a company will recruit outside for a sales supervisor to rapidly expand a young sales force. This presents an opportunity to hire some of the best competitive sales reps and supervisors who may be stymied in their careers with a slow-growth company. Once again the dangers exist of escalating the cost of salespeople in an industry and putting a price tag on loyalty. A wise sales manager will weigh the advantages and disadvantages of recruiting from the outside for sales supervisors. Nevertheless, a strong-growth company will usually attract the better sales reps and supervisors from its competitors. If expansion is rapid enough, a sales manager can promote from within to maintain high morale and selectively recruit from outside of his company.

SALES TRAINERS

Sales training managers are frequently motivated differently from salespeople and line sales managers. They usually prefer to educate rather than to sell. Often they are more loyal to their profession than to their employer. They see sales training as a career, moving to progressively larger companies, as advertising managers do, which was noted earlier.

Some sales managers use the position of sales trainer as a developmental step between selling and management. This is a good process when the sales trainer reports to someone who is in charge of this function over a long period. If not, the sales rep turned trainer may see this typical assignment of one year as a necessary evil in an upward path in management and will not be concerned with long-range planning to evaluate and improve the training function. Indeed, the trainer may never know if he or she was an effective educator but will probably be sure of being a popular one.

Modern sales managers know the value of sales training and respect the professionals in it. They readily recruit from outside the company for someone who can upgrade the training to make it more effective and more efficient. Training specialists can easily transfer their skills from one company to another and from industry to industry. Product knowledge can be taught by line management, but the sales trainers can teach psychology, effective listening, effective letter writing, effective public speaking, and many other basic skills. In addition, they can do long-range planning for the training function and are willing to be responsible for its improvement.

NONSELLING STAFF

Sales administrative positions typically call for numerous and diverse specialists. A sales analyst, for example, might require a knowledge of both accounting and data processing. A sales forecaster might benefit more from a knowledge of economics and statistics. In large sales organizations, specialists are usually demanded and hired from the outside. In small sales companies, one or two people, usually without proper background, are forced to make decisions which are over their heads.

Efficient sales managers recruit qualified administrators from outside their companies, when they can afford them, and from inside as well. Many an older salesperson, who may not have the drive and energy of youth, may be highly qualified for an inside staff job. On occasion a young, well-educated salesperson will not be effective in sales but might do an excellent job in market research or another staff function. The point is simply that modern managers will recognize and use the career branching path discussed earlier. Recruiting a nonselling staff from within an organization can be beneficial as long as those people selected do have the knowledge and skills essential for the job.

It has been a common practice in the past to fill nonselling staff positions with misfits and old-timers waiting for retirement. This is not only an economic waste but a waste of human resources as well. It is far cheaper and infinitely more humane to retire a person early than to sentence the person to five years in a job which it is known the person cannot handle.

SUMMARY

A continuous, well-planned program to recruit candidates who closely match the sales staff specification is an excellent way for a sales manager to upgrade the sales force. Over a period of time it should reduce the number of misfits and reduce turnover.

Before recruiting, the modern sales manager will analyze the company's strengths and weaknesses. He or she will determine whether or not it is possible to attract the kind of applicants the company needs and can assimilate. The manager will weigh the cost of hiring experienced sales reps against the cost of training inexperienced candidates. More than ever in the past, the attempt will be made to balance the sales force with qualified women and proportionate minority group members.

Recruiting sources often begin with the recommendations of the existing sales force and people inside the company. Educational institutions are a prime source of new people entering the job market or upgrading their job level. Some employment agencies do an excellent job of matching applicants to the company work force specifications and of seeking out employed candidates to switch jobs. The armed forces discharge centers are often overlooked, but they can provide some excellent and mature sales recruits. For good local candidates, business organizations are an easily accessible source. Advertisements are most often an expedient measure used in place of a good recruiting program, and they usually draw many unqualified applicants. Unsolicited applicants may show aggressiveness, but more often they are methodical plodders seeking any job rather than intelligently picking specific companies.

Soliciting sales supervisors from outside a company may be preferred in a rapidly expanding situation. When internal promotion is preferred, sales managers like to put social distance between the new supervisor and former friends on the sales force.

Sales trainers are becoming recognized as career specialists who can teach in essential areas in which a good sales rep usually cannot. They can also do long-range planning, which is essential to improving the sales training. For these reasons, more and more are recruited from outside the sales organization.

Sales administrative positions traditionally have been "waiting for retirement" stations with little regard for the knowledge and skill of the incumbent. Modern sales managers need a technically competent staff and will recruit from the outside if no one within is qualified. For an internal search they will recognize and utilize the career branching path. The deployment of people combines economic efficiency with good human resources management.

QUESTIONS

1 What are the advantages of having an ongoing or continuous recruiting program, compared with recruiting only when a vacancy occurs?

2 What does the Civil Rights Act of 1964 require in recruiting a sales force?

3 What does the Age Discrimination in Employment Act of 1967 require in recruiting a sales force?

4 What are the best sources of sales recruits?

5 What are the poorest sources of sales recruits?

6 When might it be more appropriate to hire competitive sales supervisors than to promote from within the company?

7 Describe the difference between a sales rep who has been promoted to do the sales training for one year and a career sales trainer.

8 Which nonselling staff jobs can be recruited from outside of the company and which would be better recruited from within the company?

SELECTED REFERENCES

Johnson, H. Webster: "Recruiting and Selecting Salespeople," chap. 3 in *Sales Management,* Charles E. Merrill Books, Inc., Columbus, Ohio, 1976.

Riso, Ovid, ed.: *The Darnell Sales Manager's Handbook,* 12th ed., The Dartnell Corporation, Chicago, Ill., 1975.

Stanton, William J., and **Richard H. Buskirk:** "Selection of Salesmen—Recruiting Applicants," chap. 7 in *Management of the Sales Force,* 4th ed., Richard D. Irwin, Inc., 1974.

Still, Richard R., Edward W. Cundiff, and **Norman A. P. Govoni:** "Recruiting and Selecting Sales Personnel," chap. 10 in *Sales Management,* 3d ed., Prentice-Hall, Inc., Englewood Cliffs, N.J., 1976.

Westing, John Howard, Isadore V. Fine, and Gary Joseph Zenz: *Purchasing Management,* 4th ed., John Wiley & Sons, Inc., New York, 1976.
Xerox Sales Training—Case History, 3/4-in. videocassette, 40 min, b&w, Intercollegiate Video Clearing House, Miami, Fla., 1976.

▶ **Case 9-1**

CONCERT WORLD, INC.

A publication, *Concert World,* deals with concerts, rock artists, their music and albums. It is printed each month and distributed free in record shops, colleges, and other locations suitable for reaching the 15 to 30 age-group target readers. One-fifth of the total monthly publication, 5000 copies, is hand-distributed at the door to patrons of rock concerts.

Advertisers are buying this target audience and distribution.

David Pirie is sales manager. The sales force consists of walk-in and phone inquiries generated by ads in *Concert World.* Little screening is done. Reps are paid a high commission and are expected to generate enough advertising to fill the paper.

Rates are published by Concern World, Inc., and sent to prospective accounts prior to a salesperson's call. There is a printed discount for consecutive ads. The sales force has no control over rates.

The past two issues have had much white space. The sales manager has been making calls on highly prospective accounts not sold by his sales representatives' repeated visits.

A new publication, *Concert World* features reprints of articles from standard news sources and is building a writing staff.

Its competition (also free) includes *Easy Times,* a two-year-old local with its own writers, and *Good Times,* a slick paper with articles of national interest put together in New Jersey and repackaged regionally with local ads.

Advertising costs much less (50 percent) in *Concert World,* yet accounts cannot be sold because of its newness.

Often all three publications are displayed for sale on the same table or in the same corner of a store.

1 What kinds of walk-in applicants would you expect to see for this publication?

2 What kinds of recruits should the sales manager be looking for?

▶ **Case 9-2**

SHERWOOD UNION, LTD.

Mr. N. G. Castagna called together an emergency meeting of the board of directors in early November 1975. "Gentlemen, as you know and are well aware, the decisions made in this meeting will have profound and far-reaching effects regarding the long-range policies and profitability of our company.

"The figures are now in, and our total losses in the United States for 1975, ending October 31, exceed $200 million. No one here needs to be informed that our United States subsidiary accounts for more than 80 percent of our entire business. Hence, the time has come for drastic actions from both an underwriting and a marketing viewpoint.

"Prior to this year the United States business had been a money-maker for five consecutive years. Our primary concern now is not whether we will maintain our position as one of the top ten property and casualty insurance companies in the world; rather our very corporate survival itself is at stake.

"My proposals to turn things around are as follows. Sherwood's business has always been placed and evaluated with its own sales force and underwriting review in Britain, Australia, and South Africa and our business on the Continent. The consolidated profitability of all business with the exception of the United States is 10 million pounds sterling and/or 20 million American dollars. Thus, our net loss worldwide for nine months ending October 31 approximates 40 million pounds sterling or $80 million. Needless to say, now is the time to turn this thing around.

"Our business in the United States has always been placed via independent agents. The only control really exercised was for our marketing reps to look in on our agents and review their book of business from time to time. Independents' commissions average approximately 18 percent of premium generated. For too long we have looked only at premium coming in, with an accent on cash flow, while at the same time virtually ignoring the risk inherently associated with the premium.

"My proposal is to obtain a better look at the business we are writing via the establishment of our own sales force in the United States. Initially this will be quite costly. Of necessity we will have to recruit sales personnel from competition. Our present marketing people will be moved into sales management positions because of their familiarity with our package programs and company procedures. They will also be able to train new personnel regarding what type of business we are looking for.

"Our internal costs for underwriting administration will be greatly reduced by our current campaign to consolidate and centralize this function. Underwriting staffing requirements will be greatly diminished by our changing our seventeen United States areas to twelve regions. Currently we have ninety-three field offices, which will be reduced to sixty.

"When these changes are accomplished, we will be in a better position to properly evaluate our business on a cost/benefit basis rather than just approving any business an independent throws our way. Our cost for our own sales staff on the Continent and in Britain for the last five years has approximated 10 percent of the premium. It is my opinion we'll be able to turn our business around by this two-pronged attack of reducing internal administrative costs while at the same time being in a better comparative position to evaluate risk.

"Our primary concern initially would be to ascertain the optimum number of salespersons necessary to staff each office. Presently, we have about 100 authorized agents for each $10 million in premiums. We believe half this business could be written directly by our offices by a mere transfer of accounts. Thus, I project the need for four salesmen for each $2 million of premium generated outside the office. We will also have to figure out an adequate compensation program for our staff. In my mind compensation should be based on a combination of commission and straight salary. That's it, ladies and gentlemen. I request your comments and suggestions."

1 What attributes in sales reps should this company be looking for when it recruits competitive salespeople?

2   How do you think Sherwood's independent sales agents will react to this change in company policy?

▶ **Case 9-3**

ED AUSTIN, INC.

Ed Austin, Inc., is an automotive supply chain. There are thirteen stores, all in the Southern states.

Each store has five employees—two counter workers, one of whom is manager, two drivers who deliver auto parts, and one salesperson. Each store grosses about $25,000 a month. After all expenses such as rent, salaries, and taxes are paid, the store's net profit is about $1800 a month.

There is a great turnover of salespeople. Each store lost three reps in the past year. The general manager of all thirteen stores hires the salespeople. The main requirement for employment is to pass a polygraph test. The new salesperson works inside the store for two or three weeks to become familiar with automotive parts and existing accounts. Then one week would be spent on the road with the manager or the sales rep who was leaving. After this one would be on one's own.

The sales rep would start at $200 a week or go on 6 percent commission. Most of the purchasing was done by phone. When the sales rep's accounts called for parts, a counter worker would take the order and the sales rep would receive 6 percent commission on it.

The first sales rep hired was from Ohio and had sold stereo equipment. He was very successful in Ohio but moved to the South for health reasons. He was given the job with Ed Austin, Inc., because he was a personal friend of the general manager. He lasted about five months.

The second salesman was the biggest flunky. He knew nothing about sales or the industry and he lasted only two months.

Only recently has the company put a foot in the right direction. The owners saw the need to create the position of general sales manager. A man who had been a very successful sales rep in one of the stores was given this position. The reason for this was that it was becoming apparent there was a need for someone successful in sales to spend time with each of the salespeople, to assist them in servicing their old accounts and securing new ones. The job of the general sales manager involved going from one store to the next to assist the sales reps. Sales would more than triple on the days the general sales manager was with each salesperson.

The whole problem was that the sales reps knew nothing about the products they were selling. Also, they did not know that many products even existed. There was a great need for the salespeople to be able to read catalogs. None of them were good at this. The sales rep would be visiting an account and have to call the store to talk with one of the counter workers to learn if a certain product was carried and its price. The sales reps carried catalogs in their cars but they would not know what catalog to use because they did not know the manufacturer of the product. The reps also needed some mechanical experience to enable them to become more familiar with automotive products.

The sales rep would visit each account one day a week. Often on the day the sales rep was supposed to visit an account, the person in charge of purchasing would call the store and give the order to a counter worker and tell the worker not to have the sales rep stop by.

The sales manager noticed that they were not selling many tools. The distributor they bought from also noticed this and had one of their sales reps go along with the Austin sales rep to help him sell to some accounts. That afternoon the Austin sales rep sold over $5000 worth of tools. In the past his store was lucky to sell $1000 of tools a month.

Things are not going to improve unless more competent salespeople are found. Instead of the general sales manager, the general manager does all the interviewing and hiring. The only way in which applicants are screened is through a polygraph test done by a private company for $25.

1 Where are good sales recruits for this company likely to be found?

2 How can a steady supply of good sales candidates be provided for?

10

Selecting the Best Candidates

▶ **Objectives**

The reader will understand how a modern sales manager judges people and predicts which recruits will be superior sales representatives by appraising the candidates' past performance in relation to the work force specification. The reader will understand how to use directive and open questions as well as elaborative, reflective, and projective questions. He or she will be able to probe sensitive areas without insulting or annoying a candidate. In addition, the reader will understand testing reliability and validity, and the legal restrictions on using tests. Finally, the reader will be able to match the candidates' profile with the profiles of the best sales reps as they appeared before hiring.

Perhaps the greatest responsibility of management is the selection of the people it hires, because they determine, to a large extent, the future of a business. This is particularly true in the selection of sales reps, because these people *are* the company as far as many customers and prospects are concerned. To a number of buyers a good sales rep is a good supplier and a poor rep is not welcome. In this sense, the individual in the field is more important to many customers than the merchandise or the company which the salesperson represents.

Given an ongoing recruiting program based on a written job description and work force specification, a sales manager normally has a choice of applicants to fill one or more vacancies. If the recruiting has been done reasonably well, there may be ten or more men and women who generally meet the needs of the manager. Deciding which one to select takes time and effort if the sales manager wants to do a good job over the long term.

PAST PERFORMANCE RECORDS

The most valid predictor of future success is one's past performance, provided, however, that the manager knows what to search for and is able to get a good reading on it. An applicant with some work experience normally is asked to record on the application form all schooling and jobs held. For example, a candidate may have completed junior college and worked for General Electric Company for three years. The important fact may be that she was a student leader at school or a customer service representative on her first job.

When an applicant has had a series of jobs, his or her past performance is usually much more revealing. During school he or she may have had a series of menial or clerical jobs to help pay the way through school. Desirably even these odd jobs should show progression in earning power and in increasing responsibility. After graduation, employment may show a series of different career attempts as the young person seeks to find a place in life. The sales manager will look for a maturing pattern which indicates that the candidate seriously considered each switch as a more favorable opportunity. The length of time spent on each job should give some clue of the applicant's persistence in pursuing a goal. The kinds of jobs should indicate a willingness to work with people and meet strangers rather than working progressively toward isolation and working with things.

Young applicants with little or no job experience also have a considerable past performance record, although many are not aware of it. If they went from high school to four consecutive years of college, for example, this might indicate they are mature enough to put off immediate pleasures for long-term gains. While in school, they may have been active in several different activities, such as sports and a chess club. This would indicate they are flexible and adaptable as opposed to others who are of single purpose. Many activities show a willingness to compete while others show a tendency to withdraw. These examples serve to point up the importance of working with a good detailed work force specification so that the sales manager will know what factors matter and what do not.

References, for the most part, will be from friendly parties who can be expected to say nice things about a candidate. They should be checked automatically, however, to screen out the applicant who may be bluffing about schooling or the time spent on different jobs. Often interesting discrepancies arise which may influence a decision if not explained in an interview.

INTERVIEWING TECHNIQUES

Most applicants for a sales job do not have enough knowledge about the job to honestly decide whether or not they are a good fit. For this reason part of the interview should include a frank discussion of the written job description. In addition, all applicants will know some things about themselves which they want the manager to know. They will know some things about themselves which they do *not* want the manager to know. Often more importantly, they will know some things about themselves that they are not aware of or cannot consciously recall. A good interview will draw out the most pertinent facts which are meaningful to the selection decision. Modern sales managers use at least six kinds of questions which are psychologically different to draw out a candidate.

Directive Questions When a manager wants to know what kinds of authority a candidate respects, often a directive question will be used. This directs the candidate's attention to a specific area without giving any clue to the desired or right answer. For example, "How did you decide to major in chemistry?" The applicant may tell of a parent's influence, or of some teacher who was admired, or of a friend's influence. The answer will give some clues about the early adult decision process and the kinds of people who have been of influence in the past.

Directive questions normally refer to a specific topic and provide the candidate with the opportunity of telling what he or she *wants* the sales manager to know. The manager might say, "Tell me about a typical day on that job." The candidate has the chance to illustrate his or her responsibility, social sophistication, independence, or whatever the person wants the manager to know. One may state that one was bored by certain routine parts of the job and that is why one is looking for a more challenging job.

Open Questions   An open question is much more general and cannot be answered by a yes or no. For example, the manager might ask, "What kind of boss brings out the best in you?" This causes the applicant to compare authority figures known in the past and to generalize experiences. The person's answer will give some clue to the type of close supervision and support which is expected or the amount of independence which is sought. An inexperienced candidate may be asked, "What kind of professor brought out the best in you?" Once again the candidate must compare and generalize. Clearly, no single question will reveal the entire truth; however, when such queries are woven through a conversation and asked in different ways, the answers should provide a basic understanding of the applicant.

Elaborative Questions   When a candidate touches upon an area of interest, the sales manager may ask the interviewee to elaborate on that subject. The manager may say directly, "Can you expand on that?" This indicates that more details are wanted about only part of what the candidate said. Or, the manager may say, "That's interesting—please go on." This would indicate general interest in an unfinished story. Another variation would be for the manager to say, "I'm not sure I understand that. Would you explain it in more detail?" This would indicate the manager wants the candidate to go back and repeat the subject but to provide more details the next time through.

Reflective Questions   When a candidate takes an extreme position or one which hints of a sensitive area, the sales manager can ask a reflective question. This simply uses the candidate's own words to reflect back to the person what was just said. For example, the questionee may say, "All my professors were big on theory, so we decided to move on." The manager might say, "*All* your professors?" Or, ". . . so *we* decided?" Hearing one's own words mirrored back may cause the candidate to modify an extreme position. For example, the person might say, "Well, not all professors, but this one really got my goat." Or the candidate might explain or justify part of the statement. For example, the answer might be, "Well, I was discouraged, and my friend and I talked it over. . . ." A reflective question permits the manager to get an idea of how strongly the candidate feels about taking an extreme position or about people who influence this person's thinking.

Projective Questions Often it is important to know personal things about a candidate which relate to the individual's honesty or stability. These are sensitive areas which may arouse hostility or blatant lies if asked directly. If the information is truly important to the selection decision, the sales manager can ask a projective question which asks the candidate to project an opinion on a stereotype group. For example, the manager might ask, "How much liquor does the average college senior drink per week?" The candidate has no way of knowing the true answer and therefore is most apt to project his or her own habits as being the normal amount. One may reply, "Oh, I don't know, I guess most have a few beers on Saturday nights."

Once again it is important to note that a good sales manager will not ask a single question and jump to conclusions based on that one answer. The manager will mentally note the answer and move on to other subjects. Later in the conversation an attempt will be made to get a better feel for the candidate by asking different questions about the sensitive area. This may be done within one interview, but normally it is done in a series of interviews.

Problem-Solving Questions Another variation used to get information from a candidate is for the manager to propose a hypothetical problem and ask the applicant to solve it. For example, the manager might say, "What would you do if your sales supervisor asked you to spy on a sales rep and report back?" This would be a test of the candidate's willingness to stand up and fight for what is believed to be ethical and right. The interviewee who would not tell the sales supervisor off in this hypothetical situation probably would not stand up to real customers who may make unfair claims against the company.

More commonly, the problem-solving question involves asking the candidate how a typical problem with customers might be handled. For example, slow deliveries may be a current problem for the sales manager, and the candidate might be asked what to say to an irate customer. If the candidate's answer indicates that the blame would be placed on production or someone else, this may mean the person is relatively insecure. If the answer indicates one would "twist the tale" or tell the customer enthusiastically that demand was overwhelming, this may indicate self-confidence and good sales sense.

Stress Interviews When a sales job demands that the sales rep perform under stressful conditions, it is ethical to stage a stress interview to see how the candidate will perform. In some sales jobs the sales rep is expected to entertain important customers who like to drink alcoholic beverages to excess. One sales manager devised a stress interview situation to weed out candidates who could not operate effectively under these conditions. The manager asked one sales supervisor to take the candidate to lunch, saying he would be along shortly. The supervisor orders martinis and invites the candidate to join in. After an hour, a second sales supervisor arrives, sending the first back to the office, and the drinking continues. In two hours the sales manager shows up, and he orders cocktails before lunch. The test is not designed to see how much the candidate can handle, but to find out how he behaves in a drinking situation. Indeed, one candidate who did not drink at all went through this test and was able to exchange jokes and get along well with those who were drinking; he was hired. Customers like him, and he is very successful. However, many drinking candidates have failed because they became argumentative and abusive after a few drinks.

Multiple Interviews Because sales managers are human, they have good days when everything seems great, as well as poor days when things all seem to go badly. This has a tendency to reflect on candidates unless the manager is careful to exercise objectivity. Experienced sales managers also require multiple interviews to overcome this problem. This may mean that the candidate has to come back on several different days, but more often it means that several supervisors and senior sales representatives interview the same candidate on the same day.

Multiple interviews have the added advantage of causing applicants to deal with different personalities and to adapt to their needs and requests flexibly much as they will have to do in dealing with different customers and prospects. Often managers in product, purchasing, and personnel can be used to interview promising candidates. They will each need the written job description and work force specification; however, they will probably use different technical terms and pose different kinds of problems for each candidate.

When this procedure is a regular ongoing practice, the time demands can be spread out over many managers so that each may have only one or two half-hour interviews per week. If requests are more frequent than that, managers decline to interview or they cannot be reached. Of course, in a small company the need should not arise very often, and the time demands then should be less.

TESTING TECHNIQUES

All testing should relate to the work force specification and should measure the degree of knowledge, skill, or aptitude the candidate has in the selected areas. For example, a large industrial company, with a sales force of over 300, tested candidates—who had survived multiple interviews—in the following areas:

- Learning ability
- Sales thinking
- Tact and diplomacy
- Understanding of people
- Supervisory judgment
- Administrative capacity
- Vocabulary

- Mechanical comprehension
- Emotional stamina
- Self-reliance
- Objectivity
- Aggressiveness
- Self-confidence
- Sociability

There are many good tests available commercially, and there are psychological testing centers in most cities. A sales manager can discuss his work force specification with a testing specialist, who will then recommend specific tests to measure that which the manager deems important. Such testing of candidates is normally done on an individual basis and takes from one to three hours. The resulting test scores provide the sales manager with objective data to reinforce or refute subjective opinions based on multiple interviews.

Reliability of Tests   The *reliability* of a test is a technical term; it refers to the frequency with which the applicant will score the same results. Sales candidates have their good and bad days; however, a good test will yield the same score, plus or minus an acceptable range. In other words, if a candidate took variations of the same test ten times, a highly reliable test would show the same basic score within a few points in nine out of ten attempts. The reliability of a test is measured on a test-and-retest basis or on a split-half basis. The results are published as a fraction of 1 since 1 would be perfect. For example, the industrial company noted earlier used a battery of tests which had the following reliability factors:

- General employment test   .92
- Sales comprehension   .71
- Social intelligence   .89
- Vocabulary   .84
- Numerical ability   .75

- Clerical ability   .71

- Mechanical comprehension   .84

All standardized tests have a proven reliability factor, and sales managers with experience learn which tests, and how accurate they must be, to use for their unique companies. If a test does not have a published reliability factor, it should not be used to select sales candidates.

Validity of Tests   While a test may be reliable, in that candidates do get basically the same scores again and again, it is not necessarily valid or appropriate to the job. *Validity* is an entirely different technical concept which means that the subject area being tested truly does relate to on-the-job performance. This technical distinction now has serious legal implications.[1]

The Office of Federal Contract Compliance (OFCC) has issued a broad range of regulations on the use of testing instruments to measure eligibility for hiring as well as for transferring, promoting, training, referring, and retaining. Included are all formal, scored, quantified, and standardized techniques used to assess job suitability. They require an employer using such techniques to have *evidence* of each technique's *validity*. This means that a company must be able to show that the test scores are predictive of, or significantly correlated with, important elements of on-the-job behavior for which the candidate is being evaluated. The testing instruments and other techniques used to select among candidates cannot discriminate on the basis of race, color, religion, sex, or national origin or against individuals aged 40 to 65 years.

For example, in technical sales a trainee may have to learn a lot of information and a technical language in a relatively short period. If testing shows that all trainees hired with a learning ability score of below the 60th percentile were not able to last one year, that evidence is adequate to reject any candidate who scores below that level. It is objective and is proven valid.

This suggests that all sales managers who have used various tests in the past now look at the records of those who survived and compare them with test results of those who quit or were terminated. If the test

[1] See *Proposed Employment Testing and Other Selection Procedures*, Office of Federal Contract Compliance, Apr. 15, 1971.

scores do not clearly predict on-the-job behavior, those tests should be discontinued. Without a prior history of using various tests, a company may have to go to an association of similar organizations to obtain evidence of a particular test's validity.

MATCHING TRAINEE PROFILE WITH BEST SALES REPS

When an attempt is being made to select the best individual candidate from a group of applicants and to upgrade the sales force in the long run, absolute test scores can be very misleading. In a similar way average scores can be misleading. In other words, the candidate with the highest test scores is *not* necessarily the best one to hire, and the average employed salesperson's scores are not the ones to match.

Most sales managers can single out their best sales reps on the basis of their proven sales ability and their capability of further growth. These are the kinds of people the manager should be looking for to add to the sales force. One of the major problems, however, is that experienced sales reps are usually very independent. They like to be out on their own, and they want the authority to make decisions out in the field without getting prior approval of the manager. In addition, some of these successful sales reps may seem overly social at sales meetings. These two characteristics, independence and sociability, may not be highly desirable for a new sales trainee. For example, an independent trainee will not readily accept training and close direction or supervision because of impatience to be on one's own. One who is overly social is too dependent upon others for approval and recognition. Such a person will not dare risk disapproval by being as aggressive as is needed.

The solution to this dilemma of trying to match the trainee profile with the best sales reps is to look at the experienced rep as the person appeared *before being hired.* A sales manager can look at the records of all reps hired in the last three to five years, for example. It is then possible to decide which of these reps are clearly outstanding today and then check their preemployment test scores. Comparing these scores with scores of reps of average ability, or less, should show some significant differences. One sales manager for an industrial manufacturer did this and found the best performers scored extremely high in emotional stamina and learning ability and either slightly low or near the 50th percentile in independence as well as in sociability before being hired. In other words, the best predictors of on-the-job performance for salespeople in this company were high emotional stamina and high learning ability together with a balanced dependent/independent score and a low or moderate need for approval and recognition. When these selected candidates were hired and trained and became experienced, they matured into independent and very productive sales reps. Their profile today really is quite different from what it was when they were first hired.

Clearly, a sales manager needs historical records to make such analyses, and for many companies the personnel department has the needed information. If such tests were never given, it will take a few years to develop data of this kind. Of all new sales reps hired this year, perhaps as many as 10 percent will be outstanding within three years. The profiles of this group before being hired can then be the basis of future comparison profiles of sales candidates.

FAILURE ANALYSIS

Another source of meaningful data is the personal histories of present and past salespeople. Analysis of personal traits will often show that good sales reps had certain characteristics which were absent in the poor ones. A failure analysis can be made of conditions which existed in the backgrounds of salespersons who were unsuccessful in their jobs and either resigned or were fired. Doubtful credit or continual financial problems might be one such indicator. Too frequent job jumping might be another. For some sales organizations, wives or husbands not supporting their spouses' desires for the job might be significant. If many poor sales representatives had the same basic problem which caused them to leave, the sales manager might include it as part of the work force specification.

Career Compensation Curve A variation of failure analysis occurs when a manager compares poor sales reps with a *career compensation curve.* This curve would normally show the average total income

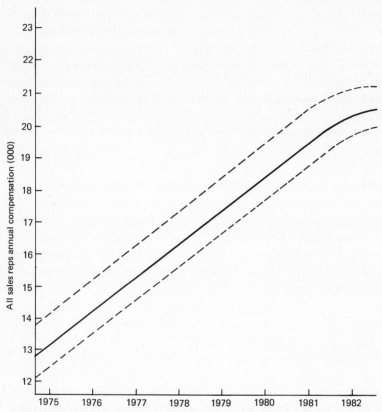

Compensation Curve. A company's compensation curve normally will show the average earnings of all sales reps as well as the range in dotted lines. This can be used in interviewing candidates to discuss their individual needs for money.

annually for all salespeople for the first ten years with the company. Any applicant who indicated he or she would not be satisfied near or under the maximum of the career compensation curve within the ten-year projection would be a poor risk. Those who indicated satisfaction well below the curve might be saying that they are not sufficiently motivated to achieve what the company considers normal. The preferred candidate is the one who sees ample opportunity for income growth within the career compensation curve. The curve can be projected into the future to offset inflationary trends so that past compensation does not look too low either today or in the next few years.

Present and past salespeople who were well below the career

compensation curve can be studied to see if they have something in common that blocks or inhibits performance. One company doing this analysis found that the majority of poor performers had significant outside income from investments in the stock market. They were more interested in the daily fluctuations of their stocks than in their selling jobs. This was then written into the firm's sales staff specification as a strong potential danger signal.

SUMMARY

Selecting the best candidates from a group of recruits who are generally qualified is a major responsibility of the sales manager. The manager's ability to judge people and predict which ones will be superior performers determines much of the future success of a sales organization.

An intelligent search of the candidate's past performance is usually the most valid predictor of future success. The manager will search for indications of success in most activities attempted, for indications of staying with a difficult assignment, for indications of variety or flexibility of interests, and for a progressive increase in responsibility and independence.

Through interviews the sales manager attempts to learn what each candidate wants the manager to know, as well as job-related things the candidate would rather the manager did not know. Directive and open questions generally will solicit much information while elaborative and reflective questions are used to probe more deeply into selected areas. Projective and problem-solving questions can be used in sensitive areas without insulting or annoying a candidate. When appropriate, a stress interview can be arranged to test a candidate's ability to handle emotionally charged situations. Multiple interviews are recommended to make the process more objective as well as to test the candidate's flexibility in dealing with different personalities.

Testing likely sales candidates is another way to obtain objective data for comparison. There are many good tests available commercially, and a sales manager can get help from psychologists who specialize in this area to match the appropriate tests with the work force specification. The tests selected should be proven *reliable* in that the candidate's score would be about the same no matter how often variations of the same test were taken. The test must be *valid* by law for most companies. The scores must be shown to have predicted on-the-job performance to a significant degree without in any way discriminating against the candidate's sex, race, color, religion, national origin, or age of 40 to 65 years.

When all the data have been collected, a profile of each candidate becomes clear which indicates the kind of person the candidate is today with various strengths and weaknesses compared with established norms. Sales managers should use caution against jumping to the conclusion that the candidate with the highest scores is the best one. An analysis can be made of the profile of the best existing salespersons as they appeared before they were hired. This often indicates more dependence, for example, when the salespersons were young and inexperienced, a characteristic which enhanced their ability to learn and to accept direction.

Selecting the best candidates takes considerable time and effort; however, it is well worth it when the sales manager can upgrade the sales force in a relatively few years. A good selection process reduces costly turnover in the long run; hence, it is justified economically and legally. Hiring good sales reps will make the sales manager's future job easier because future recruiting becomes easier and training, supervising, and motivating become easier. Better customer relations are achieved and the company goal of a high-quality sales force can be achieved.

QUESTIONS

1 How might a sales candidate's past performance indicate his or her degree of maturity?

2 Give three examples of (*a*) directive questions and (*b*) open questions.

3 Give three examples of (*a*) elaborative questions and (*b*) reflective questions.

4 Illustrate how you would use a problem-solving question.

5 Under what conditions would a stress interview be most appropriate?

6 What is the value of multiple interviews?

7 Describe the reliability of tests for sales candidates.

8 What are the legal restrictions concerning test validity?

9 What is the danger in matching a trainee's profile with those of the best sales reps as they are today?

10 How might failure analysis help a sales manager in making future hiring decisions?

SELECTED REFERENCES

Johnson, H. Webster: "Recruiting and Selecting Salespeople," chap. 3 in *Sales Management,* Charles E. Merrill Books, Inc., Columbus, Ohio. 1976.
Stanton, William J., and **Richard H. Buskirk:** "Selction of Salesmen— Processing Applicants," chap. 8, and "Selection of Salesmen—Use of Tests," chap. 9 in *Management of the Sales Force,* 4th ed., Richard D. Irwin, Inc., Homewood, Ill., 1974.
Stern, Louis, ed.: *Distribution Channels: Behavioral Dimensions,* Houghton Mifflin Company, Boston, 1969.
Still, Richard R., Edward W. Cundiff, and **Norman A. P. Govoni:** "Recruiting and Selecting Sales Personnel," chap. 10 in *Sales Management,* 3d ed., Prentice-Hall, Inc., Englewood Cliffs, N.J., 1976.

▶ Case 10-1

THE JONES INSURANCE AGENCY

Jones Insurance Agency, Inc., was formed by Ralph Jones in 1972. Mr. Jones is a general agent for a large national life insurance company. He had started as an insurance agent after two years of college. He became a general agent for another company in 1970. In 1972 he affiliated with the present company. Branch offices were established in three cities. Each office has a sales manager and ten salesmen.

The products that this agency offers are whole life and term policies and a savings program that is one of the best in the industry. Other policies are not sold, as the commission schedules are not as attractive. The main product is the savings program, which accounts for over 95 percent of the agency business.

The sales effort of this agency is somewhat unique to the insurance industry. A telephone soliciting program is used to set up appointments with prospective customers. People are told how they can save money by a book that will be dropped off by a "consultant" with no obligations. An appointment is then set up. The sales reps then call on these people, give their pitch, and try to make a sale.

Salespeople are recruited through newspaper ads, friends of present salespersons, and through industry sources. Prior sales experience is preferred but it is not necessary. Half of the present force was hired away from other insurance agencies, with the rest made up of former used car and magazine salespeople.

The training program consists of learning the sales pitch for the sales program and riding with a sales rep for a few days for people who are already licensed agents. These persons are then on their own. For those who are not licensed agents, a handbook is provided for the recruits to study for the test administered by the state, which all agents must pass before they can write business. These people ride with a sales rep for about two weeks or until they have the pitch down pat. After they are licensed, they are on their own.

The salesperson's hours are from 5 to 10 P.M. on weekdays and from 10 A.M. to 2 P.M. on Saturday. These hours are selling time. Sales meetings are held from 9 A.M. to 12 noon weekdays and from 9 to 9:30 on Saturday. At these meetings the agenda consists of talking about the previous night's sales, different techniques for overcoming objections and getting through the door, and any general business that needs to be taken care of. The salespeople then report back at 4 P.M. on weekdays to pick up their appointments, which usually number from three to six. When the salespeople go out on their appointments, they go out on the ones received that day. If they cannot get in the door, or if the people are not home, they call back on previous appointments that were missed for one reason or another.

Sales reps are on straight commission with no expense allowance and must provide their own car. They receive 40 percent of the first-year premium on savings programs and 80 percent on the whole life and term policies. The savings program is pushed because it is easier to sell and the premium dollar value is larger than for the whole life or term policies. An average sales rep should sell a minimum of $1000 of yearly premiums weekly. Commissions are received as follows: 25 percent is received on receipt of the policy application by the national company, 25 percent is received upon delivery of the policy to the client (usually two to three weeks after the sale is made), and the remaining 50 percent is received in equal payments in the ninth through the twelfth month following the sale. This last figure is not received if the salesperson should leave; it then goes to the sales manager. Mr. Jones makes approximately $60,000 a year and his sales managers make between $20,000 and $40,000. The sales managers have been with Mr. Jones from the beginning and were promoted because of their sales ability.

Since its beginning, the Jones Insurance Agency has had a turnover of 90 percent a year with its sales force.

1 What steps might be taken to select better sales representatives to reduce turnover?

2 What traits of Mr. Jones and his two branch managers would you look for in interviewing new candidates?

▶ **Case 10-2**

REDSTONE FOODS, INC.

Redstone Foods, Inc., is a large national company that produces a variety of food products. Redstone has been in business since 1905 and is known for the quality of its products. Redstone is divided into six divisions, by territory, with each division run in a semiautonomous manner. Each division has its own processing plants, warehouse, and distribution systems. The division manager is charged with making that division show a profit and is responsible for the overall operations of the division.

Each division has a number of districts depending on geographic area, number of cities, and population. Each district has two sales forces, institutional (hospitals, hotels, cafeterias, and so on) and retail (chain stores, independents, and the like). The district managers have a responsibility similar to the division managers but on a smaller scale. Each district has two sales managers, one each for institutional and retail sales reps. Each sales manager has a number of assistant sales managers depending on how large the territory is and the number of accounts and salespeople. Each assistant supervises from six to twelve people, depending on territory, the experience of the assistant, and the sales force. On a national average, the retail salespeople outnumber the institutional salespeople by a margin of three to one. Redstone uses a policy of promotion from within, as can be evidenced by the fact that over 90 percent of the corporate executives started as sales reps.

John Fecca, manager of District II of the Southwest Division, was in the process of choosing a new retail sales manager. District managers could promote sales reps to assistant sales managers without question but had to have divisional approval to promote assistants to managers. Sometimes assistants from other districts were brought in because of their past record. If this took place, both district managers involved had to agree and to receive divisional approval. Another situation was when a sales manager or assistant or sales rep wanted to be transferred to another division. This process went up through one division and down through another to find the best solution and avoid problems. In the past there had been few problems with transfers or promotions between districts or divisions. All sales managers had to come from assistant sales managers and all assistants from salespeople. Individuals could transfer between retail and institutional to gain experience and be promotable.

Jake Spangler, who was the departing sales manager, had ten years with Redstone. He was leaving to go into the nightclub business with his brother.

Mr. Fecca had followed company procedure and notified divisional headquarters of the situation. He also stated that he would recommend a replacement within two weeks. Mr. Spangler would be leaving within one month, and this had caught Mr. Fecca by surprise. Of the eight assistants to choose from (three institutional, five retail), Mr. Fecca had two in mind, Kelly Smith, assistant retail sales manager, and Brian Logan, assistant institutional sales manager. There were four other assistants; however, they did not have adequate experience or enough time with the company to warrant consideration.

Kelly Smith had been with the company five years. She came in as a walk-on and had impressed Mr. Fecca from the start. Mrs. Smith had proven to be an excellent salesperson and assistant manager. She had recently received a college degree from American Business University by going to class at night for the past six years. She had been an assistant for two years and was married with two children.

Brian Logan, a graduate of State University, had been with Redstone for six years. He had been recruited by Redstone. Mr. Logan had been an excellent retail salesperson but had trouble adjusting to his promotion to institutional assistant. However, during the past year he had done exceptionally well. He has been an assistant for three years and is divorced with three children.

While Mr. Fecca was mulling over his decision, Mr. Spangler came to his office. He had come to recommend James Jones, assistant sales manager, retail, for his job. Mr. Jones had been with Redstone for nine years and had worked with Mr. Spangler when they were both salespeople. Before being an assistant, Mr. Jones had been in retail for two years and in institutional for three. He had been an assistant for three years and was single. After reviewing the record of Mr. Jones, and because of the recommendation of Mr. Spangler, Mr. Fecca now surmised that he had three candidates to choose from. Mr. Spangler had told Mr. Jones of his recommendation.

Three days after this conference, Gary Farnsworth, institutional sales manager, came to see Mr. Fecca. Mr. Farnsworth stated that he wanted the job that Mr. Spangler was leaving. His reason was that he was experienced (he had been an assistant sales manager for four years) and that the retail job led to faster promotions than the institutional job (this is true). Mr. Farnsworth had been with Redstone for seven years and had transferred from the Northwest Division two years earlier. Mr. Farnsworth was married with three children and had recently purchased a $75,000 home. After reviewing the records of Mr. Farnsworth and looking at the situation, Mr. Fecca now had four candidates to choose from.

The next day Mr. Fecca received a call from Mike Fernandez, manager of District IV, to talk about giving Jose Sanchez the sales manager's job. Mr. Sanchez was a relative of Mr. Fernandez. Mr. Fecca and Mr. Fernandez had started as sales reps together fifteen years ago and were friends. Because of some incident in the past, Mr. Fecca owed Mr. Fernandez a favor. Mr. Fernandez wanted this favor paid off by the promotion of his relative. Mr. Sanchez had been with the company five years. He had been an excellent salesperson but was a little hot-tempered. He had been a good assistant sales manager and was married with six children. His record was on its way to Mr. Fecca, so Mr. Fecca advised Mr. Fernandez that he would consider the recommendation. Mr. Fecca now had five candidates to choose from.

1 How would you select the best candidate?
2 How would you tell the unsuccessful candidates?

Sales Training
Methodologies

▶ Objectives

The reader will now understand the need to upgrade a sales force through training and how this may be done. He or she will be able to use five different levels of sales training and to fit the level to differing needs of the individual sales representative. The reader will understand the value of television role playing and how to use it constructively. He or she will understand the difference between continuous training and retraining, as well as ways to involve experienced sales representatives.

Annual surveys of sales managers show a repeating pattern in most industries. The top 20 percent of the sales force produces about 40 percent of the orders; the middle 60 percent of the sales force produces nearly half the total sales; and the lower 20 percent of the sales force produces only 10 percent of the total sales. Typically, managers report that they would replace the lower 20 percent of the sales force if better people could be attracted to their companies.

Since sales managers can identify these poor or marginal producers, they may also be able to create a training program to increase their

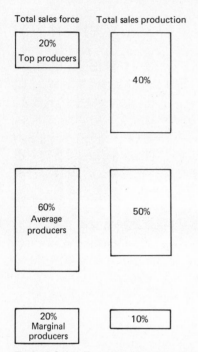

Total sales force   Total sales production

20% Top producers	40%
60% Average producers	50%
20% Marginal producers	10%

Typical Sales Force Production. Annual surveys for many industries show the above pattern repeatedly. Most sales managers report they would replace the lower 20 percent if better people could be attracted to their companies.

productivity. Moreover, any training program could also be designed to make many average producers into top sales reps. Every year that the upgraded sales reps stay with the company after training, they yield a geometric return on the training dollars invested in them.

Conversely, if salespeople do not receive good training, they run the risk of losing their effectiveness or of being outsold by their well-trained competitors. Reps who were once top producers fall back to average. Many who were formally average may become poor or marginal producers. In other words, failure to provide good training can have a direct negative impact on the profit and loss statement well in excess of the short-term positive effect of money saved by not training.

Some companies spend more on sales training annually than they spend on advertising. Xerox, for example, has proven it gets a better return on investment in sales training than it gets on spending for advertising.[1] This is the modern or enlightened approach to sales management that should be taken when the theory proves to be true for a company or an industry.

Traditionally sales managers, on the other hand, believe good sales representatives have a natural way with people and need merely to learn the product line. Typically, a sales trainee is assigned to a senior salesperson to learn by imitation. Known as the "buddy system," for many years this has been used because it is an inexpensive method of training new people. Unfortunately, it is also a dangerous method. Besides learning some good skills and techniques, the trainee also learns the informal limit on the number of calls per day. The trainee may also learn to drink martinis at lunch, to see a movie on Wednesday afternoons, or to take a full day off to play golf once in a while. Inadvertently, the senior sales rep teaches the trainee many ways to beat the system. In addition, one new trainee may learn quickly while another may be slow. The sales manager may reduce all situations to what the average trainee should learn, thereby boring the quick learner and hurting the slow learner.

LEVELS OF SOPHISTICATION

A sales manager normally has considerable discretion in determining how sophisticated the sales training may be. One who observes many salespeople in a range of industries may correctly conclude that there are thousands of ways to sell products and services. Further analysis and logic will indicate many similarities among the methods, and general categories will emerge into which most will fall:

1 Stimulus-response selling

2 Formula selling

3 Want-satisfaction selling

[1]See *Xerox Sales Training Marketing Case History,* Intercollegiate Video Clearing House, Miami, Fla., 1976.

4 Problem-solving selling

5 Depth selling

Experienced and highly successful salespeople can be found using each of these methods, and one level is not necessarily better than another level. Success depends on matching the sales strategy to the target market segment and the competence or qualifications of the sales force. In general, the sales manager tries to sharpen the sales force to an escalating minimum level of sophistication for the firm's market.

Stimulus-Response Selling   A sales presentation that is written out and memorized word for word by the sales rep is called a "canned talk." When the salesperson uses only selected parts of such a presentation and substitutes his or her own varied talks for other parts but still follows the preplanned outline, the presentation is called a "planned talk." If the prospect says one thing, the salesperson plans to answer with a particular memorized paragraph. In either form, canned or planned, the talk is a fairly standardized presentation and is given by the salesperson to all prospects. It becomes a habit of which the sales rep may not even be conscious.

The planned talk is designed to communicate rapidly to the prospect as many buying benefits as possible in an attempt to elicit a favorable buying response. The sales rep is trained to say many emotionally appealing words and to raise certain issues which will trigger a favorable response in most buyers. All the facts and emotional appeals are assembled in a logical sequence to tell a complete and persuasive story. A good planned talk has an engaging beginning, an interesting and effective presentation, often a demonstration or visual aids, and, finally, as many as ten standard phrases to use in closing a sale. Common objections are answered only when raised by the prospect, and these answers are also relatively standardized.

The canned sales presentation is widely used—intentionally and knowledgeably—by sales management in a number of industries. It is appropriate in training retail salesclerks as well as in training house-to-house outside salespeople. It is commonly used in training new people to sell insurance, mutual funds, and real estate. These are generally mass consumer markets, but stimulus-response selling is also used extensively by wholesale sales reps calling, for example, on supermarket buyers or appliance store owners; by medical detail reps doing missionary sales work with doctors and dentists; and by salespersons expected to call on time-conscious architects. There is nothing wrong with using a well-organized presentation on the proper occasion. It enables new sales reps to speak confidently without fumbling for words, which usually earns the prospect's respect, and it also assures a smooth and complete presentation. It prevents wandering off the subject or the absent-minded omission of any important points.

It is relatively simple to train new sales recruits to use a planned talk. They are asked to memorize words and phrases from a written script and to show or demonstrate certain things. By listening to records or audio tapes they can learn the proper pitch and vocal inflections for the key words. By watching sound films or video tapes they can easily learn to mimic the actors. Trainees should practice until they know every word by rote and have an actor's feeling for each line.

However, if trial closes are built into the presentation, the manager should *not* assume that trainees will know how to handle them. Many new sales recruits will not recognize when the prospect is signaling a readiness to buy. Novices are too often concerned with giving a complete sales presentation and are likely to talk themselves out of an easy sale. When a trial close elicits a favorable response, the sales rep should learn to recognize it, skip most of the remaining talk, and write up the order.

Formula Selling Probably the most popular strategy taught to salespeople is a formula of mental steps encompassing such things as gaining the prospect's favorable attention, interest, desire, conviction, and action. The formula method requires the sales rep to dominate the interview and to direct the prospect's thoughts to a desired phase of the presentation. The sales trainee is taught not to go through a planned presentation, but to build interest before moving on to the next stage. This enables the sales rep to tailor the presentation to a specific prospect and to use some degree of creativity and imagination.

Formula selling is predominant in industrial sales and is more applicable to business sales than to retail or consumer markets because it normally takes the form of a lengthy two-way conversation. Whenever the product or service is complicated and difficult to understand, or when a salesperson calls repeatedly on the same accounts throughout the years, formula selling predominates. If the salesperson has a number of products in the line, this method permits varying the talk on each visit while still maintaining a set selling pattern or organization as a guide. Industrial goods, office supplies and equipment, and petroleum and chemical products, as well as goods sold by the manufacturer to a wholesaler or by the wholesaler to the retailer, are typically sold through a formula method of presentation.

The sales trainee is taught to get acceptance on one point at a time and to focus the prospect's attention on one idea at a time. Trainees are taught to show pictures or illustrations without printed copy so that they can continue talking and directing the prospect's attention. If printed copy is shown to the prospect, the trainee is taught to remain quiet, or both the picture message and the verbal message will be lost. To pace the presentation the trainee is taught to pause after each point and frequently to ask questions to ensure the prospect's understanding and acceptance of the point being made. By knowing the prospect, the sales rep can anticipate which benefits will be most likely to be appealing and which phases of the sales talk should be played down or omitted entirely.

Training sales reps in complete product knowledge and formula application clearly takes much longer than simply having them memorize a sales talk. Recruiting will be on a higher level and selection will be more discriminating for the candidate's learning ability. A great deal of patience is required of the manager to supervise and motivate the trainee over an extended period of nonproductive activity in classes and during the early months out in the field.

Want-Satisfaction Selling The want-satisfaction sales strategy requires the sales rep to discover a want or need within the buyer's mind and then bring it to the buyer's awareness. The sales rep simply acts as the prospect's agent to show the buyer how to better satisfy this need through the purchase of the salesperson's goods or services. The sales presentation is based on the prospect's self-interest and the emotional motive that carries the strongest appeal for the prospect at that instant. Product considerations are secondary. The sales rep's job is to determine which emotional needs are likely to exist and which are the most dominant ones in relation to the products being offered.

This technique is used most effectively by experienced sales reps who have enough self-confidence to permit the sales interview to wander in many directions as a true two-way conversation. In fact, the prospect is encouraged to do most of the talking. Sales reps are taught effective listening skills to look for the keys to unlock the hidden want in the buyer's mind. While this method is most widely used by experienced sales representatives of investments, autos, and other big-ticket consumer goods, it is growing in popularity in industrial selling.

In a market where product and service differentiation is difficult or impossible to obtain, competitive sales reps are most often judged on a personal basis. The buyer looks for the rep who understands and sympathizes with the buyer's point of view. The rep is then considered a friendly source of authority—if not unbiased, at least primarily concerned with the buyer's interest.

In addition, the salesperson using this strategy will be taught in detail about the firm's products and their applications and limitations. Although the emphasis in the sales interview is on the buyer's wants and needs, whatever questions do arise about the product must be answered clearly and correctly to maintain the atmosphere of sincerity and confidence. Fundamental to this strategy is a customer-oriented prepared talk. Thus the sales manager does not build a planned talk; instead, he teaches the sales reps to probe, to recognize where their products will help satisfy needs, and to build their own customer-oriented presentation instantaneously on the spot. These are skills of a much higher order than memorizing a talk or following a product-oriented formula.

Problem-Solving Selling   Problem solving as a sales strategy is based on building a prospect's confidence in the honest service which the sincere sales reps can provide. The sales effort is dedicated to the primary benefit of the prospect by developing the prospect's true needs, thoroughly investigating all feasible solutions, projecting their applications, and selecting the most appropriate solution. The rep lets the chips fall where they may, recommending the most appropriate solution, even if it does not include the immediate purchase of any of the firm's products.

Most experienced sales reps become experts in their narrow field and are very often experts in related fields. Calling on their technical knowledge and experience, they can suggest alternate courses of action of which the prospect is not aware and can provide such a buyer with honest appraisals. Thus, problem solving can be an effective sales presentation in many nontechnical fields as well, simply because the sales force is more knowledgeable in its field than the buyers are. Many sales of accounting machines, computers, office duplicating machines, and printing machines are due to a problem-solving technique honestly applied. When the sales force is selling simple products, often nothing astonishes prospects more than the sellers' common sense and plain, honest dealings.

Clearly, the training and development of the sales force to use this strategy is very different from the sales training required for the strategies discussed previously. The sales reps are taught how to analyze an industry and a particular target company before they make any direct contact. When they make the first call, they are prepared to offer a genuine or specific service, such as a survey or audit of various processes to determine where costs may be reduced, service increased, duplication removed, and so forth.

They are taught how to conduct a legitimate study of problem areas and to project the consequences of the likely alternatives, recommending the one best serving the prospect's needs. Knowing why one product is best for a given situation is more important than knowing how to woo a prospect. In this selling method a salesperson who is gruff but technically correct is usually more persuasive than the one who is smooth-talking but too general or loose with the facts.

Second only to product knowledge in this method of presentation is the ability to educate the prospect. The sales force is supposed to be more expert in their limited area than the prospect, but they should be able to make their ideas simple and understandable to the customer. The sales force can be trained to make technical data clear and easy for the novice to understand. This skill should not be treated lightly in preparing technically educated people to sell. Such trainees should be able to state their ideas, illustrate them, and then restate them in different terms if necessary. Unless the prospect understands the suggestions and appreciates the minute technical point on which the idea swings, all the clear, scientific thinking involved may be lost.

The advantages of teaching the problem-solving sales strategy include complete customer orientation in serving the individual prospect, complete honesty in using an unbiased, two-sided argument, and an acceptable utilization of technically trained personnel in sales work. The problem-solving strategy builds long-range confidence in the source of the authority, and this is essential in most repeat sales situations and where customer loyalty is cultivated.

Depth Selling At this point the reader should see the continuum of sales strategies ranging from the completely salesperson-oriented canned talk to the completely customer-oriented problem-solving approach. Each of the four strategies was discussed in its pure form. In practice they overlap, blend, and intermingle, but generally at random and without premeditated design or purpose.

Depth selling combines the best features of all the strategies but does so with forethought and intention. It is appropriately taught to senior sales reps and those with national-account responsibility. They are taught how to diplomatically get others inside their own company to work with them to accomplish the sales objectives. Many of these experts, such as research, engineering, production, accounting, and credit personnel, will have little or no direct responsibility to the senior sales reps. Their respect and voluntary cooperation must be earned and a proud team spirit cultivated. When visiting a key-target account, the salesperson may bring along a technician to probe for information from, or to present information to, a counterpart in the prospect's company.

The depth salesperson is highly sensitive to the changing moods of the prospect and can employ whatever technique best serves the purpose at any given moment. For example, when a prospect indicates an emotional inclination toward a favorable decision, the sales rep may reinforce that attitude by using a concise stimulus-response talk which provides the essential logic. When a prospect is in an impulsive mood, the depth sales rep may use pure suggestion to activate a decision. The depth sales rep typically builds personal friendships with customers in order to gain leads and recommendations as well as repeat orders.

The preparation of sales reps to use the depth selling strategy should be a continuous program covering knowledge, skills, work habits, and attitudes. It is a large job both in time and in sales management effort. Successful salespeople in many fields have been self-educated in this method through years of trial and error. However, as sales management's knowledge increases and its attention is directed toward these training considerations, much training time can be saved.

FORMAL GROUP TRAINING

Regardless of the entry level of a new sales trainee and the initial training which he or she receives, the first few months out in the field will probably be exciting and full of challenge. In time the salesperson will become comfortable and more at ease with the work and the customers. Some salespeople will become content to stay at this level for their entire careers, but many will become bored or frustrated. When this occurs, they operate more and more automatically with as little thought as possible. Selling becomes a tedious task, with success based on the law of averages or lucky windfalls. The fun and satisfactions in life are sought away from the job. A salesperson who cannot grow is apt to wither and become cynical.

The modern sales manager is sensitive to the emotional needs of each sales rep and attempts to anticipate the rep's changing attitudes. For example, after a sales rep has been around a territory a number of times, some degree of success will be achieved. But the person will have tried and failed to sell many prospects. If the rep must go back to these same accounts again and again, using the same knowledge and skills, one can anticipate that frustration will build. The salesperson who is taught new knowledge, new skills, or new strategies, however, will again feel the excitement of challenge and will be interested in improving, growing, and realizing the pride of accomplishment.

For a sales manager to achieve good performance with high motivation and productivity from every sales rep, it is necessary to consider the various levels of training possible for each individual. As reps become less dependent on their manager, there is a danger of their behavior becoming habitual. One may become complacent with a fair amount of success. Another may work harder and harder but realize little or no progress. These signals should trigger in the sales manager a series of questions about additional training that might be appropriate.

One may need encouragement to perfect selling skills in order to become more effective. Another may need to learn new techniques to reach a higher batting average. It would be very unusual if every sales rep needed the same training. Often the sales force can be divided into several groups according to common training needs. The least experienced group might practice planned talks to answer common objections, for example. Another group might exchange successful applications of formula selling techniques. The skill of probing for information and hidden wants could be the training objective of a third group.

The training needs of salespeople do not necessarily relate to their ages or years with the company. Some young people are quite mature and some older sales reps will be very dependent on their sales manager. The effective sales manager will observe the individual rep in the field with customers and prospects. A search will be made for clues which may indicate the appropriate level of sales training for each of the representatives at that point in their careers. By matching the training to the needs of the individual, the modern sales manager can achieve better results than those predecessors who attempted to teach all salespeople exactly the same thing.

TV ROLE-PLAYING TECHNIQUES

The most common use of video tape in sales training is to record a salesperson or trainee in a role-play situation for instant replay.[2] This technique provides the salesperson an opportunity to see himself or herself as seen by others. One literally confronts oneself with a set of perceptual standards which normally are applied only to others.

Sales trainees and experienced salespeople confronting themselves for the first few times tend to be very anxious and often extremely self-critical. There is tremendous ego-involvement in watching oneself perform on instant replay. The trainee may be instructed to observe how a particular question was handled, but his or her attention is magnetically drawn to the size of the nose or a receding hairline. Many salespeople have felt that their first few exposures to this medium made them more self-conscious and awkward performers rather than better ones. Indeed, some salespeople abhor a video role-playing assignment because after their first experience the sales manager and peers have given them too much negative feedback, making them uncomfortable and embarrassed.

Self-confrontation by instant replay can be a very constructive and valuable sales training technique. The first few evaluations of taped

---

[2]See T. Stroh, *The Uses of Video Tape in Training and Development,* AMA Research Study No. 93, American Management Association, New York, 1969.

performances should emphasize the many good traits that each trainee exhibits. Little or no negative criticism should be permitted in this first phase of video sales training. After the trainees get over both the shock of seeing themselves and their preoccupation with self-centered trivia, they are ready for some carefully regulated constructive criticism.

Perhaps the only thing worse than misusing video tape in sales training is being denied the privilege of using it. Real and tremendous benefits can accrue to sales managers using this exciting medium. Nine out of ten users of video tape equipment report that the cost of their equipment is well justified and that the benefits clearly outweigh the effort involved in trying to use it effectively.[3]

The consensus among sales trainers is that video tape recording increases trainee interest and participation. It is virtually impossible for the trainee to sit back passively or to mentally tune out the picture on the television screen when the trainee is the performer. The self-interest of the trainees is so strong, in fact, that many of them ask for permission to practice with video recordings outside the normal business hours. Experienced salespeople often want to come back in the evening during a week-long training seminar to perfect their taped performance. Very few sales training methods can generate this kind of spontaneous involvement and interest.

If the sales manager wants the sales reps to be able to find out what their prospects sincerely feel about their needs, for example, the learning objectives might be stated as follows:

1 To be able to use six or more probing techniques comfortably within a fifteen-minute role play

2 To recognize sensitive areas and to probe more deeply into them without offending the prospect

3 To permit the prospect to dominate 50 to 60 percent of the interview

4 To listen well enough to recall correctly at least 80 percent of the prospect's major points immediately after the interview

[3]Ibid.

Trainees should be shown how they will personally benefit by learning the particular techniques and should be motivated to do the best job possible. They may hear lectures about the techniques, read assigned materials, and perhaps view a film on this subject and participate in a discussion afterward. When the manager feels they are ready for the role play, it is necessary to carefully explain the expected standards of behavior and precisely how the trainees will be judged. When all sales trainees understand and accept the criteria, they can proceed with the role play and instant replay. Used in this manner, the medium will enhance the learning process with a minimum of defensive reactions.

Because video tape can be erased and reused hundreds of times, it is a valuable yet inexpensive tool for self-instruction. The trainee who knows the criteria to be met or the model to be imitated can practice again and again on video tape. Instead of unknowingly making the same mistake over and over as might occur in the territory, the trainee has immediate feedback to show what must be corrected.

DEVELOPING EXPERIENCED SALES REPS

When dealing with the training and development of experienced sales reps, the sales manager is faced with two kinds of problems. The first is *continuous* training, which is needed to keep the entire sales force up to date on changing product features, changing company policies, customer or industry changes, and competitive changes. Continuous training programs are designed to improve the sales force in skills, knowledge, attitudes, and work habits in a never-ending process. Continuous training is designed to maintain a constant path toward perfection in the same job.

The second area of concern for the sales manager is *retraining* sales reps. Retraining programs are designed to prepare the sales force to handle new responsibilities or to apply known skills in a new way. Retraining most commonly occurs when an individual sales rep has mastered one selling job and is ready for more sophisticated duties and responsibilities. After one has proved he or she can handle a regular territory, one may want to handle national accounts. This new selling job probably will require different knowledge, new administrative record-keeping skills, and perhaps new selling and research skills. There is no need to have the salesperson understudy a senior national-account manager for many years or simply to transfer the person and enforce learning by trial and error. Before one is given new duties and responsibilities, one can be retrained to handle them as the sales manager wants.

Retraining experienced sales reps presents problems different from those associated with initial sales training. The sales force knows with the certainty of personal experience what works for them. They are not apt to give up selling methods which have been successful in the past in exchange for new, untried methods. It is natural to expect their attitudes to be somewhat skeptical and challenging to most instructors and managers. They are apt to be ill at ease if the new behavior they must try is contrary to their lifelong selling habits. These factors rarely appear in training new applicants to the profession.

In planning the retraining program, job descriptions can be an important analytical tool. What did the old job require? What does the new job require? What are the similarities and what are the critical differences? When these factors are identified, the program can be constructed to begin with the similarities. The experienced salespeople will be comfortable dealing with known areas, and the brief review will not offend their intelligence. As a common ground is established, the program can begin to move into the new areas.

It is important that the experienced sales reps understand in training why their old way of selling will not be very effective under the new conditions. Whenever possible, of course, old habits that can be modified to suit the new situation should be utilized. When this is not possible, the new method—the critical difference—should be emphasized with clear theory and practical demonstrations. Today, for example, they may need a basic understanding of cost accounting, which was not required or even considered five years ago. "Incremental profit contribution," "depreciation," "cost of acquisition," and "cost of life" are just a few of the terms which customers may use with salespeople. Where such expressions are used, buyers prefer a sales rep who is conversant in profit-improvement plans for the customer to the traditional "unique benefit" sales rep.

Once the critical differences have been accepted and learned, the retraining program can move much more rapidly. Experienced sales reps are quick to learn new product information, prospecting methods, and the like, because they already know how important these factors are in selling. Their questions are apt to be much more pertinent than those of new trainees, and they will understand the new concepts much faster. At this stage a degree of camaraderie will often develop and the sales manager should encourage this new team spirit. The team will often establish high standards for themselves and will persuade the more hesitant members to join the enthusiastic group.

Effective retraining does not stop at the end of a seminar. It is one thing to be enthusiastic and self-confident in the protective atmosphere of the classroom and another thing to be so in the office of a tough prospect. The salesperson's new behavior is tentative, and the temptation to revert to the old way is very strong. The experienced sales rep needs encouragement and reinforcement perhaps even more than the young trainee. On-the-job observations, praise, and coaching are all appropriate under the new conditions. Any early success should be made known to the entire team, who will try harder to prove they are as good as the few who caught on early. The naturally competitive nature of salespeople will thus encourage the desired change in behavior.

Special Seminars While an experienced sales force may be tired of learning about the basics or fundamentals of salesmanship, some of them are the very ones who may be neglecting the basics. If they are required to attend a regular sales training meeting, they may contaminate the attitude of the younger sales reps with their cynicism or ridicule. Rather than take this risk, the sales manager might consider two alternatives which have worked well for many sales organizations.

One alternative is to hold a special seminar for the most productive reps on the sales force. The top 25 percent are asked to attend a special meeting, most often on a quarterly basis. The manager reinforces the high reputation of those invited and asks their opinions on selected sales problems facing the company. For example, the manager might present a market change that has been forecasted or a new competitive challenge. The experienced sales reps then are free to exchange ideas and techniques and to suggest any number of creative approaches to the problem. While each one is a star in his or her own territory, they also realize they are with a peer group of superior performers. To be accepted by this elite group, each one wants to make a positive contribution to the discussion. It becomes an honor to be invited to attend this kind of seminar.

When handled with a proper buildup or promotion, such as a personal letter from the vice president of sales and a prestigious meeting place, the experienced sales reps enter the training program with very positive attitudes. They learn from each other, and often their suggestions become productive input for training the entire sales force. Experienced salespeople, in effect, teach each other under highly favorable learning conditions.

The second and most common alternative to boring the experienced salespersons at a routine sales training meeting is to assign each the responsibility of teaching a subject. This provides one with an opportunity to exhibit one's ability as a salesperson, an organizer, a motivator, and a trainer. Many of these abilities are required for promotion into management; hence the assignment becomes a challenge to the salesperson. To avoid appearing ridiculous in front of one's peers, the experienced salesperson will spend considerable time preparing the lesson. In the process of attempting to persuade others to use the basic techniques, the experienced salesperson is persuaded.

Several experienced sales reps can be assigned to handle one complete program in a similar way. The manager can exercise some control by outlining the specific topics which are to be covered, but the division of labor can be left up to the people involved. The manager then attends the meeting as an observer. In this way, many an otherwise reluctant experienced sales rep has been won over to the manager's position of enthusiastic endorsement of sales training.

SUMMARY

Good sales training is essential to field a competitive sales force and to attract the best applicants. The level of sophistication in training depends upon what is needed to match the sales strategy to the market segment targeted and on the competence or qualifications of the sales force.

Stimulus-response selling is a planned presentation which is product-oriented and salesperson-dominated. It can be taught to new trainees to quickly build their selling knowledge and a degree of competence. The formula method of selling permits the sales rep to tailor the presentation to a particular prospect. It guides one's pace or movement from one aspect of the sales proposition to another by keying it to the prospect's reactions. It is also product-oriented and salesperson-dominated.

In the want-satisfaction strategy of selling, the prospect is encouraged to do most of the talking while the salesperson listens for hidden wants or needs which the firm's products or services can fulfill. It is customer-oriented and customer-dominated. The problem-solving strategy of selling attempts to identify problems, such as high-expense or high-cost areas, and to present a sincere solution to achieve cost savings or greater satisfaction.

The depth selling strategy combines the best of each of the other four methods with premeditation to optimize their impact. It also calls for selected assistance, such as by an engineer or production manager, to help on a particular sales call.

Formal group training can be tailored to the needs of individual sales reps by creating subgroups with different training objectives. Attempting to teach the entire sales force exactly the same thing often leads to cynicism and ridicule.

Television role playing with instant replay is a popular sales training tool today. It provides the sales force with the opportunity of seeing themselves as others see them. Because of the tremendous ego-involvement in watching oneself perform on television, care must be taken to ensure constructive learning. Training objectives should be clear and the criteria for critique should be understood and accepted by the performers to maximize the constructive effect of this training tool.

The training and development of experienced salespeople involve continuous training to upgrade their skills on the same job, and it also involves retraining to teach skills to do a different, more sophisticated job. Experienced sales reps are reluctant to give up their old way of selling; hence, they must be made aware of the reasons for such training. Critical differences can be identified and taught to older sales reps after they accept the need to change.

Reluctant salespeople can often be won over to sales training by inviting the superior performers to special seminars where they exchange ideas and suggestions. In effect, they teach each other. An alternative to this is giving the reluctant personnel the assignment of teaching a subject. With the role reversed—with the sales rep becoming the trainer—the salesperson is not psychologically defensive and resistant. In attempting to persuade others, one persuades oneself.

Good sales training is most often tailored to the individual, with subgroups formed to meet their common needs. When it is planned in a constructive manner, the results can be readily demonstrated in the profit and loss statement.

QUESTIONS

1 How can the high cost of sales training for the entires sales force be justified?

2 Under what circumstances would stimulus-response training be most appropriate?

3 Under what circumstances would want-satisfaction training be most appropriate?

4 How might depth selling be used in selling computer services to a business woman?

5 What are the problems inherent in the sales training of large groups of sales reps?

6 What are the problems in using television role playing for sales training, and how may they be resolved?

7 What is the difference between continuous sales training and retraining? When should each be used?

8 Describe two ways to involve experienced sales reps in a constructive sales training program.

SELECTED REFERENCES

Johnson, H. Webster: "Training," chap. 5 in *Sales Management,* Charles E. Merrill Books, Inc., Columbus, Ohio, 1976.

Stanton, William J., and **Richard H. Buskirk**: "Assimilation of the New Salesman into the Organization," chap. 10, and "Developing and Conducting a Sales Training Program," chap. 11 in *Management of the Sales Force*, 4th ed., Richard D. Irwin, Inc., Homewood, Ill., 1974.
Still, Richard R., Edward W. Cundiff, and **Norman A. P. Govoni:** "Planning and Conducting Sales-Training Programs," chap. 11 in *Sales Management*, 3d ed., Prentice-Hall, Inc., Englewood Cliffs, N.J., 1976.
Stroh, Thomas F.: *Training and Developing Professional Salesmen*, AMACOM, American Management Association, New York, 1973.
Xerox Sales Training Marketing Case History, ³/₄-in. videocassette, 40 min, b&w, Intercollegiate Video Clearing House, Miami, Fla., 1976.

▶ Case 11-1

WILSON CERTIFIED FOODS, INC.

Not long ago a challenge was issued by the president of Wilson Certified Foods, Inc.: "We must search out the highest potential operating dollars on any item and construct a sales and operating program that will merchandise our product in that form." Wilson's sales department responded to this by a proposal to "Sell more: surplus items, branded items, and further-processed items."

It was decided that in order to engineer a more profitable product or sales mix the firm should train the company salespeople—offer them selling skills and product knowledge to meet the challenge at the market level.

At this point, Wilson's sales manager, Bill Young, engaged the services of Personal Dynamics, a distributor of motivational and sales training programs, to assist them in achieving their high-margin goals.

Personal Dynamics believes the approach to solving the problem is to recognize that *attitude* is the key factor in the success of any training or development.

Motivation and sales training are too often viewed as something we "do *to*" the individual. Their view is that it must be something the individual does.

Personal Dynamics works on four fundamentals of development:

1 All development is self-development.

2 All development is individual.

3 Ninety percent of development is on the job.

4 Development should be centered on the present job.

For example:

- If there are 225 selling days per year
- If 60 percent of field management time is in the field (140 days)
- If the average is ten reps under supervision (fourteen days per rep or 5 percent of each rep's time)
- If a rep averages five days in meetings (2 percent of rep's time)
- Ninety-three percent of each salesperson's development time is on his or her own

Carrying these facts to a conclusion, only a limited contribution can be made by off-the-job training, and then only if:

1 The right person . . .

2 . . . attends the right course

3 . . . at the right time

4 . . . with the right attitude.

Personal Dynamics' recommendations show how by inverting the order of conditions listed above—by placing *attitude* in the first position—and by focusing development efforts on the job, all the other "right" conditions fall into place.

Develop Field Management

Personal Dynamics' recommendations cover most of the second half of the year and are broken into three phases.

1 We suggest the company conduct a two-day seminar at head-quarters. All sales managers and district managers will be invited. The purposes of this meeting are to:

    a Improve personal management and leadership abilities.

    b Introduce product and training information.

    c Discuss management objectives and principles used in establishing goals for salespeople.

    d Sell the managers on actively supporting the motivation and sales training programs for themselves and for their salespeople.

2 Immediately following the seminar, sales managers begin work on the Sales Managers Motivation Program. The objectives of the Sales Managers Motivation Program are to:

    a Develop management skills to increase salespeople's productivity.

    b Teach management principles to increase salespeople's productivity.

    c Strengthen management orientation toward personal and corporate goal direction.

    d Organize specific plans of action for achievement of personal and corporate goals.

3 Managers will instruct a Basic Sales Training Program. By leading these programs, we ensure the manager's achieving greater understanding of the materials.

Motivation and Sales Training for Salespeople

1 A pre-program attitude survey will be conducted among all salespeople. At the end another attitude survey will be made. Adjustments will be measured and reported to the company.

2 Salespeople will attend a one-day kickoff meeting at the district level. The purpose of this meeting will be:

    a To establish individual goals for increasing profitability

    b . To introduce the Dynamics of Personal Motivation Program

    c To announce the company's plans and interest in their personal development

3 After the kickoff meeting, salespeople will begin developing attitude with Dynamics of Personal Motivation Program. This program's goals are:
   a To adjust mental attitudes toward positiveness
   b To provide a climate for self-motivation
   c To show salespeople how to set goals, and then develop plans and deadlines to be achieved

4 When the salespeople begin a Basic Sales Training Program, the program will be held on seven consecutive days. This program can accomplish its goals because of the attitude development which has taken place earlier.

5 Continuing sales training and motivation can be efficiently maintained since the vehicle is established and the habits of working with the vehicle are set.

Sources for Funding This Program

Financing will come from increased profitability. However, we suggest examination of the following:

1 Replace current special-incentive programs.
   a We propose Mr. Young issue a personal challenge to each salesperson and sales manager. Included in this challenge will be an analysis by sales territory of sales of Branded and Further-Processed items for the second half of the year.

   Each salesperson will then be asked to program a minimum increase by item and then return his or her acceptance of the challenge to headquarters.

   We believe the importance of this personal challenge and commitment will help in the attainment of the salespeople's goals.

2 Replace year-end plant sales meetings.
   a During the second half of the year the company customarily conducts annual sales meetings at each plant. We recom-

mend that sales meetings be conducted at one or more of the seven sales training sessions.

1 What is your evaluation of this sales training and motivational proposal?

2 How might you test its effectiveness before introducing it on a national basis?

▶ Case 11-2

Zimmer Golf Car Company

Zimmer Golf Car Company operates three branches in the Southeast. The home office is based in Atlanta, Georgia, and the two branches are operated only as sales offices. The golf cars are imported, and they are assembled at the Atlanta headquarters. The firm sells mostly to golf courses and country clubs. Its customers also include individuals and industries. The company has been in operation for fourteen years.

The vice president of sales, James Williams, has been with the company for three years. Prior to his employment with Zimmer, Williams was with a larger competing golf car company working as a sales rep for thirteen years. Williams is Zimmer's best producer and he considers himself a much better salesman than a sales manager.

Large purchases made by the country clubs and golf courses are usually handled by the directors of the clubs and courses. These directors are mostly middle-aged and of prominent status. Because of this fact Williams maintained that his salespeople should be around the same age as the directors. He felt that the buyers would not respect a young salesperson with little experience. For this reason Williams had a policy for hiring only salespeople with at least ten years' experience. It was preferable that the prospective salesperson also have some past experience in selling golf equipment.

The salespeople were at most times taken from other golf equipment companies. Williams would either contact them or they would contact him and an interview would be set up. The interviews were conducted by Williams. The interview was on an informal basis with a few planned questions to test the prospect on his knowledge of the golf industry. There was no formal testing.

Training was handled by Williams. Most of the training was on the job. Williams gave his new salespeople a territory at the start and would accompany the salesperson to the prospective customers. Williams also had the new salesperson accompany him on his own calls so that the new person could watch Williams in action.

Williams stated that even with the years of experience that each new salesperson had, it took a minimum of six months before the new person was productive. The average time that each sales rep was with the firm was two years. The turnover rate was 50 percent annually. Williams was concerned with the high rate of turnover and the long training program. He wanted a better way of selecting and training the new reps, but Zimmer was too small a firm to invest a great deal of time and effort in training its new sales reps.

1 How might this company train its new salespeople more effectively?

2 How do you feel about the sales manager's assumptions regarding the age and experience of recruits?

▶ **Case 11-3**

THE GREAT NORTHERN PUBLISHING COMPANY

The Great Northern Publishing Company of Chicago was experiencing difficulty in securing new sales of its books. The officials of the company were of the opinion that this difficulty was due to some inefficiencies on the part of their representatives. It seemed that the salespeople were letting many of the prospective sales slip through their hands before any specific agreement was reached. Careful analysis was made by the company in an attempt to reach some decision on how to overcome this difficulty.

At a meeting of district sales managers it was decided that the company should adopt some particular method of training their representatives to meet some of the objections that they were receiving while talking to their customers.

There were several proposals concerning possible solutions to the company's problem, but the one that was most favorably received was submitted by a branch sales manager, Neil McDonald. His proposal was that the salespersons selling their books must observe psychological principles. McDonald suggested, therefore, that the company issue to each of its representatives a pamphlet containing information that would prove helpful to each, information that would show how to use psychology in coping with various situations. The pamphlet would contain specific cases and suggestions which would help the salesperson in selling the particularly difficult prospect. McDonald suggested that if the plan were adopted, every salesperson be required to use the pamphlet, and it was also suggested that all salespeople report to their respective branch offices for explanation and demonstration of the principles contained in the pamphlet.

1 What level of sophistication is this type of sales training?

2 What might be more appropriate?

12

Compensating and Motivating the Sales Force

▶ **Objectives**

The reader will understand the advantages of compensating a sales force by straight salary, by salary plus commission or bonus, and by straight commission. He or she will also be able to recognize the difference between movement and motivation. The reader will be able to use personal satisfaction of sales representatives' strong psychological needs to produce more effectively. He or she will be able to provide for satisfaction on the job by using the tools of job rotation, job enrichment, and job enlargement. The reader will understand the appropriate use and construction of sales contests and, finally, know how to use sales meetings to develop long-term motivational programs to minimize sales expense and optimize profit.

In discussing the compensation of the sales force, there are three problem areas which have been neglected by most textbooks in the past twenty-five years. It is the sales manager's responsibility to optimize profit or the company's ROI (return on investment) in the sales force. That is to say, the sales manager should pay the sales force *as little as is necessary* for them to do the job as desired.

People who sell for a living are different in some respects from people who are happy with other kinds of employment. The top producers are generally very self-confident and willing to bet on themselves to succeed. Many have an inner compulsion to earn a lot of money—show off their earning ability as being superior to others. Many also have a compulsion to work hard and are physically uncomfortable when idle. In addition they have a tendency to regard every obstacle and threat as a challenge and to exhibit a basic need to put something over on a buyer. They also have a strong desire for recognition. These traits of top sales producers make the compensation problem much more complicated than it normally is for other groups of employees.

The second area of consideration is the modern management philosophy that people should not be seduced into working for money. People should work at what they want and because they want to do that kind of work. In other words, they should be turned on by the work itself and they should get tremendous satisfaction from achieving on the job. Notice how this modern management theory may possibly meet *some* of the needs of the top producers just noted above. This will be discussed in more detail subsequently in this chapter.

The third area of consideration is one of semantics, or the words applied to various types of compensation plans. Most writers in this field have focused on the advantages and disadvantages of straight salary, straight commission, and a combination of the two. The fact remains, however, that the top sales producers are confident they will earn a lot of money no matter what the payment system. Indeed, if they cannot do so with one company, they will leave for another. People in sales management should look at the method of paying the sales force but not exclusively. The amount paid to the top producers should be as low as possible to attract and keep top producers willing to do the job as management desires. This plan will enable the sales manager to optimize the contribution to profit by the sales force.

COMPENSATION ALTERNATIVES

Straight Commission Plan In some industries, such as real estate and automobiles, sales managers have generally preferred a *straight commission* system of compensating the sales force. It is easy for everyone to understand. It rewards directly for any given amount of sales. The selling expense is always in line as a fixed percentage of sales in good times and bad times. A top producer has no limit on the amount he or she can earn.

Some companies have modified the straight commission of a fixed percentage on every dollar of sales to a varied percentage depending on the profitability of groups of products. Frequently companies increase the percentage of commission as sales volume exceeds predetermined levels. For example, the system might call for 10 percent commission on the first $100,000 sold for one year and 15 percent on all sales over that amount in the same year. Thus a sales rep who sold $200,000 in one fiscal year would receive $25,000 in cómmissions. This system is used to encourage the sales force to work harder throughout the year rather than slack off after they have achieved some success. It also intentionally punishes the poor producers, to needle them to work harder or to leave.

Another variation of straight commission occurs less frequently and is called a "negative commission system." For example, it might call for a 20 percent commission on the first $50,000 in sales during one year, 15 percent on the next $50,000, and only 10 percent on all remaining sales. Thus if a sales rep sold $200,000 under this system, he or she would receive $27,500 in commissions. This system is used to limit the amount of compensation owed to top producers and to encourage some to go into management if they want more money.

Most manufacturers' representatives work on a straight commission basis with no defrayment of expenses by the manufacturer. Sales reps therefore pay their own expenses. This arrangement is preferred by most members of the National Association of Manufacturers' Representatives. They are fiercely independent and universally willing to bet on themselves to earn a high income. They are, in fact, in business for themselves. They frequently have an exclusive territory and can add noncompeting lines of products from other manufacturers. A number of sales engineers and other technically trained people prefer to be independent manufactuers' representatives.

Firms selling insurance, investment securities, and real estate most commonly use this form of compensation. The sales reps' nonselling duties are relatively unimportant, and sales management uses the straight commission plan to emphasize getting orders. Such plans are also common in the clothing, textile, and shoe industries, where the job demands extensive travel and time away from home. The monetary rewards for this sacrifice have to be large to attract good people. Retailers of office equipment, furniture, and business machines often pay outside sales reps on a straight commission basis.

While manufacturers' representatives frequently pay their own expenses, most employers do pay travel and other expenses at a net commission rate. Under this variation the employer has some control over the straight commission sales force employees in that it can direct their routes, acceptable means of transportation, and the like. New salespeople, in particular, prefer having their travel expenses guaranteed regardless of their sales volume. Older top producers generally prefer a higher gross commission.

From the point of view of the company, the straight commission plan is often preferred because all selling expense is a variable cost; hence, price decisions are easier to make. A small firm or one with limited capital can hire any number of sales representatives because there is no addition to the payroll until after sales are made. If markets are thin with a few customers spread over a large geographical area, this may be the only realistic plan of compensation. Manufacturers' reps do fill a real need for many companies.

The straight commission plan, however, has some obvious weaknesses. The rewards are based upon selling; hence, anything the employer wants that will use valuable selling time is fiercely resisted. Commission salespeople may use high-pressure tactics and dirty tricks to gain orders they cannot get otherwise. They will not want to take time to fill in detailed and accurate reports which the home office needs for modifying product features or forecasting sales, for example. Often their loyalty is totally with their accounts, not with the employer, and any disputes or claims are then decided in favor of the customer even when they should not be. Obviously, they will resist any proposed territory reduction or changing the product lines and the accounts which they handle. These problems have caused many sales organizations to move away from the straight commission compensation plan.

Straight Salary Compensation Plan   This is the simplest plan of all, and a generation ago it was very popular. It provides security and stability in the sales reps' income regardless of a bad month, seasonal slack periods, or sickness. It is economical to administer and provides the sales manager with the opportunity to pay at different levels for differing degrees of difficulty of the task. Some products are easier to sell than others, just as some territories are more competitive or physically more demanding. Top producers can be paid proportionately higher salaries than average producers, and many willingly work on a salary basis.

Straight salary is appropriate to compensate the sales force when the job requires considerable missionary or educational work—in drug detailing to doctors, for example. It is used to pay driver salespeople where the delivery function is as important as the selling function. It is common in industries that do heavy 'consumer advertising, in a pull strategy, so that selling is reduced to order taking.

The sales force on a straight salary plan is usually more cooperative in following management directions to push certain products, to obtain market research data, and to prepare detailed reports, for example. Personnel can be transferred more easily and there is generally less resistance to territory changes and reassigning of certain accounts. Selling expenses can be projected easily for future pricing decisions and cash flow. Many top producers prefer a guaranteed good salary over the up-and-down risks inherent in a commission arrangement.

A salary curve can be plotted showing the average compensation paid over the past five years and projected over the next five, allowing for inflation. In addition, a dotted line can indicate how much the top producers were paid and can expect to earn in the near future. When these figures are high enough to attract and keep top producers, the sales manager's job is a lot easier.

The straight salary plan has been declining in importance with most sales organizations, so that today only one in four, or one in five, pays on this basis.[1] Its apparent weakness is the lack of monetary incentives for the seller to do more than an average job. With poor administration, there is a tendency to overpay poor producers and to underpay the top producers. In addition, it is difficult to cut selling expenses when markets are depressed. These apparent weaknesses are problems in sales administration, not in the compensation plan. A modern sales manager can have a highly motivated, successful sales force on a straight salary basis.

Combination Salary Plus Monetary Incentives   Today many sales organizations use a combination of salary plus commission or salary plus bonuses. A basic salary, or a guaranteed drawing account, amounts to

---

[1] *Sales Management,* Jan. 7, 1976, p. 63.

the same thing as far as most salespeople are concerned, particularly the top producers. It must be high enough to attract and keep the top producers. Over and above this minimum compensation, the sales force can earn additional income for performing specified duties. This added compensation is most often given for exceeding sales quotas, although it may be paid for selling a certain product mix, so many new accounts, so many point-of-purchase displays, and so forth. Sales management can put the carrot, or incentive, where it wants to direct the efforts of the sales force.

Those in favor of this combination method claim it has all the advantages of a straight salary plan plus all the advantages of a straight commission plan with none of the disadvantages of either. They claim it gives the sales manager maximum control in directing and motivating the sales force. In fact, the very opposite may occur. Without extremely sensitive adjustments of basic salary and the incentive elements, the problems of both systems will recur.

Weak sales managers prefer this system because it relieves them of judging total performance and compensating proportionately. Either the sales rep achieves stated goals and is paid an agreed amount or does not reach them and is not paid. It appears simple—cut-and-dried. But it does not reward the sales rep who is working successfully on a long-term sale to a target account which may take several years. These highly profitable accounts will be sought by top producers if they receive high earnings along the way. If their earnings are penalized or withheld, they will probably leave.

The combination plan is much more expensive to monitor than either the salary or the commission plan. More detailed records must be maintained and many exceptions must be made to account for windfall sales and house accounts. The base salary or guaranteed drawing account must be high enough to attract and keep good producers; thus it may not save the company any money. The commission or bonus, typically of approximately 20 percent, for example, may not be enough to cause a greater selling effort the year around. These complications cause misunderstandings and complaints which may easily offset the supposed advantages.

Reimbursement of Expenses Most companies are quite liberal in paying sales reps for all legitimate sales expenses. These would include travel, meals, lodging, dry cleaning, laundry, and customer entertainment. In 1976 the average outside sales rep had an expense for the first three items of over $300 per week.[2] Many companies compute the selling expenses as a percentage of sales to maintain some control over abuse of the expense account.

Modern sales managers approve all reasonable expenses and accept the basic honesty of their sales force. Those few reps who attempt to abuse this privilege are quickly identified and can be put on a limited expense account with prior approval required for all unusual expenses. One of the key factors in determining what is reasonable is the customer's expectations. From personal experience, the sales manager should know what customers expect in the salesperson's appearance, method of transportation, entertainment, and so forth. With inflation these costs escalate annually. However, what is expected by customers does not change very much over the years. In addition, good sales managers make frequent trips with their sales reps and can show by example what they consider to be reasonable expenses. The sales manager who "lives it up" on the road can hardly expect the sales force to do less.

One final word of caution should be noted here. The expense account should *never* be used as a form of compensation. Once a sales manager tells a sales rep the firm cannot give a raise but will approve the padding of an expense account by $100 per week, for example, the manager has given this salesperson a license to steal. This unsavory management practice is rare, but it does occur.

MOVEMENT VERSUS MOTIVATION

Most sales managers, and all leading textbooks on the subject, equate money with incentives to motivate the sales force. This is *fundamentally wrong* if one believes in the principles of modern management as expressed by leading authorities in this field. Money, experts say, will cause a certain amount of movement. That is to say, a sales force will

[2] *Sales Management*, Feb. 18, 1976, p. 67.

make so many calls per day—they will move—to receive so many dollars' reward. Money alone will not motivate the sales force. Further, the absence of an adequate payment will cause dissatisfaction. Compensation will cause movement, not motivation.

Motivation exists within every sales rep, and it can either work for the sales manager or it can work against the manager. Assuming the compensation is adequate to attract and keep top producers, sales reps may perform adequately but still not be motivated to do a superior job no matter how much more money is promised. Motivation is caused by the internal psychological needs of the sales rep. These include the need to achieve, the need to earn recognition, the need to accept a challenge, the need to grow and develop, the need to accept responsibility, and so forth. The sales rep who feels he or she cannot satisfy these needs on the job will try to satisfy them off the job.

A sales manager can get movement by manipulating the sales force's external environment. Money, job security, work conditions, use of a company automobile, fringe benefits, and the like, can cause movement. If they are not at least competitive, they can cause dissatisfaction, poor morale, and high turnover. However, even when they are clearly *better* than competition, they do not motivate the sales force. Many top producers earning substantial compensation grow to hate their jobs and become bored doing the same things year in and year out. Sales managers, authors, and consultants who state that more money is an incentive to motivate the sales force are doing a disservice to the very people they are trying to help.

RECYCLING OF HUMAN NEEDS

Abraham H. Maslow, a distinguished behavioral scientist, has constructed a theoretical model which shows how an individual seeks to fulfill various needs at different times in life.[3] He suggests that physiological

[3]A. H. Maslow, *Motivation and Personality,* Harper & Row, Publishers, Incorporated, New York, 1954, pp. 80–85. See also Jerome E. Schnee, Harold Lazarus, and E. Warren Kirby, Part II, "Human Factors in Organizing," in *The Process of Management,* Prentice-Hall, Inc., Englewood Cliffs, N.J., 1977.

needs of the body functions are primary. These include eating, sleeping, and sex. The important point most often overlooked is that each of these needs continually recycles. One breathes and one must breathe again. One eats and one must eat again. An individual never permanently satisfies these needs. If one is near starvation, he or she cannot move to fill higher needs; but if one eats, that does not remove this recycling need. Given a temporary satisfaction of the body functions, a person will seek satisfaction of safety and security needs. In our society, this normally equates to job security or knowing that one can pay the rent or mortgage, finance a car over several years, feed and clothe the family, and so forth. Since no job is totally secure, this need also recycles. When people finally have jobs or professions in which they feel reasonably secure, their next needs are social, for example, the need to affiliate with others in a group. This, too, recycles. When one is lonely, one seeks other people. After being with them for a while, one becomes satiated and then avoids people. Being alone long enough, one again becomes lonely, and the cycle repeats.

The fourth level of need is for self-esteem and self-respect. This equates to a feeling of self-importance and is most often reinforced by recognition, partially by peers but more importantly by superiors. This need for recognition also recycles. One gets a compliment, praise, or a pat on the back, and one is pleased, temporarily. Shortly one seeks recognition again. This is a powerful inner compulsion for most top producers in sales and it constantly recycles.

The highest level of needs is said to be that of self-actualization of achievement, knowledge and understanding, and creating beauty. This supreme level enables the individual to influence his or her environment. On the job it means that one can change the company or influence the direction of the company. This need also recycles as one learns more and can envision better solutions, new ways to accomplish things, or new ways to gain greater satisfactions.

All these levels in Maslow's hierarchy of needs can be more or less active simultaneously, and they can work for the sales manager. But if one cannot get enough recognition on the job, for example, one may get it by joining a union, or from friends in a cocktail lounge. These internal psychological needs exist, and modern sales managers will do their best to see that the job offers opportunities to satisfy them.

INTERVENING VARIABLES

Between an individual's needs and their possible fulfillment lie several variables which may influence the intensity of the need. The first of these is the individual's previous experience or the degree of maturity one has reached at that point in life. For the sales manager, this equates to seeking the degree of maturity of the individual sales representative. How independent is he or she? How adaptable to new people and to new situations?

A second variable is the individual's level of aspiration. The sales manager searches for the sales rep's level of ambition or what one aspires to become in three to five years. Are his ambitions realistic? Is she content with the level of success already attained? Can the person be motivated to want more out of life? It is common in our society for the child to wish to outperform the parent. Unfortunately this situation may cause some salespersons to plateau once they have exceeded this performance level. The sales manager can point out the higher needs of self-importance and self-actualization which can be fulfilled.

A third intervening variable is the group norm or the informal work rules made by the sales reps themselves. These may work against the manager—for example, when informal leaders restrict the number of calls to be made each day. They may also work for the manager when high team spirit causes each representative to want to carry his or her share of the workload or branch quota, for example. Sales managers can influence the group norms when they become aware of them and cause them to be more in line with both the company's and the individual's objectives.

The fourth variable is the sales manager's level of expectations. If the sales manager truly believes the sales reps will perform below average and cheat on their expense accounts, for example, they probably will. Conversely, if the manager believes they will perform well above average and keep their expenses in line, they will rise to meet that level of expectation. The school system has conditioned most Americans to meet the level of expectation of the teacher. If the teacher's standards are low, little effort is made. If the teacher's standards are high, a considerable effort is made to reach them. The same thing is true on the sales job. The sales manager's attitudes and level of expectations from the sales force can influence their performance.

KITA THEORY OF MANAGEMENT

Fred Herzberg, another distinguished psychologist, has advanced modern management theory on motivation in several respects.[4] He uses the acronym, KITA, or "a kick in the behind," to amusingly represent the traditional management tools of the stick and the carrot. He maintains that all the external factors that surround the job, including money, are simply hygiene. Given poor hygiene, you will have dissatisfaction, poor morale, and poor performance. But given good hygiene, you will not

[4]Fred Herzberg, *KITA or What Have You Done for Me Lately?* B.N.A. Films, Inc., Maryland, 1971.

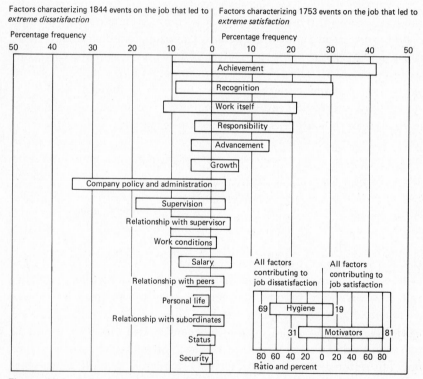

Figure 12-1 Left of center are Frederick Herzberg's hygiene factors drawn from samples of 1685 employees which he studied. To the right of center are the motivating factors which increased job satisfaction in these same studies. *Source:* Frederick Herzberg, "One More Time: How Do You Motivate Employees?" *Harvard Business Review*, January–February 1968, p. 57.

have motivation. He makes the point that all hygiene needs recycle and the *zero point escalates.* If one gets a pay raise, one quickly adjusts to the new level and becomes dissatisfied again in a short time. The higher base pay then becomes the new level, from which the individual will bargain. All compensation, expense accounts, and fringe benefits are hygiene factors with an escalating zero point, and they do provide movement but not motivation.

Herzberg insists motivation is internal and compulsive. The sales rep will do the job because he or she wants to do it, not because the sales manager wants it done. The manager can and should provide opportunities for the sales reps to satisfy their psychological needs on the job. Make the job interesting. Provide challenge to do a more complicated or more sophisticated job. Give people responsibility. Give them the opportunity to belong to a superior group of people. Give them the chance to learn something new, to grow and develop. Give them recognition for achievement.

Herzberg acknowledges that people will move for money, that he would sweep the floor if the pay were high enough. But he insists that, even if he did, he would not be motivated to do a good job. Whatever the pay rate, he would soon adjust to it and want more pay the next time he was asked to sweep the floor.

Not only do people become quickly dissatisfied with the hygiene factors, including money, but Herzberg also makes the point that it is seduction to cause a man or woman to perform a job for money. Management should be providing opportunities for people to do their jobs for reasons of personal satisfaction, achievement, and growth. Pay as much as you have to, in order to attract and keep top producers, and then do not talk about money.

JOB DESIGN AND MOTIVATION

There are five approaches which a sales manager can use to provide opportunities for the sales force to achieve satisfaction because of the job itself. The first is *job enlargement,* which might mean that the sales rep not only sells a product but he or she is given the assignment of training the user to get the most benefits from the product. As noted earlier, the sales force can be trained and used to conduct market research. The results of their findings can influence company decisions about new product lines and other changes.

Job rotation is another method of creating interesting opportunities to grow and develop. This might cause a sales rep to go from a small territory, to one with some large accounts, to specializing in sales to hospitals, government, banks, and so forth. At each new assignment, there is a challenge—an opportunity to achieve, to learn, to grow and develop.

An interesting variation of job rotation occurred in the wholesale liquor industry in New York City. The salespeople have a strong union and the best territories, in terms of highest commissions generated, for the representatives with the highest seniority. When one of these senior people leaves for any reason, each remaining sales rep has the opportunity to move up to a better territory. The entire sales force may change territories and a new trainee is hired to fill the poorest territory. The strong union imposed this technique on management.

Job enrichment is a third way that sales management can provide opportunities to activate positive motivation. As noted in the discussion of training, it discourages a sales rep to make repeated calls on people who do not buy unless the rep has something new to say or to do. When the manager teaches the reps a more sophisticated way to sell, the challenge is renewed, the opportunity to succeed is much better, and the desire to earn recognition is again activated.

Plan-do-control is a fourth approach to increasing motivation on the job. In this approach, the sales rep assumes the responsibility for what his or her job will consist of, what activities shall be emphasized, and how performance shall be measured. Assuming the manager agrees, the person does the job and monitors the ongoing progress and results. The sales reps operating under these conditions can strongly influence their world and their sense of self-importance.

Work simplification is another method of helping the sales force achieve satisfaction by eliminating many of the negative, boring tasks they are asked to perform. In most sales organizations there are numerous forms to be filled out regarding calls, expenses, forecasts, lost orders, customer complaints, sales by product category, and the like. Too often they are read by a clerk who then files them away, after which no decisions are made and no action is taken. A sales manager who wants to help the sales force will take a good look at the paperwork involved in the job. He or she will eliminate what is not used and will automate routine, boring tasks. The computer today can handle much of the detailed work and perform various meaningful analyses as well.

SALES CONTESTS FOR SHORT-TERM MOVEMENT[5]

Winning a sales contest can increase a rep's annual compensation by as much as 25 percent. There are times when a sales manager's primary need is movement, or immediate sales, for company survival, for example. He or she may not have enough time for long-term motivation and self-development of each sales rep. The warehouse walls may be about to burst with merchandise threatening to close down the production line. All of the company's funds may be tied up in an unpopular product which must somehow be converted back to cash. A company may be doing very well and its products may dominate a profitable market, but the stockholders demand faster growth or many good people will lose their jobs. Under such stormy and confusing conditions, a sales manager may devise a series of sales contests and an award system to get the essential sales productivity.

Beyond the objective of stimulating sales volume, contests can be appropriate, along with other efforts, to reduce selling costs, improve team spirit and boost morale, and to improve service to customers. A good contest can produce lasting benefits for both the sales force and the company. Conversely, when a sales contest is used as a substitute for a sound basic compensation plan, it is apt to have poor results. Clearly a good contest should be so designed as to prevent abuses of bunching sales during the contest period, overstocking customers, accepting poor credit risks, and the like.

A true sales contest offers incentives for *every sales rep to do a better job than usual.* Each contest should have clearly defined objectives and include predetermined measures of performance and limiting qualifica-

[5]This entire section is taken with permission of the editors from T. Stroh, *Effective Psychology for Sales Managers,* Parker Publishing Company, Inc., West Nyack, N.Y., 1974.

tions. For example, if the objective of a contest is to get more of an unsold market potential, then finding and selling new customers would be the measurement. The limiting qualifications might include continual selling of old repeat business and new accounts have to be of a minimum size and the initial order *restocked* within 30 days. For every new account, the reward might be a cash bonus or points accumulated toward selected prizes. The sales force might be directed toward several target segments by offering a higher prize for the most desired accounts and descending prizes for the less desirable accounts. In other words, the sales force is given an incentive to keep up their existing sales volume but to do something extra in a particular way for something extra in return.

Sales contests seem to be particularly appropriate for short-term movement or getting the sales force to put forth an extra effort for a limited time period. The incentive, the reward, is external to the sales force and they are asked for action or movement to get the prize. In this case they may willingly make the extra call per day, drive those few extra miles to see another account, or try a little harder in a certain way. When the contest is over the sales force expects to revert back to their old pace of doing business without pressure from the sales manager. This is the implicit bargain between the manager and the sales force. If the manager sets higher performance standards as a result of the short-term contest, he or she is apt to lose respect and effectiveness.

For example, if a company is overstocked, the sales manager may devise a sales contest to move the product out of the warehouse in three months. He or she may build-in various qualifications or limits regarding being eligible to earn a bonus or prize. Many of the sales force will perform well and work extra hard during this three-month period. Because they know they have to live with their accounts after the contest, they will perform with restraint, even if their consciences will not. In any event, at the end of three months, the sales force will experience a letdown emotionally and physically. This is natural and to be expected. The sales manager in this illustration would be wise to arrange some kind of celebration and afterwards go back to the regular pace of work. Company funds which were tied up in inventory are now back in the cash flow and the contest was effective. If the sales force is then punished by new, higher standards, they will have learned not to trust or cooperate with that sales manager in the future.

SALES MEETINGS FOR LONG-TERM MOTIVATION

While a sales contest can be used to get movement for a short period, most sales managers seek other techniques which provide long-term, internally generated motivation. Sales meetings which include information, training, and an awards program can be an excellent vehicle for a long-term motivational program.

Many sales reps operate on their own away from the sales office for days, weeks, or even months at a time. As noted earlier, they often do not understand the company's advertising and distribution policies, and they tend to do what is best for themselves in their limited territories. Under these conditions, it is difficult for the sales reps to identify with others in the same company. Frequently, they do not meet other reps on the same sales force except during annual national sales meetings.

But sales reps do have the need, the inner desire, to belong to a group of admirable people. If they cannot satisfy this need on the job, they will seek to realize it elsewhere. It pays, therefore, for the sales manager to construct sales meetings and award programs which will bring the sales force together as a united team. The manager should provide opportunities for the sales rep to become friendly, to share ideas, opinions, experiences, and knowledge. The sales manager who pits one sales rep against another in vicious competition is risking much more than he or she can possibly gain. Some members of the sales force may withhold leads and inquiries for each other and will keep any personal knowledge or competitive edge to themselves. Cooperation may become nonexistent and open hostility may take its place.

An awards program is basically recognition for a job well done, and it should be a regular planned part of every sales meeting. It may be the reading of a letter from a top executive recognizing and thanking a sales rep for making a significant contribution to the company. It may be the presentation of a trophy or desk clock to be displayed in the office or the sales rep's home. It may be the announcement of a banquet attended by a special few sales reps. It may be the announcement of membership in a golf club or an honorary membership in the President's Club or the Million Dollar Club, for example. The award may take the form of "Sales Rep of the Month" or "Sales Rep of the Year."

In addition to public acknowledgment at company sales meetings, winners of such awards often can and should receive publicity in the company news magazine and in their hometown newspapers as well. Such awards and recognition tend to be long-term motivators because few sales reps get enough praise. After the news becomes old, they will again seek additional recognition, and this is a healthy thing. Membership in an elite group of sales reps tends to strengthen group identity and build team spirit among the best producers. It offers promise of recognition to inexperienced reps or average producers if they become more professional.

Using sales meetings with an awards program should not be confined to the large sales organization. A sales manager of a small branch office can plan a similar recognition program and enlist the cooperation of people in the regional or home office. He or she can write letters of congratulations and offer small awards suitably engraved and framed certificates to be hung on the wall. The manager and spouse can entertain the sales rep and his or her spouse, either at home or out on the town. Even the most cynical sales force will respond to this human treatment and will frequently push themselves harder for this kind of management than they might for contest prizes.

In the past, traditional sales managers said, "Do a good job and the prize is that you get to keep your job." But good sales reps have enough self-confidence to realize they can easily change jobs; thus, to work for that kind of manager simply means that extra effort does not matter. Modern sales managers realize that good sales reps have a strong need to belong to a superior sales force, to socialize with them, and to be recognized for their superior achievements. They will work long and hard to satisfy these internal needs; therefore, the manager utilizes sales meetings with built-in awards programs to activate these needs. Such desires are continually recycling and escalating, and they operate as long-term motivators.

SUMMARY

Top sales producers are confident they will earn a lot of money no matter what the payment system may be. If they cannot do so with one company, they will leave for another. To these highly desirable people, it does not matter whether the system is called straight salary, commission, or some combination. Sales reps know that, if they have a good year, their compensation will go up, and if they have a poor year, they may be asked to leave.

It seems apparent that it is more dignified for most industries to pay a straight salary, competitive enough to attract and keep top producers, rather than a combination or straight commission. This should produce the optimum profit on sales expense dollars. It will not motivate but it will avoid dissatisfaction. A career salary curve can be constructed to show the entire sales force and new applicants what they can expect to earn if they are average and what is possible if they are top producers in future years. Men and women should not be seduced into doing a job for payment of money if they can be shown how to do the job for reasons of personal satisfaction.

All normal humans have inner psychological needs—compulsions—which they can satisfy on the job if management provides the right opportunities. Top sales producers may have stronger psychological needs than the average person, and these include interest in the job, the need to achieve, and the needs to earn recognition, to accept a challenge, to accept responsibility, and to grow and develop. These are powerful motivating factors which continually recycle and escalate.

Some of the approaches which sales managers can use to activate these psychological needs include job enlargement, job rotation, job enrichment, plan-do-control, and work simplification. Each of these approaches can provide opportunities for the sales force to satisfy their inner compulsions.

Assuming the compensation plan is at least competitive or better, to attract and keep top producers, sales contests can be used successfully to gain an extra effort—movement—for a relatively short period. The bonus or prize may have to be substantial—as much as 20 percent of annual pay—and the contest rules carefully constructed to prevent abuse. In addition, the implicit bargain is that the sales force can revert back to the old norm once the contest ends. Under certain stressful business conditions such a short-term effort can be justified by sales managers.

Most sales managers, however, search for and develop long-term motivational programs which are *not* money-oriented. The primary tools they use are sales meetings which are informative and educational and have a built-in awards program. Typically, they attempt to unite the sales force into a friendly, cooperative team of superior people. Individual recognition for achievement is generous and well publicized. Inexperienced newcomers and average producers are encouraged to become more professional and to earn the recognition that they, too, have joined the superior team. Such needs and satisfactions continually recycle and escalate. The sales manager's skillful use of such motivational factors can do much to minimize the sales expense and to optimize profit, which is his or her basic responsibility.

QUESTIONS

1 What are the advantages and disadvantages of compensating a sales force by straight commission?

2 What are the advantages and disadvantages of compensating a sales force by straight salary?

3 What is the danger in compensating a sales force by salary plus bonus or commission?

4 What are Maslow's five levels of needs, and how do they recycle?

5 What are Herzberg's hygiene factors, and what are motivational factors?

6 What are the five approaches which a sales manager can use to provide opportunities for the sales force to achieve satisfaction because of the job itself?

7 Under what conditions would a sales contest be more appropriate?

8 How can sales meetings be used to develop long-term motivational programs?

SELECTED REFERENCES

Dartnell Survey of Compensation of Salesmen (semiannual, with the 18th survey published in 1976), The Dartnell Corporation, Chicago, Ill.

Herzberg, Red: *KITA or What Have You Done for Me Lately?* 16 mm film, 30 min, color, B.N.A. Films, Inc., Maryland, 1971.

Johnson, H. Webster: "Sales Contests," chap. 9, "Compensating Salespeople," chap. 10, and "Compensation—Fringe Benefits and Expenses," chap. 11 in *Sales Management,* Charles E. Merrill Books, Inc., Columbus, Ohio, 1976.

Lombardi, Vincent: *Commitment to Excellence,* 16 mm film, 30 min, color, Bureau of Business Practices, National Sales Development Institute, Waterford, Conn., 1974.

Schnee, Jerome E., Harold Lazarus, and **E. Warren Kirby:** "Human Factors in Organizing," part II in *The Process of Management,* Prentice-Hall, Inc., Englewood Cliffs, N.J., 1977.

Stanton, William J., and **Richard H. Buskirk:** "Designing and Administering a Compensation Plan," chap. 13 and 14, "Salesmen's Expenses and Transportation," chap. 15, "Morale," chap. 17, and "Stimulation of Salesmen," chap. 18, all in *Management of the Sales Force,* 4th ed., Richard D. Irwin, Inc., Homewood Ill., 1974.

Stroh, Thomas F.: "Five Psychologically Effective Ways to Activate Salesmen," chap. 3 in *Effective Psychology for Sales Managers,* Parker Publishing Company, Inc., West Nyack, N.Y., 1974.

Something to Work For, 16 mm film, 30 min, color, Beverly Hills, Calif., 1968.

▶ **Case 12-1**

SMITH & MAKAR

This is a building supply wholesaler. They cover two counties and sell almost exclusively to contractors. The firm is twenty years old. They employ six full-time salespeople in the field. They have one full-time salesperson at their warehouse, where they have a small showroom.

The building industry fluctuates greatly with the economy. In good times their sales reps can make up to $50,000 a year and in bad times they will make only around $10,000. All salespersons receive large commissions on what they sell. Mr. Makar believes this is their prime motivator. The company also has employee medical and insurance benefits, plus many other "fringe" benefits.

There is no training program as such. A new salesperson goes into the field with an experienced one for about four or five months. The length of time really depends on how much past experience one has had. The new salesperson is usually brought in to take the position of someone who has left. One of the salespeople has been with the company for about fifteen years now. Each of the two counties they serve is divided up into three geographical territories. Each salesperson sells their entire line.

Both Smith and Makar select their salespeople personally, usually after interviews by each and then after one interview by both of them. New staff are judged on their knowledge of the industry, personal contacts that they may have, experience, and appearance. The owners look for older and experienced salespeople. They require no written tests.

Mr. Makar feels, "Money spent on advertising is pretty much wasted. You need a one-to-one relationship between sales rep and customer." Mr. Smith did say that he is starting to think differently, though, because sales are way off this year.

They both said their main problem was motivating salespeople when the economy was in bad shape.

1 Do the partners seem to understand motivation?

2 What factors have they apparently overlooked?

▶ Case 12-2

DECA SELLING ADVERTISING

As a member of the County Community College Chapter of the Distributive Education Clubs of America (DECA), Miss Kathie McManus was given a sales problem to help solve. A major source of club financing was selling advertising space in the college newspaper, *The Phoenix.* On all ads that were solicited by club members her club received 40 percent of the advertising fees. The remaining portion went back into a fund for the operation of the newspaper. In addition to selling the advertisements, the club members would lay out the ads, collect the fees due, and answer any incoming calls about *Phoenix* advertising. Because they are a sales and marketing club, they were given this opportunity. Not only would they gain financially, but they would also gain valuable business experience running the advertising section of a newspaper. However, they were not very successful. As a result of the lack of advertising in the newspaper, they began to feel pressure from the college advisor for *The Phoenix,* Mr. Ball, to improve their performance of the past and get more ads in the paper. If they could not do this, Mr. Ball said he would be forced to find another club to do the job. Realizing the potential to make money, they did not want to give up working with *The Phoenix.* They had to find a way to motivate their members.

For the last year only a few people were actually selling ads and helping with the layouts. The club's finances were lacking and the pressure from Mr. Ball was increasing. The problem as they saw it was how to motivate DECA club members to sell advertisements to local business establishments. They realized this was only part of the problem. They needed to gather facts that would convince local business people that by advertising in *The Phoenix* they were indeed reaching a market of potential buyers.

1   How can DECA members be motivated to sell more ads?

2   How can they convince the local business establishments that they will benefit from advertising in *The Phoenix?*

▶ Case 12-3

MEDIPHASICS SYSTEMS CORPORATION

Ted Klich, vice president of sales for Mediphasics Systems Corporation, is confronted with designing a new sales representative compensation system for his company. The current compensation system has caused many disputes among the salespeople concerning equitable payment for their efforts in the field. More recently the firm has experienced an increasing turnover rate of sales reps. This attracted the attention of upper management, and after two meetings with the marketing executives, a decision emerged to redesign the current compensation system.

Mediphasics Systems Corporation's main line of business is selling and installing small- and medium-scale computer systems in hospitals throughout the United States. The corporation has already successfully designed and installed computer systems in many hospitals over the past five years. The main tasks of the sales reps are twofold: (1) seeking out new accounts and submitting the proposals to marketing management for screening and evaluation, and (2) maintaining a close relationship with current clients to solicit additional services that may be performed.

The current compensation system is a combination of straight salary plus commission and some expenses. The fixed amount is intended to satisfy the salesperson's need for some stability of income. The variable amount is intended to reward and stimulate greater effort. The straight salary component represents the bulk of the salesperson's income while performing the first, foremost task as mentioned above. After a proposal is submitted, reviewed, evaluated, and approved, the commission component of the compensation plan comes into play. Here the salesperson receives a fixed percentage of the net profit received from the new client. Expense allowances for all salespersons are standardized and are intended to stimulate and reward greater effort.

In the past year, two of Mediphasics Systems' clients proved to be considerably more profitable than initially expected, causing the salespersons who worked on these accounts to reap extremely high rewards. The management of the corporation was very pleased with the progress of their relatively young business and were readily willing to meet the expenditures of the current compensation plan. Salespersons who worked at Mediphasics longer than those who were reaping the rewards harbored feelings of resentment. Over the past three months five salesmen left the firm, and this attracted the attention of upper management. In light of this fact, and the future plans for rapid expansion, management decided that it would be necessary to redesign the compensation system to help the situation in the marketing sector of the corporation.

1 What is your evaluation of their compensation plan?

2 What would you recommend for the future?

▶ Case 12-4

DRANO BUILDING SUPPLIES CORPORATION

In 1973 the construction industry was active throughout the country and especially booming in several areas. South Florida was one of these areas. In fact the South Florida area, combining Palm Beach, Broward, and Dade Counties, comprised 20 percent of the total construction volume nationwide. Most of this volume was invested in the condominium market.

Drano Corporation has been a material supplier to the building market for many years. They are one of the largest general material suppliers servicing the South Florida market. Their products included ready-mix concrete, concrete block, lumber, wood roof trusses, hardware, and other smaller-type products. Their main office, warehouse, and batch plant is located in Hollywood, Florida, which is centrally located for Dade and Broward Counties. Drano Corporation services the market by the use of outside salespeople. The salespeople are responsible for canvassing their area, finding all new projects, and dealing with the contractor/developer as the project progresses. The sales reps are able to quote prices on some items, such as most lumber prices and prices on concrete block. They must get pricing on ready-mix concrete and roof trusses from their sales manager because of pricing variations due to the size of the project and travel time for the delivery trucks. The salespeople are not permitted to reduce a price but must relay all complaints and inquiries to their sales manager.

During the boom years of 1972, 1973, and 1974 the demand for building materials exceeded the supply. All the firms were striving to increase their capacity because of this excess demand. The salespeople had to get their orders into the plant and follow them up. Any delay in the delivery was costly to the contractor and made acquiring recorders more difficult. The sales reps had to bear the brunt of all customer complaints.

In order to motivate the salespeople to develop new accounts and to service the active accounts, Drano Corporation used as a compensation basis a fixed salary with a commission for total sales reported. While the fixed salary provided some security, it was not enough for personal satisfaction. The commissions were a percentage of the total sales for each product line for a month's period. The percentage paid varied for each product as a result of the difficulty in acquiring the account. The commissions to the salespeople were computed by top management and then reduced by the expenses incurred by the firm in placing the salesperson in the field. The rep was charged with a portion of company overhead and with the expense of the company-owned automobile provided for his or her use. How management arrived at the total commission paid each sales rep was not discussed with the rep. In the big-volume years this was not a major bone of contention because everyone was making good commissions and was basically happy.

In the latter part of 1974 the market fell into a recession; the sales volume dropped, and so did the commission payments. All the salespeople complained about the decrease and wanted to know how the commissions paid were computed. They were told that the decrease was due to the reduced volume, an increase in the company overhead percentage charged to each salesperson due to reduction of outside salespeople, the charge for the company automobile, and a change in company policy concerning old accounts. Drano felt that a sales rep should not get a percentage of an account that had been established for a long time. These were referred to as "company accounts." The sales reps were responsible for maintaining the volume from those accounts but would not receive any extra compensation for their efforts. Drano felt this service should be part of the salesperson's base salary. When this became known, a number of salespeople left the firm, a couple of sales managers left, and morale dropped to a low level. Sales reps no longer wanted to service these company accounts for which they were not reimbursed while they were charged for their expense.

Because of the reduced sales, the profits for Drano have declined drastically, forcing them into major reductions. They expect their salespeople to cover more territory, service more accounts, and help out in the office. They feel the salespeople should be willing to accept a lower commission until the industry makes a recovery.

1 How can the Drano Corporation reduce the unrest between management and salespeople?

2 How can they get the salespeople to increase their workload without any extra compensation?

Part

DIRECTING
AND DECISION MAKING

Directing a sales force is the day-to-day adaptation to
a changing environment with each sales rep gaining
more experience and more knowledge. Setting
short-term targets and showing each rep how to work
smarter, not harder, is the key to efficient sales
direction. Management tools and systems are
available which can guide the sales manager in
analyzing problems and opportunities and assist in
making better decisions about what should be done.

13

On-the-Job
Coaching and Evaluating

▶ Objectives

The reader will understand the value of field sales supervisors and the purpose of on-the-job coaching with close supervision of inexperienced reps and broad supervision of top producers. He or she will be able to use the supervisor's evaluation techniques in preapproach planning, the presentation, objections, aggressiveness, close, and follow-up planning. The reader will also understand and be able to use the technique of providing negative feedback to correct a single weakness of the sales rep observed.

In many sales organizations today the traditional sink-or-swim attitude prevails, once the sales rep has finished the formal training program. He or she is expected to do the job with a minimal amount of further help. This eliminates at least one level of administrative expense—the field supervisor. Unfortunately this method may cost much more than it might save, as the result of either high turnover of new reps who cannot survive or the high cost of hiring experienced reps.

The modern approach used by many companies is to provide the new trainees with a detailed written job description which tells them exactly what is expected of them and how their field supervisor will coach and evaluate them on the job. They are assigned to a territory and given room to make mistakes, but they are also observed during calls. They expect counseling and they have an empathetic person who will listen to their problems and share their successes. They have someone close by who cares about their progress—who can accelerate their training and development. Some may need help with personal problems, and most will welcome guidance in their career-path ambitions.

CLOSE SUPERVISION VERSUS BROAD SUPERVISION

Normally a new sales rep with little or no sales experience is watched closely for the first week or two in the territory. Depending on how adequately the formal sales training program prepared them, they may ride with the supervisor and observe how he or she handles the accounts. After a day or two, the supervisor is no longer the model to be imitated but now becomes an observer of the new sales rep. After each call, or certainly at the end of the day, the results of each call are discussed in detail. The supervisor may point out many things that were handled well as well as other ways to handle the things that did not go well.

As the trainees become more proficient and self-confident, the supervisor may simply meet them at the end of the day to listen to their self-analysis of what occurred. If there are no major problems after a week or two, the supervisor may simply meet the new sales reps on Friday afternoons for several months. This loosening of control may be broadened to meeting only once a month on a regularly scheduled basis. However, the supervisor is available to help whenever asked, and he or she has the responsibility to observe directly whenever trainees feel that something may not be right.

Good field supervisors do not simply go along where the sales rep elects to call on that given day. Sales reps are normal, healthy people who will not willingly expose their faults and weaknesses to their superior. They will call on friendly accounts who make them look good. A good field supervisor will ask the rep to take him or her on several calls to unsold accounts and to places where the rep never called before in addition to a few friendly accounts.

Experienced sales supervisors also ride with the older experienced reps, but much less often, of course. These top producers are independent and resent any police action by management. The supervisor will often ask to be shown how the top producer handles certain problems so that he can teach the good technique to the newer reps. In this way the supervisor causes the top producer to show off in areas of specific interest to the supervisor. For example, a large customer may write the sales manager with a complaint about slow deliveries. The manager can ask the supervisor to ride with the top producer to see how he handles this irate customer and earns his confidence and patience.

When a top producer is skeptical about a new technique or method of selling, he or she may very well invite the supervisor to show how it will work on a particularly difficult account. The producer makes the call together with the supervisor in the role of the sales rep and with the latter as observer. In addition, top producers will ask for help in selling an account if that is what it will take to win it.

Thus, supervisors do observe all members of the sales force, closely at first until the trainees earn the supervisor's confidence. As the new rep gains experience and becomes more productive, the supervisor moves to broad or general supervision with only occasional direct observation. The emphasis is always on helping and counseling the entire sales force. While some supervisors have a checklist to be used for each individual call, the best supervisors observe the steps used or omitted, the reasoning behind the actions taken or things said, the amount of aggression shown, and the follow-up planning which may occur after the call. In addition, they will evaluate the apparent experience, sophistication, and maturity of the sales rep being observed.

PREAPPROACH PLANNING

Before making a call, the supervisor wants to know what the sales rep expects or hopes to accomplish by calling on this account now. What person or persons will the sales rep ask to visit and what tactics will he or she use with each one? How much sales pressure or aggression does the sales rep plan to exert?

Without planning, the sales rep's chances of succeeding are greatly diminished. Is the expectation of getting an order from this account today realistic? Perhaps this call should be to find out information about this account, such as who are the existing suppliers and what problems the prospect may be having. If the sales rep has only one name to ask to visit, what will he or she do if that one person is not there today? Could one realistically see several different buying influences in the same company today? Can one attempt to sell one item to the purchasing agent and also plant some money-saving ideas about other items with a department manager for future sales?

How much research has the sales rep done to understand this prospect's industry and particular company? Does he or she know of the previous dealings or sales experiences of this account? Is their credit rating and size within acceptable limits? Can they potentially buy an amount which justifies the time and effort to make a sale? What other customers' names might be used to interest or impress this prospect?

Precall planning also involves the collecting of all the catalogs, pictures, specification data, proposals, letters of testimonial, samples, and so forth. These items should be carefully selected beforehand for this particular prospect so that, if things go well, everything needed will be readily convenient. If they are not, a second call may be required, and in the meantime the prospect may lose interest.

Has the sales rep prepared to answer questions or objections this particular prospect is apt to raise? Good preparation often includes getting additional technical information and support from someone within the selling company before the call is made. Many such problems can be anticipated and preparations made to resolve them favorably.

PRESENTATION

When the supervisor knows what the sales rep plans to do in a call, he or she can listen objectively to whatever is said and done in the prospect's presence. The first five minutes of the interview are crucial because they set the tone for the rest of the sales call.[1] The sales professional will

[1] See "The Virgin Interview," in Barry J. Hersker and Thomas F. Stroh, *The Purchasing Agent's Guide to the Naked Salesman,* Cahners Publishing Company, Boston, 1975.

correctly gauge the prospect's receptivity. The first sales objective is to establish a reason or justification for the prospect's continued interest in looking at samples, catalogs, or whatever. The buyer is obligated *not* to waste time chasing merchandise or a sales proposition of questionable value.

If all has proceeded well, the buyer will now be interested and personally predisposed to keep an open mind. The sales professional's second objective is to present facts about the unique product advantages and benefits which the prospect can receive. Here a meaningful dialogue should begin. The supervisor observing the conversation will also be looking for ways that the sales professional tailors the talk to this specific buyer and industry. Does he or she show that time has been spent thinking about this special prospect?

The sales professionals are skillful in the use of questions to draw the prospect out of his or her protective shell. In addition, they are good listeners who encourage the buyer to expand or elaborate on a position or a problem. The dialogue becomes a true two-way conversation with both parties attempting to solve a problem or achieve greater efficiencies or satisfactions. Some older salespeople tend to talk too much in an attempt to dominate the conversation. A supervisor may secretly time the number of minutes the prospect is allowed to talk and later show the stopwatch to the dominating salesperson. It comes as a shock to such reps to learn that they typically talked 70 to 80 percent of the time with a buyer even when their purpose was to gain information from the buyer.[2]

THE SALES PRESSURE PRINCIPLE

Speaking in broad generalities, how "pushy" should Willy Loman be expected to be during the sales interview? Naturally, this will vary on the basis of circumstances and less definitively according to the personality of the sales rep. However, certain empirically verifiable assumptions can be made.

All things being equal, the true sales professionals will push as hard

[2]See Thomas F. Stroh, *The Uses of Video Tape in Training and Development,* American Management Association, New York, 1969, pp. 19–23.

during the sales interview as their confidence in their ability and their proposition will permit. Simply put, if they are not convinced, they will not try to bother a prospect very long. But if they are convinced they can be of service to the buyer, they will push in direct response to their own level of self-confidence.

In addition, the aggression that the professional manifests is in inverse relation to the repeat-sale potential perceived by him or her at a given point in time as it relates to the total monetary gain. Items with high repeat-sale potential (raw materials, supplies, and resale items, for example) will most appropriately be sold with a low aggression index. The professional is after a long-term relationship and cannot risk offending the purchaser. The professional is master of the "soft sell."

"One-shot deals," with no repeat-sale potential, will be sold with a high aggression index potential. If the professional does have to take no for an answer from a purchasing agent, for example, he or she has nothing to lose. Sales professionals are free to be as aggressive as their confidence, gall, and common sense permit. This is a major cause for the professional to seek some middle manager to do some "back door" buying.

High aggression may take many forms. That is, the greatest pressure in a "hard sell" may not always be recognizable as high aggression per se. It may be blatant flattery or an ego massage. It may be solving the wrong problem or be a padded service. The true sales professionals will not give up easily when they are convinced the prospect will benefit from the purchase of their goods and services. The observing supervisor will note the amount of aggression and judge its degree of being appropriate.

OBJECTIONS

Observing how a sales rep handles a prospect's objections can give the supervisor tremendous insight into the rep's knowledge, skills, and attitudes. New reps and experienced but poor producers often resent objections as an affront to their basic honesty. They feel the prospect simply does not believe they are telling the whole truth. Another common reaction of poor producers is one of frustration in failing to communicate. This is often transferred and comes out as assuming that the prospect was too dumb to understand or to see the advantages of the sales proposition.

Sales professionals, on the other hand, when faced with objections do not get rattled, confused, or abusive. They recognize that it is a common phenomenon for people to be suspicious and resist any suggestions made by strangers. Many prospects want to feel they know the sales rep and understand his or her motivation before they will warm up enough to trust what the rep says or place any confidence in the claims made for the product. They want to feel the rep is honestly looking out for their welfare.

Frequently prospects rebel against sales reps who fail to develop a personal knowledge of the buyer. The prospect may know the supplying company very well, but he or she may feel slighted if the buyer's feelings have not been given the opportunity to be expressed. The buyer's sense of self-importance has not been catered to sufficiently to justify being friendly toward the sales rep. These feelings may or may not be conscious in the buyer's mind, but they are very real and represent a considerable obstacle to any sale.

As the professional's presentation unfolds or is completed, many prospects object to buying because they do not understand the actual offer being made. When a buyer says no at this point, he may mean that the presentation does not seem complete. The professional recognizes that this type of objection is, in reality, a request for more information in order to make an intelligent decision. The prospect may be leaning toward a purchase but wants to be reassured on some doubtful points.

Other objections which are indicative of a lack of information are those which say the value offered is not equal to the sacrifice required. The prospect must believe the benefits of acquiring the product or service are greater than the loss of cash or the discomfort of doing without the product or great enough for the buyer to avoid the unpleasantness of switching suppliers. Often a buyer is weighing the benefits of acquiring product A first against the benefits of acquiring product B first, and the professional will be able to bring this out in the conversation.

Sales supervisors realize the rep must determine, during the interview, whether the objection is based on reason or on emotion. Real and emotional objections will be handled by the professional with tact and often indirectly. Real and rational objections, on the other hand, are handled openly and with logic. The observing supervisor will recognize when the professional is probing for information to make this determination. He or she will also recognize when the poor performer jumps to a conclusion prematurely and makes the wrong moves.

CLOSE

A sales trainee is observed for the number and type of sales interviews he or she conducts and the competence shown in handling the presentation and answering objections. The supervisor looks for evidence of the trainee's potential and for areas requiring possible further training. The acid test for new sales reps, however, is the total orders obtained. Closing the sale is the ultimate objective.

New sales reps are often ill at ease when it comes to the critical moment of asking for the order. They may not have confidence in their presentation or demonstration and are afraid to have their worst fears confirmed by hearing a prospect say no. Rather than risk such a major catastrophe, they rationalize their way out of the interview by promising to bring more literature or other information on their next visit. While this behavior may seem natural from their point of view, it more often than not creates doubts in the prospect's mind which may not have existed before the sales reps lost their nerve.

Sales reps who give an honest presentation have earned the right to ask for the order, and buyers respect their sincerity when they do ask for the order. The supervisor will observe how many times the sales rep asked for the order and how many different closing techniques were used. Most companies teach at least seven closing techniques which can be used within one interview. Top producers use them naturally and effectively without appearing too aggressive or boring.

Another area which the supervisor observes is how the sales rep handles the prospect who decides to buy a competitive product or service. When the prospect makes that decision, it is apt to be tentative and full of doubts. The emotionally mature sales rep will wish the lost prospect well and assure him that the sales rep will always stand ready to help him in the future. When the new supplier falls down on delivery or service, the former prospect will wish he had purchased from the friendly sales rep.

In commercial, industrial, and consumer selling, buyers return to the market again and again. The patient sales reps who can learn to be good losers as well as good winners can build their personal reputation over the years and their honesty and sincerity will ultimately ensure their success.

FOLLOW-UP PLANNING

After the call has been completed, a good supervisor will ask the sales rep what he or she plans to do on the next visit to that same account. The answers will be most revealing as to the rep's own insight into what really occurred during the interview. The discussion will also show the rep's optimistic attitude toward future success with this one account or a pessimistic attitude, and either one may, or may not, be realistic.

Potentially good producers frequently learn quickly, and immediately after the call is the best time to recognize what one has done wrong or poorly. A discussion with the supervisor may bring out some critical points which occurred during the interview. The sales rep should then be able to think of better ways to handle such points in the future. Good producers will have ideas about new ways to approach that same account or different solutions to solve the prospect's problems. They may recognize their own need to learn more and to get help from a specialist inside their company.

The poor producers will probably attempt to rationalize their mistakes away by blaming the prospect's mood and intelligence. They may complain about their own prices being too high or that their products lack certain features. Even in the rare event that one or more of these things may be true, such negative thinking is self-defeating. It builds frustration and inhibits creative thinking so that the next time they call on that same account, they are doomed to make the same mistakes again.

EVALUATING

If a knowledgeable sales supervisor travels with any sales rep from eight o'clock in the morning until five o'clock at night, he or she can compile a very lengthy list of the faults that have been observed. This is only natural. If the supervisor were to comment on every mistake throughout the day, the sales rep would soon become discouraged. Even if the supervisor confined the comments to major mistakes, it might discourage the sales rep. Any negative feedback to the sales rep during the working day is very likely to change his or her subsequent performance.

In most cases, it is best for the supervisor to observe a number of calls before providing any feedback to the rep. In this way, the chances that the supervisor will make a false snap judgment are reduced, and the sales rep will probably be encouraged to continue his or her efforts independently. Most sales reps will do many things right on every call and probably not do as well on some things as the supervisor might like on all calls. However, if the rep is totally unprepared, or if a weakness becomes painfully obvious during the morning, the supervisor might do better by calling a halt to the observations and having a serious talk with the poor producer.

The sales reps will usually ask for some feedback after each interview, even when they know the rules of the situation. An effective technique in this situation is simply to reflect the sales reps' questions back to them. For example, when the reps ask how well they did in closing the sale, the supervisor reflects, "How well do you think you did?" Obviously, favorable comments can be volunteered by the supervisor when they are honest. If the rep should press the supervisor for an opinion the supervisor can reply, "I'd rather reserve judgment until I see a few more calls; then I'll discuss it with you."

When the rep does something wrong and is obviously aware of it, the coach can comment sympathetically that he or she too has made many similar mistakes. If the rep complains about the amount of time it takes to handle all the paperwork, the coach can smile his understanding and avoid criticism or attempts to justify the system at that point. Throughout the day the coach is the friendly authority who is interested in helping each rep personally rather than the public relations officer speaking for top management or the policeman looking for petty violations.

At the end of the observation period it is preferable to have the sales reps begin the critique by describing what was accomplished that day. The kinds of things they talk about will provide the coach with some indication of the reps' self-awareness and possibly some blind spots. For example, a salesman may point with pride to the sheer number of calls he made that day. A saleswoman may take pleasure in achieving good reactions from a tough account she has been working on for months and ignore the fact that the account has little potential in relation to the time spent.

The coach may also comment favorably on a number of things that the salesperson was observed to do well. For example, one might ask, "Did you realize when Mr. Johnston really got interested in your presentation?" By praising and probing, the coach can learn more about the rep's awareness of human relations and the communication process. Occasionally, a favorable turn in a sales interview may be due to luck or to the rep's intuitive behavior. When the phenomenon is called to his or her attention during the critique, the rep may want to know more about it and how to bring it about intentionally. Obviously, the worker will be receptive to this kind of suggestion from the coach.

After the rep has discussed the good points of the day, it would seem wise to ask the rep what the rep feels are generally his or her strongest points, including those that may not have been illustrated that day. This question causes most reps to think of themselves in relation to other reps. Their response should provide some clues about their readiness to face the truth about themselves. Their self-image will probably not square exactly with the supervisor's view of them, but the two views can be compared in general. If they omit some important areas, the coach can ask them directly how they would rate themselves on these points.

Although the focus is on the positive—the good points of the day and the strengths of the rep in general—some weaknesses will naturally come out in the conversation. In addition, the reps will probably refer to some of the things they were not able to do effectively during the day. During this process, some of their hidden emotions may come to light. For example, in discussing a weakness in trying to close, one rep may say, "You know, it's strange because I never thought much about it, but I just realized that I don't feel comfortable forcing someone to make a decision." Whenever the reps can correctly identify their own weakness, the supervisor should be cautious in attempting to change their behavior. For example, if one realizes that he or she is weak in approaching new accounts, the supervisor might decide the rep needs more training in this area. On the other hand, the salesperson might decide to avoid new accounts and concentrate on getting more business out of regular accounts. In this case, training is not likely to change the rep's behavior. Once the salesperson admits a weakness, the manager might ask, "What do you think you can, or should, do about it?" The coach is really asking the rep if he or she is ready and willing to change behavior in a positive way.

If the reps do not admit to any weakness, they may justify their mediocre results by claiming that their territory is poor or that the general economic situation is bad, for example. Telling them that they are weak in an area and need training will do little or nothing for such representatives. They are not ready to accept the truth about themselves. The coach should not, however, let a rep off easy at this point. One might pinpoint one weakness which showed up on several calls and ask the rep to explain how it occurred each time. If the rep is still extremely defensive, the supervisor might explain how other reps handle similar situations much more effectively. Finally, the supervisor can offer to prove that the suggestions will work by modeling the appropriate behavior. This challenge can hardly be ignored. It is really a contingency close because the supervisor is saying, "If I can show you a better way to do this, will you admit your way is weak?" The use of audio-taped interviews will counteract the reps' defenses of faulty recall or disbelief that they really did as the coach says.

The entire process is designed to isolate one area of weakness that is seriously holding the rep back and that can be corrected by training. Going into every item on the typical checklist can destroy a poor rep's self-confidence, and this serves no purpose. The coach will achieve more positive results by focusing the critique on one key area. The supervisor might say, for example, "Let's not worry about these other points for now, Charlie. Let's look at this one thing. I believe that if we can improve your opening, you'll see a tremendous jump in your sales figures." With constructive criticism, the coach helps build the rep's self-confidence, and the rep is then able to concentrate on correcting the one area. As the rep improves, the coach can move on to the other areas—again, one at a time. Under these conditions, reps will take direction more readily as they realize that the coach is steadily helping them to grow.

When coaching an effective salesperson, the supervisor can be liberal in giving praise; however, one should not overlook minor faults simply because the rep is so good by comparison. The rep may never realize he or she has an offending habit or a distracting mannerism or whatever their minor fault may be unless the coach calls attention to it. The supervisor may prefer to treat this rep as an equal and offer a friendly tip or two in a casual way by pointing to future promotions. Every rep is entitled to constructive criticism which will enable him or her to become more effective in the future.

Contrary to popular thinking, older salespersons can learn new skills. They can learn to use computer analyses and printout information, to make forecasts, to plan their own activities, and to carry out their plans independently. They can be assigned new duties involving customers and other people who relate to older salespeople better than to young ones. Because of their age, older salespersons are often more loyal to their sales organization, and this makes them ideal for many public relations assignments. The rigorous demands of the selling profession do not lessen as a salesperson gets on in years. All salespeople need encouragement, recognition, and praise on a regular basis. When older salespeople seem to reach a plateau of productivity, they are often reflecting the sales supervisor's attitude. If the supervisor has given up trying to change the older sales rep's behavior, the person cannot be expected to change, or adapt, or to meet new challenges.

The supervisor who sincerely cares for the individual will continually encourage each rep to develop his or her potential capabilities. Many creative people do not develop their talent until later in life, after they have had considerable experience dealing with the mechanics of their profession. An older rep often has a wealth of technical product information and a knowledge of customer applications which can be used constructively in the development of new products. Some older salespersons compensate for their lower energy level by intelligently analyzing the markets and using their effort where it will do the most good.

On-the-job coaching is a natural situation for helping reps to identify and set their goals realistically. The reps cannot always do this on their own because of the day-to-day demands on their time and thoughts and because of their limited knowledge of the various opportunities within the organization. The sales manager or supervisor is in a position to guide the rep's thinking by asking specific questions regarding career goals and by providing additional information. In this sense, the long-term goals of the coach, the company, and the individual sales rep should blend into a mutual objective, with each component helping the others.

SUMMARY

While some sales organizations prefer to eliminate the cost of the administrative level of field sales supervisors, modern management recommends they be used as coaches to accelerate the growth and development of the entire sales force. Normally, close supervision is most effective for new, inexperienced sales reps and is gradually broadened as they gain skills and self-confidence. Broad supervision is usually more effective with top producers.

Areas observed by a supervisor making calls with the sales reps begin with preapproach planning of what will be the purpose of a particular call and what tactics will be used. The presentation is then observed—particularly, how it is adapted to the unique prospect or customer and how much the buyer is encouraged to participate in a two-way conversation.

How the sales rep handles the customer's objections usually reveals whether or not he or she has sufficient knowledge about the products and services of the firm and those of the competition. It also shows whether the rep knows how to probe for information to determine the validity of an objection and whether it is emotional or logical.

Throughout the sales interview, the sales pressure principle is observed to see whether the rep is acceptably aggressive when that is necessary without becoming obnoxious. The frequency of repeat sales often determines how pushy or aggressive the rep may become in an inverse ratio. The greater the repeat-sales potential, the softer the pressure.

The attitude of the sales rep toward asking for the order often determines his or her success. Supervisors recognize that high producers close often and have many different techniques which they can use in the same interview. Their self-confidence clearly shows they have earned the right to ask for the order. In addition, top producers show they can be good losers when necessary and come back again for future orders.

The final area of interest to the supervisor is how the sales rep handles the follow-up planning immediately after the sales call. This will reveal the rep's personal insight into what actually occurred as well as his or her attitude about what is possible on future calls on that same account.

Usually at the end of the day, in a relaxed atmosphere, the supervisor attempts to evaluate the individual rep and his or her readiness to accept constructive criticism. The supervisor tries to isolate one area of weakness which if improved would increase the rep's effectiveness to a large degree. By concentrating criticism on a single area, the supervisor is more apt to gain cooperation. In addition, many areas usually can and should be praised liberally to reinforce the many things which the rep does correctly. In time, when the one weakness is corrected, the supervisor can suggest another single area which might be changed for the better. The supervisor who sincerely cares for the individual will continually educate and encourage each rep to develop his or her potential capabilities.

QUESTIONS

1 What is the difference between close and broad supervision, and how are these best used?

2 What kinds of information is a supervisor checking when discussing preapproach planning with the sales rep?

3 What areas are of major interest to the supervisor when observing the sales presentation?

4 What is the sales pressure principle? Describe how a sales rep can be aggressive and still acceptable to a prospect.

5 What areas are of major interest to the supervisor when observing the sales rep dealing with customer objections?

6 What should the supervisor be looking for when observing the sales rep attempting to close the sale?

7 What can the supervisor learn by discussing the sales rep's follow-up plan after the call?

8 How should the supervisor provide negative feedback so the sales rep will accept it and change his or her behavior?

SELECTED REFERENCES

All or Nothing—Delmar Jewelry Case, ³/₄-in. videocassette, 40 min, b&w, Intercolleagiate Video Clearing House, Miami, Fla., 1976.

Haas, Kenneth B., and **John W. Ernest:** *Creative Salesmanship: Understanding Essentials,* 2d ed., Glencoe Press, Beverly Hills, Calif., 1974.

Johnson, H. Webster: "Supervising the Sales Force," chap. 6 in *Sales Management,* Charles E. Merrill Books, Inc., Columbus, Ohio, 1976.

Russell, Frederic A., Frank H. Beach, and **Richard H. Buskirk:** *Textbook of Salesmanship,* 10th ed., McGraw-Hill Book Company, New York, 1977.

Stroh, Thomas F.: "On-the-Job Coaching," chap. 9 in *Training and Developing the Professional Salesman,* AMACOM, American Management Association, New York, 1973.

————: "Seven Psychological Dependable Steps in Training and Developing Effective Salesmen," chap. 2 in *Effective Psychology for Sales Managers,* Parker Publishing Company, Inc., West Nyack, N.Y., 1974.

Thompson, Joseph W.: *Selling,* 2d ed., McGraw-Hill Book Company, New York, 1973.

► **Case 13-1**

WESTERN BELL TELEPHONE COMPANY

Miss Bernice Adams is in the Marketing Division of Western Bell based in Portland, Oregon. She is one of a team of representatives for Western Bell that sell module systems to businesses in her territory as well as watts line systems to accounts assigned outside her territory by her manager. The teams are divided by industry. Her territory consists of businesses in food (wholesale), trucking, and transportation (excluding airlines) in the metropolitan area. The division in which Miss Adams works is made up of relatively new, young people and no real conflict exists within the division.

She is assigned a bottom-line count of 300 accounts yearly and sees a minimum of two accounts per day. The objectives of her job include instituting programs for businesses by which they call their accounts on the phone rather than in person. She is to teach business personnel to use the phone for more uses, from collecting overdue accounts to contacting potential new accounts. Also, she is on a "watts line team," an activity which is outside her regular accounts.

Some of the major problems that Miss Adams encounters are involved with the first step of selling—getting in to see the prime decision makers. She stated that this is a common problem and it takes a great deal of determination and good timing to see the right people. It is a real challenge to get people to invest the time, work, and money to convert to this system. Also, it is difficult to get a cash deposit even after that sale has been made. Another problem is getting the departments in Western Bell to negotiate between themselves on the earliest date to deliver and get the system installed. There is much friction between the plant department and the marketing department. The plant department works at times almost against the marketing department and does not seem to work to give the customer the most service.

Two problems that are time-demanding are (1) that the customer calls the representative with any problems he may have rather than going through the regular channels and (2) the amount of paperwork the representative is required to do. Miss Adams estimated that almost 70 percent of her time was spent doing "busy work" paperwork which kept her from going out into the field.

One problem in this particular case is the leadership of Miss Adams's direct manager. He manages by emotion. One day he may feel that the force should "blitz the market" and the next he may tell them to concentrate only on the major accounts. This was found to be most frustrating by Miss Adams and provided no sense of direction for her.

There is a seven-step format that the rep is to follow. This does not allow for any individual style in selling. You are evaluated on how well you use this format and how well you research your customer and his needs.

Miss Adams is paid on straight salary and no commissions on her sales, although she did state that there are indirect rewards for doing outstanding work—the employee is recognized for this. She has been with Western Bell for one year and has quickly learned how important "politicking" is to her career with them. Her advice was to get to know the right people in the right places and expose yourself and your ambitions to upper management if you plan to get ahead.

1 What kind of on-the-job coaching might help this young sales rep?

2 How is she being prepared for more responsibility in sales?

14

Quotas and
Performance Appraisals

▶ **Objectives**

The reader will be able to evaluate various types of quotas and performance appraisals and to select the most appropriate ones for a given situation. He or she will recognize that dollar or product quotas do not adequately direct a sales force. The reader will be able to construct activity quotas which help the sales force achieve its objectives. He or she will be able to build a good evaluation system which will alert the manager to specific areas which need correction while there is still time to do something about them. Finally, the reader will realize that direction and corrective actions occur daily and may include sales contests, a series of sales meetings, and other activities.

Setting job performance standards and measuring the degree of achievement are relatively easy tasks in managing employees who work on the premises. It is much more difficult to set standards and appraise performance for sales representatives, for two obvious reasons. First, most of the activities of sales reps are performed without direct observation by management. Second, there are unique differences in each territory which are due to geography, competitive effort, customer profits, and so forth. Because of these differences, management cannot directly compare sales rep A with sales rep B, for example, even when they may have the same territory potential and the same experience.

Nevertheless, it is the sales manager's responsibility to direct the efforts and activities of the sales force in order to optimize the return on the investment in the sales budget. Without direction, sales reps will go their own way as they see their own selfish opportunities. While a few top producers may do very well without the sales manager's direction, the majority of the average and poor producers will be inefficient, wasteful, and not very productive, compared with their potential.

In a similar manner, the sales manager needs to establish a system as a guide to quantify data selected from the mass of information available. The ideal system will simplify evaluation of the results and clearly point to certain corrective action plans. Such a system will also adapt to individual differences between various sales reps and to the unique territory or assignment. It will clearly signal what is happening today and what might be feasible or likely to happen in the future.

SETTING PERFORMANCE STANDARDS

Traditional performance standards in the selling profession have been various quotas based on economics and resulting in dollar-volume sales targets. For example, new sales reps must sell a certain amount to cover their own direct costs of compensation and expense. They must sell an additional amount to cover the indirect expenses of sales supervision and administration. Finally, they are expected to sell another added amount to generate some profit for their employer. While this approach seems logical and easy to understand, it is loaded with problems and commercially dangerous pitfalls.

Given a quota of so many dollars of sales, most experienced sales reps will seek to increase the size of orders from existing accounts. It is usually easier to sell more to a friendly account that it is to win accounts away from competition. It is generally easier to get regular users of a product or service to use more of it than it is to sell to people who have never before used that product or service. In addition, it is easier to sell a lot of products which have a low profit margin than it is to sell a similar dollar amount of products which have a high margin.

In many industries it is common to lose 10 percent of a company's customers each year. This customer attrition rate means that the sales force must gain new accounts to the extent of 10 percent of their present customers annually just to maintain a steady volume. Clearly, one of the ways to increase sales is to earn more new accounts than are lost. Unfortunately, traditional sales quotas emphasize total sales dollars and not the source of the orders. Customer attrition rates will vary from industry to industry, but this factor should be considered before setting any quotas.

Most sales organizations offer a line of products, and each item in the line may contribute a different amount of profit. For example, some items may be sold near cost with the purpose of keeping buyers loyal. Other items in the line may provide a high contribution to profit, so that selling a balanced line of products on the average order will produce an acceptable profit. If the sales force is operating under a dollar sales quota, they will naturally push the low-profit items which the buyer recognizes as being of good value for him or her. There is no reason for the sales force to increase profit, but only to increase the size of their orders.

A third problem area with using traditional sales volume quotas is the danger of a sales rep not providing sold customers with the expected and proper service. An office machine salesman, for example, is often expected to take the time necessary to teach the clerical user to get the most benefits from the machine. But this is a nonselling activity, and the dollar quota system pulls him back to selling other accounts, leaving the poor clerk to learn by trial and error. In the long run this hurts the supplying company.

Product Quotas   A common variation of the dollar sales quota is the unit or product quota. In this system the sales reps are directed to sell a so-called "balanced" line of products so that the average order meets minimum profit expectations. For the short term of one year or less, each sales rep is given a quota of units of products in each of several categories to sell. For example, based on the firm's office products manufacturing facilities, the sales manager gives each sales rep a quota for desks, chairs, files, filing supplies, and insulated files. Because each of these five groups carries a different contribution to profit, the quotas are weighted to favor the more profitable items. Each sales rep must meet the minimum quota in each of the five categories before earning extra money, but the monetary incentive in this organization is to sell more of the higher-profit products.

While unit quotas can direct the sales force toward selling higher-profit items, notice that there is no direction given or emphasis placed on the source of the orders. Once again sales reps will tend to sell more to existing accounts rather than seek out new accounts. In addition, the expected service after the sale is ignored; thus the tendency to slight this nonselling activity continues.

Another problem occurs when management relies entirely on unit, or product, quotas. These depend on the constantly changing competitive conditions in the marketplace. A product quota in one category may seem reasonable and desirable at the beginning of a period, but a competitor may bid for a larger share of that market and begin a price war. To protect its share, the first company may have to lower prices also. The high contribution to profit may vanish through no fault of the sales force. Similar changes may occur when competition changes or modifies existing products or introduces entirely new second and third generations of improved products.

Another problem area, to both dollar and product quotas, is that of windfall orders. These are orders which are delivered in one territory but sold by a sales rep from another territory, a national account manager, or an executive of the same company. In some organizations, all credit is given to the sales rep who writes the order. In industries where service is expected after the sale, credit is often divided evenly between the two reps involved. Unfortunately it is difficult to judge when one rep, doing a good job, caused the local branch to requisition the rep's products from a distant home office. The home office may issue a purchase order to the sales rep in that city, and the latter gets the windfall sale.

House accounts are another problem of both dollar and product quotas. Many customers buy certain products and supplies over the years from standard suppliers. They will continue to buy them as long as the products are needed, competitively priced, and properly serviced. Under these conditions there is little or no actual selling effort needed and the customer will buy regardless of the sales rep who picks up the orders. Very often these accounts are given to senior sales reps as a reward for being loyal and to eliminate the risk of an inexperienced rep doing something wrong, which might lose the account. Under a dollar or product quota system, how much credit should be given to the sales rep for such orders? In many sales organizations, the sales manager or sales supervisors handle such accounts on a salary basis. In any case, most sales territories will have a number of repeat customers who were not originally sold by the sales rep now handling them. This often causes morale problems under the dollar and under the unit quota systems.

Expense-to-Sales Ratio A number of sales organizations use a combination of dollar sales volume with the sales reps' expenses. Presumably the lower the expenses for a given dollar volume, the better the sales rep looks. This does focus attention on the cost-cutting side of the sales job; however, it has all the problems discussed as inherent in dollar sales quotas. In addition, the basic expense of covering a four-state territory and of covering one-third of a single city with equal potential are simply not comparable. Under these conditions a sales manager might set up a desirable expense-to-sales ratio for each territory or for each customer segment handled, for example. The sales rep's performance then is measured against the unique quota.

The apparent advantage of this quota system is that the sales reps can improve their ratio by either lowering expenses or increasing sales, or both. Unfortunately, profit contribution is not measured, and this system may be self-defeating if profit optimization is the goal. There is also the real danger of a sales rep overeconomizing on selling expenses so that customers are not seen as often as they desire or are not wooed as they frequently expect. A "cheap" sales rep soon wears out his or her welcome, particularly when competitors are alert.

Gross Margin on Orders When a quota system is based on profit contribution alone, it does focus attention on selling both a balanced line of products and particular groups of target customers as well. A variation of this is *net profit contribution,* which adds the sales expense factor at the risks previously enumerated for the expense-to-sales ratio. The major shortcoming of either of these quotas is that they neglect the source of orders. Some sales reps will skim the best accounts and neglect smaller but still desirable ones. Others will focus on existing accounts and tend to neglect seeking new accounts.

Market Share For a number of products, there exists a system to determine market share by geographic region. When such data are available and the sales goal is to increase or maintain market share, some organizations set quotas on this basis for each territory. This is really another variation of product or unit quotas. Selling expenses, profit contribution, and new-account solicitation are neglected. In addition, the sales reps are being judged on the basis of total marketing efforts and competitive reactions, most of which are well beyond their sphere of influence.

Sales versus Potential Another common quota system is to measure the so-called effectiveness of each rep by comparing actual dollar sales with potential dollar sales. In situations where potential sales can be evaluated within an acceptable range, this quota system may indicate how effective a rep is in covering his or her territory or assigned customer targets by size or classification of account potential. It is still basically a dollar quota system although it emphasizes new-account solicitation. Sales reps still have the strong temptation to sell more to old accounts in order to increase sales, and there is no reference to profit.

Calls Made Almost every sales organization keeps track of the number of calls per day made by each sales rep. This record is desirable in establishing a norm for the sales force to encourage slow, methodical performers to increase their activities and to encourage the over-eager ones to slow down and spend an appropriate amount of time on each call. Clearly, this kind of quota should be established separately for each territory or customer category. Unfortunately, in many industries the average number of calls per day may have little or no relation to the effectiveness of the sales rep. Spending all day with one account may easily generate more sales and profits than spending one day divided amongst five accounts. This is a quantity measure which has its limited value, but in no way does it indicate the quality of calls being made.

Call Frequency Ratio Many sales managers do classify accounts by potential, as noted earlier, and some establish quotas to direct the sales force to call on each category only as frequently as the potential justifies. This helps the sales force plan their time and territory coverage in both route planning and in frequency of visiting selected accounts. While this directing of their activities is beneficial, it is also a quantitative measure of effectiveness but not of the quality of the calls being made.

Order-to-Call Ratio Many companies attempt to measure the sales reps' effectiveness by comparing the number of orders written per day, per week, or per month with the number of calls made during the same time period. This is called the sales reps' "batting average"—a good producer might sell one in three for a 0.333 average, for example. Some managers measure the order-to-call ratio for different product categories and for different customer classifications. This record often will indicate where the sales rep is weak and needs training, for example. Unfortunately, because of wide territory differences, one sales rep may come to bat only four times per day while another may come to bat eight times per day. Their order-to-call ratios may not reflect their total production. In any event, this ratio completely ignores the rep's contribution to profit.

Average Order Size Another common measurement of sales reps is made by totaling their sales for a given time period and dividing the sum by the number of orders written. The purpose here, obviously, is to reduce the small orders which generate little or no profit. This also is intended to cause the sales force to concentrate its time and effort on the potential large-order customer. This ratio is often used in conjunction with the average cost per call to emphasize the importance of making profitable sales. Unfortunately, averages tend to hide some good things and many bad things. One highly profitable large order may average out with too many unprofitable small orders, for example. The longer the time period, the greater the danger in averaging.

New Orders to Repeat Orders Ratio For some sales organizations, where customer attrition is high, this ratio can be important, as noted earlier in this chapter. The difficulty here is defining new orders, or new accounts. For some managers, any inactive account would be considered new business. For others, a single order from a new account would not qualify unless the original order was restocked within thirty days, for example. If a major competitor cannot deliver, because of a strike or a fire in the plant, for example, many windfall sales will occur on a temporary basis. In a similar way the number of canceled orders compared with total orders may vary widely for reasons well beyond the sales rep's sphere of influence.

Return on Investment In the late 1960s and into the early 1970s attempts were made to evaluate a sales rep's performance based on his or her return on investment.[1] This quantitative formula multiplies profit as a percent of sales times the sales as a percent of the territory's invested costs. Thus if one rep had $500,000 in sales which generated a net profit of $30,000, or 6 percent, and the company invested $20,000 in salary plus $15,000 in total sales expenses, or 7 percent on sales to investment, the return on assets managed would equal 85 percent. While this example might seem extreme, the numbers are very typical in the paper industry.

While this sophisticated technique might contribute to a management decision to open a new branch sales office or to fund a new territory, it is not necessarily the best way to judge a sales rep's performance. The total sales in a territory or from a group of targeted customer accounts, and the resulting profit, may have very little to do with the individual sales rep. As noted, some customers will buy from certain suppliers no matter who the sales rep may be, assuming reasonable price and service. Some accounts may be persuaded to switch suppliers only after a two- or three-year effort by an outstanding rep. None of this desirable effort would show up in any part of the ROI formula until several of the nonproductive years had passed.

PROFIT ANALYSIS AND ACTIVITY QUOTAS

No matter what traditional quota system is chosen, the top producers quickly adapt to it and rise above the pack just as they do to win most contests. Progressive sales managers today identify those behavior patterns of top producers which are different from the behavior of average producers and which make them effective. For example, the vice

[1] J. S. Schiff and Michael Schiff, "New Sales Management Tool: R.O.A.M.," *Harvard Business Review,* vol. 45, July–August 1967, pp. 59–66.

president of sales for a leading manufacturer of ladies' intimate and foundation garments realized that top producers spent considerably more time in training retail salesladies than the average producers spent in training. Then he assigned a quota to each sales rep for conducting a specific number of retail sales training courses each week. The training enables the retail salesladies to sell more expensive and more profitable merchandise, as well as to sell several additional items to customers who had planned to buy a single product. The clerks then sell more of all brands; however, they do remain grateful to the manufacturer's sales rep who trained them and tend to favor that line of merchandise over the competitive line. Thus, the sales force is directed into a nonselling activity which ultimately builds loyal retail clerks and sells more merchandise in the future.

In selling consumer products to large chains of supermarkets, heavy advertising support is the greatest marketing cost. The buyer may be persuaded to try the deal on the basis of supporting test-market results.

Often a deal is accepted to be reordered, "as branch stores reorder." The average producer might accept this situation and move on to another prospect. The top producers, however, visit each store in the chain in their territory to get increased shelf space and to physically set up substantial point-of-purchase (POP) displays of the product. When this has been done, sales have increased by as much as 200 percent over sales in stores in the same area without the POP.[2] For this reason many large manufacturers of consumer products wisely set activity quotas for the sales force to include a specific number of window displays, point-of-purchase displays, and shelf facings.

In selling office furniture and equipment to business and industry, it was found that the top producers usually accompanied each order with a detailed floor plan showing how the new equipment was to be placed and old equipment rearranged. While most sales reps offered this free service, the top producers practically insisted upon it and their customers were particularly grateful and became loyal. One such company now has set quotas of drawing so many floor plans for 50 percent of all proposals or quotations. This directs the sales force into a nonselling

[2]"Drugstore Brand Switching and Impulse Buying" and "The Effect of End Displays on Selected Food Product Sales," *Reports and Surveys,* Point of Purchase Advertising Institute, New York.

activity ultimately increases new business and builds loyalty for repeat business.

In selling lubricants to industrial accounts, it was found the top producers spent more time in surveying prospects' needs to reduce costs than the average producers spent. Quotas were set for each sales engineer to make so many surveys per week, thus directing their efforts into an area which ultimately increases business, both new and repeat orders.

The trend in sales management today is to direct the activities of the sales force by giving them a number of specific quotas other than dollar volume or unit volume. Sales managers search for areas of high leverage where a relatively small effort by the sales force will yield high returns. Frequently these areas are identified by observing what the top producers do that makes them outstanding.

Top producers are generally more independent and flexible in their thinking than the average producer. They are able to quickly adapt their selling methods to the rapid changes in the volatile world economic conditions as well as in local competitive conditions. Sales managers can take advantage of their trend-setting methods by assigning activity quotas to the entire sales force. Sales reps will readily accept this new direction of their efforts to help them become more effective. With activity quotas the sales force is being asked to work smarter, not harder.

When the assigned activity quotas really do represent the unique advantage which top producers are using, dollar sales volume goes up. Usually the sales force compensation goes up but, frequently, the overall selling costs as a percent of sales goes down, thus increasing profit. Traditional dollar and unit quotas may call attention to certain ratios which sales management would like to improve. Activity quotas show the sales force how to achieve these desired results by doing specific things. This promises to be less frustrating and much more efficient.

Reporting Objective Measurements

From the preceding discussion it can be seen there is an abundance of information within any sales organization which a manager can use to

evaluate the sales force. With the increased use of inexpensive computers, it is possible to analyze each order, item by item, for balance and
profit contribution. Totals can be derived by product category and by
territory. Expense accounting can often be allocated to specific accounts
or to categories of customers. In fact, any of the dollar or unit quotas
discussed can be computed on a weekly basis, for example, showing this
period compared with the same period last year, as well as the year to
date compared with the previous year to date. If territory potential has
been validated, and if market share can be obtained, these also can be
compared with actual results.

In addition, some sales managers require a work plan to be
submitted in advance showing where the sales rep plans to visit, what he
or she hopes to accomplish, and the sequence or route which will be
taken. This kind of report directs the sales force to do the preapproach
planning discussed in the previous chapter, and it clearly shows that
management cares about the sales force taking the time to think through
their plans for each call.

The *call report* is another common source of objective data which is
required by most sales managers. This report tells what actually happened on each call and indicates whatever progress the sales rep feels
was accomplished. The report frequently indicates how top producers are
spending their time and efforts differently from the rest of the sales
force. It also indicates where a rep is investing time in a potential sale
that the rep knows will *not* occur during this year or fiscal period. This
can be an objective measurement showing that 10 percent of the rep's
time is used in long-term selling, for example. In addition, most call
reports ask for competitive strengths and their activities. Often a
competitor's test marketing can be identified and a sales manager may
take steps to monitor the test or, in some cases, to disrupt it in order to
confuse the competitor.

Many sales managers request a *new-business report* or a list of
prospects whom the sales rep feels might be sold this month or this
quarter. It directs the sales force to look for new business from unsold
accounts. It also provides timely information about prospects whom a
supervisor or sales manager can help to sell. From past experience a sales
supervisor or the manager may have contacts and friends in the
prospect's company who are unknown to the sales rep. The sales rep
may be directed to these contacts or joint calls may be indicated. A

SALES ACTIVITY REPORT

Week ending _____

| Person and Title | Name of Company | Telephone | | First Visit | Surv. | Write Prop. | Pres. Prop. | F/U Visit | Write Letter | Remarks and Suggested Actions |
		Pl.	Comp.							
	Total for week									Total sales days

manager who attempts to take over such sales directly will soon find these reports fabricated mostly from fiction or wishful thinking rather than factual. The report should always be used to direct the sales force and secondarily to help them where possible.

Lost-sale reports and *customer complaint reports* written by the sales force can be meaningful to identify competitive actions early enough to take steps to combat them, or to identify weak products, or to indicate changes needed in customer servicing. They are rarely meaningful for evaluating the sales reps because the reps are most apt to rationalize the loss as due to almost anything other than themselves. Such reports or complaints written directly by the customers or by supervisors who directly observed what happened may be of some value in identifying sales-training needs of selected individuals.

The sales supervisor who works in the field with each sales rep, as described in the previous chapter, can also provide a wealth of objective measurements. In such cases the supervisor can report on the level of sophistication in selling, the degree of knowledge and skills observed, and the work habits and attitudes displayed, all as they compare with pre-established norms. These reports will be objective measurements of the sales force only to the extent that the supervisor is experienced and objective. There is a tendency for supervisors to be overprotective of their charges and to report only the better things they do. An experienced sales manager will recognize this when it occurs and take corrective steps to improve the objectivity of these reports.

Finally, there are external sources of information which may be highly pertinent regarding the evaluation of individual sales reps and the entire sales force as a group. There are federal and state government reports issued regularly on such factors as unemployment, changes in personal income by region, cost-of-living changes, housing starts, and the like. Dun and Bradstreet, Inc., publishes business ratios for manufacturers, wholesalers, and retailers annually in *Dun's Review.* While discussed earlier in Chapter 3, on planning for the future, it should be noted here that such data may also be used to explain or account for changes in current and past sales performance which were well beyond the control of the sales force. Clearly, sales managers should be aware of what external information is available to them and use what is appropriate.

ONGOING EVALUATION

Most quota systems include a time frame, such as monthly, quarterly, and so forth. This may inadvertently cause the sales force to work *and to loaf* in spurts as they see fit. After having just gone over quota by working hard for the last week of the period, for example, a sales rep may feel entitled to coast the first week of the new period. Other individuals may get off to a great start by working hard the first few weeks and then ease up as they see that making quota is well within their grasp. For these reasons sales managers generally prefer comparisons of current performances of this year to date with quota to date.

Ongoing evaluations should automatically alert a sales manager where trouble is apt to occur in the near future while there is still time to do something about it. The trouble may be caused by the rep's failure to take certain actions, by competitive actions, by failure of supporting advertising or sales promotions, or by changing economic conditions within customer industries, for example. A good evaluation system will both alert the manager and point to a specific area which needs correction *before* the impending event occurs.

When observing current performance of various sales reps, a manager can often recognize differences between the top performers, the average ones, and the poor performers. New managers often attempt to treat all sales reps equally, and this can be a serious mistake. Many experienced sales managers devote a disproportionate amount of their time and energy to the poor producers, and this also can be a serious mistake. Successful sales managers treat each rep and each group of performers *fairly* but not equally. Top performers who are neglected may ease off or coast to meet quota, when they are the very group that can produce the greatest improvements desired. Ongoing evaluation of their efforts should indicate some form of recognition and continued encouragement. Average performers who are on target should not be simply told they are doing all right. They may be taught new techniques which will make their jobs easier and may make some of them outstanding. The experienced sales rep who is a poor producer is perhaps the biggest waste of management time, effort, and company funds. The new sales rep who is a poor producer may need special encouragement and coaching to become productive more quickly. Assuming a good recruiting and selecting system is in effect, sales management can well afford to invest time and money in the new rep who is not yet productive.

Ongoing evaluation can be a process which indicates where a manager will direct the efforts of the sales force. However, a manager should expect different levels of performance from different groups of representatives. A good system will indicate where the manager's efforts are most apt to result in the greatest improvement and where they can be applied in time to accomplish something constructive.

CORRECTIVE ACTION

The entire reason for using quotas and appraisals is not simply to report to top management how well the sales force is doing, no matter how polite that may be. The purpose is to direct the sales force collectively and individually into better ways to achieve constantly escalating goals. While these activities are frequently called "corrective action," it should be realized that they include constructive criticism and the employment of new ideas and methods which will achieve better results. Performance appraisal is rarely a disciplinary, corrective process, as such. It is most often an opportunity to communicate, to motivate, and to educate, all in the positive sense.

Most sales organizations which operate under the management by objectives system require at least an annual formal performance appraisal inteview with each individual representative. Some require a semiannual formal review. These sessions cover what objectives and quotas were agreed to before the period began, the actual performance, and a discussion of the variations or deviations, both good ones and bad. Strengths and weaknesses are identified and plans are made for the future time period. Usually monetary considerations are discussed so that each sales rep knows what the manager is recommending and has the opportunity to influence that recommendation. As noted in the discussion on compensating and motivating the sales force, it is usually wise to dwell on the motivating factors and to talk of monetary considerations as recognition for achievement.

Most corrective action, however, occurs every day that a sales rep communicates with the supervisor and sales manager. This may involve clarification of job duties, informing the sales force of changes in company policies or products, competitive changes, sales training, or solving business or personal problems. It also includes providing opportunities for growth and development as various sales reps gain experience and maturity. These are all action activities which direct each individual sales rep to do a more efficient job and to become a better person.

Corrective action may also include the supervisor's direct assistance in selling selected accounts or in demonstrating in customers' offices how certain techniques or methods can be used more effectively. Corrective action may also take the form of more support from technical people in the home office, either educating the sales rep or actually calling with him on a customer.

As implied in the previous discussion, the corrective action called for may be from outside the sales force. A competitor's sudden lowering of prices, for example, may require a top-management decision to match the lower prices or to offer different customer services to offset the competitive advantage. In other words, when considering what corrective actions are possible, a sales manager can look to areas outside the sales force. These are particularly important when the problem or challenge is beyond the influence of the sales force.

Finally, corrective action can take the form of a sales contest or series of sales meetings, as discussed earlier. When a group has performed below expectations or perhaps is just barely meeting agreed objectives, the last quarter may provide an opportunity to boost the group's efforts or a new way to achieve much higher results. Ongoing evaluation should alert the sales manager to various alternative corrective actions while there is still time to decide, and to implement, the one or the combination which may achieve the desired results. Making these decisions and taking the necessary actions early enough are key responsibilities of sales managers.

SUMMARY

Directing and supervising a sales force is normally achieved by using various quotas and regular performance reviews. Because the sales force operates for the most part without direct observation and in territories or with groups of customers that are not directly comparable, the sales manager's job is difficult.

Sales dollar quotas, most commonly used, direct the sales force to increasing sales, but they neglect profit considerations and can negate the seeking of new accounts. Unit or product quotas direct the sales force toward selling a balanced line, but, similarly, they neglect the source of orders.

Expense-to-Sales Ratio, Gross Margin on Orders, Market Share, and Sales versus Potential quotas are all variations of either dollar or product quotas. While they may be important in sales analysis, they do not adequately direct the sales force. Calls made, call frequency ratio, and order-to-call ratio are quantitative measures of performance, but they lack giving adequate direction to the sales force. Average order size and new orders-to-repeat orders ratios offer some direction to the sales force but do so without any guidance. Return on investment shows promise in broad sales management decisions such as opening a new branch sales office; however, it measures much of what is beyond the individual sales rep's control.

Activity quotas are based upon what the top producers do differently from average producers that influences orders and profits. Activity quotas are often nonselling behavior patterns, such as training the user, sales training for the middleman, point-of-purchase displays for the retailer, and problem solving for industrial and commercial buyers. When the assigned activity quotas really do represent the unique advantage which top producers are using, sales usually go up and selling expense as a percent of sales goes down.

Whatever measurements a sales manager selects to direct the sales force, they should be objective and easy to understand. In addition to analysis of orders, items, territory, and customer sales possible, sales expenses can also be quantified and analyzed. In addition, managers frequently require work plans to be submitted in advance and call reports to explain what happened and how various reps are spending their time. New-business reports direct the sales force to obtaining new accounts. Lost-sale reports and customer complaints may often highlight problem areas which need management's attention. Sales supervisors who directly observe the sales force in customers' offices can also provide objective measurements of performance. Finally, there are some excellent external sources of objective information which can be used to explain past performance or predict future performance of the sales force.

Most performance evaluation should be done on a regular daily basis as members of the sales force naturally communicate with supervisors and management. A good evaluation system will alert the manager to specific areas which need correction while there is still time to do something about them.

Corrective action is the dynamic management phase of directing the sales force· and improving performance. Annual and semiannual performance appraisal interviews are essential under the management by objectives systems. But most corrective action and direction occur informally, whenever an opportunity arises to communicate, to motivate, to educate, and to develop the sales force. Corrective action may also include sales contests and a series of sales meetings, and, on occasion, it may call for decisions of higher management and others outside the sales force itself.

QUESTIONS

1 What should be the purposes of quotas and performance appraisals?

2 What are the shortcomings of dollar quotas and units-of-product quotas?

3 What is the disadvantage of gross margin-on-orders quotas?

4 Various measurements of calls, frequencies, and batting average all overlook what basic factor?

5 What are activity quotas, and how can they help a sales force achieve its objectives?

6 What are the sources of objective data which can be used to direct and evaluate the sales force?

7 How can giving directions and using corrective actions be a positive, likable, and constructive affair?

8 When should performance evaluation take place, and how can it help a manager decide what to do in the future?

SELECTED REFERENCES

Cummings, L. L., and **Donald P. Schwab:** *Performance in Organizations: Determinants and Appraisal,* Scott, Foresman and Company, Glenview, Ill., 1973.

Johnson, H. Webster: "Sales Quotas," chap. 14, and "Analyzing and Evaluating Salesperson Performance," chap. 7 in *Sales Management,* Charles E. Merrill Books, Inc., Columbus, Ohio, 1976.

Riso, Ovid, ed.: *The Dartnell Sales Manager's Handbook,* 12th ed., The Dartnell Corporation, Chicago, Ill., 1975.

Stanton, William J., and **Richard H. Buskirk:** "Sales Quotas," chap. 22, and "Evaluation of Salesman's Performance," chap. 25 in *Management of the Sales Force,* 4th ed., Richard D. Irwin, Inc., Homewood, Ill., 1974.

Still, Richard, R., Edward W. Cundiff, and **Norman A. P. Govoni:** "Quotas," chap. 19 in *Sales Management,* 3d ed., Prentice-Hall, Inc., Englewood Cliffs, N.J., 1976.

"Survey of Buying Power," *Sales Management* (annual), New York, July issue.

Wotruba, Thomas R.: *Sales Management: Planning Accomplishment and Evaluation,* Holt, Rinehart and Winston, Inc., New York, 1971.

▶ **Case 14-1**

JET AIR FREIGHT

Jet Air Freight was a domestic and international freight forwarder with branch offices in most major United States cities. They sold their service on getting freight from point A to point B by the quickest means available. They also handled all documentation and paperwork for international shipments. Each office had a branch manager and a sales manager. The sales manager not only was responsible for the sales force but also had a territory to maintain.

In October 1973, Ron Palmer was hired by Jet Air Freight to fill the position of sales representative at the Cleveland, Ohio, office. Ron had just completed his degree at Cleveland State University after four years in the Navy.

Ron was an aggressive individual, putting in much extra time after normal working hours and on Saturday learning the position and the company, to the pleasure of Paul Rader, the sales manager. This aggressiveness started showing by the number of new accounts that began coming out of his territory. The friction started when Ron, after each new account would show up, would jokingly tell Paul that he was after the sales manager position. What started as a joke became a full-scale attack.

After Ron had been on the job ten months, he had increased his territory yield by 150 percent, and he let it be known that he not only wanted Paul's job but deserved it. It was true that he had surpassed all the other sales reps in revenue and in obtaining one large account surpassed even Paul. When Ron confronted the branch manager with this, he was told that the fact that his sales were higher than the manager's gave him no right to the position. The branch manager then went into a long discussion with Ron about the whole matter and his actions in the last few months. Ron was politely told that if matters did not change, he would have to be let go, even though he was a great asset to the branch. The last straw came when Ron submitted a proposal to the main office in Los Angeles describing why he should be given the sales manager postion or transferred to another branch.

1 Why did the sales manager let the situation get this far? What action should he have taken?

2 What policy should the branch manager have taken when confronted by Ron?

3 What would you recommend the firm do?

▶ **Case 14-2**

THE KRAFT COMPANY

The Kraft Company (Kraftco) is well known nationally and has been long established in manufacturing in the United States as well as the world. Their major interests are with the processing of various food items in the Kraft Foods Division. They are exceptionally well known for their quality cheeses. The name "Kraft" is generally associated with quality products and goods. The prices are generally higher because of the national name brand and quality. The Kraft Foods Division processes and markets food items for consumer, institutional (hospital and restaurant), and industrial channels. The company, with its main offices in Chicago, Illinois, has several manufacturing plants spread around the country. The entire company markets in excess of 350 items, which include several complete, well-rounded product lines.

Kraft divides the country up into zones, which can cover part of one state or several states. A sales manager is responsible for each zone and reports to the home office in Chicago. Each zone is divided up into the districts. A district sales manager is in charge of the district area and reports to the zone manager. The various sales reps report to this district manager. The salespeople sell all Kraft products, no matter who the customer is. There is no product specialization in the general Kraft Foods Division. In fact, many products actually sell themselves very well. The salespersons who have been with the company the longest generally have the best territories. The salespeople are proud of the fact that their territories include mostly first-class supermarkets, which deal in larger volumes of many different types of Kraft products. Reps receive a straight salary and no commission. Bonus points may be accumulated in order to win merchandise (radios, TV sets, gifts, etc.).

Recently, a management shake-up had taken place. This occurred in the zone and district levels. The new manager at one district level is trying to make a name for himself in a short time. This is causing much friction among the salespeople. The salespeople claim that the new manager is changing old views and policies almost overnight. They claim that he makes promises and then breaks them. Some sales reps also feel favoritism. The new manager has been changing territories around, which has understandably been upsetting the salespeople further. The reps also feel that the new quotas have been set beyond their reach. Thus, the manager has been blamed for the problems of the sales force.

1　What might have caused a new manager to be sent into this district and to raise quotas?

2　What would you recommend that the district sales manager do at this point?

▶ **Case 14-3**

COMMUNICATIONS CORPORATION

Mr. Doug Smith of Communications Corporation is the regional sales manager for the state. He has just been told of a new promotional program that the company is preparing and he is considering how to present the program to his sales team.

Communications Corporation is a large manufacturer of radio communications equipment. Communications sells a complete line of mobile radios, base station radios, portable radios, and radio pagers. Mobile radios make up approximately 45 percent of the dollar volume of sales, while base stations are 20 percent, portable radios are 20 percent, and radio pagers are 15 percent. Selling prices for the products vary depending on the model and options, but mobile radios generally range from $1000 to $1500, base stations from $1500 to $4000, portable radios from $600 to $1000, and pagers from $250 to $350.

Mr. Smith, as regional sales manager for the state, is responsible for direct sales to state and local government accounts, manufacturing plants, hospitals and health care services, and all small businesses in such areas as agriculture, real estate, and services. The salespeople working for Mr. Smith specialize in one of the following areas: government, industrial, health care, or small business.

The four markets have different product requirements, and as a result the sales mix to each market is different. The government market is primarily a mobile radio market with some base station and portable radio sales. In the industrial market, the sales are primarily portable radios and radio pagers with some base stations and a very few mobile radios. The health care market buys radio pagers, primarily with some base stations, and a few portable and mobile radios. Small businesses usually buy radio systems consisting of several mobile radios and a base station.

Communications salespeople are paid a straight salary plus the use of a car and expenses, with a 5 percent bonus for making sales quota and another 5 percent bonus for making 120 percent of sales quota.

In the first quarter of 1976, Communications' products are selling at very close to the planned rate on all product lines except mobile radios. Sales of mobile radios have been only 80 percent of the planned rate, resulting in significantly lower than expected business. Because of this, the company has decided to offer a bonus to the salespeople of $10 per mobile radio sold in an effort to stimulate sales on this product line.

Mr. Smith is now preparing a presentation to announce this new sales promotion at the meeting he has called next week for all his salespeople. He is concerned that sales reps in the industrial and health care groups might not be too happy with the program. Another potential problem is the order expected from the state highway patrol for 450 mobile radios. Ralph Johnson has been working on this highway patrol system for over a year, and now the order should be placed with Communications in three to four weeks. Mr. Smith is considering exempting this one order from the bonus plan.

1   How do you evaluate this quota system?

2   What recommendations would you make for the immediate future?

▶ Case 14-4

WILSON SPORTING GOODS

Gary Ray, regional sales manager for Wilson Sporting Goods, supervises a regional sales force of fifteen representatives. Salespeople are paid on a commission basis, with allowances for expenses. The expense accounts are primarily determined by the sales reps, with minor review on control.

The problem has been continually escalating expense accounts. Gary was not extremely concerned, because of inflation, until he got word of some misuse of funds and padding of accounts.

It seemed that Robert J. was spending money entertaining not only clients, but friends and relatives also. After a careful investigation, Mr. Ray determined there had been several hundreds of dollars misused and reported as expenses over a six-month period.

It was customary to spend money at the establishments the sales-people were serving, but Robert had taken several guests to one tennis club several times. Money had been spent for food, liquor, guest fees, and tips.

The question is: What to do about Robert J.? He had been a good salesman—not in the top 10 percent, but more than adequate.

What's worse is that Mr. Ray feels many of the sales reps might be doing the same thing but have not yet been caught.

1 What expense account policy would you recommend to stop this apparent abuse of funds?

2 What would you do about the offending sales rep that was caught?

15

Directing the Sales Force
to Sell Key Target Accounts

▶ Objectives

The reader will now realize how a good sales force can be demoralized or rendered ineffective by things beyond their control. He or she will see how a key-account sales strategy program can be used to dramatically improve sales and profits. The reader will understand how an aggressive manager can influence advertising, sales promotion, and product quality. He or she will be able to use sales meetings to educate, support, and direct the sales force. The reader will be able to combine a sales contest with true long-term motivation.

Many sales reps begin each day looking for someone who will buy their products and services. Top producers begin each day planning how they can *earn* their orders. The difference between these two groups is not simply attitude and self-confidence; it is a basic realization of the value of the services which a professional sales rep can perform. This distinction shows up dramatically when both groups are asked to call on the biggest accounts in their territories or account categories. Most sales reps do not know how to crack a large account and are afraid to try. When a professional purchasing agent berates them and their company, they meekly give up trying to sell that account.

Sales managers can identify industries which can use their products, industries which are very profitable, and industries which are growing much faster than average. They can also plan and develop a promotional program to support the personal selling effort to targeted industries. However, without specific training and development, most experienced sales reps will be skeptical and they will exert little effort. Indeed, if they go back to the purchasing agent who berated them, they know with the certainty of personal experience what is most apt to happen: they will be berated again.

Directing the sales force to sell key target accounts requires a combination of training, motivation, and supervision. It is a difficult and lengthy process for any sales manager, but when successful, it produces a tremendous return for the individual sales rep and for the company. Once sales reps learn how to, and actually do, sell to one of the biggest, most desirable accounts within their responsibility, they become better producers for the rest of their careers.

A true case history will be used to illustrate how one sales manager overcame many obstacles and directed his sales force to selling key target accounts successfully within six months. The product was book paper and the targeted industry was publishers of trade and textbooks. The paper manufacturer was one of the largest and was very strong in selling to magazine publishers. Unfortunately, it had a poor history in selling to book publishers. The paper did not perform well on the presses; the company switched from selling through merchants to selling direct, and this angered both merchants and their customers; and the company periodically withdrew from this market, so that many publishers felt they could not rely on it as a long-term supplier.

An assistant sales manager in the magazine paper division was named national sales manager of the book paper division. His initial efforts were devoted to product improvement and establishing stringent quality control procedures. The manager picked four experienced salespeople from his former division and hired and trained four new people who had no previous sales experience. The ninth person transferred in from the field–technical-service group. None of these people had ever sold to a book publisher.

Wanting to build a new image in this target industry, the manager began a monthly "panel of experts" meeting. These were six authorities in all phases of book publishing, and their discussions were published monthly and distributed by mail to all book publishers. The trade quickly accepted this publication, which identified the manufacturer but had no commercial message. In addition, the manager fought for approval to publish a limited edition of a classic book which was to be given as a Christmas gift to all on the firm's mailing list. Of course, their book paper was used and it was so identified.

During this period the sales force was steadily becoming more and more skeptical as many very respectable purchasing agents berated them and their company. A national training organization was brought in for three months, but this had little effect on sales. It was at this point that the national sales manager decided to direct his nine salespeople to sell key target accounts.

BRAINWORK BEATS LEGWORK

The theme of the first monthly sales meeting in September was "Brainwork Beats Legwork," as the manager wisely chose to ask his salespeople to work smarter, not harder. He knew they were making as many calls as they could and that they were frustrated. The meeting began with a review of why each of the nine sales reps was selected. The manager reinforced each person's high qualifications and renewed some of their self-confidence. In the process he was also building a team spirit as each sales rep began to feel selected to be a part of a superior group.

The manager quickly reviewed the product-quality problems which were now resolved. Top management, including the president of the company, was now looking to this group to sell the new high-quality paper, and the group was told of this. The sales promotion program was then explained to the sales reps and the proposed advertising campaign was also discussed. The manager complimented the reps on their superior product knowledge, their sales techniques, and the tremendous effort they were making. He also acknowledged that they were not successful, himself included, and that what they needed was a strategy to crack some big accounts.

The manager pointed out that an outstanding performance by his group would be quickly identified because the president and all divisional vice presidents were scrutinizing their every move and development. He noted there was a good opportunity to expand his group as it became successful and to receive individual recognition, improved compensation, and promotions.

Then the manager challenged the group to *collectively* build a detailed sales strategy for each key target account. Each salesperson was asked to identify the ten key accounts in his or her territory which he or she would like to sell. The guildelines were profitability, growth, facilities, and competition. For each of these accounts the salespeople were asked to write up a brief outline for the next sales meeting, describing the account's needs and problems and listing as many names as possible of people within each account who might influence an order.

For the next month they were asked to plan on a call to each of the buying influences with a specific objective for each one, such as creating awareness, building friendship, or building trust. The meeting ended with the announcement that in three months' time a "Sale of the Month" contest would recognize the most intelligent and creative approach to these key target accounts. This, in effect, told the nine sales reps that he expected them to succeed within ninety days.

During the next thirty days the sales reps worked on their plans, reviewed them individually with the manager, and began calling on the key accounts. Before the second sales meeting, each of the nine salespeople sent in their outlines for selling ten key accounts in their territories. Unfortunately, each one contained only two or three names of individuals to be seen, other than a list of corporate officers.

BUYING INFLUENCES

The theme for the October sales meeting was "Buying Influences," which, of course, referred to the many people involved in making a purchasing decision.[1] The manager was prepared with the results of

[1] Barry J. Hersker and Thomas F. Stroh, *The Purchasing Agent's Guide to the Naked Salesman,* Cahners Publishing Company, Boston, 1975.

TYPICAL BEGINNING SALES STRATEGY

Account Name: E. S. Inc.   Sales representative 1

Background: Produces magazines, books of special interest, and catalogs for their newly acquired subsidiary, A.B.C., Inc. Usage is over 1000 tons a year, of which we are interested in only about half for cover stock (100-pound). Paper requirements in other areas are unknown to date. The last contact before my initial visit last month was by my predecessor three years ago.

Purchasing Department: As reported three years ago, Mr. C. F. is the man who makes the decisions to buy. He has been with this company for fifteen years and was recently named a vice president of the magazine division. A rather eccentric fellow in his late fifties, Mr. F. refuses gifts, luncheons, or anything which may sway his honest judgment to buy.

Immediate Objectives:
1. Build rapport with Mr. C. F.
2. Become acquainted with his subordinate, who will probably be doing more buying because of Mr. C. F.'s new position.

Short-Term Objectives:
1. Get C. F. to buy our paper for an upcoming catalog. This is only a once-a-year order, but it will help to establish us more firmly with the parent company.
2. Make the new buyer thoroughly familiar with our various grades, prices, quality, and services through promotional materials, printed samples, and frequent contact.

Long-Range Objectives:
1. Establish our company as a reliable source for spot orders in both coated and uncoated book grades.

Assistance: In addition to my own efforts, this prospect will be indirectly approached by two sales representatives associated with the subsidiary company. Both know Mr. C. F. and have indicated they will attempt to be of assistance. Also, I will request that the sales supervisor make calls occasionally with me to the parent company. These combined efforts will bring about more contacts and knowledge of the entire account.

Figure 15-1 A typical first effort by a sales representative in planning a key account strategy.

three studies published in various magazines, and he distributed a handout containing the following information:

1 Inertia is probably the most powerful purchasing influence; the single most important reason for selecting a supplier is that the source has been used before.

2 The role of *middle* management in initiating purchases, in selecting a supplier "pool," and in actually approving the final supplier—is all underestimated while the importance of *top* management and the *purchasing* department is grossly inflated.

3 Corporate decision makers favor suppliers who show them respect and personal consideration, and who do extra things for them. They overreact to real or imagined slights.

4 That good image qualities are said to include being "well known," being considered "big" or a "leader in the field," and having a reputation for providing good service.

5 In 88 percent of the industrial purchases studied, the initiator was a member of middle management. In 12 percent, the urge came from below that level. In no case was a member of top management or the purchasing department the source of action.

6 Naming a supplier pool in 74 percent of the purchases was by middle management. In 4 percent ranks below that did the specifying. The remaining 22 percent was handled by purchasing. Top management again took no part.

7 Middle management designated the supplier 69.5 percent of the time and collaborated with purchasing in another 12.2 percent of the cases. Alone purchasing made the selection in 4 percent of the cases.

The sales representatives were stunned and found it difficult to accept these findings. Then the manager asked what an art director for a book publisher might want in the way of papers. The reps quickly responded with various paper coatings and technical properties. The manager pointed out that not one call report mentioned that the sales rep had ever contacted an art director on any of the assigned accounts. "Why would an art director ask for our paper if he doesn't know us?" the manager asked. Gradually the reps began to see the wisdom of contacting others in middle management. They were being directed to use back-door selling or to get around the purchasing agent. At the conclusion of this second meeting, the following strategy outline was handed out to be filled in on each target account.

SALES STRATEGY OUTLINE: KEY TARGET ACCOUNT

Account Name: Sales representative:

Executives:

Middle Management Influentials:
    Product Manager
    Editor
    Art Director
    Sales Manager
    Designer

Purchasing Department:

Background:
    How many titles printed? What equipment?
    Our share or history:
    Key buying influences (from above):

Organization Chart: Who works with whom?

Strategy:
  1 Immediate
    (a) Who will be contacted and when? Who else?
    (b) Objectives of this visit or series of visits for *each* contact?
    (c) What tangible evidence will be used?
    (d) Support requested for specific purpose?
    (e) Time target for immediate sales trial?
  2 Long-Term
    (a) Build initial friendship through which buying influence?
    (b) What other areas, divisions, or buying influentials should be cultivated now for long-term friendship?
    (c) What "customer needs" are not being served now that might be in the future with different or modifiednproduct line?
    (d) Time target for major piece of business or major share of this account?

Figure 15-2 This was the "Sales Strategy Outline" form actually given to the sales rep by the author.

THE MYSTERIOUS FRIEND

In November the third sales meeting had the theme, "The Mysterious Friend," referring to the purchasing influence of a friend, expert, or relative who "told me about it." It was based on an article by Ernest Dichter.[2] A handout showed the following:

What made you buy this particular product?	
Recommended by friends	38.5%
Sharers of interest	18.0
Connoisseurs	10.0
Commercial authority	17.0
Bearers of tangible evidence	16.5
Total	100.0%

The manager explained that initially the sales rep is seen as a commercial authority or a bearer of tangible evidence. That was the reason they were asked to show good books that used their paper. After a number of calls the rep begins to share experiences of other customers with the prospect. After a time the sales rep becomes a trusted friend. "This is partly the reason entertainment and general conversation are effective," the manager concluded. He was directing the sales force to use their expense accounts on their ten key target accounts.

The outlines turned in at this third sales meeting reflected the following influences:

1 Manager of production (division or book series)

2 Plant superintendent

3 Typography and design supervisor

4 Managing editor

5 Sales manager

6 Sales service manager

7 Plant manager

8 Chief estimator

[2]Ernest Dichter, "How Word of Mouth Advertising Works," *Harvard Business Review,* November–December 1966, pp. 147–166.

9 Designer

10 Test manager

11 Pressroom superintendent (letterpress or offset)

12 Art director

13 General manager (trade or education)

FINAL SALES STRATEGY OUTLINE

Account Name: Johnson Sales representative: 9

Executives: List of all officers by title

Middle Management:
    Production Managers:

Steve	Medical books
Barbara	College and nursing books
Warren	Trade books
Ed	Elementary and high school books
Mona	Religious books
Carter	Special projects
Book Designer:	Bill, trade books
Advertising:	Audrey
Editor:	Alex, college texts

Purchasing Department: Mary Jane purchases all the paper. Her main job is to place orders for all paper for reprints which use the exact paper as the original.

Background: Over 150 titles were published last year. The trade department has the most titles followed by medical, educational, and religious. However, over the next five years they expect to quadruple their sales in elementary and high school texts.

All printing is purchased from outside sources on paper bought by this account entirely through local merchants. The majority of new texts are run offset and length of run averages 11,000 in education and 5000 or less in medical. Fall is their busy season with reprints in the spring or any time a book sells well.

Objections have never been voiced to me directly by any of the buying influences, but their secretaries tell me that our company is "too independent—will give you paper when they are ready or when it fits their plan." Also that we "drop paper grades when they are unprofitable or do not deckle," or "delivery has been poor," or that the firm is "not a reliable source of supply."

The key buying influences are the named six production managers; Alex; and

Figure 15-3 This was the "Sales Strategy Outline" submitted to the author by one sales rep at the end of the three-month period.

On each key target account the sales reps were now contacting thirteen different people in addition to purchasing agents and a few contacts with top management. Two reps had substantial trial orders as a direct result of these additional contacts, and each in turn told how the trial order was obtained. Enthusiasm spread through the entire group.

Finally, each sales rep was asked to give a brief oral description of *one* key target account on which he or she was working. The rep was

---

Mary Jane, the buyer. Many times she recommends a sheet to the production managers.

Organization Chart:
    Education:
        College—Barbara and Alex together.
        Elementary—Ed with help from Mary Jane.
        Advertising—Audrey specifies paper supplier.
    Trade:
        Warren and Bill work together. Since both men are new, Mary Jane takes care of the paper at the present time. Carter, Steve, and Mona each work on their own.

Strategy:
  1 Immediate
    (a) Continual contact with Mary Jane, the six Production Managers, Advertising Manager, Book Designer, Editors, and Art Directors.
    (b) Trial run of our paper will be this month for the college department.
    (c) Build sales volume in college area.
    (d) Get trial runs in elementary and high school books, and trade books.
    (e) No need for management support now.

  2 Long-Term
    (a) A stronger personal friendship will be developed with Ed, Warren and Mary Jane.
    (b) All the younger assistants will be cultivated for long term relationships. They will move up in the organization or move to influential jobs in competitive organizations.
    (c) The Elementary and High School Department will soon have a need for a sheet which will bulk between our X and Y sheets. We should have the plant price this soon.
    (d) As one division accepts our product we will make this known to all others as an in-house testimonial.
    (e) Invite one of their executives to participate in our monthly "panel of experts" meetings for publication to the trade.

Figure 15-3 Continued

asked to name each contact and their buying influence, the objective of each future call, an estimate of the date for a trial order, and any help he or she might want. Helpful suggestions were made by all the reps to one another. The sales manager let the reps run their own meeting at this point.

SALES OF THE MONTH

The sales reps were asked to write up a brief description of a recent sale of book paper which illustrated the various buying influences and how they handled the situation. As a result, three reps received desk-top radios with their business cards engraved on a gold plate. The theme of the fourth meeting—when the awards were made—was "Sales of the Month."

In less than six months, every one of the nine salespeople had sold several key target accounts and each had earned a trophy.

Within one year this small sales force was able to take a complete manufacturing plant from operating in the red to showing a substantial profit. At the end of this period the plant was running three shifts daily and had a three-month backlog of orders.

Each of the sales representatives earned a considerable raise in salary. One salesman, the one who had transferred in from tech-service, was made branch sales manager in a new office in the Midwest. The company modified its plans for a new production facility to include more book paper. Today they sell to almost every major book publisher in this country.

SUMMARY

This true case history illustrates the frustration of sales reps who are working hard but not succeeding. It shows how an aggressive sales manager can influence, if not direct, advertising and sales promotion programs. It shows how he was able to improve product quality. And it clearly illustrates the effective *combination* of education in sales meetings, supportive supervision, direction, a sales contest, and true long-term motivation. Incidentally, it also shows how an alert sales manager can get many good ideas from a wide variety of publications.

QUESTIONS

1 Why do average sales producers give up trying to sell large accounts who seem unfriendly?

2 How was education used to help the sales force sell key target accounts?

3 How was motivation used to help the sales force sell key target accounts?

4 How was supervision used to help the sales force sell key target accounts?

5 How did the manager direct the sales force to entertain customers appropriately?

6 Describe how a contest designed to gain short-term movement in this case was compatible with true long-term motivation.

SELECTED REFERENCES

Engineering of Agreement, 16-mm film, b&w, Roundtable Films, Inc., Beverly Hills, Calif., 1965.

Pall Corporation Marketing Case History, ³/₄-in. videocassette, 50 min, b&W, Intercollegiate Video Clearing House, Miami, Fla., 1975.

Stroh, Thomas F.: "The Crucial Psychology of Spotting and Coaxing Out Dormant Sales Capacities," chap. 8 in *Effective Psychology for Sales Managers,* Parker Publishing Company, Inc., West Nyack, N.Y., 1974.

————: "Programs for Retraining and Continuous Training," chap. 10 in *Training and Developing the Professional Salesman,* AMACOM, American Management Association, New York, 1973.

▶ Case 15-1

SYSTEMS ENGINEERING LABORATORIES

Systems Engineering Laboratories (SEL) is a small computer firm that employs about 550 people. The firm sells nationally and internationally. SEL recently expanded to include a European subsidiary. SEL's products are a standard computer and a standard computer system, as well as special systems that are tailored to the needs of the customer. Most of SEL's products are sold to major computer firms that have the prime contract for very large computer systems. Equipment to update or expand present SEL equipment or systems make up another large portion of the total sales. The selling price starts in the $200,000 range, and it is not unusual for a sale to exceed $1 million.

The entire sales organization is under the control of the vice president of sales. Under the vice president is the national sales manager. The sales force is divided geographically into regions, then into districts, and finally into account assignments. All the government contracts are handled by a special group. Technical people known as "analysts" support the salespeople. The analysts are engineers and programmers who are able to assist the sales reps work out the technical details.

SEL does not train new salespeople. The firm likes to hire "seasoned" sales reps. Sales reps are hired on the basis of their knowledge of the computer industry, their understanding of the needs of the customers in their territories, their knowledge of the capabilities of the competition, and their contacts within the market. Competition for good salespeople in the computer industry is fierce. Most of SEL's present sales force were hired from competitors and customers.

Compensation for the sales force is in the form of salary plus commission. Quotas are set on the basis of a dollar volume and on certain numbers of basic computer units sold. The salary-plus-commission structure is set up so that a salesperson who meets the quotas will have income that is about one-third commission and two-thirds salary. In addition to the salespersons, the regional managers and the analysts receive a very small commission as an incentive.

When SEL is the subcontractor to larger firms or "systems houses," sales reps must call on both the final customer and all the firms that are bidding for the prime contract. Because of the geographic locations and accounts assignments, the final customer and the prime contractor are not called on by the same sales reps. It is not unusual for a sales rep to convince a final customer that SEL is the only subcontractor that can supply the needed equipment and that SEL should be the customer's final choice of subcontractor. It is not always easy to determine which sales rep made the sale or how much influence each had on the account. This is the type of sale that runs over $1 million. Consequently, the commission is sizable. At the present time the sales rep who has the prime contractor's account receives the commission. Of course, the other sales rep feels deserving of some portion of the commission.

Another area of commission distribution that is subject to controversy is concerned with updated or additional equipment. The commission is given to the salesperson who made the most recent sale. Since the sales force is fairly new to the company, this problem has not fully developed. But as the present salespeople remain with the company, the problem could develop into a serious one. The salesperson who makes the initial sale will feel deserving of some of the commission, since the rep did sell the equipment that is being updated or expanded.

The new national sales manager, Charlotte Foster, spent the past few months recruiting top salespeople. She feels that if management does not adopt new policies concerning commission distribution, the firm is in danger of losing their reps. In an industry as competitive as the computer industry, an excellent sales force that stays with the firm is a necessity.

1 How might SEL adopt a key-account sales strategy?

2 How would you compensate the various members of a team that sells a new large order?

16

Situational Analysis and Decision Making

▶ Objectives

The reader will be able to understand and use the sales manager's decision tree to analyze difficult situations which may involve ignorance or motivational problems. The reader will be able to monitor competitive actions to improve his or her decisions on compensation, product development, and profit opportunities. One will be able to resolve problems of competitive bidding and to improve profit. Finally, the reader will know of the problems of reciprocal buying and how to handle such requests.

The sales force is very different from most other groups of people working in the same company. Sales representatives can spend company funds; they can sign contracts or letters of agreement which become legally binding on the company; they can commit company services to be freely given. Even the newest sales rep in a small territory has this authority in many sales organizations. In addition, sales reps work alone for the most part without supervision or direct observation by superiors. The very nature of the sales job attracts men and women who prefer to work on their own, independently. However, when problems arise, they are not easily recognized by the sales manager in the home office, and often the rep is too proud to ask for help.

Competitive actions and reactions are difficult to predict, although they may be crucial to the success or failure of a sales campaign. Many companies disguise their marketing plans to confuse and mislead competitors—at least until they are well under way. Other functions of management, such as production and finance, for example, depend on the sales department's figures for the making of decisions. The sales manager must deal with the unknowns outside the company.

The sales force is often involved in competitive bidding for which they are not prepared. When such opportunities arise, the sales force does not have the knowledge of how desirable an order may be at various price levels, at this time. The sales manager frequently must make these decisions based on his or her limited experience.

Another problem unique to sales management frequently occurs when sales reps report they can get a good order if their company will also buy from the customer—if they will do reciprocal buying. While this is a common problem for sales managers, and a legally complicated one, there has been little or nothing written in most texts to guide their decisions.

Sales managers can benefit by having some guidelines for analyzing the complicated problems of the sales force and competitive actions. They can use some decision-making tools to achieve better results, as compared with trial-and-error learning over a period of many years.

ANALYZING SALES FORCE PROBLEMS

Intelligent sales managers today are not concerned with what the so-called average rep will do. They search for ways to improve each individual rep. They look for ways to raise a frustrated man or woman out of a rut, to get an irresponsible young rep straightened out, to make a born loser into a winner.

To change behavior, to improve sales performance, the manager looks for ways to utilize each rep's unique strengths and minimize his or her weaknesses. Traditional sales management practices have been to reward the desired performance with money and to punish the undesired behavior with discipline, withholding money, or outright dismissal. This simplistic approach leaves much to be desired.

Human problems are signaled when someone's performance is different from what is expected of that person. For example, in a sales meeting an intelligent salesman may ask several questions which indicate he is ignorant about a certain product. Perhaps he did not hear the original introduction or did not read the sales literature. On the other hand, he may have known it well at one time and have since forgotten about it. If he is truly intelligent, his apparently stupid questions may be a form of heckling to tease the sales manager into losing his or her temper and forgetting the purpose of the sales meeting.

When a sales rep behaves differently from what is expected of the rep, the effective manager will carefully analyze the discrepancy. *The difference between what is and what should be* is the first step in identifying the problem. The difference between what is and what *might* be is part of the solution.

The first question a sales manager should answer is, "Do the performance discrepancies really matter, or should they be ignored?" If a sales rep takes too many coffee breaks, or plays golf every Thursday, or takes two-hour lunch breaks, an effective manager can look at the sales record to see if this behavior is really hurting the performance. If it does not really matter, the manager would be wise to forget it.

On the other hand, if the difference between what the sales rep is doing and what he or she should be doing is truly important, further decisions are essential. The second question on the sales manager's decision tree (see Figure 16-1) is, "Could they do it if they wanted to?" In other words, find out if the reps know how to do what is expected of them. Do they have the ability or skill required to do the job as expected? If one or more reps do not know how to do a particular job, no amount of yelling or praise will enable them to execute the job properly. Under these conditions the sales manager asks the third question, "Did they once know how to do it?" If the answer is yes, the manager is directed to retrain, provide supervised practice, or observe, test, and give corrective feedback to the sales representatives.

For example, a sales rep who performs well with existing accounts may have difficulty in getting new accounts. Perhaps he or she does not know how to get past the receptionist, so new prospects are avoided. In this case, on-the-job coaching by the sales supervisor or manager will produce the desired behavior change much more quickly than monetary rewards or punishment ever could.

If the answer is no, they never knew how to do it, the manager is directed to the branch "Provide .Training," if they can learn; or to "Modify Job" or to "Terminate or Transfer" if they cannot learn. However, sales managers should exercise caution in believing that most sales force weaknesses are training problems. In many cases the sales force *do* know how to do the job as expected but they will not do it.

If the sales force can do the proper job if they want to—a yes answer to question 2—the sales manager is directed to the alternate branch. "What happens if the sales reps perform as their manager desires?" There are three smaller branches for managers to take in question 5 concerning job motivation:

1 Zero Motivation Very often the answer to this question is that nothing happens! If a manager wants a sales rep to make eight calls per day and he or she does, this manager typically ignores the performance and picks on something else. The reps feel it really does not matter whether or not they make eight calls per day. They are being judged on some other more important criterion, such as dollar volume. The reps feel, if you do not know where the goal posts are, why run?

A salesperson who does perform as desired but is ignored will go to extreme lengths to gain satisfaction elsewhere—perhaps with friends at a cocktail lounge or with a young lady or fellow who will listen to the rep's stories. If a manager wants the rep to make eight calls per day and the rep does, the manager should praise the worker for it. The manager can keep praising until the new behavior becomes habitual.

2 Negative Motivation The second-branch possibility occurs when sales reps feel they will be punished if they do perform as desired. The sales force itself may set up unofficial limits, such as "no more than four calls per day." Any new rep who writes up six or eight calls per day is socially ostracized. They are quickly taught to observe the unwritten rules of the game or be excluded from the coffee club, the lunch group, or

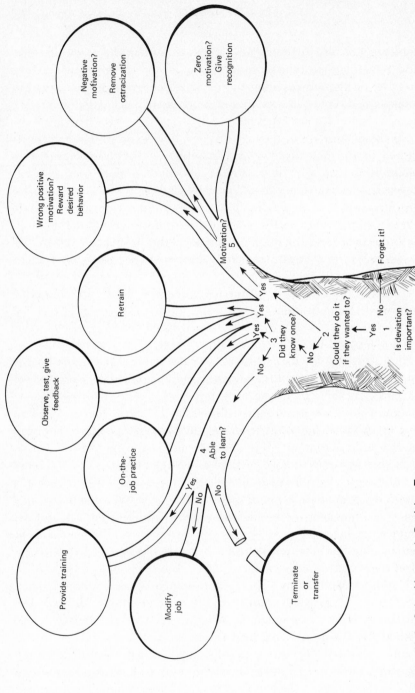

Figure 16-1 Sales Manager's Decision Tree.

the bridge team and from business cooperation. Other reps forget to give them important telephone messages, for example. Under these conditions, new trainees learn that their world is less fun if they violate the informal group norm and perform as the manager demands.

3 Positive Motivation The third-branch possibility occurs when the sales rep feels it is better to do something his or her way, in direct opposition to the sales manager's directives. Perhaps making two or three calls per day in depth generates more dollar volume for this rep than making six or eight calls per day. If the manager posts monthly dollar volume on the bulletin board and this rep ranks high on the list, one can expect him or her to boast about making so few calls per day. In other words, the rep will get more satisfaction from not performing as desired than by performing.

If sales reps do not have the potential to produce, they should be transferred to a nonsales job or terminated. The dishonest and the misfits should be blackballed out of sales and *not* be given letters of recommendation to other sales organizations. On the other hand, many good sales reps have periods of personal problems off the job which can seriously impair their judgment, emotional stability, and performance. Before firing a sales rep who has been with a company for years, it would be wise to look into his or her personal problem in more detail. There are ways a humane manager can help a good rep who develops problems.

Intelligent sales managers do not look for averages. They look at individuals. They know that a neatly dressed and smiling sales rep is the shell or facade which hides or protects the inner person. Such sales reps are probably quite confident of some of their strengths and completely unaware of most of their weaknesses. Their picture of themselves is distorted, and they are sensitive to any destructive criticism. The sales manager who knows the individual can be the friendly authority who points out the difference between what is and what might be.

RESEARCH ON COMPETITORS

Experienced sales managers constantly monitor competitive actions and regularly review their information. One of the most important areas of information desired is the compensation rate paid to top producers on the competitive sales force. Often the four or five major companies in an area will pay about the same level to their top producers, although there will be differences between individuals. A sales manager who advertises for experienced sales reps with a following, implying that they can bring accounts with them, shows his or her cards. The compensation offered will be the manager's idea of how much money it will take to get some reps to switch companies. Other knowledgeable sales managers in that industry will realize the offer is too low and no cause for alarm or that it is sufficiently high to tempt some of their reps. In the latter case, a sales manager might be wise to talk to the top producers, individually, to find out what they think of the offer.

Occasionally a weak competitor with financial troubles will promise extremely high compensation to attract top producers. A knowledgeable sales manager can inform those who might be tempted about the competitor's troubles, indicating that the promise is empty. In this situation, top producers often realize from their experiences with customers that a competitor is in serious trouble. They can inform the sales manager about it even before any advertising appears.

However, when a strong competitor offers top producers a substantial raise in compensation, they are announcing their intention to buy a larger share of that market. If there is reasonably good morale and the sales manager is respected, top producers will openly discuss the competitor's offer. Most people would prefer to stay with their existing employer rather than risk everything with another one, provided the compensation is about the same. In other words, the respected sales manager will be given a chance to match the offer before any decisions are made.

Clearly, the sales manager with adequate information will know whether competitors are in financial trouble or that they are strong and making a serious threat. This knowledge enables the manager to take decisive action. Without such information the manager is forced to make decisions blindly, from one crisis to the next.

Competitive sales reps who apply for a job without being solicited (walk-ins) are an excellent source of information. They will readily give their own compensation history (perhaps slightly exaggerated) and discuss their reasons for wanting to change. In the process they may disclose indications of competitive weaknesses or competitive changes which are planned. Whether or not the sales manager has any intention of hiring these applicants, they can provide much information to the sales manager who is willing to probe for it.

In a similar way, information about competitive starting compensation can be obtained from new applicants. While the average sales trainee may command the going rate from most competitors, an outstanding candidate may be offered substantially more by some managers. If a sales manager does not know this, and does not probe for it, he or she will miss hiring most of the outstanding candidates.

A second area of research on competitors which may be very important to the sales manager is product development. Any new products or substantial improvements over the old products may give a competitor a temporary advantage in the marketplace. If the sales manager knows the direction of competitors' research efforts, steps can be taken to alert one's own product development people. If it seems to be in a high-risk-of-failure area, some managers prefer to let the competitors take the risk. Then whenever the new product catches on, the manager's product development people are prepared to launch a similar product to take advantage of the pioneering efforts of the competition. Other sales managers may prefer to be the pioneers themselves and earn a large share of a new market before competitors can act. In either approach, knowledge of competitive product development will enhance the decision-making process.

A third area of research on competitors which may be extremely helpful to a sales manager is their choice of target-market segments. These preferences may change over time, and any early warning can alert the sales manager to future trouble or future opportunities. For example, one competitor may direct the sales force to call on another's prime target segment where tougher future competition is indicated. Conversely, they may be directed to call on an entirely different segment, in effect conceding the prime target. An astute sales manager can maintain a file on each competitor with a collection of every advertisement, indicating where it was published, and every piece of sales promotion literature, indicating whether a push strategy or a pull strategy is being used, as discussed earlier in Chapter 4. Each time a new piece is added to the file, the sales manager can review it and note any clues about competitive strategy changes. Once again, an early alert system of changes in sales strategy by competitors will enhance the manager's decision-making process.

COMPETITIVE BIDDING[1]

Competitive bidding for orders is distasteful to many sales reps because of the implied low price/low compensation ratio. Since only one bidder can win the award, more sales reps lose, and this becomes discouraging. Because it is distasteful and discouraging, many sales reps avoid accounts that require competitive bidding. When a "Request To Bid" is received, they simply turn it over to the sales manager.

On the other hand, many experienced purchasing agents firmly believe they can obtain equal quality from the lowest bidder if the specifications and other terms are written properly on the request for quotation and on the purchase order. They maintain a supplier pool of vendors who have been judged acceptable and regularly send out to them invitations to bid.

There is no doubt that many good professional purchasing agents have saved their companies substantial sums of money over the years through the use of competitive bidding. This does not mean, however, that their orders are necessarily unwanted or that they are necessarily low-profit deals for the vendor. Indeed, high-profit deals can be made by the intelligent sales manager.

Before bidding, a sales manager can learn who else has been invited to bid. In open competitive bidding—for a local government purchase, for example—the manager can learn who else has asked for the bidding forms. This information will give an approximate range of likely bids. After several such experiences the manager will see who typically bids at different levels, and he or she can then predict reasonably well how future bidding will go.

The selling is done before the specifications are written. When the

---

[1] An expanded discussion of this topic appears in Barry J. Hersker and Thomas F. Stroh, "Low Balling the P. A.," chap. 6 in *The Purchasing Agent's Guide to the Naked Salesman*, Cahners Publishing Company, Boston, 1975.

request for quotation goes out it may, intentionally or not, favor one supplier who has exclusive features, for example. All that competitors can do in this situation is to bid on basically the same items, without the exclusive features. The buyer then determines whether the exclusive features are worth the difference in bid prices. If the early selling was successful before the specs were written, the high bid has a good chance of winning the order.

A sales manager is also in a position to know if a large order has been canceled, or if the warehouse is overstocked, or if the plant is running well below capacity, for example. Any of these conditions might be just cause to bid lower than usual for a short-term gain. The sales reps out in the field usually do not have this kind of information and cannot make an intelligent bidding decision.

A sales manager may decide to bid at or near cost on a stripped-down model to get a basic order. It is then possible to direct the sales rep to call on the users to persuade them to add the optional accessories which will make their jobs easier, more comfortable, or more prestigious, or whatever benefit they can make believable. When the supplier is the only one who can provide the options to his equipment, the professional buyer may find they are expensive indeed. If those who do the requisitioning are strong enough, the sales manager will earn substantial profits on subsequent orders for the options.

When a buyer regularly asks for quotations from several vendors to keep his standard supplier honest, he leaves himself wide open to a common practice. Sales managers, with no collusion of any kind, will submit intentionally *high* quotations to accounts where they have little chance of success. If the buyer continually favors one supplier, gradually his prices will rise as competition concedes the account. The lucky supplier may remain the lowest bidder, but the buyer may never know how low it could or should be. On other accounts, the sales manager may reverse positions, so that each bidder can maintain reasonably high prices on a few accounts, as long as they bid high on other ones.

While sales reps can be taught this strategy, they usually do not have the broad view of the situation outside of their limited accounts or territories. The sales manager is frequently the only one in a position high enough to recognize where competitors are conceding business or aggressively seeking it. The manager may bid directly or may instruct a sales administrator or the territory representative to bid a certain way. This is the intelligent way to obtain high profits in competitive bidding situations. It should be honest and independent of any competitive action, but it should not be blind guessing or be left to the selfish needs of a sales rep who does not know the game.

RECIPROCITY AND IMPLICATIONS[2]

Another common problem area for sales managers today includes their decisions and handling of requests for reciprocal buying. Sales reps contact many executives, and some prospects will offer an order if the sales reps will help them get orders from the reps' company. The reps, in turn, contact the sales manager requesting the manager to talk to, or put pressure on, their own purchasing agent to buy from their potential customer.

On the surface the logic seems to be very appealing. "After all, we have to buy from someone. Why not buy from a supplier who will buy from us? One hand washes the other," are the expressions used by traditional sales managers for many years. The appeal to the purchasing agent is for him to be a good guy and help both parties. Why not, indeed?

In the first place, reciprocal buying is illegal in many cases. One who knowingly participates in such an under-the-table deal may be held legally liable. If the reciprocal buy is legal, it may create many serious problems. For example, the company auditors may question the profit involved in the exchange of orders. The people who must use the acquired products may resent the choice. The reverse is true for the supplier.

In today's climate of corporate responsibility and the public distrust of almost anyone in power, the courts are holding individuals liable for abusive actions that are judged harmful to the stockholders. The highest executives—the board of directors, who appoint and supervise the

[2]For an expanded discussion of this topic, see Barry J. Hersker and Thomas F. Stroh, "One Hand Washes the Other: Reciprocity," chap. 8 in *The Purchasing Agent's Guide to the Naked Salesman,* Cahners Publishing Company, Boston, 1975.

company president—are individually liable for corporate acts. Such boards are no longer meeting once a year to rubber-stamp plans, budgets, and decisions. They are becoming professionally involved in the daily operations of the company. Legally, they cannot tolerate any shady deals.

Most large companies today have some government contracts. These agreements normally include sections on open competitive bidding for subcontracts and materials. They often include a section on most-favored pricing and restrictive discrimination. Such legal complications may impose strict controls over how one may seek bids and place orders. Usually, if any part of an order can later be charged against the government contract, one is bound by its clauses. This might include anything charged to general and administrative expense or operational equipment used primarily but not exclusively on nongovernmental orders.

Recently, a purchasing agent for an insurance company was asked in a casual way by his president why he never ordered a certain brand of equipment. The P. A. explained that the prices were too high to justify. A few days later the president's secretary mentioned to the P. A. that the president of the supplier in question was a college classmate of their own president. This wise and experienced buyer got quotations from a number of suppliers, including the one in question. He wrote up a report concluding he could not justify the particular brand and would not buy it unless directed to do so by his president in writing. The secretary phoned the P. A. to tell him the president had the utmost confidence in him and desired him to buy what he felt was in the best interests of his firm.

While this true incident may take more intestinal fortitude to duplicate than most buyers might have, it does illustrate one fact very clearly. Top executives are very much aware of their personal liability. While they may try to influence a buyer, they will not knowingly put anything in the record that may incriminate them.

The reverse is true for the sales reps, of course. When they go to their management for approval of a reciprocal deal they have pending, they will probably receive verbal advice in private. The supplier's executives will be very wary of putting any instructions in writing regarding a reciprocal buying agreement. In this context, the sales manager and the purchasing agent dare not show that they were knowledgeable of and in agreement with any such deal.

One of the major dangers in reciprocal buying for either party is that one company is selling high-quality and often high-profit items, while the other is selling low-quality and often low-profit items. Beyond the legal implications, a sales manager does not want to get stuck on the short end of this kind of exchange. In the long run, the best possible outcome of a reciprocal buying agreement for both parties would be a fair and even exchange of products. In this very unlikely event where both parties are satisfied, what has either achieved? If two companies exchange a million dollars' worth of business on each deal at the same gross profit, neither party gains 5 cents. In fact, the commitment to tie up $1 million in this way may be very costly to one's company when future opportunities are lost because adequate funds are not available.

Reciprocity in the short run can benefit either or both parties. In the long run, however, the best that the parties can hope for is that they will break even at the risk of losing their flexibility of choice. It certainly does not make sense to take any business risk when the best possible outcome is to break even. If a sales manager is approached by a sales rep with the suggestion of a reciprocal buying arrangement, he or she should explain this break-even philosophy to the rep.

None of this commentary on reciprocal buying means one should not buy from people who also supply things to one's company. Obviously, a large company may sell its products to many customers, and some of these may also be suppliers. The point is simply that all potential suppliers should be treated openly and fairly, with no secret or special treatment and no reciprocal agreements. Reps should sell on the merits of their total product offering and not look for special-favor treatment.

SUMMARY

Analyzing the human problems within a sales force is particularly difficult because for the most part salespeople work without the direct observation of the manager. The sales manager's decision tree is offered as a way to analyze difficult situations which may involve ignorance or motivational problems. It can narrow the decision process down to likely causes of behavior deviation from the expected. It will point to corrective actions which are most apt to modify or change the behavior of the sales force or of an individual rep.

Continual research on competitors is essential if a sales manager wishes to maintain the compensation level high enough to attract and keep the high producers. A sales manager with adequate knowledge of competitors can take decisive action on compensation problems rather than act blindly from one crisis to the next. To be aware of competitive product development is also valuable in enhancing the sales management decision process. A third important area of research on competitors is their choice of target-market segments. This may signal tougher competitive actions or high-profit opportunities. It will often suggest directions for the sales force to take.

Competitive bidding is another troublesome area usually left for the sales manager's decision. Professional purchasing agents commonly require suppliers to bid for orders, and most governmental orders are on open competitive bids. High-profit orders can be negotiated in these areas by intelligent sales managers. When the selling effort is done before the specifications are written, exclusive features may permit a high bid to win the order.

If a buyer continually favors one supplier, gradually competitors will bid intentionally high to discourage further requests for future bids. The lucky favored supplier can steadily raise prices and still remain the lowest bidder. Usually the sales manager is the only one in a position to recognize where competitors are conceding this business or aggressively seeking it. Of course, all bidding should be honest and completely independent of any competitive action. However, it need not be blind guessing, as so often occurs.

In today's climate of corporate responsibility, the courts are holding individuals responsible for abusive actions that are judged harmful to the stockholders. For this reason reciprocal buying is no longer the accepted practice of "one hand washes the other." The sales force can be taught the dangers of reciprocal dealings even when they may be legal. This does not mean one cannot sell to suppliers, for obviously many do. However, all potential suppliers should be treated openly and fairly with no secret or special treatment and no reciprocal agreements, if one wishes to avoid possible legal complications.

QUESTIONS

1 Describe how the sales manager's decision tree can identify a problem and point to corrective action.

2 How can a sales manager monitor competitive action on compensation to improve his or her own decision making?

3 How can a sales manager learn of a competitor's new product developments and new targeted customers?

4 Describe several ways a sales manager can use competitive bidding to increase profitable orders.

5 What is reciprocal buying, and what are its legal implications? How should the sales manager handle requests for it from the sales force?

SELECTED REFERENCES

The Conflict Process, Conflict Resolution, and *Integrative Decision Making,* ³/₄-in. videocassettes, each 30 min, color, Intercollegiate Video Clearing House, Miami, Fla., 1976.

Filley, Alan C.: *Interpersonal Conflict Resolution,* Scott Foresman and Company, Glenview, Ill., 1975.

Hersker, Barry J., and **Thomas F. Stroh:** *The Purchasing Agent's Guide to the Naked Salesman,* Cahners Publishing Company, Boston, 1975.

Luthans, Fred, and **Robert Kreitner:** *Organizational Behavior Modification,* Scott, Foresman and Company, Glenview, Ill., 1975.

Stroh, Thomas F.: "Essential Knowledge for Successful Selling," chap. 5 in *Training and Developing Professional Salesmen,* AMACOM, American Management Association, New York, 1973.

————"How to Use Psychologically Valid Methods to Recognize Basic Strengths and Weaknesses of Salesmen," chap. 1 in *Effective Psychology for Sales Managers,* Parker Publishing Company, Inc., West Nyack, N.Y.,

▶ **Case 16-1**

MANEATER MARINE, INC.

Maneater Marine, Inc., is a Florida-based corporation engaged in the business of manufacturing boats ranging from 15 to 25 feet. Maneater was the first boat manufacturer to popularize the "open-fisherman" type of boat.

Maneater was started by Mr. Rodney ("Red") Richards in 1965. Mr. Richards was a businessman who had gained wealth from dealings in real estate. Mr. Richards had moved to Florida in 1956 because he was an ardent fisherman and Florida offered year-round fishing. Mr. Richards had purchased a number of boats but was not satisfied with their performance as fishing boats. He had also done a lot of fishing in the Florida Keys and was impressed by the way the local guides had modified their boats for fishing. Thus, the idea for the creation of his own fishing boat was started.

In 1963 Mr. Richards purchased a bare hull from a boat manufacturer and proceeded to design and build up the interior to suit himself. The finished product was unique; it had all the options that any angler could want. Mr. Richards' fishing buddies were impressed with his boat and expressed interest in owning one like it. From this Mr. Richards got the idea that his boat could be a commercial success.

Mr. Richards proceeded to hire a boat designer to incorporate his ideas into a completely new type of boat. A new type of modified deep V hull was designed to allow for running in shallow water, but it also offered a comfortable and fast ride in deep, rough water. A center console was installed to allow the angler to walk completely around the boat when fighting a fish. Features that were options on other boats were standard on this craft.

An old building in Fort Lauderdale was purchased, equipment installed, and workers hired, with the first boats coming off the production line in mid-1975. At first friends of Mr. Richards bought all the boats, which were 22 feet in length. Because of dealer inquiries and public demand Mr. Richards started designs on 17-, 19-, and 24-foot models. Additional factory space was acquired. Mr. Richards was owner, designer, and salesman for Maneater.

By 1968 Maneater boats had become so popular Mr. Richards was spending so much time with the company that he could not do any fishing. He therefore had a huge, modern factory built and hired a plant manager, a full-time design crew, and a sales force of twelve so that he could devote his time to fishing.

Six sales reps were assigned territories in Florida, and one each in the coastal areas of Louisiana, Mississippi, Alabama, Georgia, and North and South Carolina. These reps were on a straight commission plus an expense account. They were also independent, with no sales manager to report to except Mr. Richards when he wanted to talk to them. Sales representatives sold only to specific boat dealers in each territory in an exclusive dealership on a verbal agreement.

All salespeople were supplied with a master price list for all boats but were given wide leeway in the prices that they charged. This enabled the sales force to be competitive with other boat manufacturers, who by now had started to produce similar boats. Discounts were given for quantity and also to keep established accounts and to open new ones.

By 1973, Mr. Richards had little to do with the company except to consult with the design department. In the next two years sales increased substantially but profits dropped drastically. After a lengthy investigation, Mr. Richards found that the problem could be traced to some of his sales representatives.

New dealers were given rock-bottom prices by Maneater sales reps to gain new sales. Established dealers were becoming irritated because their exclusive agreements, which were between them and the sales force, were being ignored by some of the reps. Some reps had deals going with plant officials concerning preferential treatment in the shipping of boats to dealers. Some dealers and some sales reps who were not a part of this found out what was going on. Certain dealers were threatening to cancel orders, and reps were further cutting prices. Sales reps were paid a set amount for each type of boat sold regardless of the selling price or quantity sold.

Mr. Richards was in a quandry. At the present rate Maneater would be bankrupt in about a year. Dealer complaints about preferential treatment, deliveries, exclusive agreements, and prices were increasing. Some orders were being canceled. Competitors were gaining market share. The honest sales reps were threatening to quit and to bring their business to competitors.

1 How would you handle this situation if you were Mr. Richards?

2 What alternatives are possible in this real case?

▶ **Case 16-2**

ENTERTAINMENT SYSTEMS UNLIMITED

Entertainment Systems Unlimited (ESU) is a company located in Memphis, Tennessee. The primary business of the company is booking talent at major inns across the country. The company's founder and president is Joe Savarin, who used to be the head of booking entertainment for all company-owned Holiday Inns. The unique thing about the company is that instead of selling talent by way of an 8 × 10 inch glossy and a stock sales pitch, this company sells their talent by way of color videocassettes. In order to make the company a financial success, the talent pays a slightly higher commission to the agency (15 percent rather than the usual 10 percent) and must sign an exclusive contract for a period of one year. In order to keep the groups working and to know how much talent can be feasibly booked at one time, the owner of the club booking the talent must also sign a one-year exclusive contract to use the services of ESU. Each of these contracts is automatically extended for successive ninety-day periods at the end of the first year, unless terminated in writing.

The entertainment business is one of the few in which the club actually pays a certain fee for protection. This is not an add-on fee but is actually included in the price of the entertainment. A movie theater pays a certain fee for an engagement of a certain show with the understanding that the same movie will not be playing within a certain number of miles for a certain number of weeks. The same basic thing is usually adhered to in booking live talent. ESU has a policy of placing only one single, duo, trio, and group within a 25-mile area for a period of at least six months. Also, the club owner who originally bought a talent in a certain area has preference on getting that talent back when it becomes open for return engagements. This is designed to prevent a talent from making a big name in one area, and then being used in the next town 5 miles down the road six months later either as an incentive to get someone to sign up with the system or to knock out the competition.

Doug Novak is one of the sales reps for ESU. The problem he is continually running into is this: The entertainment business and its related industries are very unstable and unpredictable. The club owners have two problems that have to be handled very delicately. What happens if a certain format of music takes hold in this area and ESU does not have the talent needed to fill my requirements? The other one is this: What happens if my needs in talent change (i.e., from a single to a duo or from a five-piece group to a trio)? The way ESU has it set up, there may be only the weaker acts left to pick from if the stronger acts in my budget have played in town in the last six months. Also, if my needs stay at the new level, with the other clubs in town having first choice on the best talent when it becomes available, how will I ever be able to compete against them?

1 If you were Doug Novak, how would you field the questions from the buyers?

2 If you were Joe Savarin, how might you change the contract, offering to allow for these objections?

Part

5

CONTROLLING
AND LEADERSHIP

Continuous gains in sales productivity and profit
contribution are possible when key information is
monitored regularly to identify good opportunities
while there is still time to take advantage of them.
How the manager leads the sales force is often as
important as *what* is being attempted. Because
sales reps are different, flexibility in leadership style
seems essential. Tomorrow's sales managers may be
quite different from, and considerably better than,
today's managers.

17

Profit Opportunities
in Sales Management

▶ Objectives

The reader will understand that sales controls should provide early
warning of problem areas as well as signal profitable opportunities.
He or she will be able to analyze sales by profit contribution and to
analyze market share compared with competition. The reader will be
able to compare alternate distribution methods by their profit contribution. He or she will also recognize the need to monitor customer
attitudes, which may change before their buying behavior changes.
The reader will understand the value of optimizing profit, not maximizing it. Finally, the reader will understand how discipline and
controls can be fair and objective and also acceptable to the sales
force.

Sales control is the logical result of sales planning. Strategic control is
attempted through a tool known as the *sales audit,* which is an ongoing,
systematic, and objective measurement of sales activities and results. As
Abe Shuchman notes, an audit is intended for "prognosis as well as
diagnosis. . . . It is the practice of preventive as well as curative market-

ing medicine."[1] The sales audit tells the manager where the organization is in relation to where the plan states it should be, but it also suggests modification of the plan for the immediate future.

In the rapidly changing market environment, plans based on certain assumptions may mislead when events indicate the assumptions were false or highly inaccurate. For the next decade, world shortages of many basic raw materials will cause dramatic substitution of materials and changes in the basic design of many products. Swings in inflation and unemployment will force sales managers to adjust their plans to better fit the changing marketplace. Consumer demands and governmental controls may also necessitate radical changes in sales policies. Existing competitors and new ones entering an industry may also do a number of unexpected things, forcing a sales manager to adapt to new conditions. For these reasons a constant monitoring of the current sales effort and results is necessary to ensure that sales and profit goals will be achieved.

Performance appraisal in relation to quotas, and particulary activity quotas as discussed in Chapter 14, is of course part of the control system. However, in addition to monitoring the sales rep's individual performance, the sales audit also can keep track of sales and profits by geographic region, by product, and by customer categories. Timely early warning signals will alert the sales manager to install corrective actions and initiate positive steps to take advantage of selective profit opportunities.

Computer systems and services available today enable even the small sales organization to see what is happening in sales today and to project into the future. Such sophistication was not possible for most sales organizations five years ago. The manager can interact with the system and ask "What if . . .?" questions to stimulate alternate future actions and see their logical outcome.

Profitability control points toward corrective actions and positive opportunities to *optimize* profit. Undue pressure to maximize profit may lead to customer abuse and unethical practices which hurt the company

[1]Abe Shuchman, "The Marketing Audit: Its Nature, Purposes, and Problems," *Analyzing and Improving Marketing Performance*, Report No. 32, American Management Association, New York, 1959, p. 14. Also see Philip Kotler, "Marketing Control," chap. 20 in *Marketing Management: Analysis, Planning, and Control*, 3d ed., Prentice-Hall, Inc., Englewood Cliffs, N.J., 1976.

in the long run. The sales manager has the responsibility, therefore, to increase profit in the short run up to the point where such action will not risk losing future long-term profit. Any further action to maximize profit will be detrimental to the organization.

SALES AUDIT

In the past, most sales organizations reviewed dollar sales volume by sales rep, sometimes by item, and occasionally by customer category. Now with a data processing system management can evaluate sales on the basis of profit contribution.

The distribution of sales by items can be analyzed and shown in sequence so that the item with the largest annual sales comes first and the item with the smallest annual sales comes last. From Figure 17-1 it can be seen that the top 1 percent of all items (upper third of the data) accounts for 17.8 percent of all sales to date, as shown in the right-hand column. These six items represent nearly one-fifth of sales. Further, the top 20 percent of items (middle third of the data) accounts for 70 percent of sales to date.

Sales by individual item can also be shown comparing its cumulative sales in the current period this year with the same period last year. Year to date (YTD) compared with last year to date is shown with the percentage change indicated. See Figure 17-2.

Sales of individual items or groups of items can also be shown with gross profit, as in Figure 17-3. This type of report enables the sales manager to identify items with a high contribution of profit and to relate them to where they rank in actual sales to date in Figure 17-1. In the illustration in Figure 17-3, for example, the sales manager might direct the sales force to push the sale of acids and chemicals in order to improve overall profit contribution.

Sales analysis can be made by item class for each customer, as shown in Figure 17-4. In this illustration the customer, Tardell Hardware, purchased products in four categories with this month's sales considerably better than the same month last year. Year-to-date sales, however, show sales are off.

Using this technique, one distributor discovered he had 1300 ac-

Item No	Cumulative Count		Annual Units	Unit Cost	Annual $ Sales	Cumulative Sales	
	Rank by $ Sales	%				$	%
411045	1	.2	104,578	.966	101,023	101,023	3.8
411118	2	.4	375,959	.246	92,486	193,509	7.3
411063	3	.5	40,602	2.012	81,693	275,202	10.4
411075	4	.7	69,570	1.123	78,128	353,330	13.3
411176	5	.9	133,534	.490	65,432	418,762	15.8
411381	6	1.1	106,651	.510	54,392	473,154	17.8
411368	110	20.0	90,191	.073	6,584	1,886,385	71.0
411425	111	20.2	7,513	.800	6,011	1,892,396	71.2
411263	112	20.4	1,820	3.286	5,983	1,898,379	71.4
411503	113	20.5	10,611	.553	5,868	1,904,247	71.6
411444	545	99.2	813	.145	118	2,657,997	100.0
411465	546	99.4	4,227	.022	93	2,658,090	100.0
411243	547	99.6	90	.715	65	2,658,155	100.0
411516	548	99.8	4	2.916	12	2,658,167	100.0
411541	549	100.0	0	0	0	2,658,167	100.0

Figure 17-1 Value Analysis of Distribution by Value Report. Courtesy of IBM Corporation.

```
                        LAURENTIAN INDUSTRIES, INC.

                    COMPARATIVE ANALYSIS OF SALES BY ITEM


                         PERIOD ENDING 10/31/70                    PAGE


  ITEM                              CURR. PERIOD QUAN.  PCT    YTD QUANTITY     PCT
  NO.          DESCRIPTION          THIS YR  LAST YR    CHG   THIS YR LAST YR   CHG
  624634   D20068 OVERHAUL GASKET      10       14      29-      90      98     8-
  624832   17D0011 BELT DYNAMIC FAN   190      150      27    1,820   1,905     4-
  624901   DMK6448 HUB ASSEMBLY J2     1-        5     120-      18      18     0
```

Figure 17-2 Sales Analysis Reports. Courtesy of IBM Corporation.

```
                        LAURENTIAN INDUSTRIES, INC.

                          SALES BY ITEM CLASS

                        MONTH ENDING 03/31/70


  ITEM                        SOLD THIS   GROSS    PROFIT  SOLD THIS    GROSS    PROFIT
  CLASS   CLASS DESCRIPTION     MONTH     PROFIT   PERCENT   YEAR      PROFIT    PERCENT

   1     ABRASIVES           2,720.19   271.36      10    9,900.17    907.60      9

   2     ACIDS AND CHEMICALS 1,216.27   170.27      14    3,139.68    408.07     13

   3     BRASS               6,220.83   435.45       7   16,341.47  1,143.87      7
```

Figure 17-3 Courtesy of IBM Corporation.

```
                        LAURENTIAN INDUSTRIES, INC.

                        COMPARATIVE SALES ANALYSIS

                     BY ITEM CLASS FOR EACH CUSTOMER

                        MONTH ENDING 05/31/70                 PAGE

  CUST  ITEM   CUSTOMER/ITEM CLASS    MONTHLY SALES     PRCNT   YEAR TO DATE SALES   PRCNT
  NO   CLASS         NAME          THIS YEAR LAST YEAR   CHG   THIS YEAR LAST YEAR    CHG

  3310         TARDELL HARDWARE
         11    BUILDER HARDWARE       103.19    91.31    13     515.92    729.43     29-
         12    ELECTRICAL SUPPLIES     87.58    85.02     2     435.57    375.29     16
         13    GIFTS AND SUNDRIES      63.01      .00          315.09     490.36     35-
         14    HOUSEWARES             198.05   150.23    32     990.32   1,123.19    12-
```

Figure 17-4 Courtesy of IBM Corporation.

counts, representing 32 percent of all customers, who purchased less than 1 percent of total volume. Looking at the other end of the report, ranking customers by size of cumulative orders, he found that he had more than 1700 accounts who bought at least $1000 annually and accounted for 95 percent of the volume. Using this kind of information a sales manager can decide on the call frequency pattern for the sales force so that little time is wasted servicing small accounts which impair profitability.

The comparative sales analysis by customers for each salesman is shown in Figure 17-5. This analysis enables the rep to spot potential sales improvement for each customer. It may also alert the rep to the fact that competitors are working hard on selected accounts, and thus extra effort and service are needed quickly on those particular accounts.

A sales manager can design the report format to serve the unique needs of his or her company. Characteristic of today's computer system is an inquiry capability located in the branch, district, and headquarters offices. These terminals are connected via teleprocessing facilities to a computer, and the system can provide a broad inqugry coverage relating to sales activity updated on a daily basis.

For example, one region may be comlared with another to see if all reps are having trouble selling one product category or if the difficulty is unique to one region. If a single region is having trouble, the detailed reports of individual reps can be scanned to isolate the one or more who are having difficulties. Conversely, when one region is having outstanding performance, it can be quickly determined whether it is due to a few reps or to most of them. The manager may be able to learn what they are doing differently that increases their sales. The rest of the sales force can then be directed or trained to do the same things while there is still time to take advantage of profitable opportunities.

```
                        LAURENTIAN INDUSTRIES, INC.

                   COMPARATIVE SALES ANALYSIS BY CUSTOMER

                           FOR EACH SALESMAN

                        PERIOD ENDING 07/31/70                 PAGE

 SLMN   CUST.     SALESMAN/CUSTOMER   THIS PERIOD   THIS PERIOD   YEAR-TO-DATE   YEAR-TO-DATE
 NO.    NO.           NAME            THIS YEAR     LAST YEAR     THIS YEAR      LAST YEAR
  10              A R WESTON
        1426      HYDRO CYCLES INC      3,210.26      4,312.06      10,010.28       9,000.92
        2632      RUPP AQUA CYCLES      7,800.02      2,301.98      20,322.60      11,020.16
        3217      SEA PORT WEST CO         90.00CR      421.06         900.00         593.10

                  SALESMAN TOTALS      10,920.28      7,035.10      31,732.88      20,614.18

  12              H T BRAVEMAN
        0301      BOLLINGER ASSOCIATES    100.96         0.00         100.96           0.00
```

Figure 17-5 Courtesy of IBM Corporation.

The sales audit, then, can show where profitable sales are being made, by individual rep, by item, by territory, by region, and by customer categories. The computer system makes it possible for this information to be updated daily so that an inquiring sales manager can learn instantly where deviations from expectations are occurring. It will signal both good performance and poor performance, the timely recognition of which will enable the manager to take corrective action or to capitalize on profitable situations.

SALES ANALYSIS

While the sales audit shows where a company is today in relation to last year or in relation to expectations and quotas, sales analysis shows what happened in the past and also projects trends into the future. It also compares the situation of the company with that of competitors, the state of the national economy, or some leading indicator. For example, the sales audit may show that sales and profits are up 15 percent but that alone is not necessarily good. Perhaps competitors are up 30 percent or the national economy has swung from a recession to a boom, and sales and profits should be considerably higher.

Computer Terminal Displays Using a computer terminal display a sales manager can assess the effects of a special sales promotion, for example. Figure 17-6 shows that unit sales jumped dramatically after the fourth month, when the campaign began, and its impact carried into the ninth month. The cost of that promotional campaign can then be compared with the increase in gross profit which it generated. Historical data of this kind can be useful in making future sales management decisions regarding proposed promotional deals.

If data for some periods are missing, the system can substitute an average of the periods on either side of the missing period. For important items, terminal displays of historical data can assist in conditioning data. In the case of missing data or exceptionally high data, the sales manager can substitute demand values that may be more realistic than the averages automatically substituted by the system. For example, Figure 17-7 shows missing data in the fourth period. The system will automatically average periods three and five to fill in that point. However, the

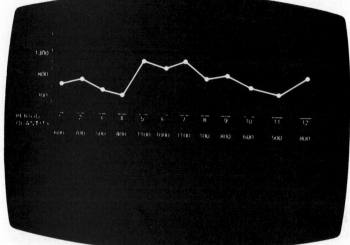

Figure 17-6 A terminal display of data points can assist in making a judgment concerning the condition of data. *Source: IBM Communications Oriented Production Information and Control System*, Vol. 3. Courtesy of IBM Corporation.

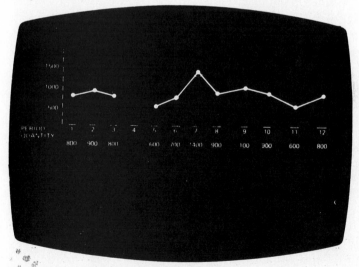

Figure 17-7 Courtesy of IBM Corporation.

sales manager may know that period four was particularly poor because of a strike or a fire, for example. A better estimate can then be substituted. In period seven, the unusual demand may have been due to a one-month sales contest, and the manager may feel that sales were held off somewhat in period six and anticipated for period eight, so that the bunched sales do not truly reflect average monthly demand. In this manner, the sales manager can interact with the data to improve the decision-making process.

In a similar manner, a terminal display can visually signal seasonal fluctuations which might not be noticed in tabulated data. If the periods are too large—yearly, for example—the significant seasonal patterns can be missed. Sales of a new product introduced with much enthusiasm may show a typical run of data. Figure 17-8 shows that periods 1 and 2 may be rejected in future forecasts because they represent the introductory period of the product's sale.

The data system will compute and display a seasonal factor to be applied to each period within the cycle (bottom line, Figure 17-9). The seasonal pattern is a supplement to the long-term trend. It appears as a periodic fluctuation around the trend. For example, in Figure 17-9 the long-term trend would indicate that the sales forecast for December of the first year is 1000. The seasonal factor for December is 0.8; hence, the actual forecast is 0.8 × 1000, or 800 units.

Market Share Analysis A measurement of sales performance relative to competitors usually avoids the contaminating effects of the noncon-

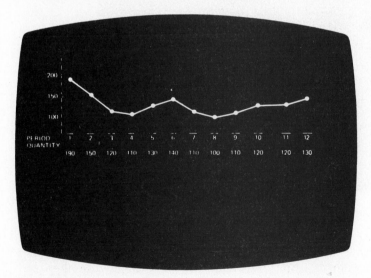

Figure 17-8 Courtesy of IBM Corporation.

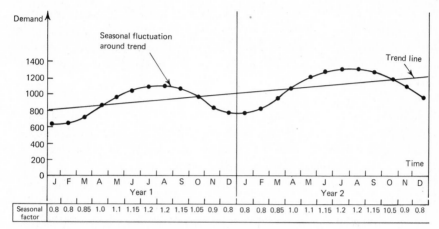

Figure 17-9 Seasonal fluctuation around the trend occurs at the same time every year. Courtesy of IBM Corporation.

trollable factors in the marketplace. Changes in the economy, inflation, unemployment, and so forth, presumably have the same impact on all competitors in one line of products. For this reason, many sales managers use market share as the key indicator to how well they are doing. For example, if sales decline from the preceding year but share of market increases, this indicates the manager did a better job than competitors under some adverse conditions which affected the entire industry.

There are thousands of trade associations in the United States, and many of them collect and report total industry sales by product line. A sales manager can easily compute his or her percentage of the total reported to find the individual share of the market. The government reports new car registrations, housing starts, and other data which may be applicable to some industries. The A. C. Nielsen Company conducts store audits in the grocery, drug, and certain other fields. The Market Research Corporation of America (MRCA) gathers information on consumer spending through a panel of consumers maintaining diaries recording their purchases. From these services manufacturers can buy data on size of total market by product class, brand share, relative importance of types and sizes of containers, and trends. Nielsen also reports on retailer inventories, out-of-stock conditions, retail prices, and point-of-purchase displays. As noted in the discussion on activity quotas, these measurements can be important to some sales managers. While share-of-market figures may indicate relative strengths and weaknesses, they should not be used as the primary measurement of sales management performance. They ignore the profitability of a product, which is the true measure of performance. For example, an expensive point-of-purchase display effort may increase sales of market, but it may also cause great losses of profit.

Distribution Cost Analysis While sales analysis is concerned with increasing revenue, distribution cost analysis is concerned with reducing expenses to increase profits. It attempts to measure the relative profitability of different ways of serving markets. For example, a manufacturer of office furniture might have a sales force to sell direct to large accounts, a dealer sales force to sell to retailers, and a catalog sales department to handle mail orders. Cost analysis would be used in this situation to determine the profitability of each method of selling. The sales manager would like to know how small an order can be in each category and still be profitable. What is the minimum size of a profitable account? Which channel generates the greatest contribution to profit?

In these problem areas the difficulty is in allocating expenses to each channel, each account, or each sales rep. For example, the home office sales management and administrative staff expense may be allotted on the basis of the amount of time these employees spend on each channel. However, this will usually vary to a large degree. Problems arise which demand much attention and effort regardless of the size of the order or its profit. If expenses are distributed as a proportion of total volume, the high sales producers are charged much more than the low producers. The direct costs of sales reps' compensation and expenses in relation to their orders can be meaningful. The indirect costs of home office support can be misleading. The nontraceable common costs, such as expenditures to maintain corporate image or to pay interest on corporate debts, for example, are usually arbitrary and beyond the control of those people or operations being measured. The full-cost approach to profitability control is subject to serious questions; however, the basic concept is sound.[2]

Most companies avoid the problem by looking at gross contribution to overhead and to net profit from a sales rep, from certain categories of

[2]Sam R. Goodman, *Techniques of Profitability Analysis,* John Wiley & Sons, Inc., New York, 1970.

products, from certain groups of customers, or from certain channels of distribution. With each of these, there will be some obvious major costs which may be compared with the gross profit. This is the basic information which a sales manager needs to make intelligent decisions. Any profit above the obvious major costs is not considered as net profit, but simply as contribution to net profit. The IBM Corporation illustrations in this chapter use the gross profit figure to compare the relative importance of sales reps, products, and customers.

CUSTOMER SATISFACTION

Perhaps the truest measure of sales performance and the best determinant of long-term profit is customer satisfaction. One indirect measure of this is the customer attrition rate, or the percent of lost accounts over a time period, typically one year. But this does not give any indication of the degree of satisfaction. Some apparently loyal customers may continue buying a product even though they have strong dislikes about it. They may feel it is simply the best of a sorry lot. Many purchases are made in spite of the sales reps, not because of them.

Asking the opinions of intermediaries (middlemen) tends to give biased results because intermediary agents are often in the role of antagonists, resisting the manufacturer's efforts. They generally want lower prices and higher support and services. Asking the sales force about the degree of customer satisfaction has the opposite bias because few reps will report anything negative about their own sales performance. To learn of customer satisfaction requires the direct solicitation of customers' opinions.

Because opinions change over time, and dissatisfaction usually precedes switching brands or products, sales managers can survey both customers and noncustomers on a current and a continuing basis. It is important to sample the nonbuyers to learn what they like about doing business with competitors or what they dislike about one's own company. The customer attitudes can reveal which product features are strongly liked, which merely accepted, and which disliked. They may reveal the importance of price or the relative value the customer places on certain products or lines of products. The quality level may be considered too high for the intended purpose, adequate, or too low.

Customer satisfaction with the sales force is also crucial information for sales management. The occasional complaint letter or praise letter to the company president should not be assumed to represent all customers. Most dissatisfied customers will quietly take their business to competitors. Those who are reasonably satisfied will quietly continue to place orders. However, buying is not a true measure of the customers' degree of satisfaction with the sales force. Too many sales reps are known as order takers who do little or no creative selling. Customers often want money-saving ideas from the sales force. They may want more service, such as training of their employees. Retailers may want help in improving their advertising, sales promotion, or point-of-purchase displays.

Customer attitude surveys should reveal how well the sales force meets customer expectations. Such surveys can be handled by market research firms, by independent consultants, by college marketing groups, and directly by the company itself. The danger in openly soliciting customers' opinions, however, is the tendency for customers to say what they think the company wants to hear. They will rarely complain in writing about their sales rep to the sales manager. More objective data and more meaningful replies can usually be obtained by going through an independent third party.

In industrial sales and in selling to intermediary agents, the sales force is in a position to help the customers optimize their purchasing and inventory policies. With data processing systems they can compute which items should be stocked in what quantities to prevent stock-outs or to provide a certain level of customer satisfaction. A paper merchant using an inventory data processing system was able to double sales without expanding inventory, and he had a stock turnover twice the industry average. A hardware wholesaler was able to handle a 20 percent sales increase while reducing his regular inventory by $150,000. A plumbing supply house reduced stock-outs from 20 percent to 5 percent without increasing inventory.

Unfilled customer needs for products and services may be revealed by attitude surveys, and these may represent profitable opportunities. The sales manager who receives timely signals such as these is in a position to innovate and fill those needs before competition does. The manager who does this regularly will build long-term loyalty with existing customers as well as win new customers.

CORRECTIVE ACTION

The purpose of controls such as the sales audit and cost analysis is, of course, to improve profit by taking corrective actions and positive steps to utilize recognized opportunities. Unfortunately, in too many organizations promotions and bonuses are based entirely on sales and profit performance. This extreme pressure from top management can lead to unethical and illegal practices throughout a sales organization.

Corrective action to improve short-term profit is often the opposite of action to improve long-term profit. For example, in a situation of short-term shortage, there is a temptation to raise prices to all the traffic will bear. In the long run, customers who feel they are being overcharged will search for substitutes and alternate sources of supply. Customer dissatisfaction may become so great that many will elect to do without the product or service altogether.

Whatever the economics of increasing profit to its maximum, consumer movements and legal restraints eventually enter the picture. High profit also attracts new competitors into an industry, and foreign competition may gain the competitive edge. Environmentalists have successfully increased legislative restraints to improve the quality of water and air. Biodegradable products and packaging are mandatory in many areas. Concern for consumer safety and health has caused many restraints to be placed on some of the largest companies in the world.

For these reasons top management and stockholders should consider the optimization of profit as the realistic selfish goal. As conditions, including taxes, exist today and as they are likely to exist tomorrow, what reasonable results can be expected? Which risks of retaliation is the company willing to take and which ones must be avoided at all costs? These are clearly top-management decisions, and the sales manager would be well advised to know their answers.

Discipline and Control   If the sales force is given a broad generalization such as "Keep all expenses reasonable," they are apt to start by spending small amounts and gradually but steadily increase the total. It would be logical for them to test the limits of the manager's permissiveness and patience.

All sales reps should know the system of rules which are designed to affect their conduct and actions. They should know how their performance will be measured and the standards of behavior by which they must abide. In addition, they should know what the rewards are and what the punishment will be if they violate the rules. Rules with controls and discipline are essential to achieve any group activity, particularly in a sales organization, in which individuals strive for independence. If the entire sales force knows the rules before the game starts, the rules are not seen as a threat but the way to play the game.

A second principle of discipline is that each sales rep should be aware that all rules will be enforced against all people equally; no one individual will be singled out as an example for all to see. They should feel confident that the sales manager will not pick on one individual because of personal bias and neglect to enforce the same rule with others. All controls can be designed to check or regulate the sales rep's behavior and keep it within prescribed limits. The discipline can be designed to enforce compliance in areas which are important to both the sales force and the company.

Enforcement of the rules can be firm and automatic without any personal malice. It need not be the manager against the sales rep, but the objective consideration whether the sales rep did or did not violate an impersonal rule. There is no need to embarrass or humiliate the sales rep, because the purpose of discipline is to make the individual a better representative within the rules of conduct.

Generally, enforcement of control and discipline in a sales situation is accomplished through the amount of discretionary power delegated to each sales rep. Each person should be given enough room to make mistakes and learn from them. In this sense, discipline is an opportunity for training in self-control and the development of strengths. The sales force is given instructions and they then practice in the field to perfect what they have learned. They expect the manager to periodically observe their behavior directly and recognize their improvement or correct their weaknesses.

Those sales reps who do not belong in sales should be weeded out quickly for their own good. Every month or year spent in the wrong occupation is wasted and can never be recovered. The savings in terminating the misfits early will be in addition to improving customer relations. Unscrupulous practices need not be tolerated in a sales force.

SUMMARY

Sales controls are used to monitor progress in an ongoing pursuit of goals in a constantly changing environment. A self-designed data system can give early sggnals of problem areas in time to take corrective action. It can also signal profitable opportunities in time to take positive steps to capitalize on them.

With modern technology even relatively small sales organizations can now evaluate sales on the basis of profit contribution, by rep, by region, by item, by product line, by customer, by categories of customers, and by alternate channels. The computer system makes it possible for this information to be updated daily so that an inquiring sales manager at a distant terminal, for example, can learn instantly where deviations from expectations are occurring.

The sales analysis looks at performance in relation to things outside the company, such as competitors' performance or changes in the national economy, for example. Using a computer terminal display, a sales manager can assess the value of special promotions, sales contests, and other sales management variables. The manager can interact with the data and modify them to better reflect reality as well as to project what is apt to happen in the event certain assumptions are changed. Seasonal fluctuations can be identified more easily, and the computer will figure the sales variation to be expected monthly, for example.

Market share analysis provides a measure of performance compared with competitors' sales under the same changing conditions in the marketplace. It should not be used as the sole criterion, however, because market share ignores the profitability of a product.

Distribution cost analysis is concerned with increasing profit by reducing expenses. It attempts to show the relative value of doing business a certain way or with selected target customers as compared with other alternatives. Most companies use gross contribution to profit as the measure of relative value, rather than using the full-cost approach to profitability. With use of a computer data system, gross profit contribution can be figured for different channels, for example, and the sales manager's judgment is then required regarding the major costs of handling each alternate considered.

One of the best measures of sales performance is a survey of customer attitudes which indicates the degree of satisfaction or dissatisfaction with the product or service. Because opinions change over a period of time, and because dissatisfaction usually precedes changing buying behavior, sales managers can survey customers and noncustomers on a current and continuing basis. Trends can be identified which will signal future trouble areas. Opportunities to provide better service can be identified and often new products can be innovated to meet unfilled needs in the market.

The purpose of all controls is to improve profit by taking corrective actions respecting negative situations and by making positive moves to take advantage of recognized profit opportunities. Undue pressure to maximize profit, unfortunately, leads to unscrupulous practices and illegal actions. Optimizing profit seems to be a more realistic goal for both short-term profit and long-term profit. Otherwise the risk of retaliation by consumers, environmentalists, new competition, higher taxes, or governmental controls is too great.

Rules with controls and discipline are essential to achieve any group activity, particularly in a sales organization. When they are fair and clearly understood by the sales force, rules are not seen as a threat but the way to play the game. Discipline can be enforced fairly to all, and it can be objective rather than subjective. A sales rep did or did not violate any impersonal rule. If he or she did, automatic penalties are invoked. Misfits, such as the dishonest or the unscrupulous, can be quickly terminated for the benefit of both the sales organization and the customers. This, clearly, is the ultimate control which a sales manager is responsible for exercising.

QUESTIONS

1 How can a sales audit of past performance help a manager make better decisions for future action?

2 How can sales analysis help direct the sales force in its call pattern and the frequency of calls?

3 Describe how a terminal display can be used to help a sales manager

determine what might happen if he or she had a sales contest or special promotion.

4 What is the purpose of a market share analysis, and what is its major weakness?

5 What benefits can be derived from a distribution cost analysis?

6 How can surveys of customer opinions predict future problem areas or profitable opportunities?

7 What are the dangers of maximizing profit?

8 How can rules with controls and discipline be made readily acceptable to the sales force?

SELECTED REFERENCES

Kotler, Philip: "Marketing Control," chap. 20 in *Marketing Management: Analysis, Planning, and Control,* 3d ed., Prentice-Hall, Inc., Englewood Cliffs, N.J., 1976.
Management Reports in Today's Business, International Business Machines Corporation, General Systems Division, Atlanta, Ga., 1973.
McCarthy, Jerome E.: "Controlling Marketing Programs," chap. 29 in *Basic Marketing: A Managerial Approach,* 5th ed., Richard D. Irwin, Inc., Homewood, Ill., 1975.
Newman, William H., and **E. Warren Kirby:** "Basic Elements of Control," chap. 21 and "PERT and Budgetary Control," chap. 22 in *The Process of Management,* Prentice-Hall, Inc., Englewood Cliffs, N.J., 1977.
Ross, Joel, and **Robert Murdick:** *Management Information Systems,* Prentice Hall, Inc., Englewood Cliffs, N.J., 1976.
Sales Management (semimonthly), Sales Management, New York. "Survey of Selling Costs," the first issue each January.
Stanton, William J., and **Richard H. Buskirk:** "Sales Department Budgets," chap. 20; "Analysis of Net Sales Volume," chap. 23; and "Marketing Cost Analysis," chap. 24 in *Management of the Sales Force,* 4th ed., Richard D. Irwin, Inc., Homewood, Ill., 1974.

Still, Richard R., Edward W. Cudiff, and Norman A. P. Govoni: "The Sales Budget," chap. 18 and "Sales Control and Cost Analysis," chap. 20 in *Sales Management,* 3d ed., Prentice-Hall, Inc., Englewood Cliffs, N.J., 1976.

▶ Case 17-1

THE APPLIANCE STORE, INC.

Billy Steadfast, newly appointed sales manager at The Appliance Store, Inc., had a problem. He had been on the job only a few weeks when it came to his attention. Billy's background had been in sales, so he had heard of cases like this before.

Joe had been one of the top salesmen in the store for a number of years. In fact, Joe had worked for the company for over ten years. In the last two years, however, there had been a marked decline in Joe's sales and his overall production record.

There had been numerous customer complaints about his work and his manners. He had been late many times—in fact, so many times that he now did not bother to come in until noon. To add to this, he often left early. There had been too much reliance on Joe's coworkers to cover for him and even to do some of his stacked-up paperwork. The problem really became noticeable when his fellows began falling behind in their work trying to keep up with his. Joe was paid on straight salary and seemed unconcerned by the remarks that were being made about him by his coworkers.

Mr. Steadfast realized that something had to be done. He approached the problem cautiously at first because he was so new. He did realize that if he did nothing, it would be a direct reflection on him. He really did not know how to approach the problem at first. After discussing it with upper-level managers, he decided to call Joe in for a conference.

With the nature of the situation, Mr. Steadfast invited in some top-level people who knew Joe. They wanted to make it precisely clear what they expected from Joe. They told him that he had been one of the best producers and that he could regain that position again. With the new sales manager on the scene, there would necessarily be some distinct changes in the work habits Joe had acquired while under the more lax sales manager. A written documentation spelling out the standards of achievement that were expected of him was shown and signed by all. There were provisions for a review of the performance in sixty days. If there had been no noticeable improvement in that time, Joe was going to be offered the option of being either demoted or released. There could be no confusion on his part about what was expected of him. It was all there in black and white.

During the evaluative period, it came to Mr. Steadfast's attention that Joe's real problem was drinking. This fact was the major contribution to the work deterioration that Joe was experiencing. For a short while Joe's work seemed to improve. At least, he seemed more alert. Perhaps the conference was going to bring him around. This was not to be.

Before the sixty-day trial period was over, Joe had lapsed into his old ways. The sales manager actually wanted to release Joe at this time. However, there were considerations over which he had no control. Joe had been with the company for ten years, and other managers felt that he should be given another chance. Ordinarily the sales manager would have final say; but in the case of this company, management tries not to release anyone with that much service to the company. That is policy. However, a person could be released immediately if there were a direct question concerning his morals or if he was caught stealing. That is policy too. Joe, therefore, was given another chance. Thus he was demoted and lost much of his responsibility. But from his standpoint, he still had a job. It paid less, but it was still a job. It is this attitude that is causing so many of Joe's problems.

Joe has been given fair warning that any further trouble—either failing to live up to goals that were set for him or lapsing into his old ways—would result in dismissal. This is where we leave Joe, on thin ice. His work really has not improved, and Mr. Steadfast would have released him long ago, but the pressures on him to keep Joe around were still great. It is hard to say who has the worst problem, Joe or Mr. Steadfast. It seems that Mr. Steadfast's authority could be undermined by having to keep this person around. What should he do? Assert authority and really try to fire Joe, or please the others and keep the keep the guy around? It seemed strange to Mr. Steadfast that all Joe's coworkers had complained so much about his lack of work until they thought that Joe could be fired. They all said, "Gee, no, we don't want that!"

1 What would you do with Joe?

2 How might you prevent this situation from occurring with other sales reps in the future?

▶ Case 17-2

PRECISION WATCHES, INC.

Precision Watches, Inc., is a commercial distributor of Seiko watches. They cover the entire state, wholesaling to jewelry and department stores. Seiko watches are classified in the $50-and-up range. This price range accounts for 18 percent of the watch units of all makes sold in the United States in 1976, or a total dollars of $55 million. Seiko's objective is to capture 10 percent of that 18 percent.

Paul Luksa is the person in charge of Precision's six-person sales force. Each sales rep takes care of roughly 175 accounts. The state is divided into six geographic sections. The sales rep should visit each account on an average of once every six weeks. With all the growth the state is experiencing, a seventh salesperson will soon be added and there will be an adjustment of the territories.

The salespeople all work on a straight commission with the sales reps paying all expenses, except when they attend national meetings. Paul speaks on the phone to each of the reps three times a week and sees them once a month. Paul will go with salespeople to larger accounts on an infrequent basis only to discuss inventory levels and co-op advertising. He hardly ever gets involved with making a sale.

When dealing with national accounts, Precision Watches must follow guidelines, set by Seiko, on how much each store or outlet is allowed to purchase. For example, if each Zales jewelry store's limit is fifty watches, Paul instructs the sales reps not to attempt to sell more, keeping with the previously arranged guidelines between Zales Company and Seiko Time Corporation.

The sales year is divided by two selling seasons: the fall—June 1 to

December 31—and the spring—January 1 to May 31. Each sales rep has a quota for a season. The salesperson is given an update every month on how he or she is doing on orders. This is where the problem stems from. There is a large difference between orders written and orders confirmed.

When salespersons write orders, 60 percent of those orders are with independent jewelers and 40 percent are with national accounts. The only reason an order would not go through when dealing with an independent would be a problem with credit. Even when this happens, the canceled order is accounted for early enough, the outcome of the order is known, and correct information is passed to the salesperson.

Not so correct information is given to the sales reps on their progress with national accounts. All orders with these accounts must have confirmation from the home office. Confirmation of the order can come within two weeks, and usually half of these orders are confirmed within this two-week period. But the fate of the other half of these orders is unknown for as long as two months.

Three main reasons cause the time delay. First, orders do not get sent to the home office as they are supposed to be. Second, stores are merchandised by dollar amounts of stock on a national-level rating—if the store exceeds this amount, they cannot buy more inventory and do not know their standing when the order is placed. The last main reason is that some stores are overinventoried in watches of competitors and the home office will not approve the order until the stores move the stock. This half of the unconfirmed orders did account for roughly $100,000 per salesperson in the spring season alone.

Paul tells each sales rep how he or she is doing in relation to the salesperson's quota, treating all written orders as confirmed orders. Although a sales rep is ahead of her quota by 10 percent, by the time the final outcome of the orders is known, she may find herself behind her quota by 10 percent. As Paul stated, "What can I do if the feedback that I give to my sales reps on their performance often restrains them from taking the appropriate action? Maybe I should just give the salespeople an update every week instead of every month."

1 How might a computer system be used to reduce or eliminate this problem?

2 How can the cost of selling be reduced in this situation?

▶ Case 17-3

PARTY CASUAL WEAR

This manufacturer's sales forecasting has been in error over a twelve-month period. The planners thought the new fad of prewashed clothes would be a hit in all types of clothes—other types as well as casual. Prewashed fabrics were a hit, but the company did not take into consideration whether people wanted this style in all items.

They forecast for the first six months of 1975 sales of $150,000, but actual sales were only $135,000; for the following six months, sales of $155,000 were forecast but recorded sales were only $140,000.

The company had presumed that people wanted the prewashed look in evening wear such as pant suits, jump suits, and dresses, which caused it to buy new machinery that was designed to run the clothes through the prewashed process. They then expanded into making swimwear and coordinated tops and blouses for girls and guys, before researching whether young people wanted to be seen in wrinkled, washed-out-looking suits.

Because of the special process of prewashing, the cost would be higher than the normal $15–$20 suit. It would mean approximately a $25–$28 retail price.

Each sales rep was asked to determine what he or she would probably sell according to last year's sales to certain companies, but of regular fashions. Obviously, the sales of prewashed clothes could not be accurately forecast if these fashions would not sell in the rep's stores.

1 How might a computer be utilized to forecast demand on a short-term basis of a few weeks or a month?

2 How might you test consumer acceptance of new fashions before national introduction?

18

Psychology for Effective Sales Force Leadership

► Objectives

The reader will understand the human side of managing sales representatives and be able to discriminate between management by objectives and management by exception. He or she will be able to recognize and use five different styles of leadership in a system appropriate to changing conditions. Finally, the reader will be able to use the integrated decision method of resolving conflicts so that both parties win.

Most control functions in sales force management are sedentary in that they are thoughtful activities such as planning objectives, designing policy and procedures, devising quotas, and monitoring performance. The active, dynamic part of control operates at the first line of supervision. How the manager handles the day-to-day control function often determines what will be accomplished.

For example, a sales rep who is criticized for making too few calls is apt to be very defensive and may easily become mentally blocked against further communication. One who cannot rationalize his or her behavior as being acceptable is apt to accuse the attacker of being stupid and not worthy of attention. With a blank stare, the rep may silently communicate this to the sales manager. The manager may interpret this behavior as evidence of a poor attitude and either lose his temper completely or dismiss the salesperson with a sense of utter frustration. Neither the sales person nor the manager will have gained anything from such a meeting. Both will have adrenalin pumping into the circulatory system, and will possibly take out their anger on someone else, or else they may keep it within and upset their digestion or other body functions.

Clearly, to be effective, the sales manager can establish a climate which will encourage honest two-way communications and understanding. Criticism can be fair and objective, and it can be made very constructive. The sales manager does not have to be a police inspector who enforces rules. He or she can be the friendly authority who is willing to help make the sales rep a better person in the future.

When dealing with control, one tends to think of improving weaknesses or eliminating faults. While these negative aspects must be recognized and corrected, this is only one-half of the human behavior of the sales force. The positive side is the recognition and implementation of the sales rep's strengths. Too often a sales rep's good points are taken for granted and relatively ignored. Because no one seems to care about such things, the sales rep is apt to neglect to do the very thing in which he or she will succeed.

Traditional management theory has been to contrast sales performance with the manager's concern for the people. While this has caused managers to become aware of how they lead, direct, and control the sales force, it has done little to improve the sales people. Since each sales rep is unique, each may require different kinds of leadership. Different situations may call for varying leadership styles. Modern sales managers are aware of this need for flexibility in their style of leadership.

Confrontation between the sales manager and a sales rep may evolve into a conflict in which one or both lose. The opposite of conflict, however, is problem solving, which may result in both parties achieving what they want. Modern management has constructed an integrated decision method which is used consciously to resolve conflicts to make both parties feel, and act, like winners.

MANAGEMENT BY EXCEPTION

When employing traditional "management by objectives" as a whip to drive the sales force, human troubles can occur, as discussed in Chapter 4. Constant pressure and ulcer-producing needling to exceed quotas increase hostility and defensive behavior mechanisms. Cynics were not born that way. They are created by poor management practices.

If competition dramatically cuts prices, for example, and the sales rep's company is not willing to meet the lower price, there is nothing to be gained by chewing out the sales force to sell harder and work longer hours to make quota. What they need is more information on how to combat the problem, such as performance test data and better guarantees. If the company feels the price cuts are temporary and more customer loyalty will be maintained by a constant fair price, the sales force should be so advised and should be trained to give convincing presentations to offset price competition.

On occasion, one sales rep may have trouble because of a depressed industry which dominates the territory. Since this is clearly beyond the control of the sales rep, it will be demoralizing if sales management holds the quota constant or berates the rep's lack of imagination in seeking new accounts. The sales rep has family and financial obligations, and he or she needs help and encouragement, not a kick when down. The manager may offer delayed billing or seasonal dating for this one territory, if it can be done legally without discriminating against other customers. Extended credit is another possibility the sales manager may wish to pursue. For some industries the manager might offer a rent-with-option-to-purchase plan. The point is simply to help a sales rep in problem areas in which he or she has little or no control or influence.

Management by exception is a much more human concept which appears most suited to managing the sales force.[1] Using this system, the sales reps are given an area of responsibility in which to operate and for which each individual alone is responsible. Within that area, each one is not only permitted but forced to operate his or her own way without interference. The manager gets routine reports of performance and progress but stays out of the way.

[1]Lester R. Bittel, *Management by Exception,* McGraw-Hill Book, Company, New York, 1964.

In this control system, the sales manager tells the reps what they must do and how the job is to be performed. This might include making twenty-five calls on stated accounts with a written report due every Friday, for an example of one phase of the total system. Now, as far as this one aspect of the job goes, the sales manager will check once each week and not bother the sales rep as long as he or she meets the stated requirements. However, if a sales rep is making only fifteen calls per week, this exception will be automatically triggered to the manager's attention. If the rep's sales are holding steady as planned but the number of calls each day is dropping off, it may signal future trouble, or it may not. The sales rep may have found a new, perhaps better, way of contacting all assigned accounts. Perhaps it is to write ten letters every day and to phone each account once every week. One may indeed be serving the customers and the company better by using time this way.

When a deviation occurs which is not what was expected, the sales manager need not look for trouble or problems exclusively. Many positive deviations are also possible. The apparent disadvantage of applying this concept is that it places the manager in the role of an error-detecting servomechanism. "It is rough on the manager, for he receives nothing but bad news all day. If things are going right, he gets no signals; all he hears about are deviations from what is supposed to be happening."[2] When the concept is applied appropriately, managers do get progress reports which are favorable. They have time to observe the personal development of individual sales reps. When asked for a report by top executives, the managers have the opportunity to show off their promising sales reps by bringing them into the conference. These are a few of the deep personal satisfactions that managers do achieve on the job. Their relief from routine processing also gives them much-needed time for long-range planning.

The limits of authority may be expanded or contracted as the sales manager sees fit. One technique used to control a sales rep's activities is the routing and scheduling plan to improve territory coverage and reduce expenses. In scheduling a new rep, the manager might designate the specific accounts to be called upon each day as well as the hour at which each call is to be made. Initially, the manager might check the new rep's reports daily to see how he or she is working and to detect needed

[2]Myron Tribus, as quoted in "The Management Machine—Can It Work?" *Dun's Review,* vol. 94, no. 6, p. 27, December 1969.

adjustments. For any variation or discrepancies noted, the rep can be asked to explain. At this early stage of development, adherence to the plans can also be enforced if the sales manager makes frequent and unannounced visits to the field.

As new reps develop good work habits and earn the trust of the manager, they may be allowed to construct their own routes and schedules and simply file their plans ahead of their trips. When the manager is informed at all times of the sales forces' whereabouts in the field, it is possible to contact them with last-minute instructions or updated information. As each sales rep becomes more experienced, detailed scheduling becomes less feasible. This is true because effective reps are better able to solve more problems for their customers and the time element becomes less predictable. Finally, the experienced and highly motivated sales reps might be asked to report only their past activities and expenses, with future planning left entirely to their own discretion.

In this system of management by exception a manager is able to devote attention to those reps who need help and guidance without neglecting the top producers or getting snowed under a pile of routine reports. The manager is able to develop a number of sales reps who are at different levels of experience and competence and who are developing at different rates of speed. As long as sales managers have a conscious system which applies to each individual on the sales force, they can easily explain the consistency of their actions on an objective and logical basis. When the sales reps perform well within the delegated area, the manager will give them a larger area to operate within their own direct discretion. Conversley, if one does not perform as expected, the manager can reduce the area of discretion to reduce errors or to control performance more closely.

Within stated company objectives and policies, the sales manager can take daily note of the sales force performance and actively invoke the expansion or contraction of assignments, responsibilities, and privileges as different sales reps grow and develop. It is a flexible system of control which minimizes the amount of detail with which the manager is required to deal. Properly designed, a management by exception system will relieve the sales manager of wasting time on routine detail work so he or she can use time more effectively in developing each sales rep individually.

Communication Climate When the sales manager plans to reprimand or discipline a rep, it is essential to establish a climate which will encourage honest two-way communications and understanding. It is easy for the sales force to forget that the sales manager is on the same side as they are when they are expecting to be chewed out for something. They are apt to be defensive and prepared with several excuses and arguments. This natural hostility must be displaced before any communication is apt to occur.

For example, if a salesman seems to be giving more discounts than he should, or if he too readily gives customers credit for damaged goods, an honest, quiet discussion is in order, not an abusive and threatening discourse by the manager. A climate can be established by the sales manager which is one of constructive criticism designed to make the sales rep a more successful and better person. By using the job description and the agreed-upon objectives, the manager can objectively point out where the sales rep may be in danger if certain actions are not taken. The manager may point out how other reps handle the same kind of problem without offending customers. In such a conversation, the manager is a sincere friend of the sales rep, and the manager is keeping in close touch to help the rep achieve his or her personal goals. This gentle reminder and advice should end on a note of encouragement with the manager's offer to help in any way possible.

The sales reps will realize the manager does watch their individual performance. They will realize that if they do not correct the faults, they may no longer have the authority to give price concessions or grant credit at their own discretion. This authority may be withdrawn and prior approval of the sales manager may be imposed. In either case, the conversation can be based upon objective facts without emotional bias. The sales rep should be able to leave the interview feeling that the manager was willing to listen and objectively discuss the goals, quotas, and performance record.

GRID THEORY AND ITS WEAKNESSES

The relationships the sales manager establishes between himself or herself and the sales force, the organization, the communications, and the ways of getting the job done are the structural aspects of how to do the sales management job. The friendships, the mutual trust between the manager and the sales force, and the climate the sales manager establishes are the human relations aspects of how to do the job.

Over the years Ohio State University has become famous for its studies of leadership behavior. Dr. Andrew W. Halpin conducted twelve studies involving groups of 1065, 1500, 2361, and 2000 subjects as diverse as aircraft commanders, factory supervisors, school superintendents, management trainees, and business managers of a large oil company. The researchers questioned each leader's work group and superiors on 1790 items. They reduced the list to 150 items and then, through factor analysis, to 40 items. For a clearer understanding, the results are clustered in two dimensions, as shown in Figure 18-1.

On the horizontal axis, "Initiating Structure in Interaction," leaders delineate relationships between themselves and their members. They establish well-defined patterns of organization, channels of communication, and ways of getting the job done. When a new problem arises, the group members are not dependent on the leader for instructions. On the

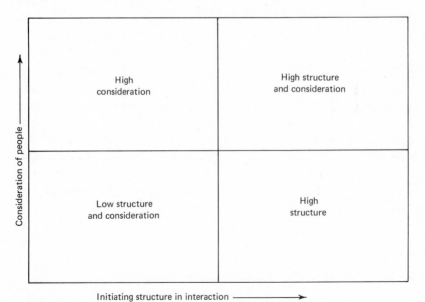

Figure 18-1   The Ohio State Leadership Quadrants. *Source:* Paul Hersey and Kenneth H. Blanchard, *Management of Organizational Behavior*, Prentice-Hall, Inc., Englewood Cliffs, N.J., 1969.

vertical axis, "Consideration of People," the leaders establish friendships and mutual trust between members of the group and between the leaders and their subordinates. There are respect and genuine warmth in all their relationships. Highly effective leaders, in all the diverse fields studied, not only scored high in both the two clusters "Initiating Structure" and "Consideration" but scored well above their peer group.

Robert Blake and Jane Mouton applied popular words to this Ohio State University concept to develop their "Managerial Grid," illustrated in Figure 18-2.

They use five leadership styles:

- *Impoverished:* This style involves the minimum effort to get the required work done appropriately to sustain organization membership.

- *Country Club:* Thoughtful attention to the needs of people for satisfying relationships leads to a comfortable, friendly organization atmosphere and work tempo.

- *Task:* Efficiency in operation results from arranging conditions of

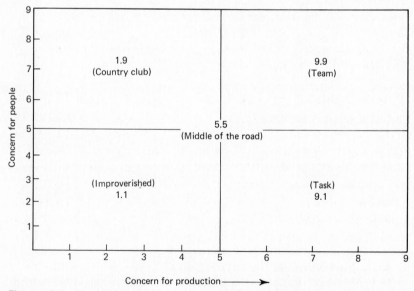

Figure 18-2 The Managerial Grid. *Source:* Robert R. Blake and Jane S. Mouton, *The Managerial Grid*, Gulf Publishing Company, Houston, 1964.

work in such a way that human elements interfere to a minimum degree.

- *Middle of the Road:* Adequate organization performance is possible through balancing the necessity of getting out work with the maintenance of morale on a satisfactory level.

- *Team:* Work accomplished comes from committed people. Interdependence through a common stake in the organization purpose leads to relationships of trust and respect.

Blake and Mouton added numerical scaling to the original concept; they stress a 9.9 or team approach to leadership rather than an extreme task orientation or an extreme concern for people. Such theories were popular through the 1960s.

Rensis Likert, an authority in this field, follows a similar pattern.[3] The implication throughout Likert's writings is that the ideal and most productive leader behavior is employee-centered, or democratic. His own findings, however, raise questions as to whether there can be a single style of leadership which can apply to all situations. For example, four of his twelve leaders using the "ideal" type of leadership had low-producing sections. In addition, one of ten supervisors using a "poor" type of leadership had a high-producing section.

In disagreement is another authority, Saul W. Gellerman, who studied leadership in a General Electric plant. He wrote:

Place an individual with strong independence drives under a supervisor who needs to keep men under his thumb, and the result is very likely to be trouble. Similarly, if you take docile men who are accustomed to obedience and respect for their supervisor and place them under a supervisor who tries to make them manage their own work, they are likely to wonder uneasily whether he really knows what he is doing. . . . The lowest morale in the plant was found among those men whose foremen were rated between the democratic and authoritarian extremes. The G. E. research team felt that

[3]Rensis Likert, *New Patterns of Management,* McGraw-Hill Book Company, New York, 1961. See also Rensis Likert, *The Human Organization,* McGraw-Hill Book Company, New York, 1967. For an update see Fred E. Fielder and Martin M. Chemers, *Leadership and Effective Management,* Scott, Foresman and Company, Glenview, Ill., 1974.

these foremen may have varied inconsistently in their tactics, permissive at one moment and hard-fisted the next, in a way that left the men frustrated and unable to anticipate how they would be treated.[4]

More recently Fred Fiedler reported that in more than fifty studies covering a span of fiteen years it was found that both directive, task-oriented leaders and nondirective, human relations-oriented leaders are successful under some conditions.[5] Leader effectiveness is a function of matching style to the situation.

THEORY H STYLE OF LEADERSHIP

Psychologists have described and labeled many stereotypes of leadership behavior for the purpose of illustration. At one extreme, and more easily recognized, is the *autocratic* sales manager. He or she is characterized by making all the decisions and parceling out the jobs in a very detailed manner. This manager often hides the overall goals to prevent anyone from challenging the actions taken. Authority, not persuasion, is used to get movement, and it is done through the use of reward and punishment. Rigid work standards are set—six calls per day, for example—many detailed rules are made often dictating precisely what should be said on a particular sales call. Often meaningless assignments are given to keep everyone busy for the sake of discipline.

The autocratic style of leadership might be *most* appropriate when:

1 The sales reps are new or inexperienced. Someone has to tell them where the bathrooms are located.

2 When disciplinary action is required, the autocratic style is very effective.

---

[4]Saul W. Gellerman, *Motivation and Productivity,* American Management Association, New York, 1965, pp. 42–43. See also L. L. Cummings and Donald Schwab, *Performance in Organizations,* Scott, Foresman and Company, Glenview, Ill., 1973.

[5]Fred E. Fielder, *A Theory of Leadership Effectiveness,* McGraw-Hill Book Company, *Harvard Business Review,* May–June 1970.

3 When a group of sales reps become complacent and lethargic, the autocratic style will shake them up quickly.

4 Clearly, in an emergency, when there is little or no time for more gentle styles, the autocrat is most effective. If a company is in danger of going bankrupt, for example, an autocratic leader may be required to get immediate results essential for survival.

Conversely, this autocratic style of leadership would seem to be *least* appropriate when:

1 The sales force is very experienced and capable.

2 In situations where teamwork and cooperation are desired.

3 When the group attitude must be won over.

4 When the group is already working well together. In this situation, this style of leadership would be disruptive and undesirable.

The second style of leadership on the scale of permissiveness is called *paternalistic* because the sales manager behaves as the friendly father or big brother. Such a manager attempts to make the sales force believe he or she is operating in their best interest but still makes all the decisions and his or her way is the only correct way. All goals are decided without talking to the sales force. There is still concern with all the minor details, and any creativity is put down or stifled. In operating this way, this manager makes the sales force totally dependent upon the "boss."

The paternalistic style of leadership might be appropriate when:

1 The sales manager senses a demand growing in the sales force. Before they present an ultimatum which may cause open anger and strife, the sales manager anticipates the demand and offers something close to what they want. One thereby proves that one really is operating in their best interests and, incidentally, cuts down the informal leaders.

2 When the sales supervisors, operating between the manager and the sales force, are weak or incapable. When such supervisors are inherited, the sales manager might be very effective in overriding such supervisors and imposing what the manager knows to be the correct way to do the job.

3 When the sales force is immature, they may want and really need a strong but friendly sales manager.

On the other hand, the paternalistic style of leadership would be *least* appropriate when:

1 The sales force is mature and independent. Such experienced sales reps want to participate in setting goals and in decision making. It would be foolish to frustrate such motivation needlessly.

2 When the sales manager has very capable sales supervisors, it might be better to let them operate in their own way without interference.

About midway on the scale of leadership styles is that of the *consultative* sales manager. He or she reserves the responsibility and the right to make all the final decisions, but the sales force is asked for their ideas and beliefs before one makes the final decision. These managers are primarily concerned with *what* will be accomplished and only secondarily with *how* the sales force will do their jobs. They encourage the sales force to be creative and to help each other at all times. They do define objectives and communicate these to the entire sales force. Because of their willingness to listen, they generate respect.

The consultative style of leadership might not be effective when:

1 The sales force is inexperienced or untrained. New sales reps have no foundation for their ideas or suggestions, and they might feel it was a case of the blind leading the blind if the sales manager consulted them before making up his or her mind.

2 A strongly independent sales force unwilling to work together as a team might give conflicting advice to their sales manager. Given two opposite and extreme positions, the manager can either choose one and be accused of playing favorites, or elect neither and compromise and displease all.

3   A sales force had previously been happy working for an autocratic sales manager who did all their thinking for them. They would not be able to work independently immediately as the new sales manager requested.

The consultative sales manager style would be very effective when:

1   The sales force is very mature and independent.

2   The sales force really works well as a team of cooperating individuals.

3   The group is well trained and experienced.

Moving toward the other extreme style of leadership, one finds the sales manager in a more passive role. Typical is the *democratic* leader. The democratic sales manager is primarily concerned with the viewpoint of the majority of the sales force. In group meetings the manager is the moderator and mediator for the entire sales force. He or she encourages discussion and creativity. The views of each sales rep are acknowledged and respected. Such managers are very permissive and accept the group's decision even when they might not personally believe it to be correct.

There are advantages to using this democratic style of leadership under certain conditions:

1   It can generate tremendous participation and commitment of a very *small* sales force.

2   It can be effective when the sales reps enjoy working together as a group.

3   It can be effective when there is lots of time for each knowledgeable rep to speak out on an issue before one must attempt to make a decision.

The disadvantages of the democratic style of leadership are caused by three major elements:

1 It is unwieldy with large groups—even six or seven, for example. Some reps may compete to take over the role of informal leader.

2 It is difficult to apply if decisions must be made quickly—which is often the case in business.

3 The democratic style cannot work when the sales force does not have enough information or knowledge to discuss an issue intelligently or make an intelligent decision.

The extremely passive end of the scale is that of the *free-rein* or substantive leader. The sales manager using this style of leadership permits the expert sales rep to control his or her work. The manager exercises little control over the sales force and acts primarily to help the sales reps achieve their individual goals. Sales reps set their own work pace and make individual decisions, reporting to the manager at their convenience. Experienced manufacturer representatives, who are really self-employed independent businessmen, often prefer to work for this type of sales manager.

This free-rein style of leadership is appropriate *only* when:

1 The substance of the work guides the sales reps more than any management directive.

2 The sales reps are truly expert in their specialty areas.

3 The sales force is willing and able to make proper decisions for the benefit of the entire organization.

Clearly, no single style of leadership is appropriate for all situations. A sales manager's effectiveness in leading a sales force is a function of matching the style of leadership to the situation. It is essential that the manager be *flexible* and change the leadership style as situations change. For example, the manager may be tough and demanding with several sales trainees and give free rein to a group of national account managers. One can be a consultative leader in developing and maturing a group of average producers, encouraging them to think more on their own. One might on occasion be democratic—in setting up a sales contest, for example.

Thus one can see how a sales manager can change the style of leadership many times in many ways all on the same day. The manager is consistent in behavior with each sales rep and each group of reps. They do learn to anticipate his or her reactions and they know what is expected of them. The effective sales manager is flexible in the use of leadership styles, which can be visualized as a four-speed gear shift or the capital letter "H." (See Figure 18-3.)

In the first and second gears, the sales manager has strong pulling power and the sales force learns to depend on him or her for rewards and punishment. In the center of the gear shift, the sales managers exert little or no push or pull and permit the sales force to influence their thinking. On the right side of the gear shift, in third and fourth gears, the managers are passive and the motivated sales reps operate relatively independently of the managers. This enables the managers to spend more time in other essential duties, such as long-range planning and developing people, rather than putting out brush fires.

A sales manager's skill as a leader of the sales force will be determined to a large extent by his or her ability to select the style of leadership most appropriate for the individual sales rep, for the particular group, and for the business situation. "Theory H" leadership combines five typical major leadership styles into a *system* of leadership where

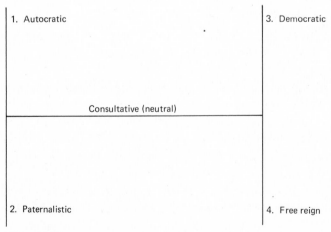

Figure 18-3

each has its purpose and correct place.[6] All sales managers have a style of leadership whether or not they are conscious of it. The question, then, is not *if* a sales manager is going to lead, but *how* he or she is going to lead the sales force.

CONFLICT RESOLUTION

There are many occasions when a sales manager views situations in a different way from the sales force. For example, the sales force often wants more money, while the sales manager wants to keep expenses down and to improve profit. The sales force may feel they are working hard, but the sales manager wants them to work harder. Individual territory or account assignments may not seem fair to the sales reps, but to the manager they appear to be practical. High producers may tend to be independent and not yield to the dictates or directives of the manager. For these and many other reasons, conflicting ideas, conflicting opinions, and conflicting behavior often occur.

Alan C. Filley has developed an enlightened theory of conflict resolution which seems to be very practical for sales managers.[7] He writes that there are three basic strategies for dealing with conflict: the win-lose strategy, the lose-lose strategy, and the win-win strategy. In the win-lose strategy a sales manager may use authority to reward or punish sales reps who disagree. Majority rule is another form of win-lose strategy in which one group wins and the other is defeated. Minority rule is another form of win-lose. For example, the manager might ask only the top producers for their ideas on a conflict and decide as they suggest for the entire sales force. However it is resolved, only one group gets its way while the other does not.

In a lose-lose strategy, neither side achieves what it wanted and both sides usually get only part of what they want. Compromise is the

[6]Jared F. Harrison and Thomas F. Stroh, *Styles of Leadership: Theory H,* Intercollegiate Video Clearing House, Miami, Fla., 1976.

[7]Alan C. Filley, *Interpersonal Conflict Resolution,* Scott Foresman and Company, Glenview, Ill., 1975. Also see *Conflict Resolution,* Intercollegiate Video Clearing House, Miami, Fla., 1976.

most common form of a lose-lose strategy. Binding arbitration is another form of this strategy where the arbitrator resolves the conflict, but rarely satisfactorily to either side. Another variation is the side payment or extra compensation paid for doing a disagreeable task. For instance, a sales manager might have to offer a sales rep a higher salary to cover a poorer territory—clearly a lose-lose strategy.

In a win-win strategy, both the sales manager and the sales reps win. Filley notes that this can take two basic forms: consensus and integrative decision-making methods. These problem-solving strategies focus initially on the goals rather than on the means—the sales manager's way versus the reps' way, or alternate A versus alternate B. The sales manager who is using the problem-solving method searches for a solution which achieves the sales reps' goals and the manager's own goals and is acceptable to both—a win-win strategy. For example, if the goal of the manager is to increase profit by 10 percent and the goal of the sales rep is to increase his or her compensation by 20 percent, an acceptable solution for both might be to work smarter—not harder—as, to sell more profitable items.

Consensus decisions occur when a final solution is reached which is not unacceptable to anyone. Either the parties involved do not care one way or the other, or they support the solution. For example, one group of young sales reps may strongly favor cash prizes in a contest while another older group strongly prefers travel incentives such as a trip to Europe. The manager may select the travel prizes with a cash conversion option.

Win-win strategies begin with the belief that there is a mutually acceptable solution available—not just the manager's way or the rep's way. If both parties can be satisfied by a solution, cooperation is more apt to result in the future. The parties see resources as abundant and have a like interest in defeating the problem, not each other. If each side changes its emphasis from argument to the achieving of a correct solution, their interactions will also shift to a problem-solving method. The sales manager must show objectivity and trustworthiness to bring out the same behavior in the sales rep. When a conflict is resolved this way, both sides know the facts and the feelings of the other. They become more committed to achieving the goals or removing the obstacles. Both the manager and the sales force feel, and act, like winners.

SUMMARY

Management by exception is a human control system which seems well suited to sales management. It should not be confused with management by objectives, which compares performance with goals and signals deviations. Management by exception gives each sales rep an area of responsibility and the authority to do the job. Inexperienced people may have a limited say in how they will cover their area. As they develop, the manager can enlarge their responsibilities and authority. It is a system which accelerates the growth and development of many sales reps at different stages of experience and maturity while minimizing the routine paperwork of reports.

The management grid theory shows the style of leadership which a manager uses, ranging from autocratic to democratic. It indicates whether a manager is more concerned with accomplishing a task or with developing people. However, studies have shown that different styles can each produce good results and that no one style is always appropriate. While the grid theory may cause a sales manager to be aware of his or her own style of leadership, it does little to help.

"Theory H" style of leadership makes the point that effective leadership is a function of matching the style to the needs of the people involved, the time constraints, and the business situation. An effective sales manager can be a demanding authoritarian with a group of sales trainees and the liberal free-rein leader with several national account managers. One should be flexible and intentionally change one's leadership style to increase one's effectiveness.

Managing a group of sales reps who are striving to be independent, as they normally should, can often create conflicts. These conflicts can be resolved by the use of power, as in, "Do as you are told!" or through reward and punishment with compensation. These are essentially win-lose strategies. They may also be resolved by compromise, where both parties settle for less than they wanted. This is a lose-lose strategy. Filley points out that the most practical strategy is a win-win one, in which the solution is acceptable to both sides. This requires an open, honest discussion of the needs of both sides with a joint search of alternate solutions beyond the immediately obvious two sides to a dispute or conflict. Problem solving is the objective way to gain a consensus agreement which benefits both parties. It shows great promise for sales managers to improve morale, commitment to goals, and performance.

QUESTIONS

1 What is the difference between management by objectives and management by exception? Can one manager use both simultaneously?

2 What is the weakness of the management grid theory?

3 Describe the five styles of leadership explained in Theory H management.

4 How can a sales manager change his style of leadership several times in one day and still appear consistent to the sales force?

5 What is the danger of using a win-lose strategy in attempting to resolve conflict?

6 In what way is a compromise a lose-lose strategy in conflict resolution?

7 How can a manager achieve a win-win solution in conflict resolution?

SELECTED REFERENCES

Cummings, L. L., and **Donald P. Schwab:** *Performance in Organization,* Scott, Foresman and Company, Glenview, Ill., 1973.

Fiedler, Fred E., and **Martin M. Chemers:** *Leadership and Effective Management,* Scott, Foresman and Company, Glenview, Ill., 1974.

Filley, Alan C.: *Interpersonal Conflict Resolution,* Scott, Foresman and Company, Glenview, Ill., 1975.

Gellerman, Saul W.: *Motivation and Productivity,* American Management Association, New York, 1965.

Hersey, Paul, and **Kenneth H. Blanchard:** *Management of Organizational Behavior,* Prentice-Hall, Inc., Englewood Cliffs, N.J., 1969.

Likert, Rensis: *The Human Organization,* McGraw-Hill Book Company, New York, 1967.

Reddin, W. J.: *Management Style Diagnosis Test: Test Interpretation Manual,* Fredericton, New Brunswick, N.J., 1965.

Stroh, Thomas F.: "Handling the New Generation Now," chap. 4 in *Managing the New Generation in Business,* McGraw-Hill Book Company, New York, 1971.

Styles of Leadership: Theory H, $^3/_4$-in. videocassette, 50 min, b&w, Intercollegiate Video Clearing House, Miami, Fla., 1976.

▶ **Case 18-1**

THE CONDOMINIUM, INC.

The Condominium, Inc., sales department consists of a male sales manager, an assistant sales manager, also male, and four saleswomen. They are aided by three female tour guides, one of whom is the assistant sales manager's wife. During busy periods the tour guides show prospective customers the condominium models.

The models are apartments, townhouses, and villas. The models range in price from about $35,000 to $70,000. The project has been selling for three months and is already 70 percent sold out. The salespeople get a 1 percent commission on all sales. The guides are paid on an hourly basis.

During slow times the guides act as secretaries for the salespeople as well as running errands for the salespeople. To the casual observer, everyone got along fairly well, except for one main problem. The assistant manager's wife would give her tours, and if the customer was sincerely interested, she would direct them to her husband. For a while this practice was unnoticed and then considered coincidental. Finally one of the saleswomen said something to the tour guide, and she denied any intentional steering of clients. This incident caused friction to develop between the salespeople and the tour guides as well as ill feeling for the assistant sales manager.

The sales manager had an office on the second floor and was virtually out of touch with the sales reps' problems and methods, as paperwork kept him tied up in the office until late in the afternoon. He worked with the salespeople only during the application of extras to the homes and the closings. Rarely were sales meetings held to discuss problems and evaluate techniques. For this reason he was almost totally unaware of the problems that were becoming more apparent.

The sales had been going so well that no one wanted to cause any trouble. But after a few more clients were steered in one direction, everyone felt a sheet of cold cover the department as relations became more strained. The sales manager tried to avoid any direct confrontation, as his personality was technical in dealing with problems and not behavioral. He knew he would have to call a sales meeting to clear the air or face a total communications breakdown in his sales force. His main problem was how to get everyone to work together again without embarrassing the members of the sales force beyond repair. He decided he would call for a meeting later in the week.

1 What style of leadership does the sales manager use?

2 What would you recommend that he do at the next sales meeting?

▶ **Case 18-2**

FREMAC'S CORPORATION

Store manager Vince Carter has been having considerable problems with his salesmen on the floor of his men's clothes store.

Fremac's is a men's clothing chain which carries quality men's clothes and accessories geared toward young and old men who prefer conservative styles.

Carter is manager of the Fremac's store located in the Sunshine Mall. He has been manager in this store for over six years and has had previous experience in men's clothes.

There is presently an assistant manager, Paul Wright, and two salesmen, Chuck Towers and Jim Newman. All are responsible to sales.

Carter hired Paul Wright in hopes he himself could spend more time with the books, and also to help set up a new store on the other side of town. Unfortunately, Paul has not turned out the way Carter hoped he would.

Paul, who is in his late thirties, has had considerable difficulty getting along with Chuck and Jim. He finds it nearly impossible to "give them orders," for they usually retort with some smart remarks. Chuck and Jim are also known for the practical jokes they play on Paul—such as hiding his cigarettes and taping tags on his back when he is not looking.

Paul refuses to take the problem to Carter, thinking he will feel Paul is unable to handle salesmen.

During this "war" many customers have been neglected and some have been offended.

Carter questioned Paul about the drop in sales—Paul just shrugged and said, "No customers."

Eventually Carter started receiving complaints from some regular customers. Presenting these to Paul, Carter questioned him again. This time Paul blamed the immaturity of Chuck and Jim. Carter said he never had a problem with them, and he begins to silently question Paul's abilities as a manager of people.

1 What kind of a leader is Paul Wright?

2 What should Vince Carter do in this situation?

▶ Case 18-3

ATLANTIC TITLE & ABSTRACT COMPANY

Josh Wilson, sales manager for Atlantic Title & Abstract Company, had just adjourned another end-of-month review with the two-man sales force. Once again the meeting had degenerated into a shouting match as credit for contracts received was argued. Josh was again faced with his monthly problem, namely, determining whether contracts received from certain accounts should be credited to the account executive who developed the account, Frank Hayes, or his new man who had taken over the accounts, Mark Wells.

Atlantic Title was started on a shoestring in 1969, and until four months ago Frank Hayes had been the only account executive. But management had decided that the rapidly expanding building and real estate industry warranted the addition of another account executive.

In the years since 1969, Frank Hayes had built up a large number of successful accounts, many of whom would automatically mail their orders to the office. This permitted Frank to make calls on these good accounts less frequently and freed more time for him to develop new accounts.

When Mark Wells joined the firm, it was agreed that he would be given certain of Frank Hayes's accounts that were highly profitable as well as some new ones that had never been called on before.

Wells's performance up to now has been as expected, and he has been receiving contracts from his new accounts. In addition, Wilson estimates that Wells has maintained the same level of volume from Hayes's old accounts. During the meeting, both Hayes and Wells expressed their reasons for claiming credit for contracts from these key accounts. Frank Hayes, who had seen his income go from under $10,000 in 1969 to just over $25,000 last year, offered these arguments:

"It took a long time to develop these accounts up to the point they're at now. . . . I didn't want to give them up, but it was necessary to allow the company to penetrate new accounts. Still, I don't think you can take away accounts that mean money to me and replace them with accounts that won't produce equivalent revenue for some time. I still deserve some credit for those contracts."

Mark Wells, who had earned almost $7,000 in the first quarter of this year, offered the following:

"When I took over these accounts, I made sure that the clients knew that I would provide the same level of service they got from Frank. And I've come through. Besides, you can't expect me to handle all new accounts and still work on straight commission. Frank developed these accounts, sure, but I deserve something for maintaining them. He can't be paid for his past performance forever."

How would you attempt to resolve this conflict?

19

Sales
Management
in the Future

▶ Objectives

The reader will understand the managerial qualifications needed in the next ten to fifteen years. He or she will be aware of increasing federal regulation and the causes of it. The reader will know of the shortages and substitutes and how they will affect sales management in the future. He or she will realize the implications of a changing population with younger people in management with different values from those of the past. Finally, the reader will recognize the need for more professionalism in future sales managers.

Hindsight is often 20-20 vision. It is relatively easy to look back, after the facts are known, and point out mistakes and show how a different action would have been better. Looking forward or forecasting with various degrees of uncertainty can be quite hazardous. Given such an obvious generalization, there are existing facts as this is being written which point to the occurrence of certain events in the coming decade. For example, all the people who will be in management in 1990 have already been born, and their personalities are now well developed and well known.

MANAGERIAL QUALIFICATIONS, 1985–1990

Successful sales managers of the future will have a broad knowledge and appreciation of social values. They will be well aware of their organization's contribution to or impact on the local, regional, and international community. They will develop ways and means to measure an organization's social capital in much more meaningful terms than today's catchall term *goodwill.*

In addition to having a broad knowledge of the social sciences, tomorrow's successful sales managers will be relatively sophisticated in the field of the behavioral sciences, including psychology, education, sociology, and other combined disciplines. The knowledgeable managers of the future will not make the mistakes of previous generations in dealing with individuals, groups, and masses of people.

A third major difference in future sales managers will be their competence in the quantitative sciences and in relating their technical competence to the real world. In management seminars today one refers to this area as SWAG, or the science of wild, asinine guesses. Technology and computer simulations will reduce guesswork in the future at the lowest level of sales management, and the quantitative sciences will replace guessing.

A fourth managerial qualification of the 1980s will be a worldwide perspective rather than today's regionalism and nationalism. Organizations such as Europe's Common Market will no longer serve the international concern operating around the world. As countries leap from an agrarian economy directly to a technological economy, they will need and demand different products, services, and financing. Government support for the importer and exporter will be essential. The more effective sales managers will be both knowledgeable and highly aware of the intricacies of operating on a worldwide basis.

A fifth qualification for tomorrow's sales managers will be understanding and willingness to accept the need for continuous learning. In a period of rapid technological advancement, existing knowledge becomes obsolete in a matter of a very few years. New management tools must be mastered as they become available. As the development of new knowledge accelerates, one can no longer afford the time-consuming trial-and-error method of learning. Obsolescence will quickly overtake the sales managers who hesitate to learn continuously.

Finally, the sales managers of tomorrow will have a strong sense of morality and humanity. In the past managers were concerned primarily with scientific management or efficiency and with improving the standard of living or the material possessions of people. Future sales managers will be concerned with protecting humanity or human decency and with improving the quality of life.[1]

INCREASED REGULATION

In the past, United States executives rarely went to jail for crimes of their companies. Chief executive officers of companies charged with price-fixing, for example, have been able to escape personal liability with the excuse, "I didn't know." The electrical industry price-fixing of the mid-1960s did send some vice presidents to prison, but the top executives were excused. Soon the codification of federal criminal laws will subject business executives to criminal penalties for a new offense called "reckless default." An officer will be personally subject to prosecution for failing to supervise properly employees who violated federal regulations.

Such legislation clearly will go beyond the traditional personal legal liability of managers for fraud against the company or its stockholders or negligence in their stewardship of assets. New laws will probably give trial judges the option of disqualifying culpable executives from holding high-responsibility jobs in the future.[2] The federal laws will not rely on

---

[1] For an expansion of this topic see Thomas F. Stroh, *Managing the New Generation in Business,* McGraw-Hill Book Company, New York, 1971.

[2] Louis B. Schwartz, University of Pennsylvania Law School, and Christopher D. Stone, U.S.C., as quoted in "The Law Closes In on Managers," *Business Week,* May 10, 1976, pp. 110–116.

the indirect effect of fines, citations, and the like, which are ineffective in making corporations more responsible. Rather, they will require direct management changes.

Companies have generally tried to shield their officers from the direct effects of liability by agreeing to indemnify them against any expenses—including fines, court costs, and attorneys' fees. But management today is not automatically shielded. Armco Steel Corporation, for example, refuses to help with the legal expenses of any employee involved in price-fixing. Their regional assistant sales manager in the Southwestern area had to pay a $5000 fine and $15,000 in attorneys' fees out of his own pocket when he pleaded no contest to a 1974 federal price-fixing charge.[3] In the past most large corporations bought directors' and officers' liability (D.&O.) insurance, but even this top-level protection will become much more difficult and costly to obtain.

In the future the manager in charge of the task will be the target for the regulators. This means that the sales manager will be responsible for the actions of the sales force and that claimed ignorance will not be an acceptable excuse. A bribe by a salesperson to get an order is likely to draw criminal prosecution of the sales executive by the Internal Revenue Service. "It is true you can't put a corporation in jail, but you can assess corporations a 50 percent civil penalty for tax fraud," says IRS Commissioner Donald C. Alexander.[4] As the IRS begins to collect such penalties, Alexander thinks, there will be an upsurge of stockholder suits against the responsible executive to recover damages in behalf of the corporation.

The newer agencies will begin to use their power to haul management into court. These today include the Equal Employment Opportunity Commission and the Office of Federal Contract Compliance, already discussed, as well as the Environmental Protection Agency, the Occupational Safety and Health Administration (OSHA), the Consumer Product Safety Commission (CPSC), and the Office of Employee Benefits Security under the Labor Department. Individual penalties for managers include substantial personal fines and jail sentences. Corporate penalties are in addition.

[3]The Law Closes In on Managers," *Business Week,* May 10, 1976.

The trend is clearly established for the next decade to hold individual managers and executives personally liable for corporate activities.

There is a need to weed out the traditional quick-buck artist from the professional sales reps and sales managers. These misfits should be identified and expelled from the profession. Since various attempts at self-regulation have not been very successful in the past, it seems most likely that federal government regulation and prosecution of individuals will increase in the next decade. Many of the penalties now make such crimes a felony rather than a misdemeanor, a regulation which automatically triggers state penalties that can range from loss of voting rights to expulsion as an officer of a country club. This is, indeed, the decade of suspicion.

SHORTAGES AND SUBSTITUTES

The world is beginning to run low of easily accessible raw materials. This means that, for the next ten years or longer, companies will have to pay more for existing supplies or for harder-to-get-at new supplies. It also means that considerable effort will be made to find substitute materials which can serve satisfactorily and at a reasonable cost. Shortages of raw materials and many components will be of a temporary nature, however, as the world's consuming patterns change and substitute materials and methods are innovated.

World population growth will continue, primarily in underdeveloped countries, and this will cause food shortages, if not famine, in many countries. This in turn will keep constant upward pressure on food prices and related farm equipment and supplies. More ocean-grown foods will be developed and fish-farming may very well become economical. As science advances, eating habits may change in the more fortunate countries which have abundant foods.

The world demand for energy will continue to increase and the environmentalists will also continue to fight pollution, ruining of the earth's surface, and threats to mankind's safety. Easy-to-get-at oil and coal will be limited and used more to make products than for fuel. Nuclear fuel plants and natural gas will become the major sources of energy, together with synthetic methane gas as a supplement. As

THE RISKS EXECUTIVES FACE UNDER FEDERAL LAW

Agency	Year Enforcement Began	Complaint May Name Individual	Maximum Individual Penalty	Maximum Corporate Penalty	Private Suit Allowed under Applicable Statute
Internal Revenue Service	1862	Yes	$5,000, three years, or both	$10,000, 50% assessment, prosecution costs	No
Antitrust Div. (Justice Dept.)	1890	Yes	$100,000, three years, or both	$1 million, injunction, divestiture	Yes
Food & Drug Administration	1907	Yes	$1,000, one year, or both for first offense; $10,000, three years, or both thereafter	$1,000 for first offense; $10,000 thereafter; seizure of condemned products	No
Federal Trade Commission	1914	Yes	Restitution, injunction	Restitution, injunction, divestiture, $10,000 per day for violation of rules, orders	No
Securities & Exchange Commission	1934	Yes	$10,000, two years, or both	$10,000, injunction	Yes
Equal Employment Opportunity Commission	1965	No		Injunction, back pay award, reinstatement	Yes
Office of Federal Contract Compliance	1965	No		Suspension, cancellation of contract	Yes
Environmental Protection Agency	1970	Yes	$25,000 per day, one year, or both for first offense; $50,000 per day, two years, or both thereafter	$25,000 per day, first offense; $50,000 per day thereafter; injunction	Yes
Occupational Safety & Health Administration	1970	No*	$10,000, six months, or both	$10,000	No
Consumer Product Safety Commission	1972	Yes	$50,000, one year, or both	$500,000	Yes
Office of Employee Benefits Security (Labor Dept.)	1975	Yes	$10,000, one year, or both; barring from future employment with plan; reimbursement	$100,000, reimbursement	Yes

*Except sole proprietorship.
Source: Business Week, May 10, 1976, p. 113.

garbage is converted to fuel, many raw materials will be recycled more economically, just as aluminum is today.

Such dramatic changes will cause many business problems, as the cost of producing will be erratic. Sales managers will be under severe pressure to increase prices at some times and to reduce the sales force size during shortages. Operating a sales force under these conditions will call for minimizing risks and stabilizing the flow of goods and materials. Customers will need several good suppliers to give some assurance of future deliveries. Good suppliers, in turn, will try to protect and serve their loyal customers.

The companies which are slow to adapt to these changes will cause their top sales producers to look to more innovative employers. These are the people who are closest to what customers are planning to do and to what competitors are doing. They can provide their sales managers with information which may persuade top management to change its course of business. For this reason alone, sales managers in the next ten years should become a power in top-management decisions.

Those companies which correctly forecast the needs of their customers and innovate new ways to serve them will enable their sales managers to attract the top producers from the competition. The sales force can be upgraded rather quickly under these conditions. There may be a temptation on the part of the sales manager to expand the sales force under these same conditions. However, every manager should exercise caution in this regard, as events can readily change and positions may be reversed. In addition, top management may prefer to skim the cream off the market with a minimum but effective sales force, as noted earlier.

Directing a sales force under such conditions will require training in how to persuade customers to accept substitute products which will still honestly serve their needs at an acceptable cost. This may necessitate the sales force's learning a new technology, such as physics or chemistry. It may involve different costing procedures; hence there would be a need for accounting information. The point is that the sales manager of the future will have to be aware of the impact of such changes on the sales force. Different target customers may become more desirable and some sales reps may be trained to specialize in new customer categories. It may be necessary to reorganize the entire sales force to better serve the changing markets and product mix.

NEW GENERATION IN CHARGE

By 1980, more than half the population will be under thirty years of age. In 1950 only one young adult in eighteen was a college graduate. By 1970, one in six had a college degree. By 1980 the number of bachelor's degrees will have increased by 73 percent while the number of master's degrees will have jumped by 90 percent.

In 1980 the middle-age group, aged 35 to 54, will *not* grow in line with the rest of the population. This is the group that traditionally provided the managers for business and industry. By 1980, there will be only a small gain in the group aged 35 to 44 and an actual drop in the group from 45 to 54. The latter is the group which has traditionally supplied the higher executives in business.

While these favored groups are diminishing, business expansion goes on unabatedly, and plans in many industries call for double or triple growth in the next decade. Corporate goals of 10 percent annual growth are both common and attainable. But during the 1970s work force shortages have begun to appear. The long period of a shortage of salespeople has now generated a shortage of sales *managers.* If one projects the population composition trends, statistics show that the population of young adults will grow twice as fast as the total population.

Combine this lag in the number of people in the desired age brackets with the intended expansion of business. Then superimpose the growing demand for managers in education and governmental areas, and one begins to see that young adults will become the new generation in charge.

What are these young adults like? They were born after World War II; hence, most have been raised on better diets than previous generations. The knowledge of the value of vitamins, together with the wherewithal of an affluent society, has permitted them to eat better and grow stronger and larger than any other generation in history. Medical knowledge and inoculations against diseases have permitted them to become the healthiest generation to date. Research has created more knowledge and methodologies to permit mass education at a higher level than had been possible in any earlier generation. As a group, these young adults are more knowledgeable than their parents were at the same age.

Every year about one family in five in the United States moves its home. Such high mobility has exposed our youth to many cultures and different social situations. Young adults are socially intelligent well beyond the level of prior generations at the same age. Sex education, the pill, and a permissive society have combined to produce a generation which can enjoy pleasures but is also able to turn its attention to more serious matters without crippling pangs of hunger, regret, or guilt.

As a group they are often more moral than any prior generation. They have been *told* that spinach tastes good, medical shots do not hurt, and hard work builds good character. Yet their personal experience has often shown that there are true differences between what authorities say occurs and reality. Authorities dispense information which is not always factual. The trick is to discover when the dispenser of information is telling the truth and when he or she is misleading for the authority's selfish benefit. These young sophisticates have heard Mom complain about housework but have seen her drinking cocktails and playing bridge all afternoon. They have heard Dad complain about slaving in the office to support his family, but they have seen the matchbook covers he brings home from the go-go places and the topless-waitress restaurants. These young adults are intelligent and sophisticated enough to question any authority, because adults have taught them to do so.

To recap, as a group, the new generation is bigger, healthier, and more knowledgeable than prior generations. Young people smoke less and drink no more than their parents did at the same age. They have read about prior generations making war to end all wars, war to make the world safe for democracy, and war to free people who did not want to be free; about economic trusts that exploit people; about freedom given only lip service as far as several minority groups are concerned; and about bribes and graft in the highest and most respected offices in government and business. If they are impatient and suspicious, surely it should not be a surprise.

Today's young adults have learned to accept atomic power, jet aircraft, a round trip to the moon, and instant communication around the world. They have not accepted poverty, starvation, race superiority, polluted air and water, or war—particularly if there is any possibility of someone in authority realizing a selfish gain from these conditions.

The young adults, including those going through college today, who will take charge in the next decade, are motivated primarily toward serving all humanity and making the world a cleaner and safer place. They believe honesty to oneself and to others is more to be revered than blind obedience to dogma, putting something over on a competitor, or abusing the environment for a profit.

It is their desire to satisfy such inner needs as sincerity, honesty, and the unselfish serving of others which makes them act as they do. They also have a strong desire to find their individual places in life where they can serve both mankind and themselves. This desire is often expressed in their concern for self-development. They want to know what kind of training they will receive and into what areas the career path may take them.

Many of these young adults feel that lower-management-level jobs are routine and without challenge. Thus, they are concerned with how long it will take to rise to a position where they can make decisions which will help humanity. They are willing to work, and work hard, for things in which they believe. If they are to work for business instead of merely tolerating it or working against it, they must be convinced that good business serves humanity.

This new generation, about to take over, can be persuaded that business does infinitely more good for the masses than it does harm. Millions of older citizens are living on funds invested in the stock of corporations; without profit, many of these retired people would be on welfare or relief rolls. It is common today for labor contracts to include guaranteed pensions, and most of the accumulated pension funds also are invested in business and finance. Thus it is to labor's advantage that our economy continue to profit and grow. For many years companies have made it a practice to hire the handicapped, and more are now giving special training to the disadvantaged. Without the assistance of business, these people would live without hope and would perpetuate the ghettos. The cost of a college education, rising every year, is offset primarily by profits from investment trusts which are owned by the colleges.

Profitable operations create a demand for equipment and land, a demand for labor, a demand for training and the constant upgrading of skills and knowledge, and a demand for highly educated leadership. Competition requires a more efficient use of natural resources, buildings, and equipment as well as of people and their individual development. Competition also creates improvements in products, systems, and services while holding costs to a minimum. Indeed, after fifty years of struggling along, the U.S.S.R. has decided to put its manufacturing plants on a profit and loss basis as an incentive to good management.

Most American companies today have an enlightened self-interest, but clearly not all of them. In other words, most companies have found it pays more to use natural resources, facilities, and people for everyone's future benefit than it pays to exploit them. For example, in the paper industry, trees are being grown faster than they are being cut down. More factories are fireproof and air-conditioned than ever before. The typical modern plant is architecturally very attractive with the surrounding area well landscaped. Waste has been reworked to remove valuable chemicals and minerals which formerly polluted the air and water.

Perhaps the new generation can come up with better answers to solve business problems for the good of all mankind and for their own selfish place in the world. Perhaps they can change the establishment for the better by increasing employment and creating more opportunities for all people to improve their lot in life. Perhaps they can develop better ways to reach and serve underdeveloped countries and to raise the standard of living around the world. Ultimately, they may find ways to reduce overpopulation, feed starving millions of people, and lessen the danger of nuclear and biological warfare. These problems are very real and truly represent a challenge to anyone. If the new generation can help solve such problems, they should be most welcome. They do have a sense of social and environmental responsibility which business strongly needs.

During the next decade people in management have the responsibility to convert the neutral or even hostile attitudes of the younger generation into positive, constructive attitudes. Business has many good causes to be championed and benefits to be rendered to humanity which must be made clear to young adults.

CERTIFIED SALES MANAGER

From the early 1950s to the mid-1970s marketing had generally replaced selling as the main tool of competitive action.[5] This led to the identifying

[5]Theodore Levitt, "Segmentation Both Good and Bad for Marketers," *Advertising Age,* Apr. 12, 1976, p. 12.

of smaller and smaller submarket segments. The marketing concept notes that a company which determines and satisfies the wants and needs of various segments in a manner consistent with its general strategies and financial objectives is headed toward success. Thus the practice of fine segmentation explains why there are so many different cars or laundry detergents, for example. This has created the proliferation of many products and varied packaging. It also created numerous advertising themes.

In the case of consumer goods the trouble lies in the incongruence between the people for whom specific products or brands are intended and the people who are exposed to advertising for those products. Levitt observed that the incongruence is inescapable, since mass media provide the cheapest way of reaching mass markets.

This suggests that what was called "wasted circulation" in 1976 is *not* simply talking to the wrong people. It is creating a growing number of complaints that there is a greater proportion of irritating advertising than in years past. While more people can buy more goods tailored to their specific needs, an almost exactly equal number of people get frustrated, annoyed, or distracted by marketing programs for what they do not want or cannot afford to have.

Advertising today is creating its own enemies. The sheer magnitude of commercial messages gets expanded as more and more products and brands scream their superiority for some small, select target audience. The smaller the target segment, the more the mass audience who get annoyed become the "wasted circulation."

In the next decade, the new generation, with its well-founded suspicions, will impose new restrictions on mass advertising. They will readily write to their representatives in Congress in impressive numbers demanding more control over these annoying practices. As mass advertising is restricted, the sales management function can fill the need.

But sales management today is not ready to challenge the marketing management. As many of the true cases in this text illustrate, sales management includes some misfits, quick-buck artists, and uneducated people who mean well but cannot cope with many of the problems. Sales management in the next decade needs to become a profession with strict standards and entrance requirements and ongoing educational upgrading. Accountants and lawyers in business have achieved professionalism and have demonstrated how sales managers can achieve the same results.

In the insurance industry, the Certified Life Underwriter (C.L.U.) is a symbol of the professionalism of the insurance specialists. In the same way the Sales and Marketing Executives International, for example, can create the Certified Sales Manager (C.S.M.), which would distinguish the elite professional from the mass of practitioners. In a ten-year period this could become so well recognized that employers might well make it a requirement to fulfill the sales management job. S.M.E.I., or a new organization, might have to "grandfather in" senior sales managers to gain initial support. In other words, it might be good politics to admit sales managers with twenty years' experience, for example, and only those others who meet the new professional requirements. Then all future applicants would have to meet these new high standards.

Surely if the sales managers do not move toward some form of professionalism, the new generation will begin to demand regulation and control of this vital activity. Then, with both advertising and sales management regulated, marketing will be very dreary. There is no need for this sorry event to take place. There is still time to make sales management a profession, but now the time is limited.

CONCLUSION

As mass marketing infuriates more and more nonprospects, it is irritating the new generation to the point where marketing will become regulated more closely. Yet sales managers today are not ready to regain the top position which they held in the 1950s. They need to become professionals in the formal sense of the word. They have perhaps ten years, at the most, to do so.

Suggested criteria for the professional sales manager of 1985 include:

1 A broad knowledge of social values

2 A broad knowledge of behavioral sciences

3 A competence in quantitative science

4 A worldwide perspective

5 Acceptance of continuous learning

6 A strong sense of morality and human dignity

Increased regulation of individuals in business began in 1965 and it will continue for the next decade. Managers can no longer hide behind the corporate façade and claim they did not know what their employers were doing. They will be fined and jailed as has rarely happened in the past. In all likelihood they will be banned from future management positions by court rule.

World shortages will become more acute in the next decades as easy-to-get-at resources become depleted. Substitute materials and methods will be innovated. Therefore, the sales force will need to be trained to handle new products and new technologies. Reorganization of the sales force may be required as customer target segments shift during these disruptive changes.

The new generation of people under thirty years of age will dominate society by 1980, as they will represent more than half the United States population. Because of a shortage of older workers, these young people will quickly move into management positions. As a group, this new generation is bigger, healthier, more knowledgeable, and more moral than prior generations. They are impatient and suspicious of big government and big business. They can be convinced that "profit" is a good word and that competition can be a healthy thing for society. They need guidance from today's managers and the opportunity to grow and develop.

The certified sales manager is one suggested way out of the dilemma of increased regulation and control. Adapting to change is essential for organizations which desire to survive and grow. Modern management principles which truly motivate the inner person and utilize more of his or her innate capabilities will produce a better, more responsive business society. They will permit the sales reps to realize satisfaction doing their jobs and, it is hoped, will enable them to live longer and healthier lives.

Perhaps most important, the young people who enter sales in the next ten years will bring a new social consciousness to business and a worldwide perspective which will be sorely needed in the 1980s. Young people can help sales management solve many of its business problems, and they should be most welcome.

QUESTIONS

1 What are the six broad managerial qualifications for the future as suggested in this chapter?

2 Do you agree or disagree that the trend to hold individual managers and executives personally liable will continue for the next decade? Why?

3 In what ways will predicted shortages and substitutes affect sales management in the future?

4 How will changes in the population over the next ten to fifteen years affect sales management?

5 Do you think profit and competition can be justified in the future, as the author contends? Why?

6 Is the suggestion to certify sales managers in the future very practical? Why?

▶ Case 19-1

UNITED GENERAL CORPORATION

One of the toughest problems facing me today is the determination of ethical standards. Being a marketing executive in the international division of the United General Corporation, my biggest concern today is developing proper business ethics when dealing with foreign business executives.

It is easy to say that an international marketing executive should act in an ethical fashion, but it is far more difficult to put this axiom into practice. Each executive as an individual usually has his or her own standards of conduct, which one believes to be ethical, and one abides by them in the administration of one's duties. It is doubtful that many people, marketing executives or otherwise, consciously engage in unethical practices. That is, most of us believe we are acting ethically by our own standards.

What is considered ethical conduct varies from one country to another, and from one situation to another. The guidelines of personal conscience are also relative and individual, even among people with a common ethical tradition. Some foreign business executives' ethical conduct allows for bribes. The problem of determining what is right and what is wrong is an extremely difficult one, yet it is one that, to a degree, is soluble.

Some of the approaches I have proposed for the international marketing executive are to evaluate the ethical status of an act by answering such questions as: Is this sound from a long-run point of view? Would I offer this to a member of Congress? Would I be offended to have this offered to me? If other people learn of this act, what would be their reactions?

Some executives in the international business field have proposed that marketing executives can develop some operational guidelines in areas from law and political theory: from law because it administers justice by means of specific case decisions. I feel that in the realm of private business power, the use of a structural limitations approach to ensure that business operates in a socially acceptable fashion is advisable.

With Congress's investigation of foreign bribes by American companies, a marketing executive's job comes under great scrutiny. Our marketing personnel have to be very careful when handling prospective foreign accounts as well as present foreign accounts. In our international marketing division we do not tolerate graft, which was pointed out in the congressional investigation. In the past we have lost large foreign accounts because of our attitude toward bribes, but in the near future we expect to capitalize on our high ethical standards.

The moral question of what is right and appropriate poses many dilemmas for our international marketer. The problem of business ethics is complex in the international marketplace because opinions of what is right and what is wrong are spread even more widely because of basic cultural diversity. Our policy of not paying bribes was not considered good business ethics in some parts of the world. In foreign countries giving business gifts of high value is not only acceptable and condoned but is also expected. My position has been made even more difficult in the past eight months because of the publicity received by American companies' bribing foreigners.

1 How would you advise this marketing executive attempting to sell expensive machinery all over the world?

2 Can he be effective if he does not match competitive bribes?

INDEX